Slavery in the Modern Middle East and North Africa

Sex, Family and Culture in the Middle East Series

This innovative series explores the connections and influences impacting ideas about marriage, sexuality, and the family throughout history in the MENA region, and until the present day. Individual volumes consider the ancient, early Islamic, medieval, early modern, and contemporary periods to investigate how traditions and practices have evolved and interacted across time and countries.

Series Editors:
Janet Afary, Professor and Mellichamp Chair in Global Religion and Modernity, UC Santa Barbara
Claudia Yaghoobi, Roshan Institute Assistant Professor in Persian Studies, The University of North Carolina at Chapel Hill

Slavery in the Modern Middle East and North Africa

Exploitation and Resistance from the 19th Century – Present Day

Elena Andreeva and Kevin McNeer

I.B. TAURIS

LONDON • NEW YORK • OXFORD • NEW DELHI • SYDNEY

I.B. TAURIS

Bloomsbury Publishing Plc, 50 Bedford Square, London, WC1B 3DP, UK
Bloomsbury Publishing Inc, 1359 Broadway, 12ᵗʰ Floor, New York, NY 10018, USA
Bloomsbury Publishing Ireland, 29 Earlsfort Terrace, Dublin 2, D02 AY28, Ireland

BLOOMSBURY, I.B. TAURIS and the I.B. Tauris logo are trademarks
of Bloomsbury Publishing Plc

First published in Great Britain 2024
This paperback edition published 2026

Library of Congress Cataloging-in-Publication Data
Names: Andreeva, Elena, 1963– editor. | McNeer, Kevin, editor.
Title: Slavery in the modern Middle East and North Africa : exploitation
and resistance from the 19th century – present day / [edited by] Elena Andreeva and Kevin McNeer.
Description: London; New York : I.B Tauris, 2024. | Series: Sex, family and culture in the Middle
East series | Includes bibliographical references and index.
Identifiers: LCCN 2023029230 (print) | LCCN 2023029231 (ebook) |
ISBN 9780755647934 (hardback) | ISBN 9780755647972 (paperback) |
ISBN 9780755647941 (pdf) | ISBN 9780755647958 (epub) | ISBN 9780755647965
Subjects: LCSH: Slavery–Middle East–History–19th century. | Slavery–Middle East–History–20th century. |
Slavery–Middle East–History–21st century. | Slavery–Africa, North–History–19th century. |
Slavery–Africa, North–History–20th century. | Slavery–Africa, North–History–21st century. |
Enslaved persons–Middle East–History–19th century. | Enslaved persons–Middle
East–History–20th century. | Enslaved persons–Middle East–History–21st century. | Enslaved
persons–Africa, North–History–19th century. | Enslaved persons–Africa, North–History–20th
century. | Enslaved persons–Africa, North–History–21st century. | Enslaved women–Middle
East–History–19th century. | Enslaved women–Middle East–History–20th century. |
Enslaved women–Middle East–History–21st century.
Classification: LCC HT1316 .S55 2023 (print) | LCC HT1316 (ebook) | DDC 6.3/620956–dc23/eng/20230713
LC record available at https://lccn.loc.gov/2023029230
LC ebook record available at https://lccn.loc.gov/2023029231

ISBN: HB: 978-0-7556-4793-4
PB: 978-0-7556-4797-2
ePDF: 978-0-7556-4794-1
eBook: 978-0-7556-4795-8

Typeset by Newgen KnowledgeWorks Pvt. Ltd., Chennai, India

For product safety related questions contact productsafety@bloomsbury.com.

To find out more about our authors and books visit www.bloomsbury.com
and sign up for our newsletters.

Contents

Part 3   Preserving Identity and Tradition

-7   Afro-Baloch communities in modern Iran and their healing traditions   135
    Maryam Nourzaei

8   Transmuted memories: Slavery and its shadow on the island of Soqotra   159
    Kevin McNeer and Sarali Gintsburg

Part 4   Slavery in a Post-Slavery World

9   Enslaved by the street: Contemporary forms of slavery among the street
    children of Cairo   187
    Dina Al Raffie

10 Yazidi women and girls held as slaves under the Islamic State: Healing
    wounds and reassessing doctrines   209
    Lana Ravandi-Fadai

Selected Bibliography   227
Index   235

Figures

Tables and Songs

Contributors

Dina Al Raffie is an assistant professor of International Relations (IR) and International Security Studies (ISS) at Duquesne University in Pittsburgh, Pennsylvania. Prior to moving to Pittsburgh in 2018, Dr Al Raffie lectured and taught in various locations across Europe at both university and practitioner levels. She has been an occasional returning adjunct professor on the George C. Marshall Center's Program on Terrorism and Security Studies (GCMC-PTSS) since 2013 and was previously a non-resident research fellow at the George Washington University's Program on Extremism (GWPoE). Dr Al Raffie has published on a variety of terrorism-related topics including the identity dynamics of radicalization, terrorist leadership, terrorist motivations and countering violent extremism (CVE), as well as non-Western counterterrorism practices, with a focus on her home country at birth, Egypt. More recent and forthcoming research addresses ideology and terrorism, and modern-day slavery in the Middle East. Additionally, Al Raffie's doctoral research, completed at the University of Navarra in Pamplona, Spain, investigated the sources of radicalization and political violence in the political theory of the Islamic Shari'a. Dr Al Raffie is a frequent speaker and participant in international workshops and conferences on related topics, and is conversant in Arabic, English and German.

Elena Andreeva received her BA and MA degrees in Middle Eastern Studies at Moscow State University and her PhD at New York University, with a specialization in Iranian studies. She is a professor of history at Virginia Military Institute where she teaches classes on Iran, the Middle East, Russia and World History. Her research focuses on the interaction between East and West, Iranian history and culture in the nineteenth and early twentieth centuries, and aspects of colonialism and imperialism in the Middle East and Asia. She has published articles on Persian and Dari literature, Russian Orientalism and Russians in Iran and Central Asia. She is the author of *Russia and Iran in the Great Game: Travelogues and Orientalism* (2007) and *Russian Central Asia in the Works of Nikolai Karazin, 1842–1908: Ambivalent Triumph* (2021), and co-editor of *Russians in Iran: Diplomacy and Power in the Qajar Era and Beyond* (2018). Her current research project is dedicated to Iran in the Second World War.

Josep Lluís Mateo Dieste (Manresa, 1968) is Serra Húnter Associated Professor in the Department of Social and Cultural Anthropology, Universitat Autònoma de Barcelona. He holds a PhD in history from the European University Institute, Florence (2002). His primary publications focus on contemporary Morocco and historical anthropology, including *In Praise of Historical Anthropology* (with Alex Coello, 2020) and *Health and Ritual in Morocco: Conceptions of the Body and Healing Practices* (2013).

Sarali Gintsburg is a researcher at the Institute for Culture and Society (University of Navarra). She holds a PhD in the humanities (Tilburg University) and MA in Arabic philology (University of Saint Petersburg). Sarali has authored over thirty scholarly publications and published on topics related to various facets of Arab Studies. Her recent publications include *Narrating Migrations from Africa and the Middle East: A Spatio-Temporal Approach* (with R. Breeze and M. Baynham, 2022) and *African Migrations: Traversing Hybrid Landscapes* (with R. Breeze, 2023).

Anthony A. Lee (History, UCLA, 2007) is retired as a lecturer at UCLA and now continues his research as an independent scholar. He is the author of *The Baha'i Faith in Africa* (2011) and general editor of the academic series *Studies in the Babi and Baha'i Religions* (1982–), now in its twenty-eighth volume. He is co-editor of the volume *Changing Horizons of African History* (2017). He has published numerous articles on his current area of research, African slavery in Iran, including 'Africans in the Palace: The Testimony of Taj al-Sultana Qajar from the Royal Harem in Iran' in *Slavery in the Islamic World: Its Characteristics and Commonality*, ed. Mary Ann Faye (2018) and 'Recovering the Biographies of Enslaved Africans in Nineteenth-Century Iran' in *Changing Horizons of African History* and 'Half the Household Was African: Recovering the Histories of Two Enslaved Africans in Iran, Haji Mubarak and Fezzeh Khanum' in *UCLA Historical Journal* (2016). He translated, with Amin Banani and Jascha Kessler, *Tahirih: A Portrait in Poetry: Selected Poems of Qurratu'l-'Ayn* (2005); also with Amin Banani, *Rumi: 53 Secrets from the Tavern of Love* (2014); with Nesreen Akhtarkhavari, *Love Is My Savior: Arabic Poems of Rumi* (2016), *Wine of Reunion: Arabic Poems of Rumi* (2017) and *Desert Sorrows: Poems of Tayseer al-Sboul* (2015); with Bilal Shaw, *The Plague of Love Selected Poems of Mir Taqi Mir* (2023).

Kevin McNeer is a writer, filmmaker and translator whose films include the award winning *Stalin Thought of You* (2008) and *On One Day of the Days of God* (2020), about traditional life on the Yemeni island of Soqotra. His most recent article is 'Shadows in the Garden' (2022–3), about female Iranian agents in the first half of the twentieth century, co-authored with Dr Lana Ravandi-Fadai. Kevin received a BA in English literature from Kenyon College and subsequently studied Persian and Arabic at the Institute for Oriental Studies and the Russian State University for the Humanities, and filmmaking at Higher Courses for Screenwriters and Directors in Moscow. He has translated numerous scholarly, fictional and dramatic texts, and is the English language editor of the ongoing multi-volume *Corpus of Soqotri Oral Literature*. His interests include language, the preservation of language and tradition, and the moving image.

Maryam Nourzaei is a field researcher at the Department of Linguistics and Philology at Uppsala University, Sweden, with a particular interest in linguistics, endangered languages, documentation of traditions and oral narration practices. She was awarded her doctoral degree from Uppsala University in 2017. Her research projects since her PhD have dealt broadly with documentation of endangered languages and ritual oral practices, focusing on topics of evolution of definiteness markers in New Western Iranian Languages; language contact and areal linguistics, orality, grammatical description, documenting endangered Indo-Aryan languages spoken in Iran; and documenting unique ritual practice traditions among Afro-Baloch communities in Iran. She has published articles on the diachronic development of definiteness in different Iranian languages. Other published papers compare linguistic features across Balochi dialects, from diachronic, areal linguistic and language contact perspectives. She has also published on the sociolinguistics of Afro-Baloch communities and their cultural traditions. In addition, she has written articles on Kholosi language and culture. Moreover, she has archived extensive data from other undescribed languages and oral practice traditions in the Endangered Languages Archive (ELAR). Since receiving her PhD, she has published thirty-one articles and established extensive international research collaborations with different universities and institutes in Germany, France, the United States, Canada and Iran.

Lana Ravandi-Fadai is head of the Eastern Cultural Center and a Senior Researcher at the Institute of Oriental Studies of the Russian Academy of Sciences, an associate professor of the Contemporary East and Africa at the Russian State University for the Humanities, a Senior Researcher at the Scientific and Educational Laboratory for the Comprehensive Study of Iran and an Associate Professor at the Higher School of Economics. She graduated from the Eastern Studies Department of Baku State University and the Moscow State Institute of International Relations. She earned her doctoral degree in 2002 in contemporary history from the Institute of Oriental Studies. She is the author of over one hundred scholarly publications. Her book, *Political Parties and Organizations of Iran* (2010), was chosen out of seven hundred candidates as runner-up for Best Scholarly Book of the Year at the Institute of Oriental Studies. Her upcoming book, *Victims of Their Faith* (2024), co-authored with Touraj Atabaki, chronicles the lives and fates of Iranian communists in the Soviet Union in the first half of the twentieth century. In addition to numerous international conferences and speaking engagements, Dr Ravandi-Fadai has taught at Virginia Military Institute in the United States and received fellowships from research institutions such as the International Institute of Social History in Amsterdam. Her works examine political and social developments in contemporary Iran – political parties and factions, government institutions, educational policy and ethnic and women's issues.

İrvin Cemil Schick holds a PhD from the Massachusetts Institute of Technology (MIT) and has taught at Harvard University, MIT and İstanbul Şehir University, as well as holding guest positions at Boston University, Sabancı University and Boğaziçi University. He is the author of *The Erotic Margin: Sexuality and Spatiality in Alteritist Discourse* (1999), *The Fair Circassian: Adventures of an Orientalist Motif* (in Turkish, 2004) and *Writing the Body, Society, and the Universe: On Islam, Gender, and Culture* (in Turkish, 2011); the editor of *The M. Uğur Derman 65th Birthday Festschrift* (2000), *European Female Captives and Their Muslim Masters: Narratives of Captivity in 'Turkish' Lands* (in Turkish, 2005), *Love for the Prophet: The Prophet Muhammad on the 1443th Anniversary of His Birth* (2014) and *The Book of Beauties in a New Style: Encomium for the Merchants and Artisans of Istanbul* (in Turkish, 2017); and the co-editor of *Turkey in Transition: New Perspectives* (with E. Ahmet Tonak, 1987), *Women in the Ottoman*

Balkans: Gender, Culture and History (with Amila Buturović, 2007), *Calligraphy and Architecture in the Muslim World* (with Mohammad Gharipour, 2013) and *The Principal Figures of Turkish Architecture* (with an editorial committee, in Turkish, 2015). His research interests include the Islamic arts of the book; gender, sexuality, spatiality and the body in Islam; and animals and the environment in Islam. He is currently completing a second doctorate at the École des Hautes Études en Sciences Sociales in Paris; his dissertation concerns occult practices in Islam with special emphasis on their legitimation.

Kadir Yildirim is a research fellow at the Center for Mediterranean Studies at Ruhr-University Bochum and a lecturer at the Institute for Turkish Studies at the University of Duisburg-Essen. He completed his PhD at Istanbul University in 2011 with a thesis focused on the development of labour organizations and worker movements in Ottoman working life from 1870 to 1922. His primary research interests lie in labour history and the social and economic history of the Ottoman Middle East. He has published several articles on Ottoman labour history and the historical formation of social and economic classes in the Ottoman Middle East. He has taught courses on economic history, history of economic thought and labour history at various universities. Currently, he is teaching Ottoman Paleography at the University of Duisburg-Essen.

Jerzy Zdanowski is Professor of Middle Eastern History at Andrzej Frycz Modrzewski Krakow University and a former Fulbright scholar at Rutgers and Princeton Universities. Select publications include 'Contesting Enslavement: Voices of the Female Slaves from the Persian Gulf in the 1930s', *Die Welt des Islams* (2015); 'The Right to Manumit and British Relations with Ibn Saud and Persia in the 1920s', *Journal of Contemporary History* (2015); *Speaking with Their Own Voices: The Stories of Slaves in the Persian Gulf in the 20th Century* (2014); and *Slavery and Manumission: British Policy in the Red Sea and the Persian Gulf in the First Half of the 20th Century* (2013).

Introduction

Elena Andreeva and Kevin McNeer

We would like to thank Janet Afary for holding the conference that became the first step toward this book and for allowing us to develop it and take it in our own direction. Having roots in a conference, the book has retained the nature of a forum for scholars from East and West to examine slavery in the Middle East and North Africa from a perspective of their choosing. The focus is on the last two centuries, which saw the endgame of institutionalized, legal slavery in the region and have seen the re-emergence of slavery and de facto slavery in places.

The result is a rich mosaic, not bound by one lens. Slavery is examined in the context of gender and racial relations, social and economic networks, cultural production (literature, music, visual arts and handicrafts), formal and informal institutions, Islamic family law, the terrors of the Islamic State and cultural heritage among the descendants of slaves today.

The contributors have sifted through government archives and statistics, and mined memoirs, interviews, photographs, drawings, music and the moving image. Much of the contemporary material has been gathered first-hand, some of it in high-risk regions, such as northern Iraq and Yemen. Not only Arabic, Persian and Turkish sources, but also a rich variety of materials in minor and endangered languages, such as Soqotri, Balochi and Sorani Kurdish, are leveraged. The voices of the slaves themselves, while largely unrecoverable from the past, sound through at times – even if muted and distorted – in folklore, poems, statements to officials and oral histories.

Commonalities emerge. Despite the diverse geographies, cultures and times studied in these chapters – from the Ottoman Empire and Qajar Iran to Egypt and Kurdistan in the present day – practices overlap, interconnected by Islam and trade. The Shari'a principle of *umm al-walad*, to cite but one example, was common to the super-region. It gave freedom and inheritance rights to the children of an enslaved mother and to the mother herself if her offspring were fathered by her master – unlike in North America, where the status of slave was passed automatically from generation to generation and governed by a rigid racial hierarchy not shared by the Muslim East. The presumption of the sexual accessibility of enslaved women, and even boys in places, was also common to the super-region, as was the presumption that slavery was a natural part of life. The gaze of 'Western eyes' produced similar narratives that often exploited slavery in the East for book sales and a sense of Western cultural superiority but also fuelled abolitionist movements and left us valuable insights. And the decline and abolishment of slavery followed similar curves – complex interactions between progressive impulses and intransigence, idealism and practicality, and pressures from within and without these societies. There ensued a contradictory and flawed freedom.

One emerging commonality today, in the – mostly – post-slavery era, is the reticence in some African diasporas to speak about their origins and the 'Africanness' of their traditions – or, in some instances, their denial of any connection to Africa – a tendency observed in Iran, Yemen and Morocco, which raises questions about how to describe the identity of these communities. This apparent 'ghosting' of the past seems connected with a sense that certain rituals and musical traditions are incompatible with, or, at least, inappropriate in Islamic society. And yet there are exceptions: in Yazd, Iran, the descendants of an enslaved matriarch were happy to discuss their African origins.

Moving from chapter to chapter, country to country, we have been struck by the massive scale of slavery and the titanic human effort required to end it – the slow restructuring of the very fabric of society and its deep-rooted habits – as well as the ease with which human beings can fall back into the old ways after so much struggle to overcome them. The two concluding chapters demonstrate that despite the abolition of institutional slavery, forms of exploitation persist.

At the same time, these histories offer moments of light: the preservation of dance and music despite the loss of language; the liberation and re-assimilation of young Yazidi women; the precious jewelled skirt a slave mother gave her son so that he might make his pilgrimage.

The book is divided thematically into four parts: Gender and Sexuality: Female Slaves; Resistance and Abolition; Preserving Identity and Tradition; and Slavery in a Post-Slavery World.

The opening chapter, 'Ziba Khanum of Yazd: An Enslaved African Woman in Nineteenth-Century Iran' by Anthony A. Lee, introduces the reader to many of the topics treated throughout the book: personal stories, suppressed or overlooked histories, emancipation and integration. There are significant gaps in our knowledge of the history of slavery in Iran, in particular of the influence of African and Afro-Iranian people on other Iranians and on Persian society and culture. The history of an enslaved African woman, Ziba Khanum, and her son, Ghulam-'Ali (Siyah) Khurasani, enhances our understanding of the history of Iran as well as of the history of the African diaspora in the Indian Ocean world. The lives of these two individuals not only have intrinsic value and human interest but, in their uniqueness and surprising fruition, also illuminate larger issues of Iranian history – issues of race, gender, religion, elite social and economic networks, the nature of slavery and the value of subaltern history.

The second chapter in the first section is 'On the Multivalence of Women's Captivity Narratives: Seventeenth to Nineteenth Centuries', by İrvin Cemil Schick. Among the earliest 'bestsellers' in the Western world were captivity narratives penned by or about individuals of European descent enslaved by native Americans, Africans and others. Some were autobiographical; many were fictional. In structure and language, these accounts prefigured the form of the novel and offered their readership exotic settings, suspense and ample opportunity for empathy. At the same time, these works were profoundly didactic, playing an important role in evangelizing, nation-building, gender-construction, warmongering and even abolitionism. This chapter is a review of the extant first-person narratives of European and Euro-American women's captivities in the Muslim World, especially but not exclusively on the Barbary Coast. It covers twelve works published between 1683 and 1875, some in numerous editions and versions, focusing on common themes such as gender, religion, race, diplomacy and eroticism, and paying special attention to the stories' veracity as well as their relevance to present-day geopolitics.

The second section consists of four chapters, the first of which, by Kadir Yildirim, is 'The Gradual Elimination of Female Slavery in the Late Ottoman Empire: Institutional Change'. As an essential institution of Ottoman social and economic life, slavery survived until the end of the Ottoman Empire. Yet for some time before this, beginning in the nineteenth century, the number of slaves had been decreasing in line with decreasing numbers of prisoners of war and the overall weakening of the slave trade. Britain's push to suppress the slave trade internationally as a step towards full abolition was paralleled by the Ottoman state enacting laws that prohibited slavery within the empire. Nevertheless, because of societal resistance to these laws, the slave trade did not die out until the end of the empire. This study makes it clear that while the change in formal institutions was more effective in ending the enslavement of Africans, the abolition of white female slavery, with Circassians and Georgians constituting the majority at that time, was only possible with changes in social and economic structures. Among those changes was the emergence of servant markets, which are discussed in their connection to manumission.

'The Social Construction of Slavery, Injustice and Manumission on the Gulf Coast of Arabia and Oman in the 1920s and 1930s', by Jerzy Zdanowski, deals with the complex attitudes towards emancipation among slaves themselves. In Arabia, slavery had been known since time immemorial, and slaves had been brought to the region from East Africa, Abyssinia, Egypt, West Africa, Baluchistan and India. On the north-eastern coast of the Arabian Peninsula, where Islamic and British manumission was practised, there was a strikingly low percentage of slaves who sought to obtain formal freedman status. The annual rate of slaves asking for manumission amounted to only 1 per cent of the slave population. This chapter analyses the economic and social aspects of slavery in the coastal areas of eastern Arabia and Oman in order to examine the question of why the majority of slaves, whose roots lay outside the region and who were aware of British manumission policy, preferred to stay in their owners' homes. This examination is conducted through the lens of statements made by the slaves themselves when applying to the British for manumission in 1908–41. These statements come from previously underleveraged archives preserved by the India Office and Foreign Office, and they demonstrate the surprising tenacity of the forces binding slaves to local communities.

'Slavery on the Central Asian Steppe in the Works of Nikolai Karazin (1842–1908)', by Elena Andreeva, examines Iranian slaves in Turkestan in the second half of the nineteenth century – a topic that has thus far received limited attention from scholars. The enslavement and emancipation of Iranians in Turkestan is presented through the creative works of Nikolai Karazin (1842–1908), a talented and popular Russian painter, writer, journalist, book illustrator, war correspondent, traveller and ethnographer.

Slavery played a significant role in Turkestan prior to the Russian conquest in the second half of the nineteenth century, and though estimates of slave numbers vary greatly, all sources agree that the overwhelming majority were Iranian. By the time Khiva fell to the Russians in 1873, there were likely around thirty thousand Iranian slaves there. This chapter places Karazin's images of Iranian slaves in the context of Russian imperialist and abolitionist policy – and in juxtaposition to Russian slaves, who were much fewer but whose liberation was a top priority for Russian military and civil authorities. The article includes songs by the captives expressing their longing for Iran and freedom, as well as the tragic story of the emancipated slaves' long and perilous journeys back home. Karazin's works in a variety of media present a vivid picture of slavery in Turkestan, illustrating the impact of the Russian conquest and administration on the institution of slavery, and emphasizing the importance of shared humanity.

The last chapter in this section, 'Mercy Releases: Manumission Practices in Tetouan, Morocco (1860–1960)' by Josep Lluís Mateo Dieste, analyses the practice of manumission of female and male slaves by notables in the city of Tetouan between 1860 and 1960, the period of slavery's demise in Morocco. It is based primarily on unpublished notarial sources combined with oral and colonial sources. During this period, neither the Moroccan authorities nor the colonial authorities – the French and the Spanish, who controlled the Moroccan Protectorate between 1912 and 1956 – formally abolished slavery, though they did prohibit the slave trade. This resulted in an ambivalent process, lasting from the end of the nineteenth to the first half of the twentieth century, of owners freeing slaves on their own initiative. The documentation indicates that until the first quarter of the twentieth century, manumission was part of what might be called a 'moral exchange mechanism' that gave masters hope of acquiring religious merit before dying and thereby of securing a reward and a place in paradise. These liberations led to divergent trajectories among the freed, the majority of whom were women: many continued to perform domestic work in the same households, while others went on to occupy subordinate jobs as cooks, ritual inviters or healers.

The two chapters of the third section explore self-perception and tradition among the descendants of slaves in Iran and Yemen. The first, 'Afro-Baloch Communities in Modern Iran and Their Healing Traditions' by Maryam Nourzaei, looks at healing dances and songs performed by the descendants of African slaves living along the coast in the Iranian province of Sistan-and-Balochistan and is based on her interviews with Afro-Baloch and time spent in their communities. While Afro-Balochi healing traditions vary across this region and have been highly influenced by Balochi themes and motifs, Nourzaei demonstrates how they share African elements brought by slaves to their new home – despite the fact that many community members do not acknowledge any African roots. This community lost its original language or languages, but its members have maintained many traditions, much like other peoples of African origin in different regions in Iran. Interestingly, many of the practices examined in this article have remained local and not spread to nearby communities such as the Jadgali or Baloch. The chapter includes a detailed description of certain ceremonies and also explores questions of the community's self-perception.

The second chapter, 'Transmuted Memories: Slavery and Its Shadow on the Island of Soqotra' by Kevin McNeer and Sarali Gintsburg, begins with an overview of the history of slavery on this Yemeni island off the coast of Somalia, relying on Arab pilot books, Soqotri oral works and Western travelogues to trace the practice through to its abolition in 1967 by Soviet-backed revolutionaries. The second part of the chapter looks at Afro-Soqotran culture and self-perception today. A generation or more removed from abolition, the Afro-Soqotran community is a part of the island's overall social fabric and yet has its own neighbourhoods, dress and customs. The authors engage a blacksmith and a musician from the Afro-Soqotran community in encounters that raise questions about how this community perceives its relationship to Africa: while elements of African culture have been preserved, there is a tendency among today's Afro-Soqotrans to de-emphasize or deny African roots, but at the same time, it is the very 'Africanness' of their performances that makes them so popular. Potential motivations for this phenomenon – also discussed in the previous chapter – are examined in the context of the island's recent history and political-cultural shifts.

The two chapters of the concluding section address modern forms of slavery, linking them to practices in the past. The first, by Dina Al Raffie, is 'Enslaved by the Street: Contemporary Forms of Slavery among the Street Children of Cairo'. While what has traditionally been understood as 'chattel slavery' is a rare occurrence in today's world, other forms of enslavement – as defined in a variety of international legal conventions – persist and tend to be overlooked. One such case is Egypt's 'street children', a group that still falls prey to human trafficking and exploitation by criminal gangs because it lacks the protection of a stable home and opportunity for upward mobility. While this topic has received little scholarly attention, it has been repeatedly dramatized in Egyptian movies and television series and discussed on popular television shows. Despite some recent advances in the legal framework for the criminalization of the exploitation of women and children in Egypt, successful prosecutions are few and far between due to the stigma attached to victims of sexual molestation, rape and forced prostitution. This chapter reviews the underlying socio-economic, political and legal causes of the problem, and shines a light on the cultural and gendered nuances that perpetuate it, before moving on to assess the government and civil efforts to address it.

The concluding chapter, 'Yazidi Women and Girls Held as Slaves under the Islamic State: Healing Wounds and Reassessing Doctrines' by Lana Ravandi-Fadai, provides an unflinching account of Islamic State (IS) sexual slavery and its aftermath, focusing on Yazidi female captives in Iraq and the debate among Islamic scholars over reforms to certain Islamic doctrines. In the summer of 2014 in the Iraqi province of Nineveh, IS engaged in genocidal violence against Yazidis that resulted in thousands of men killed and a multitude of women and children taken captive. Women and girls were subjected to physical, emotional and spiritual indignities: enslaved, raped and sold at markets. After the defeat of IS, the Yazidi and international communities worked hard to facilitate the freed women's reintegration into Yazidi society. Religious leaders relaxed traditional prohibitions on allowing women back into their community after sexual intercourse with non-Yazidis. Although many victims left for the West, especially Germany, and many others remain in refugee camps, reintegration was partially achieved. Yazidi women's children sired by Muslim fathers during captivity, however, are still struggling for acceptance in the Yazidi community. The tragedy also damaged relations with neighbouring Muslims, not only Arabs but Kurds – who share the same language and ethnicity as Yazidis.

Part One

Gender and Sexuality: Female Slaves

1

Ziba Khanum of Yazd: An enslaved African woman in nineteenth-century Iran

Anthony A. Lee

Historians have so far found little to say about Africans in Iran.[1] This is true of the history of the Indian Ocean diaspora in general and the Indian Ocean slave trade, especially as compared to the enormous amount of scholarship now available on the Atlantic slave trade and the New World diaspora.[2] There are huge gaps in our knowledge of the history of slavery in Iran in particular and of the influence of African and Afro-Iranian

I am grateful to Dr Mehrdad Amanat for his indispensable assistance with my research for this paper.

[1] The only doctoral dissertation written on the history of Iranian slavery appears to be Behnaz A. Mirzai's 'Slavery, the Abolition of the Slave Trade, and the Emancipation of Slaves in Iran (1828–1928)', PhD dissertation, York University, Ontario, 2004, published as *A History of Slavery and Emancipation in Iran, 1800–1929* (Austin: University of Texas Press, 2017). By the same author, see also 'African Presence in Iran: Identity and Its Reconstruction', in O. Petre-Grenouilleau, ed., *Traites et Esclavages: Vieux Problemes, Nouvelles Perspectives?* (Paris: Société Française d'Histoire d'Outre-mer, 2002), 229–46; and 'The Slave Trade and the African Diaspora in Iran', in Abdul Sheriff, ed., *Monsoon and Migration: Unleashing Dhow Synergies* (Zanzibar: ZIFF, 2005), 30–4; see also 'Afro-Iranian Lives' (video). Niambi Cacchioli too has done work in this area: see, 'Disputed Freedom: Fugitive Slaves, Asylum, and Manumission in Iran (1851–1913)', UNESCO (http://portal.unesco.org/cult ure/en/files/38508/12480962345Disputed_Freedom.pdf/Disputed%2BFreedom.pdf). Further, my own work on enslaved Africans in Iran: Anthony A. Lee, 'Enslaved African Women in Nineteenth-Century Iran: The Life of Fezzeh Khanom of Shiraz', *Iranian Studies* (May 2012); 'Half the Household Was African: Recovering the Histories of Two Enslaved Africans in Iran, Haji Mubarak and Fezzeh Khanom', *UCLA Historical Journal* 26, no. 1 (2016); 'Recovering the Biographies of Enslaved Africans in Nineteenth-Century Iran', in *Changing Horizons of African History*, ed. Awet T. Weldemichael, Anthony A. Lee and Edward A. Alpers (Trenton, NJ: Africa World Press, 2017); 'Africans in the Palace: The Testimony of Taj al-Sultana Qajar from the Royal Harem in Iran', in *Islamic Slavery*, ed. Mary Ann Faye (New York: Palgrave Macmillan, 2018); and chapter 2 of *The Baha'i Faith in Africa: Establishing a New Religious Movement, 1952–1962* (Leiden: Brill, 2011).

[2] A few recent works on the Indian Ocean slave trade are Shihan de Silva Jayasuriya and Richard Pankhurst, eds, *The African Diaspora in the Indian Ocean* (Trenton, NJ: Africa World Press, 2003); Edward A. Alpers, *East Africa and the Indian Ocean* (Princeton: Markus Wiener, 2009); Robert Harms, Bernard K. Freamon and David W. Blight, eds, *Indian Ocean Slavery in the Age of Abolition* (New Haven: Yale University Press, 2013); Richard Allen, *European Slave Trading in the Indian Ocean, 1500–1850* (Athens: Ohio University Press, 2014); Matthew S. Hopper, *Slaves of One Master: Globalization and Slavery in Arabia in the Age of Empire* (New Haven: Yale University Press, 2015); and Henri Médard, Marie-Laure Derat, Thomas Vernet and Marie Pierre Ballarin, eds, *Traites et Esclavages en Afrique Orientale et dans l'océan Indien* (Paris: Karthala, 2013).

people on other Iranians and on Persian society and culture. Uncovering this history will change our understanding of the history of Iran and the history of the African diaspora in the Indian Ocean world.

The focus of this inquiry

This chapter is concerned with the life of one enslaved African woman who lived in Iran, Ziba Khanum, and her son, Ghulam-'Ali (Siyah) Khurasani. Certainly, the lives of these two individuals should be recovered for their own sake. But their lives, in their uniqueness, and with all their surprises, also illumine larger issues of Iranian history – issues of race, gender, religion, elite social and economic networks, the nature of slavery and the value of subaltern history.

The scope of the Iranian slave trade

Domestic slavery has existed in Iran for centuries. By the nineteenth century, Africans were enslaved and brought to Iran in large numbers as part of the East African/ Indian Ocean trade. While there are no definite historical statistics on the number of slaves exported from Africa into the Persian Gulf, estimates among scholars for the Indian Ocean trade as a whole during the nineteenth century vary between one and two million. Possibly two-thirds of these slaves were African women and girls, who were almost always destined for residence in wealthy Iranian households as domestic servants and concubines.[3]

In 1868, a census conducted in Tehran revealed that about 2.6 per cent of the civilian population of the city was designated as African slaves or 'household servants'.[4]

---

[3] Paul E. Lovejoy, *Transformations in Slavery*, 3rd edn (Cambridge: Cambridge University Press, 2012), 60–1, 150–4; Joseph C. Miller, 'Introduction', in *Women and Slavery: Africa and the Western Indian Ocean World, and the Medieval North Atlantic*, ed. Gwyn Campbell, Suzanne Miers and Joseph Calder Miller, vol. 1 (Athens: Ohio University Press, 2007), 4–5; Helge Kjekshus, *Ecological Control and Development in Eastern Africa* (Nairobi: Longmans, 1979), 14–16; Gwyn Campbell, introduction to *Abolition and Its Aftermath in Indian Ocean, Africa and Asia* (London: Routledge, 2005), 5; and Gwyn Campbell, *Structure of Slavery in Indian Ocean Africa and Asia* (London: Frank Cass, 2004), xi. For a discussion of the number of enslaved people imported into Iran in the nineteenth century, see Mirzai, *History of Slavery*, 63–6.

[4] Thomas Ricks, 'Slaves and Slave Trading in Shi'i Iran, AD 1500–1900', *Journal of Asian and African Studies* 36, no. 4 (2001): 407–18. The categories *nawkar* (male servant), *khidmatkar* (female servant), *kaniz-i siyah* (female black slave/servant) and *khwajih* and *ghulam-i siyah* (male black slave/servant) were clearly separate from each other. There were 3,770 enslaved Africans in Tehran out of a total population of 147,256, that is, about 2.6 per cent of the city's population. The results of the 1868 census are available on the web in Persian at http://www.qajarwomen.org/fa/items/1018A2.html. Of course, the accuracy and the reliability of the census can be debated. For example, it obviously does not include the by then hundreds of African slaves living in the harem and the palace of the shah.

This count includes only urban households, not slaves who were used in agricultural work or to maintain the irrigation systems.[5] Household servants and slaves were mostly women. This 1868 census reveals the extent of domestic slavery in large cities in nineteenth-century Iran and the importance of its African population, a subject which is usually ignored in Iranian histories.[6] This chapter attempts to recover at least a part of the life of one enslaved woman, Ziba Khanum, of Yazd, the mother of Ghulam-'Ali Siyah Khurasani (1871–1949). In previous published articles, I have been able to locate seven other African slaves who appear, usually by accident, in the Iranian historical record, and to discuss their individual lives. I am interested in writing these partial biographies first for their own sake, to honour and to understand (insofar as is possible) individuals in history, as a matter of human dignity. The present chapter builds on that earlier research in hopes of constructing a history of African slavery in Iran at the level of individual biographies. An examination of Ziba Khanum's life, as well as the lives of other enslaved women in her household, can begin to fill the gaps in our knowledge of African slavery in Iran. Ghulam-'Ali's dramatic career illumines issues of race, religion and assimilation in nineteenth- and early-twentieth-century Iran.

Ziba Khanum and her son

Ziba Khanum (d. 1932), an African woman, lived as a slave and concubine of her master, Haji Muhammad-'Ali Sadiq Khurasani (known as Gunduli, 'the fat'), in the city of Yazd, central Iran, in the second half of the nineteenth century. She is absent in the documentary record.[7] Information about her life has been taken from multiple interviews with her descendants and other living relatives.[8] She is remembered by her great-grandchildren as their earliest ancestor. Her descendants relate different stories of her origins as part of family lore. Some suggest that she was purchased in Zanzibar on one of her wealthy master's merchant voyages. Others suggest Mombasa as her

---

[5] Ricks, 'Slaves and Slave Trading in Shi'i Iran'.

[6] For a brief discussion of domestic slavery in Iran, see Abbas Amanat, *Iran: A Modern History* (New Haven: Yale University Press, 2017). It is probable that cities in the southern part of Iran during this period, such as Shiraz or Bandar Abbas, would have had an even higher percentage of African slaves, being closer to the ports of import. Tehran may not have been so different in this regard from other world capital cities, however. The black populations of both London and Lisbon during the mid-nineteenth century were probably in a higher percentage range. The black population of Lisbon may have been as high as 20 per cent. See, for example, *Os Negros em Portugal: sécs. XV a XIX: Mosteiro dos Jeronimo. Setembro de 1999 a 24 de Janeiro de 2000* (Lisbon: Commisão Nacional para as comemoracões dos descobrimentos, 1999); A.P.D.G., *Sketches of Portuguese Life, Manners, Costume, and Character* (London: G.B. Whittaker/R. Gilbert, 1826); Peter Fryer, *Staying Power: The History of Black People in Britain* (Sterling, VA: Pluto Press, 1984). I am grateful to Dr Edward Alpers and Dr Gregory Pirio for this information.

[7] The only written record that I have been able to find that mentions her is on the manuscript family tree created in Germany by a distant relative that will be discussed later in this chapter.

[8] Interviews with Jalil Taqizadeh, Los Angeles, 7 April 2017, and by phone from Los Angeles, 14 November 2017 and 9 January 2018; Interview with Monir Ardekani, by phone from Vancouver, 29 September 2017; Interview with Shahnaz Khorasani, by phone from Peekskill, NY, 19 October 2017, and in Peekskill, NY, 18 November 2017. Dr Mehrdad Amanat has conducted interviews with the same informants.

point of origin. Other descendants say she was acquired in Bandar Abbas, in southern Iran, at the slave market.[9] In any case, she would have been named Ziba (beautiful) by her master after purchase. Enslaved Africans were not given (Arabic) Muslim names but were assigned Persian names as part of the process of assimilation into Persian households.[10] The name 'Ziba' suggests that Haji Muhammad-'Ali wanted to bring a beautiful African girl into his household. Enslaved African women and men, especially eunuchs, in nineteenth-century Iran were considered signs of wealth and prestige among rich merchants and aristocrats.[11] Nasir al-Din Shah brought dozens, and eventually hundreds, of enslaved African women and men into the palace as a display of wealth.[12]

Ziba, the family remembers, was purchased as a girl or young woman, possibly as a nurse for her master's ailing wife. This is also suggested by the family nickname by which she was known, Dadé (*dadih*, Persian: nanny or nursemaid). She lived in the household of her master, with his wife and children – two daughters and a son, Muhammad-Ismail Khurasani. Family lore suggests that Haji Muhammad-'Ali took her as a concubine with the permission of his wife, by some accounts, because his wife was sick and could no longer perform her marital duties. Others suggest that the master married Ziba after his wife's death, which is unlikely.

These are certainly modern rationalizations for Ziba's sexual relationship with Haji Muhammad-'Ali, a relationship which would have required no explanation or justification at the time. There were no barriers – either legal, religious or moral – to a master taking a slave as his concubine. Both slavery and concubinage were recognized and regulated by Islamic law (the *Shari'a*). A slave woman who bore a child by her master was afforded a change of status by this law. She became an *umm al-walad*[13] (mother of a son), which meant not only that she could not be sold but also that she must be freed upon the death of her master. While children born to

---

[9]   This would make a difference, since, as commodities, slaves were classified by country of origin. Lady Mary Sheil, a nineteenth-century traveller to Iran, noted that African slaves were divided into three types: 'Bambassees, Nubees, and Habeshees. The former come from Zanzibar, and the neighboring country in the interior but I don't know the etymology of the name [certainly from "Mombasa"]. The others as their names imply are natives of Nubia [Sudan] and Abyssinia [Ethiopia]' (Lady Mary Elenor Sheil, *Glimpses of Life and Manners in Persia* (London: John Murray, 1856), 243–5). The *habashis* were regarded as the most beautiful, intelligent and expensive slaves, followed by *bambasis* and then *nubis* and *zanjis* (from Zanzibar). None of these terms are ethnic designations, however, but refer only to the ports from which these enslaved Africans embarked in the slave trade. Since her descendants indicate she embarked from Mombasa or Zanzibar, at least we know that Ziba Khanum was not Ethiopian.

[10] Mirzai, *History of Slavery*, 100–1.

[11] See, for example, the memoir of Taj al-Saltana, the daughter of Nasir al-Din Shah: Taj al-Saltana, *Khatirat-i Taj al-Saltana*, ed. Mansura Ettihadia (Nizam Mafi) and Sirus Sa'dvandian (Tehran: 1361 [1982]), translated as *Crowning Anguish: Memoirs of a Persian Princess from the Harem to Modernity, 1884–1914*, ed. Abbas Amanat (Washington, DC: Mage, 1993), 112–13.

[12] For a discussion of eunuchs and enslaved women in the shah's palace, see Mirzai, *History of Slavery*, 111–22.

[13] 'Umm al-Walad: Mother of the son. Refers to a slave woman impregnated by her owner, thereby bearing a child. In the opinion of many classical jurists, such a slave woman cannot be sold. ... Children, male or female, born of this union are legally free and enjoy all rights of legitimate parentage, including inheritance and use of the father's name' (Oxford Islamic Studies Online, http://www.oxfordislamicstudies.com/article/opr/t125/e2424).

enslaved fathers were slaves and thus had no legal claim to inheritance, the child of an *umm al-walad* was born free and by Shari'a law stood to inherit the father's name and fortune in equal proportion to the father's children born into wedlock. This legal state of affairs could, naturally, prove a strong incentive for a slave woman to bear a child by her master. By doing so, the slave could move from the periphery towards the centre of the household, protect herself from sale, free her child and herself, and, finally, inherit part of her master's wealth through her offspring. The sexual aspects of the relationship were considered incidental and carried no moral stigma or social shame. It was simply assumed that a master could have sexual contact with his slaves (male or female), if he wished. But as will be seen, the law was not always applied consistently.

Ziba Khanum bore one son, who was named Ghulam-'Ali (slave of 'Ali) (Figure 1.1), by her master. This is a common enough Iranian name, since Imam 'Ali is a holy figure in Shi'i Islam. But the name has special resonance here with regard to slavery. The boy's father's name was 'Ali. So 'Slave of 'Ali' both identifies him with, and subordinates him to, his mother's master. He took his father's surname later in life and called himself Ghulam-'Ali (Yazdi) Khurasani. But he was universally known as an adult in Yazd as Ghulam-'Ali Siyah (the Black), and perhaps not even pejoratively, though his grandchildren say that no one would call him that to his face. As a teenager, Ghulam-'Ali became a Baha'i, a follower of a persecuted minority religion in Iran.[14] He eventually left home and built a career as a merchant in Bandar Abbas, travelling first to Palestine and then to India. He returned to Yazd a rich man and went on to become a personage of considerable wealth and status in the city. His mansion compound in Yazd still exists and has been turned into a modern hotel in a traditional style (Figure 1.2). Ziba Khanum lived in her son's Baha'i household after his return, with his children (her grandchildren) and his grandchildren (her great-grandchildren) until she passed away in 1932.

Conversion and pilgrimage

As his Baha'i descendants remember it, Ghulam-'Ali was converted to the Baha'i Faith in his early youth. He would accompany his father to gatherings of men that were held

---

[14] There is a considerable body of academic literature on the Baha'i religion and its history, especially in the United States and in Iran. See, for example, the twenty-five volumes of the *Studies in the Babi and Baha'i Religions* series, Anthony A. Lee, general editor (Los Angeles: Kalimat Press, 1982–). See also Peter Smith, *The Babi and Baha'i Religions: From Messianic Shi'ism to a World Religion* (New York: Cambridge University Press, 1987); Margit Warburg, *Citizens of the World: A History and Sociology of the Baha'is from a Globalization Perspective* (Leiden: Brill, 2006); Juan R. I. Cole, *Modernity and the Millennium: The Genesis of the Baha'i Faith in the Nineteenth-century Middle East* (New York: Columbia University Press, 1998); William Garlington, *The Baha'i Faith in America* (Westport, CT: Praeger, 2005); Dominic Parviz Brookshaw and Seena B. Fazel, eds, *The Baha'is of Iran: Socio-Historical Studies* (London: Routledge, 2008); Moojan Momen, *The Baha'i Communities of Iran 1851–1921* (Oxford: George Ronald, 2015); and Amanat, *Iran: A Modern History*, passim. For a full discussion of the emergence of an academic literature of Babi and Baha'i Studies, see chapter 1 of Lee, *The Baha'i Faith in Africa*.

Figure 1.1 Ghulam-'Ali Siyah (Yazdi) Khurasani who appears to be twelve or fourteen years old, *c.* 1885. His clothing indicates considerable wealth and status for the time.

Source: Khurasani family archives. In private hands.

Figure 1.2 The courtyard of Ghulam-'Ali's mansion in Yazd, which is now the Mehr Traditional Hotel. Photo 2017.

Source: Courtesy of Karnaval travel agency: https://www.karnaval.ir/stay/yazd-mehr-traditional-hotel#lg=1&slide=0.

regularly as social occasions, for business and entertainment, to smoke opium and so forth. There were Baha'is at these gatherings who would talk about their religion. This was a normal part of nineteenth-century social life among wealthy men in Iran. Ghulam-'Ali was introduced into this elite network of men very early and was accepted in these circles. In fact, Ghulam-'Ali continued this social practice in his own wealthy household in Yazd into the mid-twentieth century, entertaining men with food and conversation every night, almost to the end of his life. Ghulam-'Ali accepted the Baha'i religion as a matter of personal conviction as a teenager, but he told no one about his beliefs, not even his father. His half-brother, Muhammad-Ismail Khurasani (also known as Gunduli), became a Baha'i as well. But Muhammad-Ismail was quite open about his new faith. There were other Baha'is in their father's social circle, particularly Haji Mirza Muhammad Afshar, a wealthy merchant in Yazd who was instrumental in converting Muhammad-Ismail and who would later become important in Ghulam-'Ali's life.[15] Apparently, however, Ghulam-'Ali was converted to the new faith by Haji Mirza Muhammad-i 'Alaqiband, another wealthy merchant of Yazd.[16] So it appears that Ghulam-'Ali was deeply enmeshed in his father's business network and was connected to many wealthy merchants in Yazd.

[15] Muhammad Tahir Malmiri, *Tarikh-i Amriy-i Yazd* (History of the Cause in Yazd) (Bundoora, Victoria: Century Press, 2013), 109.
[16] His conversion by 'Alaqiband is mentioned in an editor's footnote in Sadri Navvabzadeh Ardakani, *Amr-i Baha'i dar Ardakan*, ed. Vahid Rafati (Hofheim: Baha'i Verlag, 2009), 42.

Haji Muhammad-'Ali died when his son, Ghulam-'Ali, was perhaps seventeen or eighteen years old. According to the shari'a, he should have inherited a portion of his father's fortune, land and property. But it would seem that the shari'a was ignored in this case, since Ghulam-'Ali got neither any part of his father's house nor any land, and the family has no memory of an inheritance. As the Shari'a was interpreted and administered by Shi'i clerics in Yazd, there was always room for manipulation of the law.

Ghulam-'Ali's descendants do remember that Ziba Khanum had been given a jewelled skirt by her master that was extremely valuable, embroidered with gold threads and pearls. This became her son's only inheritance. After his father's passing, Ghulam-'Ali told his mother that he was a Baha'i and that he had determined to leave Yazd and travel to Palestine to meet Baha'u'llah (1817–1892), the founder of the Baha'i Faith, who was still living in exile there as a prisoner of the Ottoman state. As a Baha'i, Ghulam-'Ali would have believed Baha'u'llah to be a Prophet of God. His mother supported his plans to make this pilgrimage and gave him her jewelled skirt, which he was able to sell for 700 *tumans* (perhaps the equivalent of $1,400, sometime in the 1880s).[17] This was a substantial amount of money at the time.[18]

The limited value of the binary concept of slave vs free

Ziba Khanum remained in the household of her deceased master and continued to live with his family in Yazd after the departure of her son. Despite the shari'a law declaring her free upon her master's death, Ziba Khanum likely remained a servant in the house and would have continued to perform her domestic duties as before. Her legal status as a free woman, if it was recognized at all by the late Haji Muhammad-'Ali's family, would have been of little consequence. She remained a dependent of the family, certainly materially and possibly emotionally, and lived in their household, with no other place to go. Her situation illustrates the problem of applying Western legal categories of 'slave' and 'free' to the lived experience of enslaved women in Iran.[19]

Historians of Middle Eastern slavery have warned about the limited value of binary legal distinctions between slavery and freedom when applied to the study of the Muslim world.[20] Such legal concepts presuppose a secular state that is able to guarantee

---

[17] Perhaps even as much as $3,500 at that time. The value of the Persian *tuman*, a gold coin, varied widely in the nineteenth century from city to city and from decade to decade. See Mirzai, *History of Slavery*, iv–v.

[18] In 1890, the average price of a house in an American city was about $10,000: 'Real vs. Nominal Housing Prices: United States 1890–2010', *VisualizingEconomics*, http://www.visualizingeconom ics.com/blog/2011/03/23/real-vs-nominal-housing-prices-united-states1890-2010.

[19] I have also discussed this theoretical problem elsewhere. See Lee, 'Recovering the Biographies'.

[20] Similar cautions are made for the study of slavery in Africa and Asia. See Miller, 'Introduction', 25–9; Gwyn Campbell, 'Introduction: Slavery and Other Forms of Unfree Labour in the Indian Ocean World', in *Structure of Slavery*, viii–xviii; and Suzanne Miers, 'Slavery: A Question of Definition', in *Structure of Slavery*, 1–14.

the lives and properties of individuals who can claim its protection. It is this guarantee of security made by the modern state which, theoretically at least, releases a free person from dependence on, or obedience to, powerful others and allows for free choices within the law. Slaves within this Western system (especially African slaves in America) were excluded from such guarantees in early-modern societies and were held as chattel property for life by their owners. They lived in a relationship of total dependence on their masters, the only relationship of theirs that the law would recognize. The slave uniquely was forced to survive without the protection of law, family or state, reliant only on the master.

Such concepts of slave and free are of limited value when discussing societies that are not constructed around the ideas of rights, citizenship or a secular state, but rather built on concepts or kinship, belonging, religious authority and hierarchies of social dependence. In nineteenth-century Iran, personal security could only be maintained by ties of kinship, household belonging, community solidarity or the protection of a powerful and wealthy patron. There was no ideal within the society of freedom from such relationships, with their implications of dependence, obedience and obligation. Furthermore, any such freedom would have left an individual isolated and vulnerable. This was true for anyone, but particularly true for women who, whether slave or free, were almost never regarded as autonomous agents but attached to a male patron (father, husband, brother, master).

All enslaved persons in nineteenth-century Iran, and for the most part all other persons as well, necessarily were embedded in Muslim households and moved along a continuum of whatever situation of power, respect, wealth and independence they might be able to negotiate within those households. Women, however, tended to occupy positions outside of the public sphere and at the margins of wealth and power, slave women especially. They moved towards the centre of their households as they performed valuable domestic duties, found favour within the family, became the master's regular sexual partner and bore the master's heirs. The most important consideration for enslaved African women may not have been their legal status as slaves, since no sharp distinction in law or practice existed. Rather, their aim would have been to negotiate the most respected position they could achieve within the family they found themselves attached to. In fact, that would have been the goal of most women, whether slave or free, in nineteenth-century Iran. The defining factor was gender rather than slavery.

Ziba Khanum's life as a 'free woman' after the death of her master, according to the shari'a, was determined by gender as much as by her previous slave status or by perceptions of race. Contrasting her life, necessarily lived within the confines of the house of her master's surviving family, with the international travels and business success of her son highlights these gender differences. As a woman, Ziba Khanum was excluded from the opportunities that her son exploited so successfully. The fact that his mother was an African slave and that he was half-African was well known to everyone. But it seems to have been of little consequence. It was not a barrier to his elite social status, his merchant career or his wealth and influence upon his return to Yazd. The important thing was that he was an elite, wealthy man.

From Yazd to Palestine and India

Ghulam-'Ali's rapid departure from the city of Yazd is explained in the family lore of his descendants as a consequence of religious devotion, simply a desire to make a pilgrimage to attain the blessings of the Baha'i Prophet. However, it might also suggest some conflict or insecurity that would cause him to leave the city, especially since he did not return after his pilgrimage. His mother's willingness to support his departure may reinforce such a suspicion. But her support may also suggest that she herself had become a Baha'i and wanted her son to make the pilgrimage as an act of piety. In any case, she supported her son's exit from the city, giving him the only asset she owned.

Yazd has a very long history of violent persecution of Baha'is.[21] From the founding of the Babi movement in 1844 in Iran, Babis and later Baha'is have been regarded as heretics and apostates from Islam. As a result, there was always a rather intolerant attitude towards Baha'is among the ulama in Yazd. While initially some clerics were unconcerned by the movement, a few of them even converting, by 1873 repression and persecution had become the norm. In 1891, this persecution led to the arrest and execution of seven Baha'i men, widespread harassment and looting of Baha'i properties.[22] If Ghulam-'Ali's Baha'i identity had become known, he may have felt threatened. Being a Baha'i would have been grounds to disqualify him from inheritance, since according to the shari'a, non-Muslims can inherit nothing from a Muslim relative.[23]

In any case, Ghulam-'Ali left Yazd with a large amount of money and arrived in 'Akka, Palestine, where he was received into the household of Baha'u'llah as a guest for several months. He was unable to meet Baha'u'llah during this visit (though he was able to do so after leaving the household and being briefly invited back).[24] But it was probably during these early months that he received a Tablet (a letter) addressed

---

[21] See Haji Muhammad-Tahir Malmiri, *Tarikh-i Shuhaday-i Yazd* (History of the Martyrs of Yazd) (Le Caire: 1926), reprinted in Karachi: Baha'i Publishing Trust, 1978, for the history of the pogroms of 1903. Also, Aqa Sayyid Abu'l-Qasim Bayda, *Tarikh-i Bayda* (Bayda's Narrative), ed. Siyamak Zabihi Moghaddam (Hofheim: Baha'i Verlag, 2016).

[22] Moojan Momen, 'Iran: Province of Yazd', draft of article for *The Baha'i Encyclopedia* (1994), https://bahai-library.com/momen_encyclopedia_yazd.

[23] *Encyclopedia Iranica*, s.v., 'Inheritance ii. Islamic Period'.

[24] Some say six months and some nine months. But there is agreement that he was not able to see Baha'u'llah because of the latter's strict terms of imprisonment. In fact, in the late 1880s and early 1890s, when Ghulam-'Ali would have arrived in Palestine, Baha'u'llah was not under strict confinement. More likely, Ghulam-'Ali had arrived at the Baha'i headquarters unannounced and without permission, which was strictly forbidden by the Prophet. He was received into the household, but he was not allowed to see Baha'u'llah until he left and was invited back. See H. M. Balyuzi, *Bahá'u'lláh: The King of Glory* (Oxford: George Ronald, 1980), 362ff. on the conditions of Baha'u'llah's confinement during this period. Nonetheless, upon arrival in the household, Ghulam-'Ali gave his 700 *tumans* to 'Abdu'l-Baha (1844–1921), the eldest son of Baha'u'llah, who was in charge of household affairs. This may have been intended as a contribution, since the 700 *tumans* were returned to him, only over his protests, when he left Baha'u'llah's household. He finally agreed to accept 600 *tumans* back. After he left Palestine, he travelled first to Alexandria, Egypt. While there, within a day or two, he received a message that Baha'u'llah was able to receive visitors and he was invited back to the Holy Land. On the second visit, he met with Baha'u'llah. His descendants proudly insist, therefore, that he was able to achieve two pilgrimages during his lifetime.

to him by Baha'u'llah.[25] In the message, Baha'u'llah laments that earthy treasures have corrupted most people and caused them to turn away from God. He urges Ghulam-'Ali not to grieve over the sorrows that come to him in this world or the changes and chances of this world. These remarks certainly reflect general Baha'i teachings of detachment and resignation in the face of adversity. But in the specific case of Ghulam-'Ali, Baha'u'llah's words seem to suggest that in Yazd he had experienced a loss of wealth about which he remained in turmoil. Again, disinheritance, family disputes and religious persecution might be what Baha'u'llah is alluding to. The Tablet continues with a prayer for steadfastness for Ghulam-'Ali to recite.[26]

Return to Yazd

Ghulam-'Ali did not return to Yazd immediately after his stay in the Holy Land. He left Palestine for India. He seems to have been well connected to Baha'i networks, at least in Palestine and in South Asia. He worked as an agent of the previously mentioned Haji Mirza Muhammad Afshar, the Baha'i in Yazd, for his trading company in India. With the money he received from his mother, he would have been a junior partner in his mentor's business. He was able to accumulate more capital and eventually established a business of his own in Bandar Abbas, apparently importing and exporting goods between India and Yazd. When he returned to Yazd, sometime later, he brought Ziba Khanum into his home, where she lived as his dependent. He was very rich; family lore has it that he returned to Yazd with forty camels loaded with valuables, merchandise and household goods.[27] He was able to buy land and build a big house where he lived

---

[25] This was considered a great honour among Baha'is, and a blessing, since all of the writings of Baha'u'llah were considered sacred scripture by the Baha'is (and still are).

[26] The Tablet reads in full:

> He is the Witness, the All-Informed. All created things bear witness to the revelation of the Creator of the heavens, and the concourse on high is stirred up by the sweetness of the celestial call, and yet the people, for the most part, perceive it not. Verily, the treasures they have laid up have drawn them far away from their ultimate goal, and vain imaginings have debarred them from turning towards God, the Help in Peril, the Self-Subsisting. They cast behind their backs the Book of God, cleaving fast unto their idols and idle fancies.
>
> In truth, thy name was mentioned before this Wronged One. Thereupon, the Ocean of utterance surged, the Countenance of the Ancient of days turned towards thee and revealed for thee that which enraptureth hearts and souls. Grieve thou not over the changes and chances of the world. In all thy affairs, put thy reliance in God, the Lord of the Promised Day.
>
> Say: Praise be unto Thee, O Lord of Names, and glory be to Thee, O Creator of Heavens. I beseech Thee by the lights of the Throne, and the mysteries of the Cause, to enable me to hold fast unto the cord of steadfastness in thy love, and to cleave to that which Thou hast commanded me in Thy Tablets. Thou beholdest, O my God, Thy servant detached from all except thee and earnestly seeking thy bounty and favor. Ordain then for him that which beseemeth the heaven of Thy grace and the ocean of Thy bounty. Powerful art Thou to do what pleaseth Thee. There is none other God but Thee, the Forgiving, the Gracious.

I am grateful to Dr Nader Saiedi for translating this passage into English from the original Arabic. The Tablet has been published in the original language (Ardakani, *Amr-i Baha'i*, 43).

[27] Certainly, the forty-camels tale should not be understood literally. No doubt, Ghulam-'Ali did return to Yazd with camels. The date of his return is unclear. Forty probably simply indicates a large number.

Figure 1.3 Ghulam-ʿAli Siyah Khurasani with his wife, Munavvar Khanum (centre, front), and their children and grandchildren in their home in Yazd, taken September 1940. Back row (L to R): Iraj Turkzadih, Paridukht Haqiqat, Iran Haqiqat, Parvin Haqiqat, Hushang Khurasani, Jalal Taqizadih, Muhammad Khurasani, Furugh Taqizadih, Turan Turkzadih, Afaq Taqizadih. Front row (adults, L to R): Shamsi Khurasani Tadayuni, Nusrat Khurasani Turkzadih, Suraya Khurasani Haqiqat, Munavvar Khurasani, Ghulam-ʿAli Khurasani, Malikih Khurasani Taqizadih, Muluk Khurasani Sarraf, Safa Khurasani (a relative). Front row (children, L to R): Arassa Khurasani, Nasir Turkzadih, Mahvash Taqizadeh, Farhang Sarraf, Mihrbanu Khurasani. Images identified by Monir Ardekani. Note the two large and matching Persian carpets used as a backdrop, and as a display of wealth.

Source: Khurasani family archives. In private hands.

with his mother, his wife, his children and his grandchildren (Figure 1.3). By the end of his life, he was the largest landowner in the city and extremely influential in politics and business affairs. It seems that he also acquired three slaves of his own, or at least three African women who lived in his house as dependents and were known as *kaniz*: Fezzeh (silver), Zaffaron (saffron) and Shireen (sweet).

Scholars of Iranian history have sometimes puzzled over what they regard as the almost complete disappearance of the African diaspora in Iran.[28] Ziba Khanum's descendants demonstrate how fully Afro-Iranians were incorporated into Iranian society, especially among the wealthy classes, without regard to race. All of Ghulam-ʿAli's adult children married into well-to-do Iranian families, and their children are indistinguishable from other Iranians. Moreover, none of Ghulam-ʿAli's family make

---

[28] Ronald Segal, *Islam's Black Slaves: The Other Black Diaspora* (New York: Farrar, Strauss and Giroux, 2001), 127. See also Eduard Jakob Polak, *Persien: Das Land und seine Bewohner* (Leipzig: Brockhaus. 1865), 250 (I am grateful to Sara Zavaree for bringing Polak's assessment to my attention). Such a judgement rests on the assumption that a racial classification of the Iranian population into contemporary Western categories is viable.

any attempt to hide their African descent, or of Ziba Khanum's identity as an enslaved African woman. Similarly, all of her master's, Haji Muhammad-'Ali's, descendants, including the children and grandchildren of his Iranian wife, acknowledge Ziba Khanum as a member of their family and a forebear. A genealogy of the family, produced in Germany, includes Ziba Khanum and her descendants, who make up a large portion of the tableau (Figure 1.4).

There is no one alive today, however, who remembers meeting Ziba Khanum, and there are no documentary records of her life. All information about her must be gleaned from family traditions. Her descendants universally insist that she was always respected as a member of Ghulam-'Ali's household in Yazd. They describe

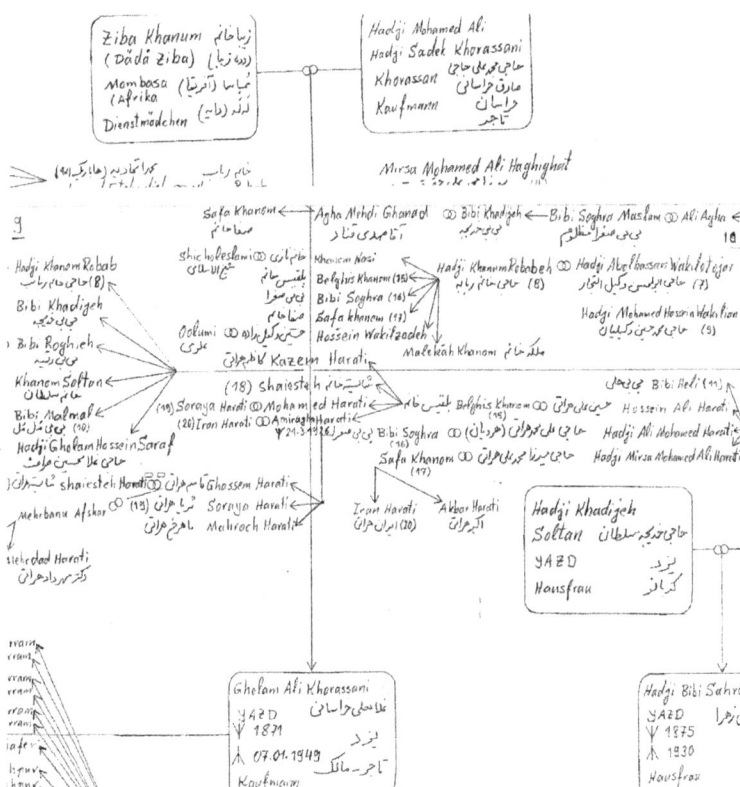

Figure 1.4 Detail of the Herati–Khorasani family tree in German and Persian, drawn up recently in Germany by the descendants of Haji Muhammad-'Ali Sadiq Khurasani. Ziba Khanum (top left) is shown as the mother of Ghulam-'Ali (bottom centre). The document suggests that Ziba was from Mombasa. She is designated with the name 'Dadé' (nanny), as she was known by the family. She is also designated here as *lalih* (nursemaid) and as *dayih* (wetnurse) by occupation (suggesting, perhaps, that the author was unsure of her role in the family in her time). No marker of race is included for her or her descendants.

Source: 'Familien Tafel: Stammbaum des Dr. Nasser Torkzadeh', 1995. In private hands.

her as gentle and loving, a typical grandmother figure. Living in her son's house, she may have indeed overcome her status as a slave. Sadly, it has proven impossible for me to recover even one word that Ziba Khanum spoke during her lifetime, and so it would seem that her voice is permanently lost to history. She remains silent and subaltern. The one act of agency that can be identified is the gift of the jewelled skirt to her son, which enabled him to make his Baha'i pilgrimage and possibly provided him with capital to go into business. More tentatively, we might include her move into her son's house upon his return to Yazd and her possible conversion to the Baha'i Faith. In any case, towards the end of her life, she was living in her son's Baha'i household and would have been regarded a Baha'i, as much as any other member of the family.

Will the subaltern speak?

The voiceless Ziba Khanum presents the historian of slavery with a dilemma. How should her life be represented and understood? Gayatri Spivak aggressively raised this challenge in her noted essay, 'Can the Subaltern Speak?',[29] in which she questions the use of subaltern subjects in writings about the history of India. She forcefully, and sometimes poignantly, demonstrates the appropriation of the subaltern voice in the service of the British imperialist 'civilizing mission', by Indian nationalists conducting an armed insurgency against the British Raj and by contemporary historians and Marxist theorists in support of revolutionary ideologies. Representations of the absent and silent subaltern, it would seem, can be fashioned and refashioned to support any position whatsoever. Spivak comes close to suggesting that a history of subaltern people, either as individuals or conceived as a class, cannot be written at all and should not be attempted. She seems determined, at least in this essay, to insist that subaltern persons, and especially women, will never be able to speak or represent themselves. She declares bluntly that 'the subaltern female cannot be heard or read'.[30] Spivak's challenge is of direct relevance to my own attempt to recover at least a part of the life of Ziba Khanum from family memory and tradition.

Eve Troutt Powell has raised Spivak's arguments with regard to the attempt by historians of slavery to recover the voice and history of Africans in the Middle East.[31] Troutt Powell, however, does not reach the same bleak conclusions. She does warn of the tendency in the historiography of slavery to impose artificial frameworks and constructions on subaltern subjects, particularly the danger of applying American abolitionist narratives and assumptions of Atlantic slavery to very different situations in Islamic realms. Edward Alpers and Matthew Hopper raise the same issue with

---

[29] Gayatri Chakravorty Spivak, 'Can the Subaltern Speak?', in *Marxism and the Interpretation of Culture*, ed. C. Nelson and L. Grossberg (Basingstoke: Macmillan Education, 1988), 272–313.

[30] Ibid., 104.

[31] Eve M. Troutt Powell, 'Will the Subaltern Ever Speak? Finding African Slaves in the Historiography of the Middle East', in *Middle East Historiographies: Narrating the Twentieth Century*, ed. Israel Gershoni, Amy Singer and Hakan Erdem (Seattle: University of Washington Press, 2006).

regard to slave testimonies recorded by the British agents in western Indian Ocean ports.[32] They conclude that even when faced with transcripts of interviews which claim to represent the voices of former African slaves, the historian must exercise extreme caution, allowing for errors of translation and distortions of interpretation and interference by both indigenous and British officials. This conclusion is, however, closer to the ordinary care and caution that historians must exercise when examining any document.

Only there are no documents even claiming to have captured Ziba Khanum's first-person voice. Nor were any of her words preserved in the recollections and oral traditions of her family, who apparently found such words unimportant. So, is there any way to hear her voice? Or, to make Spivak's question specific: Can Ziba Khanum ever speak? Sadly, my answer is no. Her voice is lost; we have no access to her thoughts or her inner life.[33] But that does not mean that her life is without meaning or value to history. We must listen for the African voice in Iran, even when it cannot be heard. Ziba Khanum's silent voice therefore is reduced to only a presence. That presence informs us that there were African women who were enslaved in Yazd in the middle of the nineteenth century, that these women served as domestic servants and concubines, that they had children by their masters and that they could sometimes act to support and protect their children (who were legally free). These Afro-Iranian children remained in Iran, married local people and, although they might be identified as black (*siyah*), could live normal lives as Iranians. Sometimes these Afro-Iranians might become wealthy and notable men. Some percentage of the Iranian population, as a consequence, is of African descent, although this heritage has never hardened into a clear racial category within the society.

I maintain that historians should continue to recover what can be recovered of the lives of enslaved Africans in Iran as individuals for their own sake – to understand and to honour those who were taken from their African homelands by slave traders and sold in Iran, to rescue them from anonymity and to restore their human dignity. Doing so, we must take these persons seriously, acknowledge their presence, listen for their voices and regard them as actors, making choices (even when we cannot see their choices) among the options that were available to them, in an effort to gain as much dignity, status and autonomy as might have been possible under the circumstances of their enslavement. Such a history of African slavery in Iran is possible and should be written.

---

[32] Edward A. Alpers and Matthew S. Hopper, 'Speaking for Themselves? Understanding African Freed Slave Testimonies from the Western Indian Ocean, 1850s–1930s', *Journal of Indian Ocean World Studies* 1 (2017): 60–88.

[33] Of course, I have not interviewed every descendant and distant relative of Ziba Khanum, and so I still hope that we do not yet know everything that can be known about her.

2

On the multivalence of women's captivity narratives: Seventeenth to nineteenth centuries[1]

İrvin Cemil Schick

> *Valcour, ils sont affreux! Sur un triste rivage,*
> *Loin de toi je languis, je meurs dans l'esclavage.*
> *Seule dans l'univers, je n'ai devant les yeux,*
> *Au lieu de mon amant, qu'un maître impérieux.*
> *On me défend les pleurs, & même le murmure;*
> *J'ai perdu tous les droits que donne la nature;*
> *Et j'éprouve, soumise à de barbares loix,*
> *La crainte & le mépris, inconnus dans les bois.*[2]

Captivity narratives are central to European and Euro-American literatures – some consider them the precursor of the novel.[3] In fact, many early examples of the genre from *Don Quijote* (1605) to *Robinson Crusoe* (1719) feature a European hero taken prisoner in a strange land. The most common settings for such narratives are Northwest

---

[1] This chapter is a slightly updated and much abridged translation of the Introduction to my book *Avrupalı Esireler ve Müslüman Efendileri: 'Türk' İllerinde Esaret Anlatıları* (European Captive Women and Their Muslim Masters: Narratives of Captivity in 'Turkish' Lands) (Istanbul: Kitap Yayınevi, 2005), a collection of captivity narratives set in North Africa and the Middle East and attributed to women. A comparable collection was subsequently published in English by Khalid Bekkaoui as *White Women Captives in North Africa: Narratives of Enslavement, 1735–1830* (Basingstoke: Palgrave Macmillan, 2011).

[2]
>   Valcour, they are horrible! On a sad shore I am languishing far from you, I am dying in slavery. All alone in the universe, I have before my eyes not my lover but an imperious master. They forbid me to cry and even to whisper. I have lost all the rights granted by nature. Subjected to their barbaric laws, I am experiencing fear and contempt, unknown in the woods (Claude-Joseph Dorat, *Lettre de Zeïla, jeune sauvage, esclave à Constantinople, à Valcour, officier françois* (Letter from Zeïla, Young Savage, Slave in Constantinople, to Valcour, French Officer) (Paris, 1764), cited here from the third edition. (Geneva: Bauche, 1766), 24)

[3] See, for example, George A. Starr, 'Escape from Barbary: A Seventeenth-Century Genre', *Huntington Library Quarterly* 29 (1965): 35–52.

Africa (the 'Barbary Coast') and North America, but there are many others set all over the world.

Although Europeans and Euro-Americans were not the only ones to be taken prisoner throughout history, others seldom recorded their experiences, and there was neither a reading public in their home countries thirsting for their misadventures nor a publishing industry standing ready to quench that thirst. By contrast, what Benedict Anderson has dubbed 'print capitalism'[4] fulfilled its nation-building role in part by constructing foreign peoples as Other, and narratives of captivity contributed to producing a sense of nationhood and solidarity in opposition to that Otherness.

It is only during the last several decades that the importance of this corpus has come to be appreciated, and a number of important studies have appeared, largely inspired by feminist and postcolonial theories. The emphasis has been principally on 'Indian'[5] captivity narratives, but the genre was imported into North America from Europe, and the first early modern narratives were penned by Europeans taken captive by 'Turks'.[6]

Initially an expansionistic and militarily successful power, the Ottoman Empire took many prisoners from among the peoples it subjected. Some were forced into slavery, and of those who eventually regained their freedom – whether through manumission, redemption or escape – a number wrote and published memoirs, notably Johannes Schildtberger (*c.* 1380–*c.* 1440), Bartolomej Georgijević (*c.* 1505–*c.* 1566), Johann Michael Heberer (*c.* 1567–1623), Václav Vratislav (1576–1635), John Smith (1580–1631) of 'Pocahontas' fame and Joseph Pitts (1663–*c.* 1735).

In addition to such prisoners of war, numerous merchant ships, their crews and passengers were captured by Ottoman pirates and privateers based on the Barbary Coast. Many of these captives were sold as slaves; for example, a Portuguese source

---

[4]   See Benedict Anderson, *Imagined Communities: Reflections on the Origin and Spread of Nationalism* (London: Verso, 1983), especially chapter 3.

[5]   I know that this is a misnomer, but it is the term by which North American captivity narratives are usually known.

[6]   I have placed 'Turks' in quotes because the term is often used generically in contexts where the individuals in question may not be ethnically Turkish at all. For example, Maria ter Meetelen persistently refers to her captors as 'Turks' and to their language as 'Turkish' even though she was held captive in Morocco, a country that was never part of the Ottoman Empire. Historically, 'Turk' has often been used by Europeans as synonymous with 'Muslim'. For North African captivity narratives, see also Albert Savine, *Dans les fers du Moghreb: Récits de chrétiens esclaves au Maroc, XVIIᵉ et XVIIIᵉ siècles* (In the Irons of the Maghreb: Narratives of Christian Slaves in Morocco, Seventeenth and Eighteenth centuries) (Paris: Société des Éditions Louis Michaud, 1912); Herman Hardenberg, ed. and annot., *Tussen Zeerovers en Christenslaven: Noord Afrikaanse Reisjournalen* (Between Buccaneers and Christian Slaves: North African Travel Journals) (Leiden: H. E. Stenfert Kroese, 1950); André Vovard, *Les Turqueries dans la littérature française: le cycle barbaresque* (Turqueries in French literature: The Barbary Cycle) (Toulouse: Privat, 1959); Albert Mas, *Les Turcs dans la littérature espagnole du Siècle d'Or* (The Turks in Spanish Literature of the (Spanish) Golden Age) (Paris: Centre de Recherches Hispaniques, 1967); Guy Turbet-Delof, *L'Afrique barbaresque dans la littérature française aux XVIᵉ et XVIIᵉ siècles* (The Barbary Coast in French Literature during the Sixteenth and Seventeenth Centuries) (Geneva: Librairie Droz, 1973); Paul Baepler, ed., *White Slaves, African Masters: An Anthology of American Barbary Captivity Narratives* (Chicago: University of Chicago Press, 1999); Joe Snader, *Caught between Worlds: British Captivity Narratives in Fact and Fiction* (Lexington: University Press of Kentucky, 2000); Daniel J. Vitkus, ed., *Piracy, Slavery, and Redemption: Barbary Captivity Narratives from Early Modern England*, with an introduction by Nabil Matar (New York: Columbia University Press, 2001).

estimated that some twenty thousand captives lived in Algiers between 1621 and 1627, at least half of whom were Christian.[7] Such was the case with Cervantes (1547–1616) who was taken prisoner in 1575 on his way back from the Battle of Lepanto and spent five years as a captive in Algiers.[8]

An interesting group of captivity narratives were written by or are attributed to women. They are particularly common in the North American context, since most of those captured by natives were settlers, including many women.[9] In the case of North Africa and the Middle East, some narratives are attributed to women captured by pirates and privateers and redeemed by their families or Christian charities.[10] I focus here mainly on first-person captivity narratives attributed to women, although there is no doubt that many, if not most, are works of fiction, and many were probably written by men.

The corpus

The anonymous *Ravissement de l'Hélène d'Amsterdam, contenant des accidens étranges tant d'Amour que de la Fortune, arrivez à une Demoiselle d'Amsterdam en plusieurs endroits du monde, & principalement en Turquie où elle a été Esclave* ('The Ravishment of Hélène of Amsterdam, Containing Strange Mishaps of Love as Well as Fortune That Befell a Maiden of Amsterdam in Numerous Places across the World, and Principally in Turkey Where She Was a Slave') was published in Amsterdam in 1683. While there

---

[7] Cited by Fernand Braudel, *The Mediterranean and the Mediterranean World in the Age of Philip II*, vol. 2 (New York: Harper & Row, 1976), 885. On Barbary pirates and their slaves, see Charles Penz, *Les captifs français du Maroc au XVIIᵉ siècle (1577–1699)* (French Captives in Morocco during the Seventeenth Century) (Rabat: Institut des Hautes Études Marocaines, 1944); H[enry] G. Barnby, *The Prisoners of Algiers: An Account of the Forgotten American-Algerian War, 1785–1797* (London: Oxford University Press, 1966); Stephen Clissold, *The Barbary Slaves* (New York: Barnes & Noble, 1977); Ellen G. Friedman, *Spanish Captives in North Africa in the Early Modern Age* (Madison: University of Wisconsin Press, 1983); Emilio Temprano, *El mar maldito: Cautivos y corsarios en el Siglo de Oro* (The Cursed Sea: Captives and Privateers during the (Spanish) Golden Age) (Madrid: Mondadori España, 1989); Salvatore Bono, *Corsari nel Mediterraneo: Cristiani e Musulmani fra Guerra, Schiavitù, e Commercio* (Privateers in the Mediterranean: Christians and Muslims between War, Slavery, and Trade) (Milan: A. Mondadori, 1993); Daniel Panzac, *Les corsaires barbaresques: La fin d'une épopée, 1800–1820* (Barbary Privateers: The End of an Epic) (Paris: CNRS Éditions, 1999); Robert C. Davis, *Christian Slaves, Muslim Masters: White Slavery in the Mediterranean, the Barbary Coast, and Italy, 1500–1800* (Basingstoke: Palgrave Macmillan, 2003); Linda Colley, *Captives: Britain, Empire, and the World, 1600–1850* (New York: Anchor Books, 2004); Jennifer Lofkrantz and Olatunji Ojo, eds, *Ransoming, Captivity & Piracy in Africa and the Mediterranean* (Trenton, NJ: Africa World Press, 2016).

[8] See, for example, Fernando Arrabal, *Un esclavo llamado Cervantes* (A Slave Named Cervantes) (Madrid: Espasa, 1996); María Antonia Garcés, *Cervantes in Algiers: A Captive's Tale* (Nashville, TN: Vanderbilt University Press, 2002).

[9] Collections of North American women's captivity tales include Frances Roe Kestler, ed., *The Indian Captivity Narrative: A Woman's View* (Mattituck, NY: Amereon House, 1990); and Kathryn Zabelle Derounian-Stodola, ed., *Women's Indian Captivity Narratives* (New York: Penguin Books, 1998).

[10] Friedman, *Spanish Captives in North Africa*, 119. Based on archival research, the author estimates that women constituted some 5 per cent of redeemed Spanish captives. Since those who were sent to the capital or sold into local harems could not be redeemed, however, this figure may underestimate the overall fraction of women captives (146–7).

are earlier narratives attributed to men, this undoubtedly fictional text appears to be the earliest first-person narrative of Turkish captivity attributed to a woman. The book's rarity today suggests that it may not have circulated widely; still, the existence of translations into German, Italian and Dutch indicates that it did command some interest.

Another early and doubtless fictional narrative is that of Mrs Villars, part of *The Voyages and Adventures of Captain Robert Boyle, in Several Parts of the World*, which first appeared in London in 1726 and was republished over forty times in Britain and the United States. Translations appeared in French, German, Italian and Dutch, this latter bearing the subtitle *De nieuwe engelsche Robinson* ('The New English Robinson'). Indeed, the book was long believed to be the work of Daniel Defoe; sometimes attributed to Benjamin Victor, it is now believed[11] to be by William Rufus Chetwood (d. 1766), whose *The Voyages, Dangerous Adventures and Imminent Escapes of Captain Richard Falconer, Intermix'd with the Voyages and Adventures of Thomas Randal* (1720) and *The Voyages, Travels and Adventures, of William Owen Gwin Vaughan, Esq., with the History of His Brother Jonathan Vaughan, Six Years a Slave in Tunis, Intermix'd with the Histories of Clerimont, Maria, Eleanora, and Others* (1736) also speak of North African captivity.

Wonderbaarlyke en Merkwaardige Gevallen van een Twaalf Jarige Slaverny, van een Vrouspersoon genaemt Maria ter Meetelen, Woonagtig tot Medenblik ('The Wondrous and Remarkable Story of the Twelve-Year-Long Slavery of a Lady Named Maria ter Meetelen, a Resident of Medenblik'), published in Hoorn in 1748, appears to be mostly factual.[12] Herman Hardenberg writes that Maria ter Meetelen was baptized in Amsterdam in 1704, got drafted into the army as she travelled around Europe dressed as a man, eventually married a sea captain, was captured by pirates and lived as a slave in the Moroccan city of Meknes between 1731 and 1743 before regaining her freedom and settling in Medemblik.

Another eighteenth-century first-person account is *The Female Captive: A Narrative of Facts, which Happened in Barbary in the Year 1756*, published in London in 1769. The title page only bears the rubric 'written by herself', but both manuscript notes by Sir William Musgrave in the British Library copy[13] and archival

---

[11] Philip Babcock Gove, *The Imaginary Voyage in Prose Fiction: A History of Its Criticism and a Guide for Its Study, with an Annotated Check List of 215 Imaginary Voyages from 1700 to 1800* (London: Holland Press, 1961), 251.

[12] Exceedingly rare today, it is better known through its inclusion in Hardenberg, *Tussen Zeerovers en Christenslaven*, 73–147, and the French translation *L'Annotation ponctuelle de la description de voyage étonnante et de la captivité remarquable et triste durant douze ans de moi, Maria ter Meetelen, et de l'hereuse délivrance d'icelle, et mon joyeux retour dans ma chère Patrie, le tout décrit selon la Vérité et mon expérience personnelle* ('The Precise Record of the Astonishing Voyage and Remarkable and Sad Captivity during Twelve years of I, Maria ter Meetelen, and of the Happy Deliverence from It, and My Joyful Return to My Dear Motherland, All of It Described Truthfully and According to My Personal Experience'), trans. and annot. G[eorges]-H[enri] Bousquet and G[ertrude] W[ilhelmine] Bousquet-Mirandolle (Paris: Éditions Larose, 1956). Another edition of the Dutch text was published by Laura van den Broek, Maaike Jacobs and Gerard van Krieken in *Christenslaven: de Slavernij-ervaringen van Cornelis Stout in Algiers (1678–1680) en Maria ter Meetelen in Marokko (1731–1743)* (Christian Slaves: The Experiences of Slavery of Cornelis Stout in Algiers and Maria ter Meetelen in Morocco) (Zutphen: Walburg, 2006).

[13] Shelfmark Gen. Ref. Coll. 1417.a.5.

evidence[14] confirm that the book was written by one Elizabeth Crisp, née Marsh, born in Portsmouth in 1735. Unfortunately, the text is remarkably uninformative as to the actual circumstances of the author's captivity, instead describing at length her gripes against fellow-prisoners, consuls and other local residents.[15]

The tale of Polly Davis was first published around 1799 in Hanover, New Hampshire, as part of *Narrative of the Captivity of John Vandike, Who Was Taken by the Algierines in 1791: An Account of His Escape in 1791, Bringing with Him a Beautiful Young English Lady Who Was Taken in 1790; the Ill Usage She Received from Her Master; the Whole in a Letter to His Brother in Amsterdam*.[16] Apparently the first American narrative of a woman's Barbary Coast captivity, it followed the first narrative of Indian captivity (1682) by more than a century, and this delay requires an explanation. Unlike native Americans who were viewed by European settlers as mere 'savages', Muslims were acknowledged to constitute a rival – albeit 'inferior' – civilization; this may be why a white, Christian woman's captivity and abuse at the hands of Muslims may have long been considered too challenging a subject to broach in print.

A first-person narrative involving a Christian woman who was not European but Georgian appeared in two versions, *The Adventures of Gen. Hutchinson and Serinda, the Fair Georgian; Containing an Account of their Captivity, Their Escape from Aleppo, in the Disguise of Pilgrims, and the Extraordinary Vicissitudes which They Afterwards Experienced, till Their Accidental Meeting in London...* (London, 1802) and *Love and Honour; or, the Adventures of Serinda, a Beautiful Slave, Who Was Carried off from a Harem in Aleppo, by General Osmond, a Prisoner of War; with an Account of Their Arrival in Russia, Their Marriage, and the Tragical Death of General Osmond* (Liverpool, undated). Along with Circassians, Georgians were reputed for their fair skin and beauty and are a staple of Orientalist painting and literature.

An Affecting History of the Captivity & Sufferings of Mrs. Mary Velnet, an Italian Lady Who Was Seven Years a Slave in Tripoli, Three of which, She Was Confined in a Dungeon, Loaded with Irons, and Four Times Put to the Most Cruel Tortures Ever Invented by Man is considered the prototype of North American women's narratives of Barbary Coast captivity (Figure 2.1).[17] Its first edition, published in Boston, is undated. Although some have suggested that it appeared in 1800, the text mentions the Swedish blockade of Tripoli which only took place in 1801–2. Furthermore, Thomas Jefferson called for decisive action against the Barbary states during his first speech as president of the United States in December 1801,[18] and this narrative may have been intended to

---

[14] In particular, see Jeremy James Heath-Caldwell's useful web page, http://jjhc.info/marshelizabeth1 7xx.htm (accessed 16 June 2019); also Linda Colley, *The Ordeal of Elizabeth Marsh: A Woman in World History* (London: HarperPress, 2007).

[15] Facsimile reprints (e.g. Eighteenth Century Collections Online by Gale), in addition to Khalid Bekkaoui's edition (Casablanca: Moroccan Cultural Studies Centre, 2003) and his *White Women Captives in North Africa* (121–61), have made this text accessible to modern readers.

[16] Baepler writes of two editions published in Leominster, Massachusetts, including one of 1797 that I have been unable to trace (*White Slaves, African Masters*, 304).

[17] Keith Huntress, *A Checklist of Narratives of Shipwrecks and Disasters at Sea to 1860, with Summaries, Notes, and Comments* (Ames: Iowa State University Press, 1979), 47.

[18] Robert J. Allison, *The Crescent Obscured: The United States and the Muslim World, 1776–1815* (New York: Oxford University Press, 1995), 24–7.

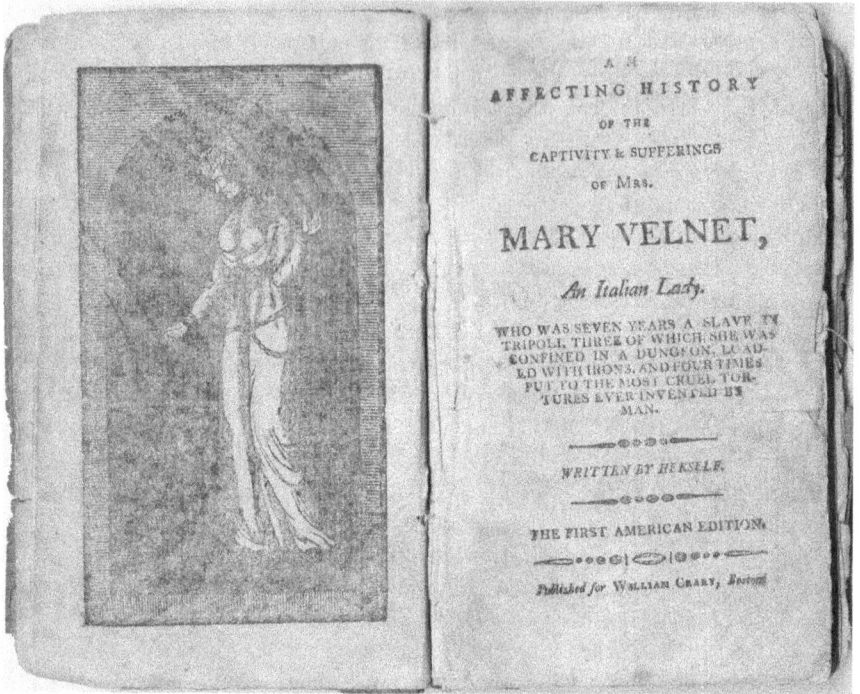

Figure 2.1 Frontispiece and title page of *An Affecting History of the Captivity & Sufferings of Mrs. Mary Velnet, an Italian Lady Who Was Seven Years a Slave in Tripoli, Three of which, She Was Confined in a Dungeon, Loaded with Irons, and Four Times Put to the Most Cruel Tortures Ever Invented by Man* (Boston: William Crary, c. 1801–2).

Source: Author's collection.

give his hawkish faction ammunition for its political struggle against the Federalists. Two more Boston editions followed, and another from Sag-Harbor, New York. The same account was also published under the name Mary Gerard (Boston, 1810). It presents an interesting combination of Gothic[19] and Orientalist elements, thus straddling two prominent branches of the European discourse of alterity prevalent at the time. As Edward Said has noted, 'popular Orientalism during the late eighteenth century and the early nineteenth attained a vogue of considerable intensity … [that] cannot be simply detached from the interest taken in Gothic tales, pseudomedieval idylls, visions of barbaric splendor and cruelty'.[20] Some have even posited a genre dubbed 'Gothic orientalism'.[21] With its sexualized horror and blood-curdling torture scenes, the narrative of Mary Velnet may be considered an example of this genre.

[19] Baepler, *White Slaves, African Masters*, 16.
[20] Edward W. Said, *Orientalism* (New York: Penguin, 1979), 118.
[21] See, for example, Michael Franklin, 'Orientalism', in *The Handbook to Gothic Literature*, ed. Marie Mulvey-Roberts (New York: Palgrave Macmillan, 1998), 168–71.

The most popular[22] among women's narratives of Barbary Coast captivity is that of Maria Martin which first appeared in Boston in 1806, followed by at least eleven more editions. The same account was also published under the name of Lucinda Martin (Boston, 1810), bringing the total to thirteen editions in as many years. The titles changed over time, evidencing various degrees of sensationalism:

> *A History of the Captivity and Sufferings of Mrs. Maria Martin, who was Six Years a Slave in Algiers, Two of which She was Confined in a Dark and Dismal Dungeon, Loaded with Irons* (Rutland, VT, 1815);

> *History of the Captivity and Sufferings of Maria Martin, who was Six Years a Slave in Algiers; Two of which She was Confined in a Dismal Dungeon, Loaded with Irons, by the Command of an Inhuman Turkish Officer* (Brookfield, MA, 1818);

> *History of the Captivity and Sufferings of Mrs. Lucinda Martin, who was Six Years a Slave in Algiers; Two of which She was Confined in a Dark and Dismal Dungeon, Loaded with Irons, for Refusing to Comply with the Brutal Request of a Turkish Officer* (Boston, 1810).

All these editions were published in the north-eastern United States, the region most actively involved in foreign trade; furthermore, the first edition appeared in the immediate aftermath of the First (Tripolitan) Barbary War (1801–5) and the last one shortly after the end of the Second (Algerine) Barbary War (1815), highlighting their probable role as wartime propaganda.

An Authentic Narrative of the Shipwreck and Sufferings of Mrs. Eliza Bradley, the Wife of Capt. James Bradley of Liverpool, Commander of the Ship Sally which was Wrecked on the Coast of Barbary, in June 1818 was first published in Boston in 1820, followed by at least fourteen more editions. This, and the fact that the title is still widely available in the antiquarian book trade, suggest that it was published not only in many editions but also in relatively large print runs. Although the preface claims the book had been previously published in Britain to great acclaim, that seems to be a marketing fib. The narrative is almost certainly fictional: Keith Gibson Huntress has pointed out that the archives of Lloyd's of London and British Customs make no mention of a shipwrecked vessel named *Sally*, that parts of the narrative were lifted verbatim from the captivity narrative of John Riley (1817) and that even the publisher's name, James Walden, appears to be spurious.[23] Given that the Barbary Wars were over, it is likely that this popular work served a different purpose than wartime propaganda; the tone of the text, and the fact that it was regularly assigned in Sunday schools,[24] suggest that its purpose was evangelical.

Turkish Barbarity: An Affecting Narrative of the Unparalleled Sufferings of Mrs. Sophia Mazro, a Greek Lady of Missolonghi, who with her Two Daughters (at the Capture of that

---

[22] Baepler, *White Slaves, African Masters*, 147.
[23] Huntress, *A Checklist of Narratives of Shipwrecks and Disasters at Sea*, 110; also Huntress, Preface, *An Authentic Narrative of the Shipwreck and Sufferings of Mrs. Eliza Bradley...* (Fairfield, WA: Ye Galleon Press, 1985).
[24] Baepler, *White Slaves, African Masters*, 17.

Fortress by the Turks) Were Made Prisoners by the Barbarians, by Whom their Once Peaceable Dwelling Was Reduced to Ashes, and Their Unfortunate Husband and Parent, in His Attempts to Protect His Family, Inhumanly Put to Death in Their Presence was apparently published only once, in 1828, in Providence, Rhode Island. The purpose of this little book was to raise funds in support of the struggle for Greek independence (1821–30) from the Ottoman Empire. The story's setting, the town of Missolonghi, was an obvious choice given its symbolic importance for Philhellenism: it was there that Lord Byron had died in 1824, and the massacre perpetrated by the Ottomans two years later had been powerfully immortalized by Delacroix in his 1826 painting La *Grèce sur les ruines de Missolonghi* ('Greece on the Ruins of Missolonghi').

Another first-person (epistolary) narrative published in 1828, this one in London, is the anonymous *The Lustful Turk: A History Founded on Facts, Containing an Interesting Narrative of the Cruel Fate of the Two Young English Ladies Named Silvia Carey and Emily Barlow…*, which was also inspired – albeit indirectly – by the Greek War of Independence. Although some may be tempted to dismiss this book as 'mere pornography', that would be a mistake as its storyline is closely linked to the historical context in which it was published. It can hardly be coincidental, for example, that the novel ends with the Ottoman governor of Algiers being castrated by his Greek captive! The book was printed twice by the original publisher and many more times by later publishers.

Neapolitan Captive: Interesting Narrative of the Captivity and Sufferings of Miss Viletta Laranda, a Native of Naples, Who, with a Brother, Was a Passenger on Board a Neapolitan Vessel Wrecked near Oran, on the Barbary Coast, September 1829, and Who Soon After Was Unfortunately Made a Captive of by a Wandering Clan of Bedowen Arabs, on Their Return from Algiers to the Deserts, and Eleven Months after Providentially Rescued from Barbarian Bondage by the Commander of a Detached Regiment of the Victorious French Army was published in New York (1830) and then in Middletown, Connecticut. Although this New York edition claims to be the third printing, I have not been able to trace the first two and neither, apparently, has Baepler;[25] once again, this may just have been a marketing ploy intended to suggest that the book was popular. Parts of it appear to have been pirated from the narrative of Eliza Bradley. The publication date of 1830 is important in that it corresponds to the invasion of Algeria by the French, bringing an end to Barbary Coast piracy. The rescue of Miss Laranda by the French army signals that captivity narratives now functioned to legitimize colonialism.

Finally, *Marche´ aux esclaves et harem: Épisode inédit de la piraterie barbaresque au XVIIIᵉ siècle* ('Slave Market and Harem: An Unpublished Episode of Barbary Coast Piracy during the Eighteenth Century') by 'Mlle Sidonie B***' was apparently published only once, in Paris in 1875. Decades after the end of Barbary piracy and the occupation of Algeria by France, this erotic novella might be thought devoid of a political agenda; once again, I would disagree. It is noteworthy, for instance, that race plays a very important role in this narrative, echoing the increasing popularity of racialism during the nineteenth century. The fact that this narrative was produced

---

[25] Baepler, *White Slaves, African Masters*, 310.

by Ernest Leroux, a relatively serious French publisher of ethnographic books, gives another reason not to dismiss it as purely prurient.

The texts listed above cover almost two centuries (1683–1875) and reflect changing relations between Christendom and the Muslim World. There are other tales involving European women captured by Barbary pirates. For example, *La belle captive, ou Histoire du naufrage et de la captivité de Mademoiselle Adeline* ('The Fair Captive, or Story of the Shipwreck and Captivity of Mlle Adeline'), published in Paris in 1785 and attributed to Pierre-Sylvain Maréchal (1750–1803) or Jacques Grasset de Saint-Sauveur (1757–1810), was actually based on the true story of Mlle de Bourk, an aristocratic young girl captured in 1719, whose story was told in a variety of venues from 1721 on.[26] It is not, however, a first-person narrative.

The question of veracity

In all, some twenty distinct narratives of North African captivity were published in North America alone, in at least 149 editions.[27] Some were bestsellers, and the reason for their success is that they served several functions at once: education, entertainment, warmongering, evangelism, social criticism, gender construction, eroticism and more. It is often difficult to determine which captivity narratives are veridical and which are not, so it is important to take them not as factual accounts representing the reality on the ground but rather as reflective of the mindset prevailing in the Western societies in which they were produced. In this respect, Moulay Belhamissi was right to pose the question, 'histoire ou hystérie?' (history or hysteria?).[28]

Published accounts of captivity and slavery were by their nature disturbing, particularly as they described the oppression, enslavement, torture and violation of people who are white, Christian, European or Euro-American – that is, from the viewpoint of the readers, of 'us' – by people who are brown, Muslim, African or Asian – that is, 'them'. That the texts were at all deemed socially acceptable derived from the fact that, as Mary Louise Pratt put it, 'the very existence of a text presupposed the imperially correct outcome: the survivor survived, and sought reintegration into the home society. The tale was always told from the viewpoint of the European who returned.'[29] In other words, the narratives invariably ended with deliverance and restoration of the universal order; this is why they were widely read and considered not only diverting but also instructive.

It has been noted that 'cultural representations of suffering – images, prototypical tales, metaphors, models – can be (and frequently are) appropriated in the popular culture or by particular social institutions for political and moral purposes. For this

[26] For an example published in London in 1735, see Bekkaoui, *White Women Captives in North Africa*, 46–57.
[27] Baepler, *White Slaves, African Masters*, 303.
[28] Moulay Belhamissi, *Les captifs algériens et l'Europe chrétienne (1518–1830)* (Algerian Captives and Christian Europe) (Algiers: Entreprise Nationale du Livre, 1988), 48.
[29] Mary Louise Pratt, *Imperial Eyes: Travel Writing and Transculturation* (London: Routledge, 1992), 87.

reason, suffering has social use'.[30] Tales of suffering must therefore be handled with care, not in the sense of denying the victims' pain but rather of approaching the material in a holistic manner and not as an encyclopaedic collection of positive facts.

Ellen Friedman has challenged Spanish popular views of Barbary captivity, noting that the captors valued their prisoners as sources of labour and ransom and made every effort to safeguard their well-being. Thus, she writes, 'while instances of cruelty undoubtedly did occur, in general the treatment of captives in North Africa was at least consistent with the standards of the age. ... [T]he evidence does not add up to a systematic pattern of brutality'.[31] Even contemporary commentators cautioned readers that captivity narratives were not always truthful and that their authors often had ulterior motives. In his *Histoire du Royaume d'Alger* ('History of the Kingdom of Algiers') (1725), for instance, the former French consul Laugier de Tassy wrote that captives in Algiers were 'not by far as miserable in slavery as one would believe from the fabulous accounts of the Monks or of those who have been slaves, who have reason to impose on the Public'.[32] Still, these books were produced for a popular audience, and it is safe to assume that most readers would have taken them at face value.

What ties together the narratives discussed here is that they all contributed to the production of identity and alterity in the countries in which they circulated. Such dichotomies as male/female, Christian/Muslim, European/North African, merchant/pirate, countryman/enemy, slave/master and abolitionist/slave owner are centrally important to them all. But they were never absolute. There were women who far exceeded men in cruelty; Christian converts to Islam; Jews who straddled the line between captors and captives; a heterogeneous collection of Turks, Arabs, Bedouins and Berbers indiscriminately grouped together as the 'enemy'; an equally heterogeneous collection of European and Euro-American Christians belonging to different nations and denominations and separated by sundry mutual antipathies and rivalries; collaborators and interpreters who bridged the divide between masters and slaves; consuls and clergymen who shuttled back and forth between Europe, North Africa and the Middle East; and European 'renegades' who worked with and sometimes even led Europe's antagonists. It is this wealth and complexity that gives the narratives a fascinating heteroglossia composed of the voices not only of captors, captives, translators, emissaries and redemptionists but also of the authors themselves, of the publishers' deliberate or unconscious interventions, of the didactic texts added by editors as prefaces or postfaces and of the historical, geographical and ethnographical information with which the narratives were often padded.

---

[30] Editors' Introduction in Arthur Kleinman, Veena Das and Margaret Lock, eds, *Social Suffering* (Berkeley: University of California Press, 1997), xi.

[31] Friedman, *Spanish Captives in North Africa*, 55–6, 73.

[32] [Jacques Philippe] Laugier de Tassy, *Histoire du Royaume d'Alger; Avec l'état présent de son gouvernement, de ses forces de terre & de mer, de ses revenus, police, justice politique & commerce* (History of the Kingdom of Algiers; with the Present State of Its Government, of Its Land and Sea Forces, of Its Revenues, Police, Political Justice, and Commerce) (Amsterdam: Henri du Sauzet, 1725), 275.

The element of gender

Is it significant that the narratives discussed here are all attributed to women and built around women's experiences? Put another way, do they have characteristics that set them apart from men's captivity narratives? Might they have had a part in constructing or reconstructing gender relations in the societies in which they were written, published and read? The narratives in question played two mutually contradictory roles: while some confirmed and reproduced traditional values and conceptions, others staged alternative realities that implied the possibility of challenging and even transgressing them.

In most Indian captivity narratives, women are helpless and incapable of defending themselves; they are captured and tormented by the natives until finally saved by an external force – a white man or Providence. In some, however, the female heroine departs from white society's sanctioned gender roles, and this is an aspect of Indian captivity narratives on which feminist analyses have focused. Thus, Christopher Castiglia has argued that the genre gave women opportunities to go beyond traditional gender norms, becoming self-sufficient, exercising aptitudes they were assumed not to possess and reaching social positions denied to them in their societies of origin. Moreover, the very act of crossing over from one culture to another suggested a certain cultural relativism that made it possible for female readers to question gender relations in their own societies.[33] To denote such 'idealized worlds of female autonomy, empowerment, and pleasure', Pratt has coined the term 'feminotopia'.[34] Whether fictional or otherwise, Indian captivity narratives often featured such spaces of difference where alternative gender relations could exist.

Given the Western perception of the harem as a site of oppression and cruelty, a microcosm of 'oriental despotism',[35] captivity narratives staged in North Africa and the Middle East could not credibly suggest that European women might find more favourable conditions in Muslim societies than in their own. Yet this was not entirely unknown in real life: Lady Montagu (1689–1762) tells of a Spanish woman who, having been captured and violated by an Ottoman privateer, spurned her family's attempts to ransom her and opted instead to marry him and stay behind (Figure 2.2). There was a certain logic to this decision, however abhorrent it may seem to a modern reader: as 'damaged goods', she would have no doubt been forced by her family to spend the rest of her life in a convent had she returned to Spain.[36]

Explicitly fictional narratives conjured utopic sites where traditional gender relations could be transcended and women could reinvent themselves as free and powerful. Perhaps the most striking examples are in the works of Eliza Haywood

---

[33] Christopher Castiglia, *Bound and Determined: Captivity, Culture-Crossing, and White Womanhood from Mary Rowlandson to Patty Hearst* (Chicago: University of Chicago Press, 1996), 4–7.

[34] Pratt, *Imperial Eyes*, 166–7.

[35] See Alain Grosrichard, *Structure du sérail: La fiction du despotisme asiatique dans l'Occident classique* (Structure of the Seraglio: The Fiction of Oriental Despotism in the Classical West) (Paris: Éditions du Seuil, 1979), 147–9, 156.

[36] Lord [James Archibald Stuart-Wortley-Mackenzie] Wharncliffe, ed., *The Letters and Works of Lady Mary Wortley Montagu*, rev. by W. Moy Thomas, vol. 1 (London: Swan Sonnenschein, 1893), 363–4.

Figure 2.2 'Arrivée d'un marchand d'esclaves à Constantinople'.

Source: Illustration from Eugenio and Raffaele Fulgenzi, *Collection de costumes civils et militaires, scènes populaires, et vues de l'Asie-Mineure* (İzmir: Fulgenzi & Fils, *c.* 1836–8). Harvard Fine Arts Library Special Collections FAL-LC XCAGE GT1400 .C65 1838.

(1693?–1756), where the theme of captivity is taken up again and again.[37] In *Idalia; or, The Unfortunate Mistress* (1723), the Venetian heroine is victimized by a succession of European men, but when she is captured and taken to the Barbary Coast, her captors show her nothing but friendship and respect. In *The Fruitless Enquiry* (1727), set in the Maldives, a European woman becomes queen and rules over men. Both there and in *Philidore and Placentia* (1727), set in Persia, European male captives are weak and incapable of heroism while the harem is redefined as a site of female empowerment and male subordination. Captives are oppressed and ultimately emasculated by the women in scenarios that authorize the casting of 'castration as an ironic analogue for rape, as a violent sexual subjugation that defines the male as a patriarchal victim'.[38]

---

[37] *The Fair Captive; A Tragedy* (London: T. Jauncy and H. Cole, 1721); *Idalia; or, the Unfortunate Mistress* (London: D. Browne junr., W. Chetwood, and S. Chapman, 1723); *Philidore and Placentia: or l'Amour trop delicat* (London, 1727); *The Fruitless Enquiry; Being A Collection of Several Entertaining Histories and Occurrences, which Fell under the Observation of a Lady in Her Search After Happiness* (London: J. Roberts, 1727). For a detailed discussion, see Snader, *Caught Between Worlds*, 158–68.

[38] Snader, *Caught Between Worlds*, 161. The forcible circumcision of Christian male captives is also suggestive of this idea (81).

While some captivity narratives thus challenged traditional gender relations, many served instead to reinforce them, and, here, it is important to bear in mind the social context within which the tales were fashioned: men and women were profoundly unequal; men were responsible for production and women for reproduction; men were mobile and women sessile; and women were deemed to require the protection of men (against other men). Violators of these norms deserved punishment, and so captives were sometimes blamed for their own misfortunes: Hélène of Amsterdam and Haywood's Idalia had both disobeyed their parents and followed their hearts, while Maria ter Meetelen had rambled about in Europe dressed as a man. They paid for these transgressions with their freedom.

In patriarchal society, a woman's body is subject to strict public control, the loss of which – worse still, a woman falling under the control of foreign men – mobilizes a discursive power that men's captivity narratives can never muster. Just as gender provided narratives with a backdrop, the narratives in turn helped reproduce gender relations. They cast every woman as a potential victim in need of men's protection and her body as potentially the object of appropriation by men. At the end of *La belle captive*, the author wrote of female readers:

> May the example of the virtuous Adeline give them courage: in times of danger, let them remember this young heroine of virginal purity; let them tell themselves: Adeline found herself alone in a barbaric country, separated from her mother and far from her relatives, at an age where passions are at their zenith and face to face with those of an African despot; as the monarch's favorite, she was subjected to the most cruel and shameful instruments of torture, yet she was able to preserve her honor and thwart her captor's intentions. Therefore nothing can stay in the way of a woman's virtue.[39]

Another interesting element of women's narratives of North African captivity is that the heroines systematically depict native women in extremely unfavourable terms. The following passage from the narrative of Viletta Laranda is typical:

> The females of Arabia are not so tall as the men, and their features much harder and more ugly. In person they are extremely disgusting. ... [They] are very filthy in their persons, and are covered with vermin, not even cleansing themselves with sand. The harsh treatment which they continually receive from the men, has worn off that fine edge of delicacy, sensibility, and compassion so natural to their sex, and transformed them into unfeeling and unpitying beings, so much so that their conduct towards such of those unfortunate persons as fall into their hands, is extremely brutal, and betray the extinction of every human and generous feeling.[40]

Bearing in mind the fact that the authors of these narratives were probably men, the frequent repetition of this trope may be explained in at least two ways. First, the motif

---

[39] Maréchal or Grasset de Saint-Sauveur, *La belle captive*, 95–7.
[40] *Neapolitan Captive*, 27–9.

of the ugly, brutish and cruel Arab woman may have served as a foil for European identity construction. The rising Western middle classes defined themselves in part by their women's femininity: a woman must be tender, compassionate, loving, sentimental, elegant, beautiful and well kempt. Disparaging descriptions of Arab women thus served to signify the unbridgeable distance between Europeans and their Others.

A second possible explanation has to do with the idea of gender solidarity, or rather with the wish to argue against it. When Mary Velnet and her fellow-captives are taken to the slave market, she looks at the spectators: 'Among them I recognized many of my own sex, which gave me fresh hopes of protection: but alas! This fond hope was of but short duration, for so far from exhibiting any symptoms of pity for me, they seemed rather to exult in my miseries!'[41] Later she relates how 'an overseer, a woman of the Algerine nation', would 'torture and punish us by every means her inventive faculties could give birth to', describing those means quite graphically.[42] Given that Mary Wollstonecraft (1759–1851) had recently published her controversial *A Vindication of the Rights of Women* (1792), it seems possible that these descriptions were meant to emphasize the non-existence of natural solidarity based on gender.

On the other hand, some early feminists like Wollstonecraft and Charlotte Brontë (1816–1855) used the condition of women in the Muslim World as a tool with which to mark the oppression of women as alien to civilized Europe while rendering feminism less threatening by displacing its target to distant lands.[43] Thus, it is stated in Serinda's narrative that 'the violation of female liberty, so general throughout the Turkish dominions, is pregnant with evil'. The heroine goes on to say, 'Oh! my dear young friends, you have reason to rejoice that you were born in a country where woman is treated like a rational being; where she sweetens existence and embellishes society.'[44] This gushing statement would have come as a surprise to Wollstonecraft, whose argument was precisely that women should be educated and treated as rational beings!

Religion and evangelism

It is no accident that the first book on Barbary captivity published in North America was by the puritan minister Cotton Mather (1663–1728).[45] Leitmotifs in captivity narratives included trust in God, the power of faith to overcome hurdles, withstanding pressures to apostatize, miraculous portents and providential deliverance. That captivity and slavery are a test of faith over which true believers shall triumph by divine providence was frequently their central idea.

---

[41] *An Affecting History*, 13.

[42] Ibid., 35.

[43] Joyce Zonana, 'The Sultan and the Slave: Feminist Orientalism and the Structure of *Jane Eyre*', in *Revising the Word and the World: Essays in Feminist Literary Criticism*, ed. VèVè A. Clark, Ruth-Ellen B. Joeres and Madelon Sprengnether (Chicago: University of Chicago Press, 1993), 165–90.

[44] *Love and Honour*, 13.

[45] Cotton Mather, *The Glory of Goodness: The Goodness of God, Celebrated; in Remarkable Instances and Improvements Thereof; and More Particularly in the Redemption Remarkably Obtained for the English Captives, which Have been Languishing under the Tragical, and the Terrible and the Most Barbarous Cruelties of Barbary* (Boston: T. Green & Benjamin Eliot, 1703).

In the dedication of her *The Noble Slaves* (1722), a novel containing several captivity narratives, Penelope Aubin (1679–1731) requested her patroness's protection against 'atheists, who deride God's Providence, which this History was chiefly designed to vindicate and to excite Men to put their Trust in, at this time when they scarce know how to trust one another'.[46] She described another novel also inspired by captivity narratives, *The Strange Adventures of the Count de Vinevil and his Family* (1721), as 'a Story, where Divine Providence manifests itself in every Transaction, where Vertue is try'd with Misfortunes, and rewarded with Blessings; In fine, where Men behave themselves like Christians, and Women are really vertuous, and such as we ought to imitate'.[47]

The evangelical function is most evident in the narrative of Eliza Bradley, where the relationship between the heroine's gender and her devoutness is stressed by the publisher right from the outset: 'We recommend [the book's] perusal to the attention of our young females, in particular manner, as Mrs. Bradley sets a shining example to her sex, in her struggles against the calamities of life, under circumstances the most uncomfortable'.[48] Eliza Bradley's piousness is evident: she frequently prays, cites the Scriptures, exhorts her fellow captives to be faithful and forbearing and comforts her husband, 'assur[ing] him that if we put our trust in God, He certainly would remember mercy in the midst of judgement, and would so far restrain the wrath of our enemies, as to prevent their murdering us'.[49] The land where she is held captive is described in religious terms as 'a distant heathen clime, a land of darkness, where the enemy of souls reigns triumphant, and where by an idolatrous race the doctrines of a Blessed Redeemer are treated with derision and contempt'.[50]

This attitude is not unique to Eliza Bradley; in *La belle captive*, the Turks discuss what to do with their captives: 'Some demanded that they be killed in accordance with their false religion so that, by sacrificing Christians, they would find a place for themselves in Muhammad's paradise; others opposed this out of self-interest, hoping to obtain a large ransom'.[51] To be sure, anti-Islamic polemics had been widespread since the Middle Ages, spurred by the Crusades and the conquest of Constantinople, and they had only intensified in the sixteenth century as Ottoman armies seized control of the Mediterranean and seemed poised to conquer Vienna. But what about the United States in the early nineteenth century? Other than a handful of ships captured

---

[46] Mrs [Penelope] Aubin, *The Noble Slaves; or, the Lives and Adventures of Two Lords and Two Ladies Who Were Shipwreck'd and Cast Upon a Desolate Island near the East-Indies, in the Year 1710... How, in Their Return to Europe They Were Taken by Two Algerine Pirates Near the Straits of Gibraltar. Of the Slavery They Endured in Barbary; and of Their Meeting There with Several Persons of Quality, Who Were Likewise Slaves...* (London: E. Bell, 1722), vi. For the first-person captivity narratives of Eleonora and Anna, see pp. 61–80.

[47] Mrs. [Penelope] Aubin, *The Strange Adventures of the Count de Vinevil and His Family. Being an Account of What Happen'd to Them whilst They Resided at Constantinople. And of Madamoiselle Ardelisa, His Daughter's Being Shipwreck'd on the Uninhabited Island Delos...* (London: E. Bell, 1721), 6.

[48] *An Authentic Narrative*, 4.

[49] Ibid., 23.

[50] Ibid., 42.

[51] Maréchal or Grasset de Saint-Sauveur, *La belle captive*, 47–8.

by privateers, Americans had no obvious reason to promote such prejudices. Robert J. Allison offers an interesting explanation:

> Americans and Europeans had distorted ideas about Islam, but they found these ideas useful. Enlightenment writers created a picture of the Muslim world that served as a sober warning about the dangers of submitting to despotism, about the dangers of suppressing public debate, and about the twin evils of tyranny and anarchy. ... Americans of different political philosophies disagreed on the particular lessons drawn from Muslim history. But all of them, Tories and Patriots, Republicans and Federalists, agreed that Islam fostered religious and political oppression. ... The Muslim world was a remarkably useful rhetorical device that could be used by libertarians like Mathew Lyon and Thomas Paine and by conservatives like John Adams and Alexander Hamilton. With a popular image of Muhammad and the Muslim world firmly established in the public mind, it was enough to mention either one as a starting point for a political argument.[52]

In other words, Islam was not a reality for American public opinion but an abstraction – not unlike the present day. It was taken to be the antithesis of everything that American political culture held dear. Thus, for example, Susanna Haswell Rowson (1762–1824) wrote in the preface of her *Slaves in Algiers; or, A Struggle for Freedom* (1794) – a play based on the 'Captive's Tale' in *Don Quijote* – that she intended her work to 'contain no one sentiment, in the least prejudicial, to the moral or political principles of the government under which I live'. On the contrary, she had endeavoured 'to place the social virtues in the fairest point of view, and hold up, to merited contempt and ridicule, their opposite vices'.[53] Her Muslim characters were the incarnation of everything that was considered anathema to the 'moral or political principles' the United States stood for; only later were captives able to convince them of the error of their ways, thus enlisting them in the cause of freedom.

Soirées algériennes by the French clergyman Léon-Nicolas Godard (1825–1863) went through at least eleven editions between 1857 and 1886. Written in the form of dialogues between the author and a priest named Dom Gervasio Magnoso who had spent some fifty years in Algiers, the book presents the ultimate in moralizing and didacticism – Barbary captives are equated with early Christian martyrs, and their redemption with the struggle between Christianity and paganism.[54] While this may seem over the top, it is, in fact, only an extreme case of a common pattern in the corpus of captivity narratives, many of which approach their subject from a strictly religious angle. Carefully chosen biblical verses are interspersed throughout the texts, drawing parallels between the bondage of Israelites in Egypt or Babylon and the experiences of European captives in North Africa and the Middle East. As Gary Ebersole notes,

---

[52] Allison, *The Crescent Obscured*, 35, 59.

[53] Mrs [Susanna] Rowson, *Slaves in Algiers; or, A Struggle for Freedom: A Play, Interspersed with Songs, in Three Acts* (Philadelphia: Printed for the author by Wrigley and Berriman, 1794), ii.

[54] Léon[-Nicolas] Godard, *Soirées algériennes: Corsaires, esclaves et martyrs de Barbarie* (Algerian Evenings: Privateers, Slaves, and Martyrs of the Barbary Coast) (Tours: Alfred Mame et Fils, Éditeurs, 1886), 55.

the captives' travails and the Bible were used to gloss one another: 'This important dialectical relationship between the captive's reading of the Bible and her experience of her body in captivity needs to be recognized.'[55]

Stressing that she read the Bible twice during her captivity and praising it for the solace it afforded her, Eliza Bradley exclaims,

O, how precious, how exceedingly valuable is the word of God! how exceedingly precious is the religion of Jesus – how unlike that of Mahomet, how different from any which the carnal heart can invent! – O, it was this that sustained me in the hour of affliction, in the day of my captivity.[56]

Nor was she the only one who saw the light: after weeks of trekking through the desert, struggling with hunger and thirst, and coming face to face with death, her fellow captives had also seen the light. 'O that they may continue to be ever grateful to Him for past favors,' she says, 'and learn to trust in Him for the time to come – surely then above most others they have reason to say "it is good for us that we have been inflicted".'[57]

Captivity narratives typically had long titles that summarized their most salient points, and their endings were, of course, known beforehand. They were read not for suspense but for the lessons they taught; when interpreted in the light of the Bible, the narratives became parables and the captives exempla.[58] Together, the retelling of the sequence of events, the didactic prefaces and postfaces, and the Bible itself constitute a heteroglossia that needs to be appreciated and parsed as such if the narratives are to be understood as intended.

Captives in Indian narratives sometimes questioned their faith and rebelled against God for subjecting them to such suffering, but it would have been unthinkable for them to abandon Christianity in favour of animism or idolatry. In this respect, North Africa and the Middle East were quite different in that Islam figures in both narratives of captivity and the writings of redemptionists as an imminent danger that may tempt Christians and condemn their souls to eternal damnation.[59] Moreover, the threat was not necessarily that captives would willingly convert but rather that they might be compelled to do so by their captors. This is why priority was given to the ransoming of women and children who, it was assumed, would not be as able to resist the cruelties to which they were subjected as the men. It was in order to save their souls rather than easing their earthly pain that they had to be redeemed as soon as possible.[60]

There is no doubt that Christian captives were occasionally pressured to convert to Islam; archival evidence shows, for example, that a young Spanish woman named

---

[55] Gary L. Ebersole, *Captured by Texts: Puritan to Postmodern Images of Indian Captivity* (Charlottesville: University Press of Virginia, 1995), 36.

[56] *An Authentic Narrative*, 64–5.

[57] Ibid., 47. The verse is Psalms 119:71.

[58] Ebersole, *Captured by Texts*, 23.

[59] On the representation of Islam as a seductive threat in English literature, see Daniel Vitkus, *Turning Turk: English Theater and the Multicultural Mediterranean, 1570–1630* (New York: Palgrave Macmillan, 2003), especially chapter 5.

[60] Laugier de Tassy, *Histoire du Royaume d'Alger*, 283.

Bernarda de la Torre who was held captive between 1666 and 1669 was tormented because she refused to convert and marry her master.[61] For her part, Mrs. Crisp relates how, as she mechanically repeated what some native women were saying without understanding it, she happened to pronounce the Profession of Faith upon which she was taken to have converted, and when she denied it, was threatened with execution.[62] These incidents were the exception, however, and this was stressed by many commentators. For instance, James Wilson Stevens emphasized that natives never forced their captives to convert, since that would cost them the ransom money.[63] As Samuel Chew put it, 'the general impression in England that Moslems practised forcible conversion was probably founded upon the reports of escaped or ransomed captives who hid under the plea of compulsion their voluntary lapse from Christianity for the sake of ameliorating their condition.'[64]

Naturally, the role of religion in captivity narratives was not static. While the earliest narratives were approved by religious institutions and often used by them for fundraising, the gradual secularization of publishing brought about changes in their tenor and content. The new, fictional narratives 'rel[ied] on human agency rather than God's providence to forward the plot. Becoming increasingly secular, they focus[ed] on the rescuer's initiative rather than on the trials the captive endures while waiting on the Lord for rescue.'[65] The narratives of Mrs Villars and Polly Davis are good examples of cases where the female captive is saved and the tale brought to a happy ending by the clever and valiant actions of (male) heroes.

Abolitionism

A pamphlet published in 1700 compared African slaves in America to white captives on the Barbary Coast.[66] In an article that appeared in 1790, Benjamin Franklin attacked southern rationalizations for slavery from the pen of an imaginary Algerian.[67] And in *An Historical and Geographical Account of Algiers* (1797), Stevens attacked slavery as 'incontestible evidence of the remains of barbarism in those nations who sanction so diabolical a principle', asking, 'With what countenance then can we reproach a set of

---

[61] Friedman, *Spanish Captives in North Africa*, 89.
[62] [Mrs. Crisp], *The Female Captive*, vol. 2, 27–41.
[63] James Wilson Stevens, *An Historical and Geographical Account of Algiers; Comprehending a Novel and Interesting Detail of Events Relative to the American Captives* (Philadelphia: Hogan and M'Elroy, 1797), 242.
[64] Samuel C. Chew, *The Crescent and the Rose: Islam and England during the Renaissance* (New York: Oxford University Press, 1937), 375.
[65] Barbara Mortimer, *Hollywood's Frontier Captives: Cultural Anxiety and the Captivity Plot in American Film* (New York: Garland, 2000), 16.
[66] [Samuel Sewall], *The Selling of Joseph: A Memorial* (Boston: Bartholomew Green & John Allen, 1700). On this subject, see also Martial Poirson, 'L'Autre regard sur l'esclavage: Les captifs blancs chrétiens en terre d'Islam dans le théâtre français (XVIIᵉ–XVIIIᵉ siècles)', in *Littérature et esclavage, XVIIIᵉ–XIXᵉ siècles*, ed. Sarga Moussa (Paris: Éditions Desjonquères, 2010), 77–98.
[67] Benjamin Franklin, *Writings* (New York: Literary Classics of the United States, 1987), 1158.

barbarians, who have only retorted our own acts upon ourselves in making reprisals upon our citizens?'[68]

Another voice of abolitionism was Charles Sumner (1811–1874), whose *White Slavery in the Barbary States* – first delivered in 1847 as a lecture before the Boston Mercantile Library Association – clearly intended to hold up a mirror to American society. North African piracy had ended with the French occupation of Algiers in 1830, and Boston merchants no longer had reason to fear Barbary captivity. Emphasizing that African slaves in the United States were no less victims than American slaves on the Barbary Coast, Sumner noted that the slaveholding southern states were at the same latitude as North Africa: 'Perhaps the common peculiarities of climate, breeding indolence, lassitude, and selfishness, may account for the insensibility to the claims of justice and humanity which have characterized both regions,'[69] he wrote, echoing Hippocrates's (*c.* 460–*c.* 370 BCE) postulation of a relationship between geography and temperament – a notion often taken up by Orientalists during the eighteenth and nineteenth centuries.

In this context, the title of a former slave's memoirs is especially significant: *Narrative of the Sufferings of Lewis Clarke, during a Captivity of More than Twenty-Five Years, among the Algerines of Kentucky, one of the So-Called Christian States of North America* (1845). The reference to Kentucky slaveholders as 'Algerines' would not have failed to highlight the idea that slavery was a barbaric practice unworthy of civilized Christians. Indeed, Sumner said he intended 'to exhibit the pointed parallels ... between Algerine and American slavery', writing, 'The conscientious man could not plead in behalf of the emancipation of his white fellow-citizens, without confessing in his heart, perhaps to the world, that every consideration, every argument, every appeal urged for the white man, [h]old with equal force in behalf of his wretched colored brother in bonds.'[70]

In the novel *The Algerine Captive* (1797) by Royall Tyler (1757–1826), one Dr Underhill who worked on a slave ship is captured by pirates. The cruelty to which he is subjected arouses feelings of remorse for what he has done, and he prays to God 'who hath made of one flesh and one blood all nations of the earth' that his own suffering 'may expiate for the inhumanity I was necessitated to exercise towards these my brethren of the human race'.[71] When an African offers him help, Dr Underhill feels 'oppressed with gratitude' and implores God to give him a chance 'once more to taste the freedom of my native country, and every moment of my life shall be dedicated to preaching against this detestable commerce'.[72]

The motif recurs in Rowson's *Slaves in Algiers* and in many other plays, in terms sometimes moderate and sometimes quite radical.[73] Bernardin de Saint-Pierre

---

[68] Stevens, *An Historical and Geographical Account of Algiers*, 234–5.
[69] Charles Sumner, *White Slavery in the Barbary States* (Boston: John P. Jewett and Company, 1853), 11–13.
[70] Ibid., 83.
[71] [Royall Tyler], *The Algerine Captive; or, The Life and Adventures of Doctor Updike Underhill, Six Years a Prisoner Among the Algerines* (Hartford, CT: Peter B. Gleason, 1816), 100–1.
[72] Ibid., 111.
[73] For a detailed survey, see Benilde Montgomery, 'White Captives, African Slaves: A Drama of Abolition', *Eighteenth-Century Studies* 27, no. 4 (1994): 615–30.

(1737–1814), the author of the well-known novel *Paul et Virginie* (1788), noted in his posthumously published play *Empsael et Zoraïde* that he wished to exhibit slavery from the viewpoint of the slave.[74] The publisher of the 1815 Rutland edition of the Maria Martin narrative added a section that discusses at length the savagery of North African natives, only to conclude, 'For this practice of buying and selling slaves, we are not entitled to charge the Algerines with any exclusive degree of barbarity.'[75] This remark could not have failed to leave its North American readers deeply shaken.

It is worth noting that harems were often equated in the West with slavery, so that many anti-slavery activists viewed them as naturally within the purview of abolitionism. Thus, the Anti-Slavery Society established in London in 1823 by William Wilberforce and Thomas Clarkson worked to end slavery in the Ottoman Empire, focusing also on the institution of the harem. The society's secretary Louis Alexis Chamerovzow (1816–1875) edited not only *Slave Life in Georgia: A Narrative of the Life, Sufferings, and Escape of John Brown, a Fugitive Slave, Now in England* (1855) but also *Six Years in Europe* (1873), the sequel to Melek Hanım's *Thirty Years in the Harem* (1872) which ranks as one of the most bitter memoirs of harem life ever to appear in print.[76] Captivity by Muslims remained a powerful weapon in the hands of abolitionists until quite late into the nineteenth century.

Diplomacy and war

Many captivity narratives functioned as political propaganda – some exhorting their readers to help drive North American natives ever further inland and open the continent to white settlement, others calling for war against the North African pirates who impeded free trade. It is no coincidence that several narratives of Barbary captivity were written before and during the Barbary Wars.

After gaining independence in 1776, the United States of America found itself a fledgling former colony with neither army nor navy. Due in part to British provocations, its unprotected merchant ships were regularly attacked by North African

---

[74] Bernardin de Saint-Pierre, *Empsael et Zoraïde, ou Les Blancs Esclaves des Noirs à Maroc* (Empsael and Zoraïde, or the White Slaves of Blacks in Morocco), ed. Maurice Souriau (Caen: Louis Jouan, Éditeur, 1905), 3.

[75] *An Historical Account of the Kingdom of Algiers; Including a Description of the Country, the Manners and Customs of the Natives, Their Treatment to Their Slaves, Their Laws, Religion, etc. To which Is Annexed, a History of the Captivity and Sufferings of Mrs. Maria Martin, Who Was Six Years a Slave in Algiers, Two of which She Was Confined in a Dark and Dismal Dungeon, Loaded with Irons* (Rutland, VT: Fay & Davison, 1815), 14–15. This sentence appears verbatim in Mathew Carey's *A Short Account of Algiers: Containing a Description of the Climate of That Country, of the Manners and Customs of the Inhabitants, and of Their Several Wars...* (Philadelphia: Printed by J. Parker for M. Carey, 1794), 18. Such 'borrowings' are very common.

[76] Melek Hanım (Marie Dejean) was the former wife of Grand Vezir Mehmed Pasha the Cypriot. See *Thirty Years in the Harem; or, the Autobiography of Melek-Hanum, Wife of H.H. Kibrizli-Mehemet-Pasha* (New York: Harper & Brothers, 1872); L[ouis] A[lexis] Chamerovzow, ed., *Six Years in Europe: Sequel to Thirty Years in the Harem; the Autobiographical Notes of Melek-Hanum, Wife of H.H. Kibrizli-Mehemet-Pasha* (London: Chapman and Hall, 1873). On Melek Hanım and her memoirs, see my Introduction to the reissue of *Thirty Years in the Harem* (Piscataway, NJ: Gorgias Press, 2006), v–lx.

privateers. Debates between Republicans and Federalists on how to respond to these attacks reflected broader disagreements over the powers that should be granted to a central authority and the legitimacy of overseas military intervention.[77] Some found it necessary to convince the American public that the country was under threat, and narratives of Indian captivity once again became the model of choice for hawkish propaganda. In the years leading to and during the First and Second Barbary Wars, the capture of white women by pirates in Morocco, Algiers, Tunis and Tripoli remained a topic that commanded much attention.

An amusing example of the political use made of female captives is the changing persona of Roxelana (Hürrem Sultan, d. 1558), the Ruthenian chief consort of the Ottoman sultan Süleyman the Magnificent (r. 1520–66), in a sequence of Western plays. Jean-François Marmontel's (1723–1799) short story 'Soliman II', first published in 1756, tells of a European woman named Roxelana who is captured and taken to the imperial harem. Refusing to submit to the will of the sultan, she teaches him Western ways, instils in him egalitarian ideas and eventually marries him as his 'queen and equal'.[78] The story was adapted for the stage by Charles-Simon Favart (1710–1792) as *Les trois sultanes, ou Soliman Second* and performed in Paris in 1761; its plot was largely unchanged, except for the fact that Marmontel's 'European' Roxelana was now French.[79] A few years later, Isaac Bickerstaff's (1735–1812) *The Sultana* (1775) was staged in London, and once again the story was the same except that Roxelana was now English.[80] And finally in 1794, as war against the Barbary States was being debated in the United States, John Hodgkinson's (c. 1767–1805) adaptation *The American Captive* was staged in New York and Roxelana was now American![81] Chameleon-like, the 'female captive of the Turks' motif was thus constantly re-circulated in the service of a variety of political agendas.

In 1830, the French invaded and occupied Algiers. Ann Thomson has noted the presence of a 'special antagonism towards Algiers' in writings on North Africa, venturing that 'the most obvious reason can be summed up in a single word: corsairs'. If only Ottoman rule could be overthrown, many believed, the problem of piracy and captivity would be resolved. Yet, Barbary piracy had declined by the early nineteenth century, and the number of captives still held there was insignificant. According to Thomson, the real reason for the colonization of North Africa was economic: 'The question of the pirates or the need for a crusade against the infidels, or the liberation of the "white slaves", however much they may have captured the popular imagination, were to a certain extent screens for the more down-to-earth motives of commercial

---

[77] See Allison, *The Crescent Obscured*, 3–34.

[78] [Jean-François] Marmontel, *Contes moraux* (Morality Tales) (Amsterdam: Marc Michel Rey, 1779), vol. 2, 42–69.

[79] [Charles-Simon] Favart, *Les trois sultanes, ou Soliman Second: Comédie en trois actes et en vers* (The Three Sultanas, or Süleyman the Second: Comedy in Verse in Three Acts) (Paris: Barba & Hubert, 1817).

[80] Isaac Bickerstaff, *The Sultan; or, A Peep into the Seraglio: A Farce*, ed. Thomas Dibdin (London: Printed at the Chiswick Press by C. Whittingham for Sherwood, Neely, and Jones, 1817).

[81] No copies of John Hodgkinson's adaptation appear to be extant, but the play is known to have been performed at least twenty-two times between 1794 and 1840. See Allison, *The Crescent Obscured*, 69 and 237 n. 16).

interest.'[82] Captivity narratives were just elements in the legitimating discourse of colonialism.

James Leander Cathcart, a captive in Algiers from 1785 to 1796, made clear this political dimension when he wrote in his memoirs: 'I could not conceive that a more humiliating situation than mine was in existence. I was convinced that *the honor of our country* was connected with our redemption.'[83] Considering the gendered nature of 'honor' in patriarchal societies, it is hardly surprising that narratives of women's captivity also partook in this discourse. The trope of Muslim men violating Christian women was a battle cry calling Europeans to action. At the end of *La belle captive*, the anonymous author asks, 'How can it be that, on a coast separated from Europe by a narrow band of water, such horrors and cruelty have been allowed to take place for so long? Why is orderly Europe not taking up arms to teach these ruffians the first lesson of the heart, which is humanity?'[84]

In the works of Aubin, Chetwood and others, the virtue of European women captured by Muslims was considered equivalent to the honour of Europe and all of Christendom.[85] In her *The Strange Adventures of the Count de Vinevil*, for instance, the eponymous hero goes on business to Istanbul accompanied by the beautiful Ardelisa and their good friend, the Count of Longueville, who is in love with her. The latter expresses his fear that Ardelisa's beauty may be their undoing, 'should some lustful *Turk*, mighty in Slaves and Power, once see that lovely Face; what human Power could secure you from his impious Arms, and me from Death!'[86] Alas, a Turkish officer named 'Mahomet' does see Ardelisa and resolves to possess her. As the young lovers prepare their escape, Longueville says,

> May Angels guard you and conduct you to my longing Arms again; but if some dreadful Chance prevents our meeting, remember both your Duty to yourself and me. Permit not a vile Infidel to dishonour you, resist to death, and let me not be so compleatly curs'd, to hear you live, and are debauch'd. My Soul is fill'd with unaccustom'd Fears; forgive me, Ardelisa, I know your Virtue's strong, tho you are weak, but Force does oft prevail.[87]

A similar story is told in *La belle captive*, where Adeline's captor tries to seduce her. As he declares his love, 'he ha[s] the temerity of crossing the bounds of decorum', but Adeline proudly rejects him: 'Despite the misfortunes, terrors, and misery that she

[82] Ann Thomson, *Barbary and the Enlightenment: European Attitudes towards the Maghreb in the 18th Century* (Leiden: E.J. Brill, 1987), 124, 128, and 141. On the growing importance of trade in the pre-colonial period, see pp. 133–42.

[83] J[ane] B[lancker Cathcart] Newkirk, ed., *The Captives, by James Leander Cathcart, Eleven Years a Prisoner in Algiers* (La Porte, IN: Herald Print, [1902]), 43, italics mine.

[84] Maréchal or Grasset de Saint-Sauveur, *La belle captive*, pp. 100–101. Similar sentiments were also voiced centuries earlier, e.g. by European Christian captives of the Ottomans in a sixteenth-century German Protestant hymn; see Sydney H. Moore, *Sursum Corda. Being Studies of Some German Hymn-Writers* (London: Independent Press, 1956), 121.

[85] Snader, *Caught between Worlds*, 149–53.

[86] Aubin, *The Strange Adventures*, 18.

[87] Ibid., 27–8.

had undergone, this beautiful French girl had still managed to retain the nobility and loftiness that behoved her, her station, and her nation.'[88]

In these stories – just a few of many examples of the somatization of political conflicts – international struggles were reduced to personal relations between slaves and their cruel masters, as female captives were identified with their country, Europe or Christendom. Rebecca Blevins Faery's description of Indian captivity narratives also holds for those centred on North Africa:

> The captive woman was made into a metaphor: she was herself the emblematic territory for control of which the two sides fought. The conflict between colonial and Native cultures contracted, during the time of her captivity, into the space she herself occupied; her body, both actual and textual, was a border zone, a mediating space between emergent races and cultures in conflict, a terrain for which and on which the ideological struggle between the two cultures took place.[89]

When Christophoros Plato Castanis, who had been taken captive by the Ottomans after the Chian massacre of 1822, published his memoirs in 1845, he dedicated the book to those who sympathized with the island's beautiful girls.[90] When the book was reissued in 1851, it was rededicated to those who had rescued 'the persecuted daughters of Greece'.[91] Emphasis was placed on the female gender (even though Castanis himself was a man) because there was much more political capital to be made from identifying Greece with its suffering women.

Captivity narratives were also mobilized by Philhellenes to garner support first for the Greek struggle for independence and then for the young kingdom of Greece. The narrative of Sophia Mazro, published in 1828, is a case in point. While it differs somewhat from other captivity tales – the family's two daughters are captured and taken away, but their actual experiences are not described – the booklet was clearly modelled on Indian and Barbary narratives not only by its title and premise but even by its physical format. It contains two captivity tales, one related by a woman who escaped the massacre in Missolonghi (1825–6) and the other by a survivor of the massacre on Chios. It is clear that the book was published for fundraising, and it is thus not unlike those produced by Trinitarian or Mercedarian monks in Britain, France and Spain to support redemptionist efforts.

---

[88] Maréchal or Grasset de Saint-Sauveur, *La belle captive*, 66–7.
[89] Rebecca Blevins Faery, *Cartographies of Desire: Captivity, Race, and Sex in the Shaping of an American Nation* (Norman: University of Oklahoma Press, 1999), 41.
[90] *The Greek Captive: A Narrative of the Captivity and Escape of Christophoros Plato Castanis, during the Massacre on the Island of Scio by the Turks* (Worcester, MA: Henry Howland, 1845), 7.
[91] *The Greek Exile, or a Narrative of the Captivity and Escape of Christophorus Plato Castanis, during the Massacre on the Island of Scio, by the Turks* (Philadelphia: Lippincott, Grambo, 1851), iii. Note both the Latinization of the author's first name and the substitution of 'exile' for 'captive', as Castanis had been living in the United States for many years by the time the book was reissued.

Romance and sexuality

Some first-person narratives of Barbary captivity were explicitly erotic – for example, *The Lustful Turk* and *Marché aux esclaves et harem*. As I have argued elsewhere,[92] sexuality was widely used to produce 'spaces of otherness', in contrast to which Europeans defined themselves and the lands that they could be mobilized to conquer and colonize. Captivity narratives were an important element in this literature, and even those that were not erotic often had sexual undertones.

By their very nature, tales of captivity feature settings where familiar social rules do not apply, settings that entail hostility and danger. Moreover, most of the narratives discussed here involve capture by pirates, a category considered beyond the pale of civilized society whether in social, economic, political, cultural or sexual terms.[93] It was, therefore, perhaps inevitable that the threat of sexual violation would be present in these works. Some narratives made this explicit and some did not, but even if only by way of reassuring the reader that the captive had not been raped, sex (and particularly sexual violence) is present in many if not most.

Sexual violence in captivity tales is occasionally directed against men[94] or children,[95] but the threat/attempt/act of rape was generally reserved for young women.[96] In some narratives, description of the captive's rape borders on the pornographic. For example, Francis Brooks writes in *Barbarian Cruelty* (1693) of a young girl captured by Moroccan pirates in 1685 while on her way from London to Barbados. Found to be a virgin, she was sent to the royal harem:

> Thus this beastly and inhuman Wretch by all ways he could invent, fought to force her to yield, which she resisted so long, till Tortures and the hazards of her Life forced her to yield, or resign her Body to him, tho her Heart was otherwise inclined. So he had her wash'd, and clothed in their fashion of Apparel, and lay with her; having his Desire fulfilled, he inhumanly, in great haste forc'd her away out of his Presence; and she being with Child, he sent her by his Eunuchs to Macqueness.[97]

---

[92] See my *The Erotic Margin: Sexuality and Spatiality in Alteritist Discourse* (London: Verso, 1999).

[93] See, for example, B[arry] R[ichard] Burg, *Sodomy and the Pirate Tradition: English Sea Rovers in the Seventeenth-Century Caribbean* (New York: New York University Press, 1984); Hans Turley, *Rum, Sodomy, and the Lash: Piracy, Sexuality, and Masculine Identity* (New York: New York University Press, 1999). And for this reason, no doubt, piracy has provided a fertile setting for sadomasochistic novels such as Jean de la Beuque's *Esclaves et pirates* (Slaves and Pirates) (Paris: Amateur-Biblio, 1926) and *Femmes et corsaires* (Women and Privateers) (Paris: Amateur-Biblio, 1931).

[94] See, for example, Baepler, *White Slaves, African Masters*, 45; Turbet-Delof, *L'Afrique barbaresque dans la littérature française*, 98–9; Snader, *Caught between Worlds*, 148, 165; Colley, *Captives*, 128–30.

[95] Temprano, *El mar maldito*, 57.

[96] See, for example, James R. Lewis, 'Images of Captive Rape in the Nineteenth Century', *Journal of American Culture* 15, no. 2 (1992): 69–77.

[97] Francis Brooks, *Barbarian Cruelty: Being a True History of the Distressed Condition of the Christian Captives under the Tyranny of Mully Ishmael, Emperor of Morocco and King of Fez...* (London: S. Phillips, 1693), s. 34.

In the narrative of Polly Davis, the captive is more forbearing and resists her captor for a long time. Begging him to pity 'the poor and helpless innocent maid' standing before him and not to do 'so base a thing, which cannot do you any good, and which takes from the virgin all that is praise worthy, in the woman', she points out that 'it is not lawful for men and women to copulate together until marriage, which is an institution appointed by God himself; neither do I think, that a man has any business with more wives than one; and there is no rule for it, in all the new-testament, but much to the contrary'.[98] Alas, these supplications do not move the captain, whose behaviour is described in words that would not feel out of place in a work of Victorian erotica:

> He flung me on the bed, and was so rude that I screamed very loudly, upon which, he was very much affronted, and told me, that another such noise would cost me my life. I told him, that did not affright me, for I had rather that he would plunge his dagger into my heart, than to be deflowered, in such a manner. ... [H]e told me that he would have his will of me, if it should take four of his servants to hold me; therefore I had better surrender quietly, than expose my nakedness to the other servants.[99]

In *La belle captive*, Adeline's master fails to convince her to submit, so he calls for a Christian woman who has been a slave for some time to be brought to him: 'The shaykh fully satiated his savage passion with her, right next to Adeline, as she closed her eyes and shrouded herself with her virtue.'[100] This, of course, does nothing to reduce Adeline's determination.

Not all captivity narratives were as explicit. Those intended for a general audience tended to be more reserved, and sometimes the same basic text was modified to suit the intended readership. For example, the narrative of Maria Martin was published several times not only with different titles but also with slightly different illustrations. Thus, the Boston edition shows the heroine with bared breasts, while the Rutland edition has her in exactly the same setting and pose but fully clothed. Moreover, she is Italian in the former and English in the latter; presumably the sexualization of a darker, Mediterranean, Catholic woman would have been found less threatening by rural New Englanders than that of her fair, British, Protestant counterpart.

Another way in which captivity narratives engaged in 'sexploitation' is in descriptions of torture. The narrative of Mary Velnet includes no less than four blood-curdling torture scenes involving fantastical devices:

> On my arrival, orders were given to the four Turks selected to execute the Bashaw's barbarous laws, to strip me; after being divested of my clothing, one of the monsters seizing me by the hair, at the same time another taking me by the feet, stretched me on the platform of the horrid machine! the spears or spikes which it contained, soon pierced my flesh to the bone; four ropes were then made fast to my wrists

[98] *Narrative of the Captivity of John Vandike*, 10.
[99] Ibid., 11.
[100] Maréchal or Grasset de Saint-Sauveur, *La belle captive*, 74–5.

and ankles, and drawn taught by means of the four posts turning like a windless as before mentioned, and which were turned at intervals until every bone in my arms and legs were wrenched out of joint, the spikes on which I lay at the same time tearing and hackling my flesh in a manner not to be described.[101]

This torture device and others like it recall both those of the Inquisition and the automaton fad of the eighteenth century, not to mention the Marquis de Sade (1740–1813) who was still alive at the time the narrative was first published. There is no trace of Sade's radical cynicism and moral relativism in this account, however, and closer cognates may be found in some Indian captivity narratives.[102]

Miscegenation was perhaps the most important cultural taboo during the age of colonialism. The rape or seduction of white women captives by their brown captors was therefore depicted in the narratives as a recurrent and particularly dire threat. There was, however, a way in which the racial interdiction could be cast aside, and that was by the conversion of the non-believing partner to Christianity. This motif is often encountered in romances involving a European man and a Muslim woman, as well as in North African and Middle Eastern captivity narratives. Thus, in Cervantes's 'Captive's Tale', Zoraida falls in love with the narrator, helps him and his fellow captives escape, and converts to Christianity.[103] In Alexandre Hardy's (*c.* 1570–*c.* 1632) *Elmire, ou l'Heureuse bigamie* (1628), the daughter of the sultan of Egypt likewise falls in love with a Christian, frees the captives, converts and marries her beloved.[104] *The Life and Adventures of the Prince of Salermo* (1770), published under the pseudonym Marquis de Vere, presents a particularly complicated story in which a Christian captive falls in love with the wife of his master, and his master in turn falls in love with the captive's sister; after a divorce, two conversions and two marriages, all ends well.[105] Yet again, not all stories have happy endings: in both Voltaire's (1694–1778) *Zulime* (1740)[106] and Laugier de Tassy's *Histoire du royaume d'Alger*,[107] Muslim women who fall in love with their infidel captives end up dead.

Aubin's *The Strange Adventures of the Count de Vinevil* interestingly complicates matters. While Ardelisa has managed to protect her virtue, Violetta has succumbed and married a Turk. She feels guilty and says to her confessor that she should have instead opted to die.

The Priest answer'd, 'Madam, you are deceiv'd: in Ardelisa, who was marry'd to another, it would have been a horrid Crime to suffer another Man for to possess; but as you were single, a Virgin, and made his by the Chance of War, it was no Sin

[101] *An Affecting History*, 78–9.
[102] See Nathaniel Knowles, 'The Torture of Captives by the Indians of Eastern North America', *Proceedings of the American Philosophical Society* 82, 2 (1940): 151–225.
[103] Book 1, parts 39–41.
[104] *Le théâtre d'Alexandre Hardy* (Paris: J. Quesnel, François Targa, 1624–8), vol. 5, 113–96.
[105] Marquis de Vere, *The Life and Adventures of the Prince of Salermo: Containing an Account of His Adventures at Venice and in Hungary, His Captivity at Damas, and Amours with an Ottoman Princess, Together with His Return to Italy...* (London: J. Roson, 1770).
[106] *Œuvres complètes de Voltaire*, ed. Louis Moland (Paris: Garnier Frères, 1877–85), vol. 4, 1–90.
[107] Laugier de Tassy, *Histoire du Royaume d'Alger*, 171–99.

in you to yield to him, and it would have been wilful Murder to have kill'd him, or but conspir'd his Death: nay, a Sin not to have been faithful to his Bed, whilst he is living you ought not to marry, you might have been a means of his Conversion; you ought to pray for him, and consider he acted according to his Knowledge and Education.'[108]

Under different circumstances, the priest would have undoubtedly argued that abstention from earthly pleasures would lead one to heaven and debauchery to hell; but the hope of helping convert a Muslim and thereby 'save his soul' was enough to absolve Violetta of any sin.[109]

Conclusion: The currency of history

Captivity narratives must be analysed not just as simple chronicles of events – whether true or fictional – but as complex intertexts comprising elements of gender, religion, politics and sexuality. But that is not all. Reading those narratives today entails confronting an intertext that also includes the discursive uses to which they have been put in contemporary politics. As Liliane Weissberg put it,

> Events can be recalled only if they (or their mode of narrative) fit within a framework of contemporary interests. Society, in turn, modifies recollections according to its present needs. Social beliefs are collective recollections, and they relate to a knowledge of the present. Collective memory adjusts to, and shapes, a system of present-day beliefs.[110]

Memory, in other words, is a two-way street between the past and the present: what is remembered shapes, and is in turn shaped by, current concerns. Captivity narratives partake in the production of a collective memory that influences the ways in which we perceive the present, naturalizes and legitimizes existing or desired power relations and helps to mould the ongoing Cold War against the Muslim World.

Take, for example, the capture and rescue of Jessica Lynch during the Second Gulf War. Ambushed and injured on 3 March 2003, Lynch was taken to and cared for in an Iraqi hospital and, after nine days, 'delivered from captivity' in a televised and highly sensationalized military operation. In her first interview following her recovery,[111] she

---

[108] Aubin, *The Strange Adventures*, 91–2.
[109] Interestingly, Martin Luther stated in 'Vermahnung zum Gebet wider den Türken' ('Admonition on Prayer against the Turks') (1541) that a married Christian woman separated from her husband by virtue of captivity could, if her Turkish master so ordered, submit to his will; however, even if she yields her body, she should never surrender her soul. See John W. Bohnstedt, 'The Infidel Scourge of God: The Turkish Menace as Seen by German Pamphleteers of the Reformation Era', *Transactions of the American Philosophical Society*, new Series, 58, no. 9 (1968): 22.
[110] Liliane Weissberg discussing Maurice Halbwachs in her Introduction to *Cultural Memory and the Construction of Identity*, ed. Dan Ben-Amos and Liliane Weissberg (Detroit: Wayne State University Press, 1999), 15.
[111] Interview with Diane Sawyer on ABC's 'Primetime Live', 11 November 2003.

stated that news about her ill-treatment and rape in captivity were all untrue, and that her rescue had been exploited for propaganda. Her case was just a cynical replay of a centuries-old script wherein a fair-skinned, blond-haired woman was taken captive by swarthy men and delivered by the grace of God – and, in this instance, the prowess of the American military. That so much attention was lavished on Lynch at a time when numerous other soldiers (and civilians) were being killed or injured shows the hold that narratives of women's captivity continue to have on Western collective memory.

Part Two

Resistance and Abolition

3

The gradual elimination of female slavery in the late Ottoman Empire: Institutional change

Kadir Yildirim

As an essential institution of Ottoman social and economic life, slavery survived until the end of the Ottoman Empire. Yet for some time before this, beginning in the nineteenth century, the number of slaves had been decreasing in line with decreasing numbers of prisoners of war and the overall weakening of the slave trade. Britain's push to suppress the slave trade internationally as a step towards full abolition was paralleled by the Ottoman state's enactment of laws that prohibited slavery within the empire. Nevertheless, due to societal resistance to these laws, the slave trade did not die out until the end of the empire.

This chapter considers the process of eliminating female slavery in the Ottoman Empire by applying the concept of institutional change. According to Douglass C. North, institutions form the 'rules of the game' in a society, and thus institutional change is the key to understanding historical change. Institutions structure incentives in all human exchanges, whether political, social or economic.[1]

Those rules that constitute the political, legal, economic and social environment such as a constitution or legal regulations are referred to as formal institutions. They entail an official, formal enforcement mechanism when violated. Morals, norms, habits, values, conventions, traditions and codes of conduct, however, also influence human behaviour in a society. These cultural and social factors are called informal institutions.[2] Changes in formal and informal institutions are closely related, though the former can be changed more easily and quickly, while informal institutions are more resistant to change. Gerard Roland classifies all institutions into two types: 'slow-moving' and 'fast-moving'. Culture – including values, beliefs, and social norms – is an ideal example of a slow-moving institution for which change may take quite a long time. Conversely, fast-moving institutions can change far more rapidly – sometimes overnight. Political institutions are typically viewed as fast-moving institutions.[3] Institutional transplantation – replicating

---

1 Douglass C. North, *Institutions, Institutional Change and Economic Performance* (New York: Cambridge University Press, 1990), 3.
2 Constanze Dobler, *The Impact of Formal and Informal Institutions on Economic Growth: A Case Study on the MENA Region* (Frankfurt: Peter Lang International Academic Publishers, 2011), 15.
3 Gerard Roland, 'Understanding Institutional Change: Fast-Moving and Slow-Moving Institutions', *Studies in Comparative International Development* 38, no. 4 (2004): 109.

institutions or institutional practices from other countries – has been a historically common method of achieving such rapid change. As a result of being influenced (or forced) by the practices of other countries, many states have changed a native institution by changing the political and legal bases of that institution.

In line with this theoretical approach, this chapter underscores the role of informal rather than formal institutions in explaining the demise of female slavery in the late Ottoman Empire. Moves towards the abolition of the slave trade in the empire first began with the legal regulations enacted in 1847 (formal institutions) as a practice of institutional transplantation, which, after prolonged conflicts, continued until the end of the empire. Societal acceptance of these changes, however, was gradual. In other words, the traditions, religious beliefs and habits of society (informal institutions) were slow to accept the legal regulations prohibiting slavery.[4] While these changes to formal institutions were more effective in ending African slavery, the abolition of white female slavery, mostly involving Circassian and Georgian female slaves, was only possible through reform of the social and economic structure. Therefore, after briefly providing an overview of slavery in the late Ottoman Empire, this chapter will discuss the abolition of African and white female slavery as two separate topics. Emphasis will also be placed on the importance of emerging servant markets in the empire as an indicator of changes in societal preferences to better understand how white female slavery finally came to an end.

Slavery in the nineteenth-century Ottoman Empire

Slavery took on many forms in late Ottoman society. Slaves laboured in every capacity, skilled and unskilled, intimate and remote, respected and degraded. While they served in various fields – as guards and lackeys, porters and miners, masons and musicians – the majority worked in households in a wide range of capacities: from house stewards, gardeners, eunuchs and wet nurses to laundresses, maids, cooks and concubines.[5]

---

[4] For some studies dealing with the importance of legal regulations in ending slavery. see Y. Hakan Erdem, *Osmanlı'da Köleliğin Sonu 1800–1909* (Istanbul: Kitap Yayınevi, 1990); Gülnihal Bozkurt, 'Köle Ticaretinin Sona Erdirilmesi Konusunda Osmanlı Devletinin Taraf Olduğu İki Devletlerarası Anlaşma', *OTAM* 1 (1990): 45–77; Zubeyde Gunes Yagci, 'Istanbul Esir Pazari', in *Osmanlı Devletinde Kölelik, Ticaret, Esaret, Yasam*, ed. Z. G. Yagci and F. Yaşa (Istanbul: Tezkire Yayınları, 2017), 57–90; Gul Akyilmaz, 'Osmanlı Hukukunda Köleliğin Sona Ermesi ile İlgili Düzenlemeler ve Tanzimat Fermanı'nın İlanından Sonra Kölelik Müessesesi', *Gazi Universitesi Hukuk Fakultesi Dergisi* 9, nos. 1–2 (2004): 213–38. For studies emphasizing the resistance of Ottoman society to the abolitionist legal regulations, see Terence Walz and Kenneth Cuno, eds, *Race and Slavery in the Middle East: Histories of Trans-Saharan Africans in Nineteenth-Century Egypt, Sudan and the Ottoman Mediterranean* (Cairo: American University in Cairo Press, 2010); Abdullah Martal, '19. Yüzyıl'da Kölelik ve Köle Ticareti', *Tarih ve Toplum* 121 (1994): 13–22; Ehud R. Toledano, *The Ottoman Slave Trade and Its Suppression: 1840–1890* (Princeton: Princeton University Press, 1982); Ehud R. Toledano, *As If Silent and Absent: Bonds of Enslavement in the Islamic Middle East* (New Haven: Yale University Press, 2007); Erdal Tasbas, 'Osmanlı Devleti'nin Ortadoğu'da Köle Ticaretini Engelleme Çalışmaları', *Akademik Incelemeler Dergisi* 13, no. 2 (2018): 119–57.

[5] Madeline C. Zilfi, *Women and Slavery in the Late Ottoman Empire: The Design of Difference* (New York: Cambridge University Press, 2010), 99.

Slaves were also utilized in state factories.[6] Agricultural slavery, which had almost ceased in previous centuries, reappeared with Circassian migration from the Caucasus in the 1860s. The main reason for this was that immigrants were allowed to bring their slaves to work on land granted to them.[7]

The two most important modes of enslavement in the Ottoman Empire were elite (military-administrative slaves and their wives and consorts, mainly categorized as *kul/harem* slaves) and non-elite (domestic or menial slavery). *Kul/harem* slavery diminished steadily and accounted for a smaller proportion of the overall slave population in the nineteenth century. Another demarcation of slavery in Ottoman lands can be made with regard to gender. In this case, the majority of slaves were women who served in domestic positions.[8] According to official records, there were 52,000 slaves in Istanbul alone in the 1850s. Of these, 5,000 were African slaves, and 47,000 were mostly female white slaves.[9] As concubines, they also served their masters by performing an early modern version of sex work.[10]

From the early modern era to the end of the First World War, as men moved into other types of employment, domestic service became increasingly feminized in Europe. Similar feminizing trends were also evident in Ottoman slavery from the seventeenth through to the nineteenth centuries. By the end of the eighteenth century, the slave trade was increasingly driven by the enslavement of women for domestic labour and sexual exploitation. The restructuring of the professional military, with free soldiers taking the place of an already declining number of slaves in the nineteenth century, along with the demilitarization of grandee households, were the decisive factors behind this trend. As a result, a new norm appeared: household labour, which often meant house slaves, came to be associated with women.[11]

---

[6] The wage records of Hereke textile factory in 1852 show that nineteen slaves, both male and female, laboured in the factory (Tevfik Güran, 'Tanzimat Döneminde Devlet Fabrikaları', in *150. Yılında Tanzimat*, ed. Hakkı D. Yıldız (Ankara: Türk Tarih Kurumu, 1992), 249). In the 1830s, slaves and prisoners were also employed in a haircloth factory in Sliven (Olcay P. Yapucu, '19. Yüzyıl Osmanlı Sanayii'ne Bir Örnek İslimiye Çuha Fabrikası', *Tarih ve Toplum*, 28, no. 167 (1997): 21).

[7] Ehud R. Toledano, *Osmanlı Köle Ticareti 1840–1890* (Istanbul: Tarih Vakfı Yurt Yayınları, 2000), 6–7.

[8] Michael Ferguson and Ehud R. Toledano, 'Ottoman Slavery and Abolition in the Nineteenth Century', in *The Cambridge World History of Slavery Vol. 4 AD 1804–AD 2016*, ed. D. Eltis, S. L. Engerman, S. Drescher and D. Richardson (Cambridge: Cambridge University Press, 2017), 200–1.

[9] H. Abdolonyme Ubicini, *Osmanlı'da Modernleşme Sancısı* (Istanbul: Timaş Yayınları,1998), 359–60. At that time, the population of Istanbul was between 350,000 and 450,000 (Zafer Toprak, 'Nüfus', in *Dünden Bugüne İstanbul Ansiklopedisi 6* (İstanbul: Tarih Vakfı Yayınları, 1994), 109). According to these figures, slaves comprised approximately 12–15 per cent of Istanbul's population in the middle of the nineteenth century.

[10] Suraiya Faroqhi, 'Slavery in the Ottoman World: A Literature Survey', in *Otto Spies Memorial Lecture 4*, ed. S. Conermann and G. Şen (Berlin: EB Verlag, 2017), 7. Not just Muslims but also other ethnic and religious groups held slaves for sexual purposes. For example, slaveholding was widespread in Jewish households in urban centres. These slaves were usually female. Prestige, sexual fulfilment and obedient domestic help were the main reasons for slaveholding in the Jewish community (Yaron Ben-Naeh, 'Blond, Tall, with Honey-Colored Eyes: Jewish Ownership of Slaves in the Ottoman Empire', *Jewish History* 20 (2006): 73–90).

[11] Madeline C. Zilfi, 'Servants, Slaves, and the Domestic Order in the Ottoman Middle East', *Hawwa Journal of Women of the Middle East and Islamic World* 2, no. 1 (2004): 26; B. W. Higman, 'Demographic Trends', in *The Cambridge World History of Slavery Vol. 4*, 38–9.

Since the majority of slaves were now women, female slaves were at the centre of conflicts between slaves, owners, slavers and the state in nineteenth-century Ottoman society. Below, I will discuss how slavery functioned on a day-to-day basis for women in this period.

Female slaves, slaveholders and traders: Some individual cases

In 1799, two men went to court to ratify an agreement they had made privately. According to the terms, Kahveci Mehmed had paid 60 *guruş*[12] to Numan Agha, *Kethüdâ* (the head of the guild) of candlemakers. The reason for the initial conflict was that Numan Agha had accused Mehmed of having sexual intercourse with his female slave, Alime. When Alime realized that she was pregnant, she used drugs to abort the baby but tragically died as a result. Mehmed rejected the allegations at first, but then he and Numan Agha arrived at an understanding and applied to the court to have it put down on paper.[13] Only Alime was now dead and had left behind many unanswered questions. Had she consented to sexual relations with Mehmed or been abused? Had she wanted to abort the child or been coerced? Did Numan or Mehmed bear any responsibility for her death? Unfortunately, we can never know the answers. What we do know is that suffering sexual abuse as a female slave was not just Alime's story.[14] Physical and sexual violence is frequently found in the Ottoman archival documents on slavery throughout the nineteenth century.

Ottoman court records show that the men who were involved in the sexual abuse of female slaves can be classified into three groups:

1. Owners and the relatives of the owners (husbands, sons, brothers, fathers-in-law, nephews, sons-in-law);
2. The male servants, friends, business partners and employees of the owners; and
3. Slave traders (*esirci*), their male servants and known/unknown foreigners and guests in the places where female slaves were kept for sale.[15]

The law itself supported the rights of owners to have sexual access to female slaves. When an owner had a child from his female slave and accepted paternity, the child took its status from the paternal line and became free. In this case, the mother was known as *umm al-walad* (mother of a child), and she also had the right to be freed following the death of the owner. If the father was someone other than the owner, however, then the child took its status from the mother, and both remained slaves. In

---

[12] 60 *guruş* was worth 7.5 Venetian Ducats at that time.
[13] Yahya Araz, 'Cariyeler, Efendiler ve Pusuda Bekleyenler: Osmanlı İstanbul'unda Hamile ve Çocuk Annesi Cariyeler Üzerine Düşünceler (1790–1880)', *Kebikeç* 37 (2014): 233–4.
[14] For a similar case, see Ehud R. Toledano, 'Shemsigul: A Circassian Slave in Mid-Nineteenth-Century Cairo', in *Struggle and Survival in the Modern Middle East*, ed. Edmund Burke III (Berkeley: University of California Press, 1993), 59–74.
[15] For a list of specific cases, see Araz, 'Cariyeler', 252–7.

that case, the owner could either emancipate them or compel his female slave to marry a free man or another slave. Nevertheless, the owner's rights of possession continued; offspring and mother were still the owner's property. In other words, female slaves could marry and start a family but remained slaves regardless of their marital status. Any property they obtained through marriage also redounded to their owners.[16]

Nor did impregnation by one's owner automatically confer the status of *umm al-walad*. It was also common for owners to force concubines to have abortions. In 1849, a concubine named Mahire escaped from her master in Istanbul and requested the help of officials. She claimed that she had been illegally forced to have an abortion by Latif Aga, the *Esirciler Yiğitbaşısı* (the officer from the Slave Traders' Guild[17] responsible for enforcing market regulations). According to the Ottoman law of the time, it was illegal to have an abortion, and the penalties included imprisonment or exile. There were many midwives, however, who performed these operations in secret. Latif Aga took Mahire to a midwife, and there they forced her to take some kind of drug. Mahire, who had previously been forced into a similar procedure, understood what was being done to her and refused to take the drug.[18]

There were also several cases when the owners intended to sell their pregnant female slaves. In theory, a slave who conceived by his or her master should have been given freedom, but in practice, things were often different. Due to intrafamilial pressure and a desire to escape responsibility, many slave owners sold their pregnant slaves. If the master denied paternity, the concubine had to prove it in court; the courts usually decided in favour of the owners in these cases. In 1870, Halime, a slave who was six months pregnant at the time, told a court that her owner, Hadji Mehmed, had impregnated her and then wanted to sell her. A year later, in 1871, Gülbuy, a Circassian slave, charged her former owner, Shaikh Mustafa Efendi, with selling her, even though he knew that she was pregnant with his baby. Although she told him several times that she should be taken as an *umm al-walad*, he nevertheless sold her, and then the new owner, Saide Hanoum, wanted to do the same. In another case, in 1827, Esma Hanoum complained that her Circassian female slave Pervin had repeatedly disobeyed her. When the *kadi* asked her the reason, she said that she was pregnant by her previous owner, Hussein, and as an *umm al-walad* should be returned to him. The interesting detail in this case was that Hussein was Esma's husband. So, everything had been 'in the family'. After analysing court records on pregnant slaves between 1790 and 1880, Yahya Araz concluded that most of the court decisions (including the cases mentioned above) displayed a similar tendency. According to the courts, the accusations by the slaves were not *meşru* (legitimate) or *iltifata şayan* (notable). In most cases, the *kadis* counselled the slaves to obey their owners.[19]

---

[16] Zilfi, *Women and Slavery*, 109–11, 162.
[17] The slave dealers in the empire were organized in each city as a special guild headed by a sheikh and a *Kethüda* (warden). They regulated the slave markets and audited the lawfulness and legitimacy of the slave trade. Although they continued to exist, these guilds weakened significantly in the second half of the nineteenth century due to the ban of the slave markets (Toledano, *Ottoman Slave Trade*, 60–1).
[18] Araz, 'Cariyeler', 248–9.
[19] Ibid., 239–40.

In some cases of sexual abuse, the economic loss caused by a female slave's pregnancy (or resulting death, in the case of Alime) was the most critical issue for owners. The complaint was usually resolved through compensation paid by the abuser who caused the loss. For example, a female slave owner sued a man who raped her young virgin slave and won 500 *guruş* in compensation. The justification for the payment was that the slave had lost her financial value through the loss of her virginity. Ottoman juristic opinion (*fetvas*) literature mentions many similar cases in which inquiries were submitted and answered regarding disputed paternity, prostitution, adultery, joint ownership of slaves, marriage, childbirth, violation by someone other than an owner and sexual relations with a wife's female slave.[20] There were also cases where the defendants and complainants were members of the same family. In 1833, a man named Mehmed Ali forced Hurican, a Greek female slave of his wife, Hatice, into sexual intercourse, resulting in the loss of her virginity. Since that meant a significant economic loss for Hatice, she had a heated debate with her husband. In the end, her husband paid 4,250 *guruş* as the cost of the virginity of Hurican. A month and a half later, Mehmed Ali and Hatice divorced due to irreconcilable differences.[21]

Cases of sexual abuse of slaves were not always limited to the actions of one individual. In some situations, the ambition to make money at any cost knew no limits and human dignity was disregarded. One such event in Smyrna in the 1850s is detailed in the archival documents as follows:

> Some wealthy and greedy slave owners in the Smyrna province are forcing their African male slaves and concubines to have sexual intercourse with each other, without their consent and against Shari'ah. They force them to live and work like animals on their farms and lands. They are also wrenching the children born from these couplings as pitilessly as if they were separating lambs from ewes to sell them.[22]

Although it is claimed that conditions for slaves were better in the Ottoman Empire than in Europe and the Americas,[23] cases such as the one above reveal that slavery, regardless of where it took place, could make the lives of its victims extraordinarily difficult. Wolf von Schuerbrand, a correspondent for the *New York Times* in Istanbul in the 1880s, had the chance to visit a house where female slaves had been secretly traded in Istanbul and

---

[20] Zilfi, *Women and Slavery*, 205.

[21] Araz, 'Cariyeler', 243. Literature on slavery focuses on recapturing the voices of slaves in the empire and shows us many similar cases. For some of these studies, see Y. Hakan Erdem, 'Magic, Theft, and Arson: The Life and Death of an Enslaved African Woman in Ottoman İzmit', in *Race and Slavery in the Middle East*, 125–6; Eve M. Troutt Powell, *Tell This in My Memory: Stories of Enslavement from Egypt, Sudan and the Ottoman Empire* (Stanford: Stanford University Press, 2012); Toledano, *As If Silent*; Özgül Özdemir, 'African Slaves in the 19th-Century Ottoman Empire', unpublished master thesis (Istanbul: Bogazici University, 2017), 58–67; Evren Dayar, 'Mancarcık Kuyusu Cinayeti: 19. Yüzyılda Antalya'da Hovardalar, Azatlı Köleler ve Rakkase Kadınlar', *Cihannüma Tarih ve Coğrafya Araştırmaları Dergisi* 4, no. 2 (2018): 61–81.

[22] Prime Ministry Ottoman Archives (hereafter BOA), *A.MKT.UM.* 231/46, AH 27 Rajab 1272 (3 April 1856).

[23] Murat Sarıcık, *Batılı Kölelik Anlayışı Karşısında Osmanlı'da Kölelik, Cariyelik ve Harem* (Isparta, 1999), 323–5; Ubicini, *Osmanlı'da*, 359–64.

noted correctly, 'True, slavery, on the whole, is of a mild and rather humane form with the Turks. But still, it is slavery.'[24] As one of the British Anti-Slavery Society reports on female slavery in the Ottoman Empire observed, 'It is true the "wife" or "concubine" may be very kindly treated, and the slave may occasionally have found a good owner; but the position as a future wife, concubine, and slave is absolutely uncertain.'[25]

Due to these uncertainties, many slaves were willing to take enormous risks for the chance of escape. Being subjected to violence or a decision by an owner to sell a slave or his/her family was among the main reasons to abscond. For example, in 1857 in Tripoli, an owner decided to sell the mother and child but keep the father of a family of three enslaved Africans. Due to his objections, the father was locked in a dungeon for fifteen days. After managing to escape, he reunited with his family and sought refuge in the British consulate. When another owner wanted to sell the three children of a female slave, she also resorted to the protection of the British consul in Damascus. In 1867, two Ottoman officials brought six of their eleven Circassian slaves – all from the same family – to Istanbul to sell. When the family applied to the Shari'a court to prevent themselves from being sold or split up, the court ruled in favour of the owners. Persistent objectors could sometimes save their families from such situations with the help of the Ottoman Treasury, which compensated the owner monetarily.[26] In another case in 1893, a Circassian slave named Hasan accused a slave trader of selling his six daughters. Denying the accusations, the slave trader claimed that he had obtained the girls from Hasan's Circassian owner. According to the owner, this was an ancient tradition among Circassians, and he thus had the right to sell his slave's children.[27]

Despite the significant uncertainties of remaining enslaved, the risks were even higher after escape, especially for former female slaves. Many had been born into slavery or had been captured at a young age. They had little knowledge of their origins or their homelands. Under these circumstances, running away was a dangerous strategy. Worse still, freedom without a home, occupation, work or income was immensely risky. For the majority of former slaves, their lives as free men and women resulted in marginalization, criminalization, begging, prostitution and theft.[28]

The 'uncertainty of independent living'[29] was not easy to handle for emancipated slaves, especially for female slaves.[30] This was certainly true in the case of Mecbure,

[24] Wolf von Schuerbrand, 'Slaves Sold to the Turk: How the Vile Traffic Is Still Carried On in the East', *New York Times*, 28 March 1886, 6.
[25] 'Conference at Constantinople', *The Anti-slavery Reporter* 20, no. 7 (1 January 1877): 167. Uncertainty was exceptionally high for many slaves in the long-term. For example, a female slave named Nevres lived in the Erzurum governor's house for nineteen years. The governor had treated her as an adopted child rather than as a slave. However, after the death of the governor, uncertainties arose for her. The governor's wife and son intended to sell her as a concubine (BOA, *BEO.* 474/35520, AH 13 Rabī'al-Awwal 1312 (14 September 1894)).
[26] Toledano, *As If Silent*, 92–106.
[27] BOA, *DH.MKT.* 181/34, AH 3 Jumādā al-Ūlá 1311 (12 December 1893).
[28] Stephanie Cronin, 'Islam, Slave Agency and Abolitionism in Iran, the Middle East and North Africa', *Middle Eastern Studies* 52, no. 6 (2016): 961–3.
[29] Powell used this term for the manumitted female slaves (Eve M. Troutt Powell, 'Slaves or Siblings? Abdallah al-Nadim's Dialogues about the Family', in *Race and Slavery in the Middle East*, 223).
[30] Kozma tells about similar stories of six manumitted slaves, Saluma and her friends, who were kidnapped to be sold as slaves as they were looking for employment in Egypt in 1877. Most female

a female African slave. Like many emancipated slaves, she found herself alone and homeless (*bîkes* and *bîmekân*), as well as helpless and destitute (*âciz* and *bîvaye*). After the Haseki Women's Hospital rejected her request for treatment, in 1887 she turned to the police for help. She was referred to the Istanbul municipality, *Şehremaneti*, which was also responsible for providing food and security to helpless and destitute people. Mecbure's story was not unique. When slaves became old and useless as labourers, many risked ending up alone, homeless, helpless and destitute.[31] For example, one of the older enslaved servants of the imperial harem, Sırrıcemal, found herself on the street, homeless and penniless. In another case, Nazmiye, a slave of a former pasha, also found herself homeless with her eight-month-old child, poverty-stricken and without family and friends.[32] After manumission, many former slaves struggled to make a living. Since they had no source of income or livelihood, they became trapped in debt. Many married other liberated slaves and entered downward spirals with no prospect of escaping poverty. For this reason, numerous liberated slaves became involved in crime and earned a bad reputation in society.[33]

State vs. society: The official abolition of slavery and ensuing social disruption

The abolition of the African slave trade

Slave markets were banned for the first time in the Ottoman Empire in 1847.[34] A stronger law was then enacted in 1857 reaffirming the ban on the African slave trade and instituting penalties on slave traders.[35] The new law provoked sharp reactions, especially in the Arab regions. In Mecca, the *kadi* who read the edict prohibiting the public sale of slaves was severely beaten, and rioting ensued.[36]

Despite these prohibitions and measures, including the appointment of officers to monitor the African and Red Sea coasts, the slave trade continued throughout the Red Sea region.[37] Since new slave markets did not cease to open regardless of the bans,

---

former slaves experienced months and years of employment uncertainty after their manumission (Liat Kozma, 'Black, Kinless, and Hungry: Manumitted Female Slaves in Khedival Egypt', in *Race and Slavery in the Middle East*, 197–215).

[31] Özdemir, 'African Slaves', 12.

[32] Ceyda Karamürsel, 'The Uncertainties of Freedom: The Second Constitutional Era and the End of Slavery in the Late Ottoman Empire', *Journal of Women's History* 28, no. 3 (2016): 143–4; there were also emancipated concubines who wanted to return to their homelands. For example, a female Circassian concubine named Nahlikemal wanted to spend the rest of her life close to her relatives, and, therefore, she was allowed to go to the Caucasus (BOA, *A.MKT.NZD.* 157/8, AH 18 Zilkade 1271 (2 August 1855)).

[33] Dayar, 'Mancarcık', 71–2.

[34] 'Abolition of the Slave Market of Turkey', *The Anti-slavery Reporter* 2, no. 15 (March 1847): 37; Cevdet Türkay, 'Esircilerle İlgili Bir Belge', *Belgelerle Türk Tarihi Dergisi* 11 (1968): 60.

[35] 'Esaret-i Zenciye Tacirlerinin Mücazatına Dair Ferman', *DUSTUR* 1, no. 4 (AH Jumādá al-Ākhirah 1273 (January/February 1857)): 368–70.

[36] 'The Jedda Massacres and Slavery in the Red Sea', *Macmillan's Magazine* 49 (1 November 1883): 384.

[37] BOA, *A.MKT.NZD.* 215/5, AH 1 Rajab 1273 (25 February 1857).

two additional regulations were implemented in 1871 and 1879.[38] Moreover, a treaty was concluded between England and the Ottoman Empire in 1880 reaffirming the prohibition on the slave trade, forbidding the importation of African slaves into any part of the empire or its dependencies and mandating the punishment (according to Ottoman law and the 1856 *ferman*) of any person subject to Ottoman tribunals who was directly or indirectly implicated in the African slave trade. It was also forbidden to export African slaves from Ottoman territory to a foreign country, except in the case of their having to accompany their masters or mistresses as domestic servants. And it was the Ottoman government that bore responsibility for taking the necessary measures to free and take care of illegally captured slaves. Thus, in all Ottoman territorial waters, the right to detain and search Ottoman vessels suspected of engaging in the slave trade was extended to English ships.[39]

Slave traders, however, were quick to adapt. They changed routes, preferring small ports where warships could not enter and military control was weak, and they found safer bays. Thus, they were still able to land their illicit cargoes safely and move completely undetected at numerous points on the coast.[40] Slaves were also shipped from Tripoli and other places to central ports as free travellers.[41] They were brought in small numbers to give the impression that they were the slave merchant's wives, relatives, adopted children or servants.[42] At the end of the nineteenth century, British Anti-Slavery Society agents asserted that there was scarcely a single vessel leaving Tripoli without slaves on board. Local authorities were also involved, imposing fines for fake emancipation letters.[43] The slave traders, after drawing up illegal agreements with local authorities,[44] obtained valid manumission documents for their slaves. If anti-slavery agents or soldiers suspected that slaves were being transported, the coerced victims would claim or even swear that they were traveling on their own volition in search of work. Evidently, the so-called emancipation documents were taken from them as soon as they arrived at their destinations. As these slaves were not able to read Ottoman Turkish, the dealers told them that the papers were passports and hence useless once they had reached their destinations.[45] An observation by English Consul-General Stanton summarizes the situation at that time: 'What was said concerning Constantinople and the cities of Turkey in Asia is equally applicable to Cairo and the cities of Egypt. Freedom is a word and not a right.'[46]

[38] Gökçen Alpkaya, 'Tanzimat'ın "Daha Az Eşit" Unsurları: Kadınlar ve Köleler', *OTAM* 1 (1990): 7–8.
[39] 'Anglo-Turkish Convention for the Abolition of the African Slave-Trade', *The Anti-slavery Reporter* 22, no. 1 (March 1880): 5–6; 'Slave-Trade Convention between England and Turkey', *The Anti-slavery Reporter* 1, no. 11 (November 1881): 200.
[40] 'The Jedda Massacres', 390; Benjamin J. Reilly, 'A-Well Intentioned Failure: British Anti-slavery Measures and the Arabian Peninsula, 1820–1940', *Journal of Arabian Studies* 5, no. 2 (2015): 94.
[41] 'Anti-slavery Society to Foreign Office', *The Anti-slavery Reporter* 24, no. 3 (June 1904): 100.
[42] 'Slave-Trade at Salonica (Turkey)', *The Anti-slavery Reporter* 20, no. 7 (1 January 1877): 171.
[43] 'The Slave-Trade under the Turkish Flag', *The Anti-slavery Reporter* 13, no. 1 (January–February 1893): 41–2.
[44] BOA, *DH.MKT.* 434/3, AH 6 Rabī' al-Ākhir 1313 (26 September 1895).
[45] 'Slaves in Tripoli', *The Anti-slavery Reporter* 23, no. 5 (November 1903): 147; BOA, *DH.MKT.* 1555/12, AH 11 Safar 1306 (17 October 1888).
[46] 'Egypt. Slavery and the Slave-Trade', *The Anti-slavery Reporter* 20, no. 7 (1 January 1877): 171.

Some local government authorities did, however, liberate slaves they saved from traders. In Yemen, for example, eighteen slaves and twenty-two concubines were released, and some were given to well-off families to work as servants.[47] Shortly afterwards, in what must have been a recurring nightmare for the African men and women involved, the same families re-enslaved and sold them in other regions.[48] Local officials also gave slaves whom they had 'rescued' back to their former owners as servants. Many were promptly re-enslaved and sold again.[49] Similar complaints came from Benghazi. Some former slaves were taken to Istanbul to be sold by the wealthy families they served as servants, despite having emancipation documents granted by the government.[50] As the slave trade was a very profitable business, civil servants were also involved. For example, when 110 African slaves were deposited in Hodeida in 1888, the port chief, customs officers and soldiers took a bribe to remain quiet about it.[51] The captains of state ships also brought slaves from Benghazi and other regions and sold them in major cities.[52]

Once the slaves were brought to the cities, it was in private houses and through private dealings that the slave trade was sustained and the norms of servile employment were shaped.[53] In fact, these allegedly private houses were not really all that private, either in Istanbul or in other cities. Augustus B. Wylde, an English vice-consul, described the situation in 1876: 'At Jeddah, although the slave market is still closed, the sale of human beings goes on in some private houses adjoining the old market. The town is absolutely full of fresh-run slaves; these could not have entered within the walls without the knowledge of the officials.'[54] The private depots for newly arrived slaves were well known, and the traffic went on nearly as openly as in the old *Esir Pazari*.[55]

Many individuals in influential positions maintained the domestic institution of slavery.[56] A report of the British Anti-Slavery Society from 1877 explained that 'the maintenance of slavery is the cause of the slave trade in the empire, and its extinction impossible as long as slavery is permitted to exist'.[57] Neither the society nor the local/central state officers were enthusiastic about the extinction of the trade. Furthermore, the traders and suppliers were eager to profit from continuing strong demand.

For all of these reasons, in 1889 a new prohibition on the trade, importation and transport of black slaves in the empire and its dependencies was introduced, with more severe penalties.[58] Persons who engaged directly or indirectly in the slave trade, persons

[47] BOA, *DH.MKT.* 1318/20, AH 18 Rabīʿ al-Awwal 1294 (2 May 1877).
[48] BOA, *DH.MKT.* 1672/37, AH 14 Rabīʿ al-Awwal 1307 (8 November 1889).
[49] BOA, *DH.MKT.* 1692/42, AH 1 Jumādá al-Ākhirah 1307 (23 January 1890).
[50] BOA, *DH.MKT.* 1535/54, AH 15 Dhū al-Ḥijjah 1305 (23 August 1888).
[51] BOA, *DH.MKT.* 1459/23, AH 14 Safar 1305 (1 November 1887); BOA, *DH.MKT.* 1519/118, AH 27 Shawwāl 1305 (7 July 1888).
[52] BOA, *DH.MKT.* 151/2, AH 8 Shawwāl 1311 (14 April 1894).
[53] Zilfi, 'Servants', 7.
[54] 'The Slave-Trade in the Red Sea, Turkey', *The Anti-slavery Reporter* 20, no. 7 (1 January 1877): 171.
[55] James C. McCoan, 'Slavery and Polygamy in Turkey', *Fraser's Magazine* 18, no. 106 (1878): 405.
[56] 'The Nemesis of Slavery and the Slave-Trade', *The Anti-slavery Reporter* 20, no. 6 (November 1876): 144.
[57] 'Conference at Constantinople', 168.
[58] 'Üserâ-yı Zenciye Ticaretinin Men'ine Dair Kanun', *DUSTUR* 1, no. 6 (AH 22 Rabīʿ al-Awwal 1307 (16 November 1889)): 486–7.

who assisted in that trade, or captains of ships carrying slaves, were to be sentenced to a year in prison for the first offence and double for the second. The slaves found in their possession were to be confiscated and certificates of manumission delivered to them.[59] Attending the Brussels Anti-Slavery Conference the same year, the Ottomans agreed to end slavery once more.[60] Yet despite these new prohibitions, even clergymen continued the African slave trade. A Catholic pastor in Benghazi bought African children in the region and sold them as slaves in Naples in 1894.[61] This example demonstrates how embedded the slave trade was in society and how difficult it was to extirpate it.

Another controversial issue concerned the status of existing slaves after the trade was banned. After a discussion on this topic in Izmir in 1868, it was declared that abolition was not valid for slaves acquired before the ban or purchased for household service.[62] The subject had been a persistent problem in discussions between the Ottomans and European countries at international anti-slavery conferences. The Ottoman representatives were against the emancipation of existing slaves. Caratheodori Efendi, an Ottoman minister and representative at the Brussels Conference in 1889–90, stated that his country was ready to endorse all other provisions of the Belgian plan but would not allow the vested rights of current slaveholders to be affected. He also asserted that the slaves were well treated and far happier than they would be if freed and returned to Africa.[63] According to the Ottoman statesmen, 'the slaves of Turkey are the most favored and the happiest people of the empire. A slave in a Turk's family is almost invariably considered as a member of the family … manumission, however, they generally refuse when it is offered to them, as they know that, by changing their condition, they could not improve it.'[64] It would be fair to describe these comments as an extremely generous view of slavery in the empire.

Despite all of these attempts to ban and curtail the African slave trade, as the lieutenant governor of the Hejaz mentioned in 1910, slavery continued in the region. After emphasizing that the existence of slavery in the city centres and within the desert tribes should be handled separately, he stated that immediate abolition would be dangerous due to the possible violent reactions of the tribes. The slaves were the tribes' most important means of economic production. He therefore recommended a ten-year postponement for these groups.[65] The emancipation of 272 slaves in Benghazi in 1909, 60 slaves in Jeddah in the same year and 13 slaves in Medina in 1913 illustrates that slaves were still being traded in the region.[66]

---

[59] 'Turkey and the African Slave-Trade', *The Anti-slavery Reporter* 9, no. 6 (November 1889): 274–5.
[60] 'Men'i Esaret Hakkında Kaleme Alınan Sened-i Umuminin Hükümet-i Seniyye Murahhası Tarafından İmzası Hakkında Mazbata', *DUSTUR* 1, no. 6 (AH 16 Dhū al-Qa'dah 1307 (4 July 1890)): 672–4; 'Brüksel Konferansının Sened-i Umumisi', *DUSTUR* 1, no. 6 (AH 16 Dhū al-Qa'dah 1307 (4 July 1890)): 676–702.
[61] BOA, *DH.MKT.* 162/33, AH 21 Rajab 1311 (28 January 1894).
[62] Alpkaya, 'Tanzimat'ın', 7.
[63] 'The Anti-slavery Conference at Brussels: Domestic Slavery in Turkey and Persia', *The Manchester Guardian*, 1 March 1890, 8.
[64] 'Turkish Slaves', *The Anti-slavery Reporter* 1, no. 12 (December 1846): 205.
[65] BOA, *DH.MUİ.* 7/47, AH 29 Safar 1328 (12 March 1910).
[66] BOA, *DH.İD.* 71/1, AH 24 Safar 1330 (13 February 1912).

It can be concluded that the abolition of African slavery in the Ottoman Empire was primarily due to the practice of institutional transplantation. However, such institutional transplantation was severely tested by the social and economic values of Ottoman society and showed the strength of informal institutions and the barriers they created to hinder the enactment of legal regulations to abolish the African slave trade. Many different ethnic and religious groups resisted abolition until the end of the empire. In terms of white slavery, the state itself was part of the resistance to abolition for a long period of time.

Attempts to end white slavery: Circassian and Georgian slaves

The period of the Crimean War (1853–6) saw progress made towards full abolition of slavery in the Ottoman Empire. Shortly after the first legal arrangements to ban the African slave trade, the Ottoman state took steps targeting the trade in white slaves. First, in 1854, a *ferman* was issued for the Circassians who sold their children and parents as slaves. The main goal of the edict was to instruct the Circassians to end this trade. The majority of slaves sold in this way were women of childbearing age.[67] Another decree, issued in the same year, prohibited the sale of women and children brought from Georgia. Yet despite these proclamations, Ottoman law continued to accept and even protect slavery, especially white slavery for domestic service, as a legitimate practice. The Ottoman legal order, 'modernized' and 'westernized' in the period following the proclamation of the Tanzimat, aimed to protect the lives, property and honour of citizens but excluded slaves. Instead, the status of slaves continued to be regulated by traditional rules.[68]

While the Ottoman Empire was reluctant to meet the demands of foreign states regarding the abolition of white slavery, it needed the help of France and Britain in its war against Russia, and so a decree was issued to prevent the continuation of the slave trade from Circassian, Abkhazian and Georgian shores. It was stated that measures should be taken to avoid the purchase and sale of slaves in the public streets of Istanbul. According to the decree, the trade should be hidden and undertaken more secretly in private homes.[69]

Beginning in 1858, several years after the Crimean War, large numbers of people began migrating from the Caucasus to Ottoman lands. By 1907, the number of immigrants had reached six hundred thousand.[70] Throughout the war and the Circassian expulsion that followed – a period in which 'even people of moderate means were able to pay for a slave with a few pieces of gold' – the imperial harem, as well as many elite households, consisted almost exclusively of young Circassian women.[71]

---

[67] Toledano, *Osmanlı Köle Ticareti*, 97; BOA, *İ.HR.* 115/5601, ᴀʜ 7 Rabīʻ al-Awwal 1271 (28 November 1854).
[68] Alpkaya, 'Tanzimat'ın', 6–7.
[69] BOA, *İ.HR.* 14/5553, ᴀʜ 28 Dhū al-Ḥijjah 1270 (21 September 1854).
[70] Although the Ottoman official records stated that 150,000 of them were slaves, many scholars find this figure exaggerated (Rahmi DenizÖzbay, 'Osmanlı İmparatorluğu'nda Köle Emeğinin İstihdamı ve Mükâtebe Yöntemi', *Kocaeli Üniversitesi SBE Dergisi* 17 (2009): 158).
[71] Karamürsel, 'Uncertainties of Freedom', 140.

According to von Schuerbrand, the great favourites with slave owners had always been beautiful Circassian girls, blonde, blue-eyed and wavy-haired. Numerous Circassian chiefs, who often had favours to ask in Istanbul or who wished to expedite important matters, furnished such girls in lieu of cash as *backsheesh*. Debts, too, were frequently settled in the same manner.[72]

Some migrants even advertised their daughters or sisters for sale as slaves in newspapers. For example, in 1860, a Nogai emigrant in Istanbul listed in *Ceride-i Havadis* that he would sell his sister, a beautiful and literate sixteen-year-old, for 3,000 *guruş*. Some indication of the acceptance of such behaviour can be seen in the fact that he also informed the Immigration Commission about this sale and even announced that interested buyers should apply directly to them. In another case, five children – four of whom were only seven years old – were sold to a slave trader who intended to take them to Egypt for resale. The dealers in this transaction were all siblings and relatives of the children: brothers, a cousin and an uncle.[73] As a response to such cases, a decree was issued in 1862 that declared the Circassian tradition allowing the sale of one's own children and relatives into slavery as being incompatible with human dignity.[74] All the same, the practice continued unabated until the end of the empire.

Slavery was extremely widespread among Circassian groups, and they strongly opposed any policy that forced them to part with their slaves upon immigration into Ottoman lands. For this reason, there were even armed clashes between those who refused to remain slaves and their former masters.[75] In 1866, when a court in Edirne freed Circassian children whose parents were slaves, around four hundred armed slave owners in the region rose up against this decision and insisted on maintaining their traditions. The conflict could only be ended with the intervention of the security forces. However, the governor was concerned that there might be new conflicts.[76] According to Circassian customs, the children of their slaves became their slaves, and they believed that they had the right to sell them, especially the girls, as such. They also put in a claim for half of the grain harvest produced by the slaves and seized the land that had been given to slaves by the state as part of its programme of granting land to all migrants.[77]

Circassian women were forced to allow their female children to be sold as concubines.[78] One of them, Circassian Naziktar, lost her husband and children after coming to Bandırma and was sold as a concubine together with her five-year-old

[72] Von Schuerbrand, 'Slaves Sold to the Turk', 6.
[73] Abdullah Saydam, *Kırım ve Kafkas Göçleri (1856–1876)* (Ankara: Türk Tarih Kurumu, 1997), 196–7.
[74] BOA, *A.MKT.MVL.* 140/4, AH 23 Rajab 1278 (24 January 1862); BOA, *A.MKT.NZD.* 396/97, AH 3 Sha'bān 1278 (3 February 1862).
[75] Ufuk Tavkul, 'Osmanlı Devletinin Kafkas Muhacirlerinin Kölelik Kurumuna Yaklaşımı', *BILIG* 17 (2001): 34–47.
[76] Toledano, *Osmanlı Köle Ticareti*, 136–7.
[77] For a discussion on the slavery-related conflicts between the Circassian migrants in the Ottoman Empire and specific cases, see Ceyda Karamürsel, 'Transplanted Slavery, Contested Freedom, and Vernacularization of Rights in the Reform Era Ottoman Empire', *Comparative Studies in Society and History* 59, no. 3 (2017): 696–711.
[78] BOA, *A.DVN.* 149/21, AH 1 Jumādá al-Ākhirah 1276 (26 December 1859); BOA, *A.MKT.MHM.* 176/37, AH 9 Rajab 1276 (1 February 1860); BOA, *A.MKT.NZD.* 383/13, AH 3 Jumādá al-Ākhirah 1278 (6 December 1861).

daughter. She described her years as a slave in the following strong words: 'Let alone human beings, even an animal cannot stand the cruelty I have been subjected to.'[79] Local governments were not sure how to address the situations caused by this tradition. When some Circassians wanted to enslave other migrants on the grounds that they were their slaves, the governor of Thessaloniki asked the capital how to treat them. He complained that the *beys* beat slaves in Varna and took away their engaged daughters to sell as concubines. According to the *beys*, it was their right to do so.[80]

Another major factor supporting the continuation of Circassian slavery was poverty. Despite its risks, slavery was seen as a solution to the economic problems experienced by expatriated Circassian families. After the massive Circassian migration,[81] many poor Circassian girls in need of protection were given to well-off families, such as local state officials. Over time, many Circassian girls complained about the sexual abuse they had experienced from members of these families.[82] Life was certainly economically difficult for Circassian immigrants in their new land, but greedy individuals also took advantage of their poverty. For example, some women deceived young, poor Circassian girls in Istanbul and then sold them as concubines there or in Egypt. According to police reports, they convinced low-income families to allow the girls to be given up by saying that they would take them to the sultan's palace.[83]

White slavery was legally banned only in 1909, far later than African slavery.[84] All the same, the societal response was similar, and the ban was largely ignored. Several Circassians who had refused to stay slaves complained to legal authorities about being tortured by their owners.

As Ceyda Karamürsel has shown, there were cases when slave owners didn't accept the claims of freedom made by their slaves after the 1908 revolution, despite the fact that the revolution had occurred under the slogans of freedom, equality and justice. As a result, slaves such as Fatma Leman, a female slave of Circassian origin, demanded emancipation. According to the Circassian Mutual Aid Society, however, Circassian

[79] BOA, ŞD. 1284/30, AH 19 Rabī' al-Awwal 1298 (19 February 1881).
[80] Tavkul, 'Osmanlı', 49–50.
[81] Involving a programme of subjugation and expulsion, Russian military conquests of the Crimea and Caucasus caused forced deportation of millions of Muslims from these regions into the Ottoman territory. Following the Crimean War in 1856 and lasting until the end of 1870s, an estimated two million to five million emigrants were torn from their lands and migrated to the Ottoman Empire (David C. Cuthell Jr, 'The Muhacirin Komisyonu: An Agent in the Transformation of Ottoman Anatolia 1860–1866', dissertation (Columbia University, 2005), 1–3).
[82] In one case, after buying a Circassian concubine and having sexual intercourse with her, Mehmed Ali Bey, governor of Bayburt, tried to give her back and reclaim his money. He mentioned that the slave trade was forbidden in the Ottoman lands and he therefore wanted to return the concubine (BOA, *DH.MKT.* 1515/100, AH 15 Shawwāl 1305 (25 June 1888); BOA, *Y.MTV.* 31/15, AH 11 Jumādá al-Ākhirah 1305 (24 February 1888)). For the case of Reshad Bey, governor of Latakia, who was accused of raping Fatma, a Circassian girl under his care, see BOA, *DH.MKT.* 386/20, AH 24 Dhū al-Ḥijjah 1312 (18 June 1895). For the case of Hilmi Bey, who was accused of raping Ayşe, see BOA, *DH.MKT.* 361/29, AH 14 Shawwāl 1312 (10 April 1895).
[83] BOA, *DH.MKT.* 139/42, AH 28 Rabī' al-Ākhir 1311 (8 November 1893); BOA, *DH.MKT.* 416/67, AH 4 Safar 1313 (27 July 1895). There were also similar cases in 1908 (BOA, *DH.MKT.* 2676/53, AH 13 Dhū al-Qa'dah 1326 (7 December 1908)).
[84] 'Çerkes Vesâir Köle ve Cariyelerin de Üsera-yı Zenciye Gibi Men-i Bey' ve Şerâsı Hakkında İrade-i Seniyye', *DUSTUR* 2, no. 1 (AH 15 Shawwāl 1327 (30 October 1909)): 831.

slaves and concubines were the only people who saw no benefit from the peaceful atmosphere of the new era: 'The Constitution and the Islamic rules which protected even the animal rights did not include these poor helpless people.'[85] Since their owners did not want to free them, some slaves resorted to absconding to other cities, yet even this did not guarantee their absolute freedom from their owners. A former Circassian slave, Osman, who lived in western Anatolia, accused the wife of the Diyarbakir governor of coming to his village to seize all of his properties. She also took his three daughters. She claimed that as he was a slave of her father, his property and daughters were also hers to do with as she pleased. She took the girls to sell as concubines and told him, 'You will always be in my servitude.'[86]

Despite the protests of the slaves, the slave owners asserted that it was their legal right to buy, sell and employ their slaves. In a petition dated 13 August 1909, thirteen Circassian *beys* wrote that these rights had been passed down from their ancestors. Any decisions and regulations that went against these rights would be contrary the Shari'a and the *Kanûn-ı Esâsi* (constitution).[87] Other former slaves joined the army. Their former owners still pursued them and appealed to military authorities, demanding that their runaway slaves be returned. The use of physical violence against Circassians who refused slavery was a common complaint.[88] In 1913, the governor of Sivas reported that there were 1,559 slaves in the province: 590 of them were concubines and 969 were male slaves. The governor was concerned about potential conflict between owners and slaves in the wake of collective emancipation.[89]

Due to unresolvable conflicts between slaves, owners and public authorities, the complaints continued up until[90] and even after the First World War. During the war, the number of orphans and widows increased as men lost their lives. This was seen as an opportunity by those who benefitted from the slave trade. They deceived widows and orphan girls of poor Anatolian families with promises of marriage and took them to remote regions, such as Java, to sell as concubines.[91]

Nevertheless, in the last years of the nineteenth century, it was not easy to find girls to purchase as concubines. In 1891, an encrypted letter sent from the Sublime Port to the Konya governor ordered him to find some young and healthy Circassian girls over

[85] Karamürsel, 'Uncertainties of Freedom', 138, 152. BOA, *BEO.* 3710/278209, ᴀʜ 17 Safar 1328 (28 February 1910). Even after a half-century, some Circassians born in the Ottoman lands and their children were being treated and forced to work as slaves due to the former slave status of their ancestry (BOA, *DH.MKT.* 2723/41, ᴀʜ 7 Muharram 1327 (29 January 1909)).
[86] BOA, *DH.MUİ.* 7/24, ᴀʜ 1 Ramaḍān 1328 (6 September 1910). Holding and having enslaved girls meant power and prestige in Ottoman society. Therefore, women from different ethnic and social backgrounds and elite women from the palace exploited the slave network for their benefit. For a discussion of the women as slave traders and slave owners in the late Ottoman Empire, see Ceyda Karamürsel, ' "In the Age of Freedom, in the Name of Justice": Slaves, Slaveholders, and the State in the Late Ottoman Empire and Early Turkish Republic, 1857–1933', Publicly Accessible Penn Dissertations (Pennsylvania, 2015), 108–52.
[87] Karamürsel, 'Uncertainties of Freedom', 149. BOA, *BEO.* 3565/267343, ᴀʜ 13 Rabī' al-Ākhir 1327 (4 May 1909); BOA, *DH.MKT.* 2739/67, ᴀʜ 25 Muharram 1327 (16 February 1909).
[88] BOA, *DH.MUİ.* 7/24, ᴀʜ 1 Ramaḍān 1328 (6 September 1910).
[89] BOA, *DH.İ.UM.EK.* 84/14, ᴀʜ 25 Dhū al-Ḥijjah 1336 (1 October 1918).
[90] BOA, *DH.HMŞ.* 10/62, ᴀʜ 24 Rabī' al-Awwal 1331 (3 March 1913).
[91] BOA, *MV.* 219/82, ᴀʜ 4 Shawwāl 1338 (21 June 1920).

fourteen years of age. The girls were to be taken to the palace for training as concubines. Despite all of his efforts, the governor, who searched not only in his region but also in other provinces, had difficulties meeting the demands of the palace. He offered high fees but was only able to obtain a small number of prospective concubines.[92]

Such official collusion in the continuation of the slave trade reduced the legitimacy of the measures taken to end the enslavement of white women. The famous Ottoman philosopher Ali Suavi noted, 'The grand vizier himself, who forbade us to buy a concubine, leads a life of pleasure with fifty concubines.'[93] Suavi pointed out that the legal prohibitions to end white female slavery were less effective than measures to end African slavery, not only in societal terms but also because of the support for such practices by statesmen. Ultimately, the main factors in the cessation of white female slavery were the difficulty in finding slaves and changes in the social and economic nature of the Ottoman Empire.

In lieu of a conclusion: The rise of servant markets and the end of slavery

As stated in a British Anti-Slavery Society report published in 1846, 'the bare idea of the disturbance and rout that would be produced in every Turkish household by the abrogation of slavery, causes here a very keen distress'. The Ottomans insisted that the abolition of slavery would entirely break the economy of their domestic life. There was no ready replacement, as females in the country were entirely unaccustomed to domestic service.[94] This was a key reason for the failure of Ottoman efforts to end the slave trade and, in particular, female slavery. Therefore, the imperial decrees of the sultan to prohibit the slave trade in Georgia and the use of Circassian slave girls were frequently 'dead letters'.[95]

Yet the phasing out of female slavery in the Ottoman lands was not just the result of constant European pressure in the nineteenth century; it was also a result of the changing political, social and economic nature of the Ottoman Empire. As Stephanie Cronin emphasizes, political and legal changes cumulatively transformed the relationship between slaves and their owners and the perception of both by society at large.[96] In the context of white and mostly female slaves, the changing structure

---

[92] Toledano, *Osmanlı Köle Ticareti*, 155–9. Nevertheless, concubine recruitment to the palace continued in subsequent years. However, it can be seen from archival documents that the numbers decreased considerably. From an encrypted telegram in 1900, we see that six concubines were taken to the palace (BOA, *Y.PRK.ASK.* 159/65, AH 18 Dhū al-Qaʿdah 1317 (20 March 1900)). In 1908, fourteen additional concubines were taken. The parents, all of Caucasian origin, confirmed that their daughters had never previously been concubines in the service of someone else and had lived with them since they were born. They also added that 'their daughters happily accepted to enter the sultan's service with their own consent' (BOA, *Y.PRK.ASK.* 255/2, AH 11 Safar 1326 (15 March 1908)). Such written confirmation from the parents was probably considered as a precaution against possible problems in the future.
[93] İsmail Parlatır, *Tanzimat Edebiyatında Kölelik* (Ankara: Türk Tarih Kurumu, 1992), 19–29.
[94] 'Turkish Slaves', 205.
[95] Charles K. Tuckerman, 'White Slavery in Turkey', *New Review* 5, no. 26 (July 1891): 23.
[96] Cronin, 'Islam, Slave Agency', 972.

of cultural and economic relations and the emergence of servant markets were also crucial factors. British ambassador Sir Henry Elliot foresaw this development as early as the 1870s. He wrote the following with regard to the white Circassian slaves on 24 March 1876: 'No measures are in progress for their emancipation, but the feeling is gradually becoming general that the employment of free persons is more desirable, and the number of slaves is daily diminishing.'[97]

We can also see the signs of change in literary works of the era. The works of the Ottoman intelligentsia began to field strong criticisms of concubinage and enslavement. Many writers such as Ahmed Mithad and Samipashazade Sezai (whose mothers were both concubines), Recâizade Mahmud Ekrem, Abdulhak Hamid and Namık Kemal heavily criticized slavery in their work. To raise public awareness, they depicted many tragic cases involving the fates of concubines and slaves.[98]

As discussed earlier, when the supply of slaves became more difficult – even for the palace – alternative methods were developed to fill the gap in the labour markets in this period. One of these was to increase the number of wage servants. Towards the end of the century, female slaves were gradually replaced by paid servants, cleaners, launderers and handmaids who performed domestic services.[99] Having servants in middle- and upper-class homes became a matter of economic preference and social status. The cultural influence of Europe and changing social and economic realities, which began after the Tanzimat era and continued to strengthen, turned hiring maids into a matter of social prestige, just as owning slaves had been in the past.[100] In the new era, servants were rapidly replacing slaves.

There was a continuously growing demand for maids to perform domestic service, and failures of supply were addressed by the emergence of public and private employment agencies. The Istanbul Servant Agency (*Dersaadet Hidmetkâran İdârehanesi*), already active in the 1880s, hired out maids to fill the growing demand.[101] There were also private agencies of various sizes, distributing advertisements and placing women and girls with interested families. Many of these agencies operated without legal permission.[102] Strong market demand encouraged

[97] 'Slavery and the Slave-Trade in the Ottoman Empire', *The Anti-slavery Reporter* 20, no. 7 (1 January 1877): 169–70.

[98] For further information on the studies of late Ottoman intellectuals on slavery, see Parlatır, *Tanzimat*; Ehud R. Toledano, 'Late Ottoman Concepts of Slavery (1830s–1880s)', *Poetics Today* 14, no. 3 (1993): 477–506.

[99] In one of her studies on domestic work in US history, Phyllis Palmer emphasizes the importance of three factors that linked housework to slavery: 'not treating domestics as people independent of their employers, designing housework to give domestics the physically hardest tasks, and demanding almost unlimited working hours' (*Domesticity and Dirt, Housewives and Domestic Servants in the United States, 1920-1945* (Philadelphia: Temple University Press, 1989), 73).

[100] Yavuz Selim Karakışla, *Osmanlı Hanımları ve Hizmetçi Kadınlar (1869-1927)* (Istanbul: Akıl Fikir Yayınları, 2014), 12–30.

[101] BOA, *Y.A.RES.* 26/8, AH 10 Muharram 1302 (30 October 1884).

[102] BOA, *DH.MKT.* 2007/73, AH 17 Aylül 1308 (29 September 1892). In this period, the guild of servants was also still active. The *Kethüdâ* of the guild often complained about the activities of private institutions working without legal permission (BOA, *DH.MKT.* 1672/151, AH 16 Rabī' al-Awwal 1307 (10 November 1889)). One of the main complaints from the houses where the servants worked was theft (BOA, *BEO.* 77/5776, AH 5 Rabī' al-Awwal 1310 (27 September 1892); BOA, *BEO.* 644/48228, AH 27 Dhū al-Ḥijjah 1312 (21 June 1895)).

those who saw an opportunity in contracting maids to act illegally, just as the slave traders had in the past.

In the 1910s, as it became more and more difficult to find slaves, the demand for servants grew and the number of agents on the market increased. Needy Circassian women and girls under the care of *Darulaceze*, a public charity, began to be employed as maids in private homes.[103] The number of widows and orphan girls was also increasing due to the effects of war. As the number of women and girls in *Darulaceze* increased, a specific programme was launched in 1913 to train them as maids.[104]

Many *müstahdemîn idârehaneleri* (servant agencies) were established in this era. The most important of these was *Umûm Hidmetkâran İdârehanesi* (the General Maid Agency), which was set up in 1911. According to the founder, Osman Bey, there was a need for a reliable provider in the market as some agencies were essentially trafficking white females under the name of maid recruitment.[105] Although the number of public and private agencies increased, it was still difficult to meet demand, especially in Istanbul; orders were, therefore, sent to regions in Anatolia, such as Trabzon, Kastamonu, Hüdavendigar, Samsun, Karesi and Izmit, to boost the number of women and girls available to work as maids.[106]

All of these developments pointed to the emergence of a new servant market. This was not only a result of the decreasing female slave trade but also one of the underlying reasons for ending slavery. Since slavery was such a long-established institution in the Ottoman Empire, this change occurred amid much resistance; but it proceeded, however slowly, and slavery in the empire was on its way out.

---

[103] BOA, *ZB*. 329/196, AH 1 Kānūn ath-Thānī 1324 (14 January 1909); BOA, *DH.MKT*. 2718/13, AH 2 Muharram 1327 (24 January 1909); BOA, *DH.MKT*. 2704/97, AH 19 Dhū al-Ḥijjah 1326 (12 January 1909).

[104] BOA, *DH.ID*. 161–1/6. 14 Ramaḍān 1331. 17 August 1913.

[105] BOA, *DH.EUM.VRK*. 7/47, AH 20 Safar 1329 (20 February 1911). For example, four women who were deceived by the claim that they would make a lot of money as servants were sold to brothels in Galata in 1909 ('Sefil bir Ticaret', *Tanin* 459 (AH 29 Tishrīn ath-Thānī 1325 (12 December 1909)): 3).

[106] BOA, *DH.ŞFR*. 103/77, AH 12 Dhū al-Ḥijjah 1337 (8 September 1919).

4

The social construction of slavery, injustice and manumission on the Gulf Coast of Arabia and Oman in the 1920s and 1930s

Jerzy Zdanowski

Introduction

Slavery in Arabia and the Persian Gulf region has existed since time immemorial, and at the beginning of the twentieth century, public opinion in the Arabian ports of the Persian Gulf and Oman was still strongly in favour of slavery.[1] Traffic of slaves and unfree labour was an important part of the socioeconomic system of the region based on pearl diving and the cultivation of palm trees. While this system had existed for ages, it was threatened by an economic crisis in the 1920s and 1930s. At the end of the 1920s, slaves from the Gulf coast of Arabia and Oman began to run away from their masters and approach British agencies in Bahrain, Kuwait, Muscat and Sharjah (Shargah) to ask for manumission. By 1946, around one thousand applications had been submitted for a manumission certificate.

Data from the applicants' statements show how slaves' status was defined by largely unwritten rules stemming from what amounted to a social contract. Masters were obliged to provide their slaves with food, clothes, shelter and even husbands and wives. Slaves' explanations for fleeing their masters often tell us which rules they considered their masters to have violated and thus how the slaves themselves understood the status of 'free' and 'enslaved'.

Slavery was a social norm accepted by Islam. The centrality of norms in providing social consensus and system equilibrium has been much discussed by sociologists. Emile Durkheim's fundamental conception stresses that any social action should be conceived within a normative framework. When carrying out their duties as members

---

[1] Foreign Office, Memorandum Concerning the Existence of Slavery and Slave Trading along the Eastern and South-Eastern Coast of Arabia, 27 March 1930, FO 371/14475 E 1658/1054/91; From Political Agent, Bahrain, to the Political Resident, Bushire, received on 15 March 1938, R/15/1/227 5/193 III (B 46) (India Office Records (IOR)); Office of the Political Resident in the Persian Gulf, Camp Bahrain, to the Secretary of the Government of India, New Delhi, 22 March 1938, R/15/1/227 5/193 III (B 46) (IOR); From Political Resident, Bushire [Bushehr], at Bahrain, to Secretary of State for India, London, Bahrain, 27 March 1938, R/15/1/227 5/193 III (B 46) (IOR).

of a family, residential group or ethnic or religious community, individuals fulfil the obligations imposed on them by an unwritten social contract or the objective reality transmitted to them through education and 'endowed with an imperative and coercive power'.[2] Thus, social organization is founded on 'collectively recognized and supported norms which create an "axionormative order"'.[3] Slavery was one of the norms that provided system equilibrium to the societies on the Gulf coast of Arabia and Oman. In short, slavery was part of the fabric of everyday life and must have seemed as natural as marriage and childbirth to many.

The change of a norm is a complex phenomenon as it refers to other normative clusters, and it can be understood as 'the emergence, replacement or modification of components of the normative structure: norms, values, roles, institutions'.[4] Robert Merton has proposed a concept of a normative deviation when 'behavior departs from what is required by cultural goals' and suggested considering deviance as critical for the change of norms. It is important, however, to distinguish new forms of behaviour still within prescribed norms and those that breach those norms.[5] While the first represents 'variant' behaviour, the second falls into the category of 'deviant' and can be a prelude to a change in norms. Was the manumission movement on the Persian Gulf coast of Arabia and Oman in the 1920s and 1930s a 'deviancy' that eventually grew over the following decades to create a new social norm undermining society based on slavery?

Slave importations to the north-east coast of the Arabian Peninsula

Slaves on the Arabian coast of the Persian Gulf and Oman were divided into three categories: (1) those imported from the interior of the Arabian Peninsula and East Africa, (2) those imported from Makran, the coastal part of Baluchistan, and (3) those who were born on the coast.

Until the 1870s, slaves were imported to the Gulf coast of Arabia mainly from East Africa via the Omani ports of Sur and Muscat, and partially to the small Arabian ports of Sharjah, Dubai or Ras al-Khaimah. Slaves were also traded directly between the Persian Gulf ports of Bandar Abbas, Lingah, Ras al-Khaimah and Basrah.[6] There is a broad range of estimates of the number of slaves who passed annually from the coast of

---

[2] Emile Durkheim, *The Field of Sociology*, in *Emile Durkheim: Selected Writings*, edited, translated and with an introduction by Anthony Giddens (Cambridge: Cambridge University Press, 1972), 63–4.

[3] See Talcott Parsons, *The Structure of Social Action* (New York: McGraw Hill, 1937), 91; Florian Znaniecki, *The Social Role of the Man of Knowledge* (New York: Columbia University Press, 1940), 8, 11–12, 72.

[4] See Piotr Sztompka, *The Sociology of Change* (Oxford: Wiley-Blackwell, 1993), 251.

[5] Robert Merton, 'Social Conformity, Deviation and Opportunity Structures', *American Sociological Review* 24, no. 2 (1959): 181.

[6] Arnold B. Kemball, 'Suppression of the Slave Trade in the Persian Gulf', in *Selections from the Records of the Bombay Government, No. XXIV. – New Series. Historical and Other Information Connected with the Province of Oman, Muscat, Bahrein, and Other Places in the Persian Gulf* (Bombay: Education Society's Press, 1856), 647.

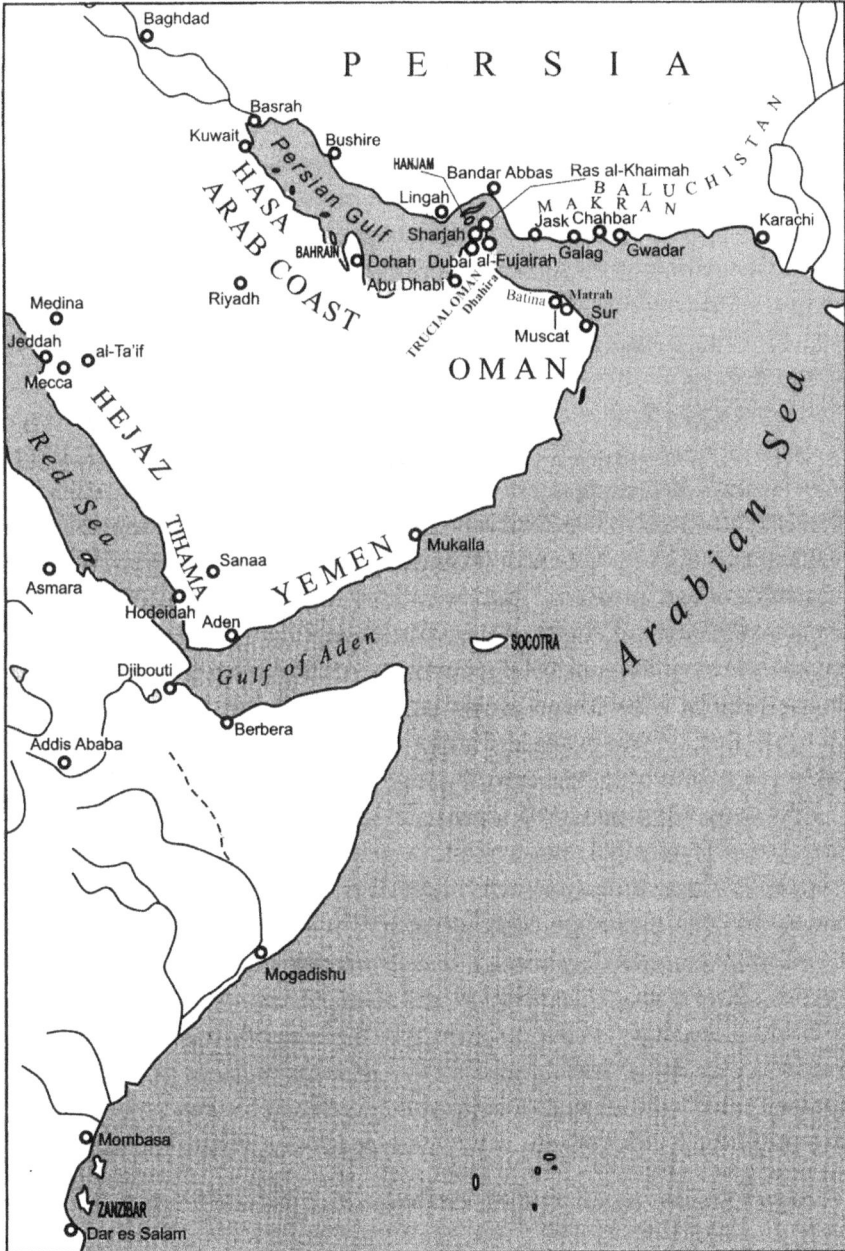

The Arabian Sea Region

Figure 4.1 The Arabian Sea Region.

Source: Map provided by the author.

Africa to Zanzibar and to points north between 1800 and 1870: from 6,000 to 20,000. Between 1870 and 1876, the year the slave trade was abolished in Zanzibar, 300,000 slaves were sent to the island and to Arabia, Persia and India. These figures give a total East African Arab slave trade of 1,257,100.[7] According to even higher estimates, over 2 million slaves were sent abroad from Zanzibar between 1830 and 1873, when the exportation of slaves by sea was forbidden.[8]

At the turn of the twentieth century, the traffic in slaves from Makran to Arabia was carried out by people from the Jask, Galag, Chahbar and Gwadar districts who were purchasing slaves from the inhabitants of Makran and Baluchistan and were selling them to merchants from the Omani coast. The trade was largely driven by local chiefs scouring the country with armed retinues and forcibly enslaving and selling Baluchis. This went on despite the fact that the enslavement of free Muslims was contrary to the law of Islam. Although *mullas* in Jask voiced frequent objections, the rulers concerned refused to desist.[9]

In the 1920s, slaves were still imported to Kuwaiti markets from the Hejaz and Nejd in western and central Arabia. They were often kept in the shops of local merchants.[10] In 1928, it was estimated that there were about 2,200 slaves in Kuwait, plus 2,000 who had been granted freedom. Their number was gradually decreasing, however, because of the lack of regular supply.[11] In Trucial Oman, slaves were sold unofficially as the sale of slaves was prohibited by a formal agreement between the British government and the sheikhs of Trucial Oman.[12]

---

[7] Murray Gordon, *Slavery in the Arab World* (New York: New Amsterdam Books, 1989) (first published as *L'Esclavage dans le monde arabe* (Paris: Edition Robert Laffont, 1987)), 186–7.

[8] Ralph Austen gives more conservative estimates and thinks that 800,000 slaves were exported from East Africa to the Muslim world in the nineteenth century. They were transported to the north: 30,000 of them across the Red Sea and Gulf of Aden, and the rest from the Swahili coast. According to Thomas M. Ricks, annual importations to the Persian Gulf in the nineteenth century were much greater than in the previous one. In 1772–82, the annual import covered 500–600 slaves, and in 1782–1842, it was 800–1000, while in 1842–72 it reached up to 3,000. The total imports were accordingly 30,000–36,000 slaves for 1772–82, 48,000–60,000 for 1782–1842 and 60,000–90,000 for 1842–72. In 1872–1902, the total imports decreased to were 1,500–3,000 slaves or 500–1000 per year. Around 80–90 per cent of the imported slaves, especially in the period of the dramatic increase of the number in 1842–72, were most likely re-exported from the Gulf into the Ottoman and Iranian hinterland to work as cash-crop or irrigation canal workers in Fars and Kirman. This data corresponds with other estimations. According to Arnold B. Kemball, British Resident in the Persian Gulf, around 3,500 slaves were imported annually in the second quarter of the nineteenth century. Ralph Austin, 'The 19th Century Islamic Slave Trade from East Africa (Swahili and Red Sea Coast): A Tentative Census', in *The Economics of the Indian Ocean Slave Trade in the Nineteenth Century*, ed. William G. Clarence-Smith (London: Frank Cass, 1989), 21–44; Thomas M. Ricks, 'Slaves and Slave Traders in the Persian Gulf, 18th and 19th Centuries: An Assessment', in *The Economics of the Indian Ocean Slave Trade in the Nineteenth Century*, 60–7; Kemball, 'Suppression', 647.

[9] John G. Lorimer, *Gazetteer of the Persian Gulf, Oman, and Central Arabia*, vol. I *Historical*, vol. II *Geographical and Statistical* (Calcutta: Superintendent of Government Printing, 1908, repr. Archive Editions, 1986), vol. I *Historical*: 2510–11.

[10] Political Agency, Kuwait, to The Political Secretary to H.E. The High Commissioner, Kuwait, 13 May 1921, R/15/1/207 5/161 VI, 168 IX, 179 II (IOR).

[11] Political Agency, Kuwait, to the Secretary to the Political Resident in the Persian Gulf, Kuwait, 29 September 1928, R/15/1/229 5/196 I (IOR).

[12] The Residency Agent, Shargah, to the Political Resident, Bushire, 22 August 1928, R/15/1/229 5/196 I (IOR).

The largest number of male slaves sent to the Gulf coast of Arabia was absorbed into the pearl fishing industry. Pearl diving was the most important industry in the Persian Gulf region. The outcome of the pearling season determined the livelihood of merchants, boat-owners, creditors, brokers, sailors and divers. Every year, the season's catch was bought by dealers from India and Europe. Some Gulf pearls were taken directly to Europe; others were sent to Bombay to be pierced, graded and then exported to Europe. Paris was the European centre of Persian Gulf pearls. Shipments were also made to Zanzibar, but the volume was comparatively insignificant.[13]

Slave presence on the Gulf coast of Arabia and Oman at the turn of the twentieth century

People of African origin constituted a significant part of the population of Kuwait, Qatar, Bahrain and Trucial Oman. According to John G. Lorimer, the Sunni Arabs of Bahrain tended to intermingle with African slaves to the extent that 'there was a noticeable infusion of Negro blood' among them. Male slaves were generally married to slave wives by their masters, who took possession of the offspring, but there were a few cases of slaves married off to free women.[14] In 1904, Africans from the Swahili coast still comprised a considerable part of the total population of Ajman, Abu Dhabi, Dubai, Umm al-Qaiwain and Sharjah. Lorimer points out that African slaves were exceptionally numerous in the coastal towns and that the Swahili language survived among full-blooded African slaves.[15]

The African population was also very conspicuous in Oman. This country had a long history of contacts with Zanzibar and the East Africa coast. Most of male slaves imported to Oman were employed on date plantations. Lorimer stressed that the number of Africans and half-caste (*mawalid*), both bonded and free, was large. The majority came from the Swahili coast and there were a few Ethiopian women and Nubians. The Arabs of pure blood were very few because of concubinage with slaves or marriages with free African women. A heavy infusion of African blood was evidenced by a large proportion of people of mixed blood among the population of Sur on the southern coast of Oman. This port had close commercial relations with Africa, and its inhabitants were involved in slave trade.[16]

Lorimer's figures, which are sometimes considered inflated, show that the African presence on the Gulf coast of Arabia and Oman in 1904 varied from 7 per cent in

---

[13] On the pearl fisheries industry and the exportation of pearls, see Lorimer, *Gazetteer*, vol. I, Appendix C *The Pearl and Mother-of-Pearl Fisheries of the Persian Gulf*, 2220–36; *Annual Report on the Administration the Persian Gulf Political Residency and Muscat Political Agency for the Year 1877–78*, Appendix A. *Memorandum on the Pearl Fisheries of the Gulf by Captain E.L. Durand, 10 Assistant Political Resident, Persian Gulf*, in the *Persian Gulf Administration Reports, 1873–1947*, 10 vols. (Gerrards Cross, Buckinghamshire: Archive Editions, 1986), vol. 1 (1873–9): 31–2.

[14] Lorimer, *Gazetteer*, vol. II, 241, 1051, 1531; Abdul Sheriff, 'The Slave Trade and Its Fallout in the Persian Gulf', in *Abolition and its Aftermath in the Indian Ocean, Africa and Asia*, ed. Gwyn Campbell (London: Routledge, 2005), 109.

[15] Lorimer, *Gazetteer*, vol. II, 1437.

[16] Lorimer, *Gazetteer*, vol. II, 296–7, 1183–5, 1198–2000.

Table 4.1 African Presence on the Gulf Coast of Arabia and Oman in 1904

	Number of slaves (1904)	Total population (1904)
Kuwait	4,000	35,000
Qatar	4,000	27,000
Bahrain	6,000	45,000
Trucial Coast	10,400 (1881)	32,000 (1881) and 72,000 (1904)
Muscat	10,000	40,000
Matrah	2,480	34,000
Total	36,880	253,000*

* Lorimer, *Gazetteer*, vol. II, 241, 1051, 1531.

Matrah to 11 per cent in Kuwait, 13 per cent in Bahrain, 14 per cent in Qatar, 25 per cent in Muscat and 28 per cent on the Trucial Coast (in 1881). The total number of slaves can be estimated at 36,880 out of a total of 253,000, which gives an average percentage of 14.5 for the region (including Kuwait, Qatar, Bahrain, Trucial Coast, and Muscat and Matrah) (Table 4.1).[17]

Possession of slaves brought prestige and was considered a mark of prosperity. In Nejd, the average was two slaves for every wealthy household. Tribal chiefs kept slaves, but the number differs according to the position of each chief.[18] Undoubtedly, the slave trade was very profitable.[19] The statement of thirty-two-year-old slave Mubarak bin Yahya Yamani recorded at the Political Agency in Bahrain on 22 April 1930 indicates that he was sold six times over a 26-year period of enslavement (between 1904 and 1930), and the total earned by the brokers and owners from the consecutive sales of him and his wife was 15,400 rupees. This was a huge sum of money.[20]

The possession of a slave was an investment. He or she could be sold at any time for an excellent profit, or could yield an income employed as a labourer.[21] He or she could be sold if the situation of the owner worsened.[22] Slaves were frequently transferred to other owners for a partial payment of debts, and sometimes, they admitted to having debts of their own.[23] In the late 1930s, the barter of slaves in partial liquidation of debts

---

[17] Calculations of Abdul Sheriff based on Lorimer's estimates: Sheriff, 'The Slave Trade', 112.
[18] Foreign Office Memorandum (Mr. Hamilton Gordon), 'Slavery in Abyssinia', 27 August 1927, FO 371/12287 J 2405/55/1.
[19] Statement of slave Bakhit bin Mubarak, born at Bisha (South Hijaz), aged about 28 years, recorded in the Political Agency Bahrain on 6 November 1937, R/15/2/1827 (IOR).
[20] Statement of slave Mubarak bin Yahya Yamani, aged about 32 years recorded at the Political Agency, Bahrain, on the 22 April 1930, R/15/1/205 5/161, IV (IOR).
[21] Statement made by Alia bint Isa bin Buti of Ras al-Khaima, recorded at Shargah on 29 July 1941, R/15/1/212 5/168 VIII (IOR). This was the equivalent of approximately 1,800 pounds. In 1904, 1 pound was worth 15 rupees, and in 1930, 13⅓ rupees. For comparison, in 1937 in Abu Dhabi, a bag of rice cost 10 rupees, and a diver's earnings for the summer pearl fishing season were 70 rupees.
[22] Statement of slave Zayed bin Salmin, aged about 38 years, 13 December 1932, R/15/2/1825 (IOR).
[23] Statement of Sultan bin Abdullah, aged about 40, recorded in the Political Agency, Bahrain, 1 November, 1937, R/15/2/1827 (IOR).

became more common because of the effects of the general trade depression.[24] The common practice everywhere on the north-eastern coast of Arabia and Oman was to mortgage slaves, which practically amounted to selling them. This practice prevailed in the Trucial Coast sheikhdoms. A slave woman, Halimah bint Sarur from Sharjah, born at Addis Ababa, who applied for the manumission certificate in August 1937, had been mortgaged several times. Her first master mortgaged her to another for 400 rupees. She stayed with the second master for six months, after which he mortgaged her to Shaikh Sultan bin Saqr, ruler of Sharjah, for an unknown amount. After a year, she was mortgaged by the ruler to a company for 300 rupees. Then the woman escaped and came back to her first master, who mortgaged her to a man from Sharjah for 223 rupees. She served him four months and when he intended to sell her, she ran away and arrived at the British agency in Sharjah.[25]

Slaves were a part of the community of divers. They dived about nine months of the year. During winter, some slaves on the Trucial Coast were employed on plantations, in fisheries, as camel-drivers and as cattle herders. Many were allowed to perform whatever additional work they could find for clothes and pocket money, but they were fed by their masters. The industrial slaves received no wages but were given food and clothing, and, in theory, it was in the master's interest to keep them fit. With the approach of the pearling season on the Trucial Coast, there was a great yearly migration north from Oman. Batinah produced the best divers, sending as many as 5,000 of them. Another 2,100 were said to come from Dhahirah and Sharjah. Of this total number, not less than 1,000 were believed to be slaves.[26]

The lot of slaves

Opinions about the nature of slavery on the north-eastern coast of the Arabian Peninsula vary. British consular officers in the region stressed that domestic slavery as practised on the Gulf coast of Arabia and Oman was comparatively more humane than in other parts of the world. 'There was no question of keeping the slaves as prisoners or working them in a gang under overseers: the conventional "Uncle Tom's Cabin" picture that was called up in some people's minds by the word "slavery", according to a political resident's report from 1935.[27] In some reports, the social position of slaves in Arabian societies was even seen as equal to that of their masters. British agents could not discern major signs of stigma or degradation attached to the position of slaves. Slaves could pray by the side of their masters and dined at the same table with

---

[24] From the Commanding Officer, HMS Lupin at Sea, to the Senior Naval Officer, Persian Gulf, HMS Shoreham, 10 May 1934, R/15/1/209 5/168, V (IOR).

[25] Translation of statement made by Halimah bint Sarur of Addis Ababa, age about 28 years, recorded at Shargah on the 15th August 1936, R/15/1/210 5/168, VI (IOR).

[26] From Lieut.-Colonel H. V. Biscoe, Political Resident in the Persian Gulf, to the Foreign Secretary to the Government of India, New Delhi, No. 637 of 1930, Bushire, 18 March 1930; Domestic Slavery in the Persian Gulf, R/15/5/311 9/1 (IOR); From Political Agent, Bahrain, to the Resident, Bushire, No. C/78–20/, Bahrain, 16 February 1936, R/15/1/226 5/193 II (B 38) (IOR); From Political Agent, Muscat, to British Consul, Bushire, C/28, 11 February, 1936, R/15/6/414 13/1 (IOR).

[27] The Residency, Bushire, to the India Office, Bushire, 20 July 1935, R/15/1/226 5/193 II (B 38) (IOR).

the most respectable free men. A slave could transact business, buy and sell in his own name and on his own initiative. He could buy property in his own name, although such property was legally considered as belonging to his master. There were instances of freed slaves who acquired through their manumission all the rights and privileges of a free man. There were many cases of slaves who took refuge at the British agency in the heat of the moment but later changed their minds and returned to their masters. There were examples of dhows manned by slaves who traded on the African coast and returned to their masters after several months with profits earned.[28] Some slaves were sent to schools and received an education. Some owners took a particular interest in their slaves' education as these slaves could do more valuable work.[29] Slaves used to have disputes with their masters, and when they did not want to stay with them, they asked to be sold to someone else. In most cases, however, they failed to convince their masters to grant their wish.[30]

These British views should be approached with caution, however, and assessed in the context of the general British policy in the region. For Great Britain, the main strategic goal was to ensure the safety of the sea route through the Persian Gulf from India to Mesopotamia.[31] For that reason, and on account of the difficulty of intervening with any beneficial effect in the internal affairs of independent and quasi-independent states, the British government generally abstained from active interference in Arabia, domestic slavery being no exception. Thus, opinions about the mild nature of slavery justified the policy of non-intervention. All the more so because the British administration in the Persian Gulf did not believe in the possibility of the complete eradication of domestic slavery due to the fact that slavery was accepted by Islam and the rulers and inhabitants of the countries surrounding the Persian Gulf strongly favoured the continuation of slavery.[32]

Moreover, many statements made by slaves to British authorities when applying for a certificate of freedom paradoxically emphasize a strong attachment to the home in which they were born and raised and to the family of their owner. Some slaves declared a desire to return to their owners if they changed their attitude towards them. On the other hand, these statements show that they were beaten, forced into labour, sold or put to work for other owners without consent, and held in solitary confinement for not following orders. William G. Clarence-Smith, a slavery scholar, stressed that 'domestic slavery', a phrase so frequently repeated in studies on the attitude of Islam to slavery, is to some extent a misleading term, as the duties of a domestic slave covered a range of

---

[28] Mr. Bond (Jeddah) to Foreign Office, No. 60, 6 March 1930, FO 371/14475 E 1541/1054/91.

[29] Statement of slave Nasib bin Muhammad, aged 22 years recorded in the Political Agency, Bahrain, 14 May 1938, R/15/207 5/161 VI, 168 IX, 179, II (IOR).

[30] Statement made by slave Faraj bin Nasib, 23 February 1929, born in Shehr, aged about 50 years, R/15/1/216 5/190, II (IOR).

[31] From the Deputy Secretary to the Government of India to the Political Resident in the Persian Gulf, Simla, 13 October 1898, R/15/2/1826 (IOR).

[32] Foreign Office, 'Memorandum concerning the existence of Slavery and Slave Trading along the Eastern and South-Eastern Coasts of Arabia', E 1658/1054/91, 27 March 1930, R/15/1/2265/193 II (B 38) (IOR); League of Nations, Advisory Committee of Experts on Slavery, Note by the Secretariat, C.C.E.E./70, 'The Aspect of Slavery in Muhammadan Law', Geneva, 15 February 1936, R/15/1/2265/193 II (B 38) (IOR).

purely productive tasks.[33] This remark perfectly reflects the situation on the Gulf coast of Arabia in the period under study. Male slaves were used there as divers in summer and as house servants in winter without the opportunity to choose for themselves the nature of their labour.

Despite these conditions, ingrained tradition worked to protect slaves in many ways. They knew that their master would avenge any harm inflicted upon them. The killing or kidnapping of a slave reflected badly on the owner's honour, though this was not the same, to be sure, as the dishonour involved in something similar happening to one's son. On the other hand, masters and family members believed that slaves had to be continually kept in check and reminded of their position. A predominant opinion was that a slave, even a beloved one, needed to be kept in a proper state of mind, and the best way to do this was to use a heavy hand.[34] The system of slavery worked ruthlessly and was well protected by tradition as well as by religion. There were slaves who escaped from their masters and were working for themselves as labourers, divers or sailors. If they were found by their masters or recognized as slaves, they were arrested and sent back to their masters.[35] In some cases, slaves lived separately from their masters, who used them periodically as a labour force.[36]

Slaves enjoyed a certain freedom of movement, but as labourers they operated within a network of social bonds and norms. Whoever broke these norms was ostracized and excluded from the economic system. Male slaves were an important part of the pearl-diving community, and they were sent for diving by their masters from all parts of the Arabian coast and Oman. As the main pearling season lasted from May to September and the boats stayed in the fisheries for up to 130 days, free divers were given cash advances by captains of their boats to support their family while they were out at sea. When the diving season was over and the pearls were sold, they received another payment, and in winter they were given some pocket money. They were generally indebted to *nakhudas* or merchants, and their debts were inherited by their sons or brothers. The debts were registered in special pearling courts and nobody could avoid paying them.[37] Slave divers received no cash advances but were given food and clothing from their masters, who were receiving their advances and payments. The masters were also responsible for the families of slave divers when they were away from home. Theoretically, this system provided slaves with a livelihood, but in practice, the owners still tried to earn as much as possible from the labour of their

[33] William G. Clarence-Smith, *Islam and the Abolition of Slavery* (London: Hurst, 2006), 3.
[34] Ibid., 178–9.
[35] Statement of Gharib bin Sayeed, place of birth Sinas (Batineh district), aged about 38 years, name of master Sultan bin Zaid, chief of Abu Dhabi, Bandar Abbas, 11 December 1924, R/15/1/216 5/190, II (IOR).
[36] Translation of a statement made by the slave Suwaid bin Marzooq, born at Mekalla, aged about 65 years. Recorded at Shargah on 10 January 1941, R/15/1/212 5/168, VIII (IOR).
[37] Mohammed G. Rumaihi, *Bahrain: Social and Political Change since the First World War* (London: Bowker, 1976), 46; From Lieut.-Colonel H. V. Biscoe, Political Resident in the Persian Gulf, to the Foreign Secretary to the Government of India, New Delhi, No. 637 of 1930, Bushire, 18 March 1930, R/15/5/3 11/9/1 (IOR); From Political Agent, Bahrain, to the Resident, Bushire, No. C/78–20/, Bahrain, 16 February 1936, R/15/1/226 5/193 II (B 38) *Slavery in the Gulf, 1 Jan. 1930–18 Sept. 1936* (IOR); From Political Agent, Muscat, to British Consul, Bushire, C/28, 11 February 1936, R/15/6/414 13/1 *Slavery in the Gulf, 11 Dec. 1934–30 Jan. 1939* (IOR).

slaves at the expense of the latter. When the masters' fortunes began to fail due to the crisis in the pearl industry, slaves were still sent for diving but they no longer received sufficient assistance from their masters. They tried to borrow money from captains or merchants, and slave diver debt – which had been an incidental occurance before – in the 1930s became commonplace.[38]

Slave divers generally refused to pay their debts, arguing that it was the duty of their masters who were taking their earnings. The lenders considered this argument valid and demanded that a slave's debt be repaid by his owner; but until this happened or until the master made a commitment to repay the debt, the indebted slave was not allowed to fish for pearl oysters, and that meant a dramatic worsening of his and his family's situation.[39] Since the British authorities also believed that slaves' debts should be paid by their owners, cases where indebted slaves reported to the British agency for the certificate of manumission became more frequent. These petitioners believed that the British document would protect them from the claims of their creditors and allow them to work on the boats fishing for pearl oysters. Their hopes did not materialize, however, and they were still treated in the pearl fisheries as indebted slaves whose fortunes depended on their owners paying their debts.[40]

Perhaps not surprisingly, there were cases when free divers indebted to their captains posed as slaves and applied for a British certificate in an attempt to annul their debt. In October 1937, a Baluchi named Mas'ud bin Gundan came to the Political Agency and asked for a manumission certificate. He was about forty years old and stated that he was a slave and had run away from his master because of his cruelty and intention to sell him. The agent noted that the slave showed no marks of ill-treatment.[41] Upon further inquiry, it was found that Mas'ud bin Gundan was a free man and a diver, and that he owed a huge sum of 640 rupees. The man did not receive the certificate of freedom and his debts were registered in the pearling court.[42]

Islamic manumission

Release of slaves was a part of Islamic norms. Although Islam did not abolish slavery, it recommended freeing a slave as an act of piety and charity. At least two *hadiths* refer to slave manumission. The *hadith* entitled 'The Excellence of Emancipating a Slave' says, 'Abu Huraira reported Allah's Messenger as saying: If anyone emancipates a Muslim slave, Allah will set free from Hell an organ of his body for every organ of his (slave's)

[38] The Residency Agent, Sharjah, to the Political Resident, Persian Gulf, Bushire, 27th December 1921, R/15/1/216 5/190, II *Manumission of Slaves at Muscat: Individual Cases, 7 Sept. 1921–12 May 1929* (IOR).
[39] Political Agency, Bahrain, to the Secretary to the Political Resident in the Persian Gulf at Bushire, Bahrain, 23rd January 1926, R/15/1/208 5/168, IV *Manumission of Slaves in Arab Coast: Individual Cases, 19 Feb. 1925–18 March 1931* (IOR).
[40] Ibid.
[41] Statement of the slave Mas'ud bin Gundan, aged about 40 years, recorded on 15 October 1937, R/15/1/219 5/190, V (IOR).
[42] Translation of letter No. 307 dated 21 April 1938 from the Residency Agent, Shargah, to the Political Agent, Bahrain, R/15/1/219 5/190, V (IOR).

body.'[43] Another *hadith* declares, 'It (freedom of a slave) has not the reward even equal to it, but the fact that I heard Allah's Messenger say: He who slaps his slave or beats him, the expiation for it is that he should set him free.'[44]

Thus, Islam also stressed fair treatment of slaves, including adequate food and clothing and support for old slaves. Islam prescribed several ways of manumitting slaves, including the possibility of the slave buying his or her own freedom. This type of freed slave was known as *mukatib*. Under this arrangement, a contract was made between the owner and his slave, usually for the payment of a particular sum of money, and after payment was completed, the slave was free.[45] In other cases, the owner made a promise to the slave that he or she would be free after the death of the owner. A slave who was promised manumission was called *mudabbar*. After such an assurance was given, the *mudabbar* slave could not be sold but continued to work for the master. In the case of marriage between owner and slave, Islamic law required that offspring be freed and granted rights fully equal to those of the offspring of free mothers.[46]

Under certain circumstances, however, these rules were not followed. A man could retract his last will and testament if he wished, including the provision to emancipate a slave. A slave could not be made *mudabbar* unless he/she fell within that third of the estate over which the testator had powers of independent allocation. A *mudabbar* could be sold if his/her owner was in financial difficulties, regardless of any promise of freedom. A debtor whose property did not cover his debts was not eligible to free a slave. And again, if someone owned a part of a slave (when the ownership was shared between two or more people) and freed the slave, the latter did not become free until due compensation was paid to the co-owner.[47] Freed slaves enjoyed the legal rights of the freeborn, but their former masters remained their patrons.[48]

Although Islamic law provided for manumission, there were very few domestic slaves among those emancipated on the Gulf coast of Arabia and Oman at the turn of the nineteenth and twentieth centuries. The practice of emancipating domestic slaves was a rather new phenomenon in the region. It first became socially acceptable in Muscat in the 1890s, where it happened occasionally that, with the consent of the sultan, domestic slaves proven to have been badly treated or unclaimed by any owner were manumitted by the Islamic court; and if they were returned to their masters, they received a guarantee of kind treatment. An attempt to introduce the manumission of domestic slaves in Trucial Oman in 1899 failed because the sheikh of Sharjah declined to entertain such a proposal by the British Resident in the Persian Gulf on the grounds that his subjects would demand compensation from him for

---

[43] *Sahih Muslim Being Traditions of the Saying and Doings of the Prophet Muhammad as Narrated by His Companions and Compiled under the Title Al-Jami'-us-Salih by Imam Mulim Rendered into English by Abdul Hamid Siddiqi* (Lahore: Sh. Muhammad Ashraf, 1976), vol. II, Chapter DXCI, 790.

[44] *Sahih Muslim*, vol. III, Chapter DCLXII, 882.

[45] Humphrey J. Fisher, *Slavery in the History of Muslim Black Africa* (London: Hurst, 2001), 75.

[46] Bernard Lewis, *Race and Slavery in the East: An Historical Enquiry* (Oxford: Oxford University Press, 1990), 8–9. Several *hadiths* speak of the possibility of selling a *mudabbar* – see *Sahih Muslim*, vol. IV, chapter XII: The Book of Oath.

[47] Fisher, *Slavery*, 74.

[48] Frederick Cooper, *Plantation Slavery on the East Coast of Africa* (Portsmouth: Heinemann, 1997), 242–3.

every slave manumitted.[49] Another British agent pointed out in 1936 that an owner who emancipated his slave would be considered a man of exceptionally piety, but it seems that these formal acts of Islamic manumission often had no significant social consequences for the slaves: slaves who received their promised freedom at the time of their owner's death nonetheless remained at the house of their deceased owner and performed the same duties as before. They were still viewed as slaves in the neighbourhood, and the heirs usually treated them as part of the inheritance of the deceased and often wanted to sell them, which meant re-enslavement.[50]

The role of the British

The British policy on the Gulf coast of Arabia and Oman aimed at several goals, and suppression of the slave trade was among them – the result of a global shift in British policy. 'An Act for the Abolition of the Slave Trade', passed by the British parliament in 1807, made it illegal for any vessel to transport slaves from any port in British dominions. In 1811, traffic of slaves was declared a felony in order to prevent commercial transactions in slaves by British subjects. The next step was made in 1833 with the abolition of proprietary rights to slaves throughout British dominions. The final liberation of all slaves took place in August 1838.[51]

In addition to the suppression of the slave trade, the British practiced manumission. On the Trucial Coast, manumission was based on the Agreement of 1847, which was reaffirmed by the rulers of Sharjah and Abu Dhabi in 1873.[52] Certificates were granted by or on the specific authority of the resident after an investigation, or based on the report of the British political agent, and after consideration of the views of the rulers of Sharjah and Abu Dhabi.[53]

The chief institution responsible for manumission was the British Residency in Bushehr on the Persian coast. The history of the Residency goes back as far as 12 April 1763.[54] By 1825, British agencies staffed by political agents were established in Bahrain, Muscat and Sharjah (initially in Qatif).[55] The first agreement on the slave trade in the

---

[49] Lorimer, *Gazetteer*, vol. I, 2514–16.

[50] From Political Agent, Muscat, to British Consul, Bushire, C/28, 11 February 1936, R/15/6/414 13/1 (IOR).

[51] Marika Sherwood, *After Abolition: Britain and the Slave Trade since 1807* (London: I. B. Tauris, 2007), 1–2, 15–17.

[52] Charles U. Aitchison, *A Collection of Treaties, Engagements and Sanads* Relating *to India and Neighbouring Countries*, vol. XI, *The Treaties Relating to Aden and the South Western Coast of Arabia, the Arab Principalities in the Persian Gulf, Muscat (Oman), Baluchistan and the North-West Frontiers Province, Revised and Continued up to the End of 1930 under the Authority of the Government of India* (Delhi: Manager of Publications, 1933), 178, 184.

[53] Manumission of Slaves, R/15/1/234 5/202 (IOR).

[54] 'CXXIV, Extract of a Letter from Commission and Instructions to Mr. William Andrew Price, Provisional Agent of Persia, dated 22 January 1763', in *The Persian Précis, 1, Selections from State Papers, Bombay, Regarding the East India Company's Connections with the Persian Gulf, with a Summary of Events, 1600–1800*, ed. Jerome A. Saldanha (Calcutta: Superintendent of Government Printing, 1908), 162–3.

[55] James Onley, *The Arabian Frontier of the British Raj: Merchants, Rulers and the British in the Nineteenth-Century Gulf* (Oxford: Oxford University Press, 2007), 66–93.

Persian Gulf was the General Treaty of 1820 signed with the sheikhs of Trucial Oman.[56] New agreements with the sheikhs of Ajman, Dubai, Abu Dhabi, Umm al-Qaiwain and Ras al-Khaimah were signed in 1839, 1847, 1856 and 1873, in which the five sheikhs of Trucial Oman committed to prohibit the exportation of slaves from aboard vessels belonging to themselves and their subjects.[57]

The duty of the agency in Sharjah was to insist on sheikhs observing the agreement. If the political agent came to know about the importation of slaves from outside the region, he asked the sheikh of the town where the slaves had been imported. He then assisted the sheikh's men in arresting the slave traders and either handed over the slaves to the sheikh or sent them by ship to the port whence they had been brought. In the first case, the slaves remained in the sheikh's household and the British authorities were not interested in their fate. In the event that the slaves freed from the hands of the kidnappers came from another town in the region, they were sent to their owners.[58] The general attitude of the sheikhs of Trucial Oman towards slavery was favourable, and their cooperation in granting manumission was considered rather poor. Nevertheless, if a slave took refuge at the British agency, his or her statement was taken and submitted to the Political Residency in Bushehr in order to grant him or her a manumission certificate. The sheikhs' cooperation was not quite wholehearted but enough to maintain an official prohibition on the sale of slaves in their territories. The business of trading in humans, however, continued privately between the inhabitants of the territories.[59]

British manumission statistics

The practice of British officials freeing slaves started in 1852, and by 1908, 693 slaves had been rescued at sea and 1,853 released at the demand of British authorities.[60] Generally, until 1924, the number of applications submitted yearly to the British agencies in the Persian Gulf for manumission was not considerable. It rose sharply, however, after 1925, and it was exceptional by the end of the 1930s. If in 1924, only 9 applications for freedom were submitted to British agencies, this number increased to 24 in 1925, 32 in 1930, 52 in 1934, 91 in 1937 and 158 in 1938. Altogether, between

---

[56] The text in *Treaties, Agreements, and Engagements between the Honorable East India Company and the Native Prices, Chiefs, and States, in Western India; the Red Sea; the Persian Gulf, etc. and also between Her Britannic Majesty's Government, and Persia, Portugal, and Turkey, Compiled under Instructions from the Government of Bombay by R. Hughes Thomas, Uncovenanted Assistant to the Chief Secretary, with Notes and Memoranda by the Compiler* (Bombay, printed for the Government at the Bombay Education Society's Press, 1851), 23; see also Aitchison, *A Collection*, vol. XI, 245–9.

[57] The texts in *Treaties, Agreements, and Engagements*, 26–31; Kemball, 'Suppression', 669–78.

[58] Translation of a letter No. 275, dated the 6th September 1910, from the Political Resident in the Persian Gulf to Sheikh Mubarak, Chief of Koweit, R/15/5/85 29/2 (IOR); From the Senior Naval Officer, Persian Gulf, to the Commander-in-Chief, East Indies Station, 19 December 1928, R/15/1/223 5/191, III (IOR).

[59] The Residency Agent, Shargah, to the Political Resident, Bushire, 22 August 1928, R/15/1/229 5/196, I (IOR).

[60] Lorimer, *Gazetteer*, vol. I, 514–16.

Table 4.2 Number of Applications for Freedom in 1921–1946

Year	Number of applications	Sex of applicants	
		Female	Male
1921	7	2	5
1922	1	0	1
1924	9	2	7
1925	24	15	9
1926	29	10	19
1927	21	4	17
1928	30	6	24
1929	57	6	48
1930	32	6	26
1931	49	7	42
1932	46	5	41
1933	32	4	28
1934	52	4	48
1935	17	5	12
1936	58	16	42
1937	91	28	63
1938	158	65	93
1939	124	53	71
1940	55	26	29
1941	20	7	13
1942	12	3	9
1944	7	1	6
1945	5	1	4
1946	6	0	6
Total	**956**	**283**	**673***

* No applications were found for 1923, 1943, 1947 and 1948.

1921 and 1946, at least 956 applications were made by slaves at the British agencies on the Gulf coast of Arabia and Oman (Table 4.2).[61]

Regarding the geographical origin of slaves applying to British agencies for a certificate of freedom, out of the total of 956 statements, 393 were made at the agency at Sharjah. This does not, however, mean that all applicants were inhabitants of the Trucial Coast. Some of them came from Oman, Buraimi, Bahrain and Bandar Abbas. On the other hand, inhabitants of the Trucial Coast were among those applying for manumission in Muscat, Bandar Abbas and Bushehr. The open geography of the Persian Gulf was conducive to travel, and people there moved around with relative freedom.

---

[61] My own calculations based on statements found in the archives.

Most striking was the change in the attitude of domestic slaves. If by the mid-1920s the general number of applications for release was small, with only isolated cases of applications by domestic slaves, then from the second half of the 1920s and into the 1930s, this number increased significantly, including the proportion of domestic slaves, both male and female. In the years 1925–40, when British agencies saw the greatest increase in applications, the overwhelming majority of applicants were slaves born into slavery in the region. Slaves brought from Hejaz, Nejd, Makran, Yemen and India, where they had been bought or kidnapped, formed only the second-largest group of applicants. The number of female slaves applying for British manumission had always been lower than that of men, yet between 1935 and 1939, this number jumped. In the case of the British agency at Sharjah, to which there were more applicants, the increase in applications from women was striking. Out of 393 applications submitted to the British political agent at Sharjah, 199 were made by women, which exceeded the 194 applications by men.

Why did the slaves, and especially women, choose to flee from their masters? An explanation commonly used in the literature has been the collapse of the pearl fisheries. Indeed, as the pearl fisheries employed the majority of male slaves, the industry's collapse was critical for the slave divers and their families. In 1924, Japanese pearls were introduced on the international markets for the first time, and this posed a threat to the Persian Gulf's pearl trade. In 1925, the local pearl market deteriorated seriously, and in 1926, it became even worse because of the low catch and the decrease in European purchases. The *nakhudas* had to accept less cash, and the advance for the divers was, thus, reduced. In 1927, the catch was better, and in 1928 and 1929, everything appeared to be back to normal. However, the global recession of 1930 brought a slump in the pearl trade. Only a few merchants in Bahrain managed to sell pearls because of the recession in the markets of Paris and Bombay. The number of boats operated by the banks decreased and the majority of divers were paid no profits because the expenses of diving were higher than the revenue. The situation worsened in 1931, and during the 1932 main season, the industry experienced a low catch. The downward slide continued during the years 1930–4, and the future of the industry was becoming increasingly uncertain with the main trend being one of gradual decline.[62]

There is no doubt that the decline of the pearl industry had a decisive impact on the erosion of slavery. At the same time, an analysis of the number of applications for manumission and the reasons given by the slaves provides unexpected insights. First of all, there is no correlation between the waves of the economic crisis and the number of the application submissions. When we look at the table displaying the fluctuations in application submissions, we see that despite the fact that the crisis in the pearl industry had already deepened in 1930, the number of manumission applications was stable until 1936 and then increased sharply in the years 1938 and 1939. This proves that it was not the crisis waves themselves but their common perception that influenced the decision to flee. The first deterioration of the local pearl market took place in 1925, but in 1927, the catch was better and in 1928 and 1929, everything appeared to be as

---

[62] See Mahdi A. Al-Tajir, *Bahrajn 1920–1945: Britain, the Shaikh and the Administration* (London: Groom Helm, 1987), 116–22.

usual. The downward slide of the industry continued during the years 1930–4, and the future of the industry was becoming increasingly uncertain, although there was still a chance for improvement. Masters and slaves were still hoping for a better future, and in fact, the years 1935, 1936 and 1937 saw some slight improvements. In 1938, however, it became evident to all that the industry was entering its death throes. In 1939, the Residency Agent reported that the slave owners in the Trucial Coast towns were 'cashing in' on their slaves.[63] This was an important signal that slave owners had lost all hope of improving the situation and did not have the resources to keep their slaves. The 'cashing in' meant that wives were separated from husbands and children were separated from their parents. Consequently, the threat of being separated from family became real, and flight and appeals to the British for emancipation spiked.

Another aspect of the erosion of slavery in the wake of the collapse of the pearl industry is revealed by an analysis of slave complaints against their owners. The British demanded that the escaped slaves give reasons for their escape, and these reasons underwent quite noticeable fluctuations over time. In the 1920s, the argumentation was focused on cruel treatment by individual masters or on quarrels within owner families. For example, in 1925, there were twenty-five statements made by both men and women, and each case was different in terms of the reasons that pushed those people to leave their masters. Two of the men had already been manumitted by their masters but were afraid of being re-enslaved by the heirs. One man swam off to a man-of-war as he was ill-treated and wished to be repatriated to Zanzibar. One woman was kidnapped when her husband left for diving, and there were two Abyssinian girls kidnapped and recovered by the British agent. Thus, there was no dominant reason for submitting an application.

In the 1930s, the arguments changed. The applicants still complained of 'ill-treatment' but now understood it in a more general context. Almost half of the slaves who asked for British citizenship in 1938–9 complained of being 'ill-treated' by their owners. If before, 'ill treatment' was understood as beating and chaining, now there were only a few such examples. The argument that they were not fed or clothed and 'not being paid' for the diving season was the most common. Applicants generally stressed that their masters' obligation was to provide them with food and clothing. Some were simply turned out of the house by masters who could not do this. 'Not being paid' signified that they were not getting the advances before the diving season that allowed them feed themselves during diving. The fact that the owners failed to fulfil these obligations was assessed by the slaves as an injustice. Some of them declared that they would like to return to their owners' homes if they were provided with food, clothing and, in the case of the divers, advances.

The largest group of applicants for British manumission, however, constituted those who were afraid of being sold and separated from their families. These were mostly women. The youngest female petitioner of African origin was Hallum bint Jumah from Dubai, just ten years of age. She reported to the British agency in Sharjah on 28 August 1938 and explained that she had run away because she was afraid of being sold. She had

---

[63] *Slavery in the Gulf, 3 April 1938–31 July 1939*, Office of the Political Resident in the Persian Gulf, Camp Bahrain, to the India Office, London, 17 February 1939, R/15/1/228 5/193, IV (B 55) (IOR).

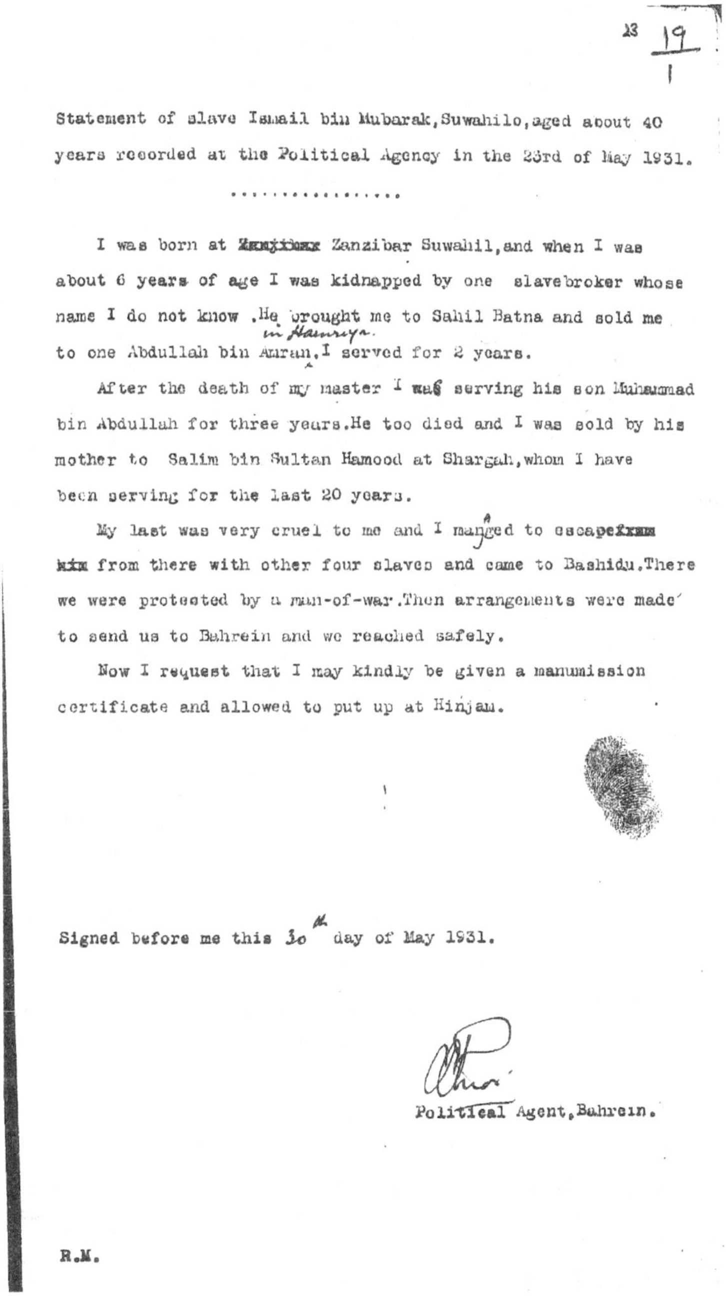

13 19

Statement of slave Ismail bin Mubarak,Suwahilo,aged about 40
years recorded at the Political Agency in the 23rd of May 1931.

. . . .

I was born at ~~Zanzibar~~ Zanzibar Suwahil,and when I was
about 6 years of age I was kidnapped by one slavebroker whose
name I do not know .He brought me to Sahil Batna and sold me
to one Abdullah bin Amran. in Hamriya. I served for 2 years.

After the death of my master I was serving his son Muhammad
bin Abdullah for three years.He too died and I was sold by his
mother to Salim bin Sultan Hamood at Shargah,whom I have
been serving for the last 20 years.

My last was very cruel to me and I managed to escape~~from~~
~~him~~ from there with other four slaves and came to Bashidu.There
we were protested by a man-of-war.Then arrangements were made
to send us to Bahrein and we reached safely.

Now I request that I may kindly be given a manumission
certificate and allowed to put up at Hinjam.

Signed before me this 30th day of May 1931.

Political Agent,Bahrein.

R.M.

Figure 4.2 Statement by a slave named Ismail bin Mubarak.

Source: Courtesy of the British Library Board (R/15/1 Political Residency Bushire 1763–1947).

followed her older sister, who had already been manumitted by the British.[64] One of the oldest female applicants was Fatimah bint Ahmad, who came from Dubai but was born in Yemen. She was about fifty-five and worked as a servant. She asked for manumission on 29 December 1938 after she had been beaten for protesting against the sale of her daughter.[65] One of the most dramatic scenes took place at the British Agency in Sharjah on 24 October 1938. A woman entered the agency crying, 'I am a free-born woman and not a slave of anyone!' Her name was Manyuh bint Khalfan from Dibbah, and her fate encompassed many problems experienced by enslaved women. She was born in Dibbah in the house of her master, Abdullah bin Muhamad. When she was young, she was manumitted along with her mother by their master. They stayed in Ras al-Khaimah, but after some time her mother died, and she travelled to Dubai, where she remained. Then she fell ill and needed money for her recovery. She mortgaged herself for 200 rupees to an old woman who was originally a slave of the wife of a Dubai merchant. When she recovered from her illness, the old woman mortgaged her to a certain Said bin Dhabi of Dubai who, after a short period, mortgaged her to Alluh and Salmin, both sailors. Fifteen years later, they mortgaged her to Said bin Muhammad al Mansuri of the Manasir tribe. Manyuh remained in the service of Said, who died ten days before she applied at the agency. Alluh and Salmin then both alleged that they had not received anything from her late master, Said. This was on account of her having been mortgaged, and they had in their possession some papers in support of their claim. They intended to enslave her, but she considered herself a freeborn woman. Because she was afraid that she would be sold, she came from Dubai to Sharjah in order to take refuge at the agency and asked to be granted a manumission certificate so that no one could interfere with her liberty.[66]

Applicants also often complained of masters failing to fulfil their obligation to arrange for marriage despite the fact that the slaves' earnings were sufficient to maintain a family.[67] This complaint, however, was not so much due to the economic crisis as to a general shortage of new slaves in the area. This problem became significant as early as the beginning of the twentieth century, when the influx of fresh slaves from Africa was blocked by the British Navy. The common practice was to formalize a marriage of a male slave with a female slave belonging to the same owner. In this case, the master took possession of the offspring. The other option was to marry a male slave to the female slave of another master. Both practices became increasingly difficult owing to the scarcity of fresh slaves.

---

[64] Statement made by Hallum bint Jumah, aged about 10 years. Recorded at Shargah on the 28th August 1938, IOR: R/15/1/211 5/168 VII *Manumission of slaves in Arab Coast: Individual Cases, 28 July 1938–28 June 1939.*

[65] Statement made by the slave Fatimah bint Ahmad, aged about 55 years. Recorded on the 29th December 1938, IOR: R/15/1/220 5/190 VI *Manumission of Slaves at Muscat: Individual Cases, 15 Jun 1938–7 May 1942.*

[66] Statement made by Manyuh bint Khalfan, born at Dibbah, aged about 35 years, recorded at Shargah on 24 October 1938, R/15/1/211 5/168, VII (IOR).

[67] Statement of Saleha bint Saad resident of Umm al-Qaiwain, age 25 years, recorded on the 12th August 1937, IOR: R/15/1/219 5/190 V *Manumission of Slaves at Muscat: Individual Cases, 10 Sept. 1935–24 Nov. 1938.*

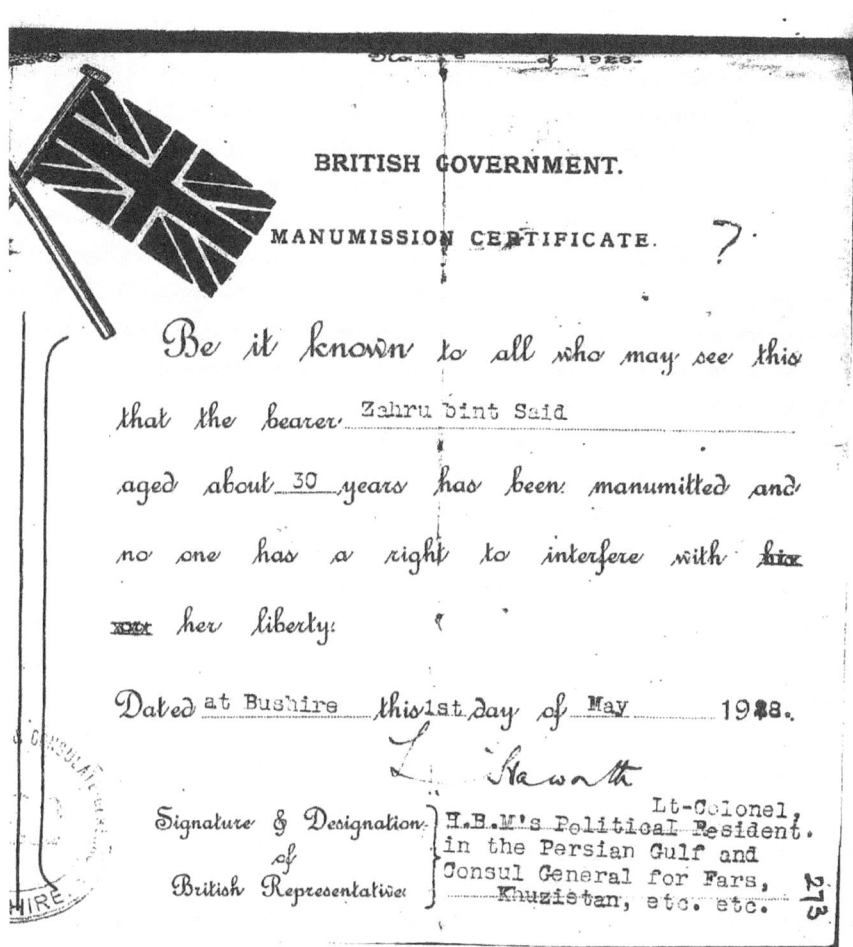

Figure 4.3 A British manumission certificate from 1928.

Source: Courtesy of the British Library Board (R/15/1 Political Residency Bushire 1763–1947).

Conclusion

The slaves' statements prove that the collapse of the pearl industry, which depended on the labour of slaves employed in the oyster fisheries, set a series of dramatic events in motion. The owners of the boats and their crews were left without jobs and livelihoods. The slave owners were unable to support their slaves, and when it turned out that there was no hope of reviving the pearl industry, they began to get rid of slaves – either by selling them or throwing them out of the house one by one. As a result, more and more slaves turned to British agencies for a certificate of freedom, complaining of ill-treatment by their owners and hoping to improve their desperate situation. While male applicants had hoped that as free people they would receive fair payment for their work – the same as the free pearl divers – their hopes would remain only hopes in the face of the pearl industry's collapse and the absence of other jobs. Fortunately for them and for the entire region, during the economic crisis caused by the collapse of the pearl industry, oil production began on the Arabian coast of the Persian Gulf, and in the years that followed, many freed slaves found employment in oil companies as labourers, keepers of oilfield equipment or drivers. But at the time they were applying for freedom, their economic situation was hopeless. Women applying for the British document were afraid that the slave owners would sell their children and other family members. In this case, the certificate offered real protection, as it obliged British agents to start looking for sold slaves, even if these searches were not always successful. Many slaves believed that a British certificate of manumission made them British subjects and required British authorities to provide them with work. These assumptions were immediately disowned by British officials. The position of the Government of India was that the British manumission certificate only entitled the bearer to British assistance in the case of interference with his or her liberty.[68]

It is important to stress that the slaves who asked for British manumission represented only a small segment of the slave population. Comparing the number of applications with the estimated number of slaves in the region in the years 1936–8, that is, the years with the highest number of applications, demonstrates that only 1–2 per cent of the slave population asked for manumission. In other years this percentage was even lower. Most of the slaves remained in slavery, and there were several possible reasons for this. One of the explanations could be the lack of information about the possibility of obtaining freedom, but this wasn't the case. The British were disseminating anti-slavery proclamations in the Arabian sea ports of the Persian Gulf and Oman on a regular basis, and their content was passed orally throughout the entire region. Some petitioners who reported at British agencies were from quite remote areas in the hinterland, and yet they still knew about British manumission. There was, of course, also a deep cultural divide at play: the native and slave populations had difficulty understanding the nature of the liberation of slaves by the British authorities. Since their masters were not freeing them in accordance with Islamic law, the status of slaves manumitted by the British changed only in terms of foreign law. Most locals saw emancipation by the colonial government as no more than a purchase and referred to slaves manumitted in such a manner as 'slaves of the government' or 'slaves of the Consul'.[69]

The low demand for manumission was interpreted by British officials as indicating a comparatively low standard of living among free labourers.[70] In fact, free people who were employed in pearl oyster fishing were paid so little that they could hardly make ends meet and were permanently tied to their captains by debt. As noted earlier, there

---

[68] Manumission of Slaves, R/15/1/234 5/202 (IOR); Manumission Procedure in Kuwait, R/15/5/85 29/2 (IOR); Circular Memorandum in Cancellation of the Memorandum of 1913 Concerning Manumission of Slaves', British Residency and Consulate-General, Bushire, dated 1 August, 1938, R/15/2/1843 (IOR).

[69] Cooper, *Plantation*, 242–3.

[70] Minute, file XIII/3, Muscat, 9 August 1948, R/15/6/418 13/2 II (IOR).

were cases when free divers pretended to be slaves and demanded a British certificate of manumission in an attempt to avoid paying debts to their captains.[71]

Slave divers did not receive remuneration from the captains of fishing boats, because these were taken by their owner, but they did not have to worry about collecting them as it was the owner's responsibility. The fact that the lot of the slaves was more comfortable compared to the free labourers certainly did not act as a stimulus for slaves to run away from their masters. It should be remembered that on the north-eastern coast of the Arabian Peninsula, slavery was part and parcel of a relatively poor society that functioned in a harsh, gritty environment. The financial situation of the slave owners was not much better than that of their slaves. When the owner of a slave approached a British agent with his slave, the only indication of who was the owner and who was the slave was, usually, skin complexion. They were both attired in similar poverty and shod in similarly poor footwear.

There is evidence that the poor economic situation stimulated slaves' integration rather than dis-integration with their masters. After manumission, only very few domestic slaves decided to leave the region for their countries of origin. This observation also applied to those who had been kidnapped. British manumission procedures stipulated that a refugee kidnapped from outside the Gulf could expect the agency to help with repatriation, but the majority of African slaves preferred to stay on the Gulf coast of Arabia and Oman. Many were afraid of being re-enslaved in Africa: the route was long and dangerous, and generally they no longer had homes in their countries of origin.[72]

To return to the lens of the axionormative framework for social actions, the manumission movement of the 1930s was a case of nonconforming behaviour aimed at questioning slavery as a standard of normality and thus breaking with one of the fundamentals of the existing social order. The application for British manumission was an expression of dissent, and this dissent was not hidden from the public. The slaves reported to the British agencies in broad daylight, bypassing the local authorities – the sheikh of the town and the judge of the religious court – and this act was not publicly condemned by local communities. The ostracism that slave divers experienced in pearl oyster fisheries was not because they applied for a British manumission certificate but because they did not pay the boat masters their debts. Further evidence that the abandonment of slave status took place with public consent was the masters' reaction to their slaves' request to be manumitted. Only a few owners asked the British agencies to cancel the release of the slaves. Most accepted the departure of their slaves and even felt relieved to be rid of household members they could not feed. In fact, some of those slaves who petitioned British authorities had been previously thrown out onto the street by their owners due to the deep economic crisis.

---

[71] The Residency Agent, Sharjah, to the Political Resident in the Persian Gulf, 20th September 1928, R/15/1/204 5/161, III *Manumission of Slaves at Bahrain: Individual Cases, 28 Dec. 1924–14 Dec. 1929* (IOR).

[72] The Residency Agent, Shargah, to the Political Resident, Persian Gulf, 19 November 1925, R/15/1/208 5/168, IV (IOR). The Residency Agent, Shargah, to the Political Resident, Persian Gulf, 19 November 1925, R/15/1/208 5/168, IV (IOR).

But was the manumission movement of the 1930s Merton's 'deviant' behaviour – a sort of prelude to the change in norms – or did it remain a 'variant' behaviour that coexisted with the prescribed norm? An unequivocal answer to this question is not easy. Slaves who were petitioning the British for manumission represented only a small segment of the slave population, and the majority of them accepted their status. The institution of slavery was coming to its end gradually – and though the applicants' numbers in the 1930s were low, they were nevertheless symptomatic. On 23 May 1959, the British Resident in the Gulf sent a report to the Foreign Office on slavery in the Persian Gulf. He stressed that slavery in the common sense of the word no longer existed on the Gulf coast of Arabia and Oman. There was no open trade in slaves and there were no established slave routes in the region any longer. At the same time, the British Resident pointed out that domestic slavery was still practised in most of the sheikhdoms.[73]

---

[73] British Residency, Bahrain, to Foreign Office, 23 May 1959, FO 371/140305, No. 44 (2188). Saudi Arabia and Yemen abolished slavery in 1962 and Oman in 1970.

5

Slavery on the Central Asian Steppe in the works of Nikolai Karazin (1842–1908)

Elena Andreeva

Slavery constitutes one of the major themes woven into Nikolai Karazin's artistic panorama of Turkestan, which aspired to a realistic reflection of Central Asia but was simultaneously enmeshed in the colonial projects of the time. Karazin's Central Asia is filtered through his role as a participant, if a comparatively benevolent one, in Russian imperial conquest and colonization. Slavery not only receives direct and unflinching treatment in a number of his literary and visual works but also generates an undercurrent of fear, given the constant danger of capture by the Turkmen and clear understanding of the consequences of such capture.

A fascinating and complex character, Nikolai Nikolaevich Karazin (1842–1908) was a gifted and popular painter, writer, journalist, book illustrator, war correspondent, traveller and ethnographer. At the same time, he was a soldier who served in the Russian military campaigns in Central Asia – and later in its exploration – during the second half of the nineteenth century. During the Bukhara campaign in 1868, he demonstrated such exceptional courage that General K. P. von Kaufman, the first governor general of Turkestan, awarded him a golden sabre engraved with the words 'For courage'.[1] In 1874 and 1879, he was invited to join Russian Geographical Society scientific expeditions to the Amu-Darya with the purpose of studying possibilities for navigation and railroad construction there.[2] In 1888, he was a guest at the opening of the Transcaspian railroad and travelled along it.[3] In all, Karazin spent more than ten years in Turkestan, and his extensive experience in Central Asia and his lifelong passion for the area and its peoples illuminated his visual and literary works.

The recipient of many awards and widespread recognition during his lifetime, Karazin was an immensely popular and prolific artist who published extensively in

---

[1] P. A. Korovichenko, 'Karazin, Nikolai Nikolaevich', in *Voennaia entsiklopediia*, ed. K. I. Velichko, V. F. Novitskii, A. V. fon-Shvats, V. A. Apushkin, and G. K. fon-Shul'tsl, vol 12 (St. Petersburg: T-vo I. D. Sytina, 1913), 375.

[2] Ibid.

[3] Vladimir Shumkov, 'Zhizn', trudy i stranstvovaniia Nikolaia Karazina, pisatelia, khudozhnika, puteshestvennika', *Zvezda vostoka* 6 (1975): 224.

various Russian and foreign periodicals.[4] He created around four thousand drawings and watercolours and over one hundred paintings; he also illustrated dozens of books.[5] Karazin's visual works are kept in over twenty galleries of the former Soviet Union, including the Tretyakov Gallery in Moscow and the State Russian Museum in St. Petersburg. The complete collection of his literary works, ranging from novels and short stories to essays and travelogues, numbers twenty-five volumes. His visual works comprise large oil paintings, watercolours and sketches, his series of oil paintings depicting the conquest of Turkestan garnering him the most fame.

Several generations of the Russian literary public discovered Central Asia and its peoples through these works – it was his visions that shaped their views. He played a mediating role between Central Asia and the public's perception of it, providing a prism through which Russian readership looked at its new frontier society. Karazin's Central Asia – with its horsemen and soldiers, masters and slaves, endless and foreboding steppe – enchanted and educated several generations of devoted audiences for whom his descriptions or detailed sketches never felt tedious: in his very best works, he was 'simultaneously realistic, fantastic, and picturesque'.[6]

Despite the outstanding role he played in the cultural history of Russia in the second half of the nineteenth century, Karazin remains largely unknown to the Western public, having likewise received limited attention from Western scholars. With the exception of two books and an essay, none of Karazin's works has been translated into English thus far.[7] Sources published in Russian on his life and activities, including those related to Central Asia, are also limited.[8]

While providing specific and detailed information on slavery and slaves, Karazin also demonstrated a peculiar approach to Turkestan, the only 'real' Russian colony.[9] As with other contemporary Russian artists, Karazin 'endorsed [Russian] imperialism in certain ways, while taking issue with others'.[10] What seems to be a contradiction to the modern observer was a reflection of the maze of Russian national identity – itself a product of Russia's distinctive (but not unique) position between East and West, its geographic position and historical development culminating by the late nineteenth century in the creation of its huge Eurasian empire. This curious feature marking

[4] *Biobibliograficheskii slovar'. Khudozhniki narodov SSSR*, vol. 4, book 2 (St. Petersburg: Gumanitarnoe agenstvo Akademicheskii proekt, 1995), 208.

[5] E. V. Nogaevskaia, 'Nikolai Nikolaevich Karazin, 1842–1908', in *Russkoe iskusstvo. Ocherki o zhizni i tvorchestve khudozhnikov. Vtoraia polovina deviatnadtsatogo veka II*, ed. A. I. Leonov (Moscow: Iskusstvo, 1971), 358.

[6] A. A. Sidorov, *Russkaia grafika nachala XX veka. Ocherki istorii i teorii* (Moscow: 'Iskusstvo', 1969), 53.

[7] *Dvunogii volk*, translated by Boris Lanin as *The Two-Legged Wolf. A Romance* (University of California Libraries, 1894); *Na dalekikh okrainakh*, translated by Anthony W. Sariti as *In the Distant Confines* (Authorhouse, 2007); 'N. Karazin. Camp on the Amu Daria', translated by Elena Andreeva and Mark Woodcock, *Metamorphosis* (Spring 2010).

[8] See detailed bibliography in Elena Andreeva, *Russian Central Asia in the Works of Nikolai Karazin (1842–1908): Ambivalent Triumph* (Palgrave, 2021).

[9] Daniel Brower, *Turkestan and the Fate of the Russian Empire* (London: Routledge, 2003), XI.

[10] Jonathan Arac, 'Introduction', in *Macropolitics of Nineteenth-Century Literature: Nationalism, Exoticism, Imperialism*, ed. Jonathan Arac and Harriet Ritvo (Philadelphia: University of Pennsylvania Press, 1991), 1, quoted in Susan Layton, *Russian Literature and Empire: Conquest of the Caucasus from Pushkin to Tolstoy* (Cambridge: Cambridge University Press, 1994), 9.

Russian 'writing on the borders' has been analysed by a number of scholars, primarily in relation to the Caucasus.[11] Karazin's works about Central Asia are marked by a consistent inconsistency: on the one hand, he hails Russian imperialism in Turkestan; on the other, he is highly critical of many aspects of the Russian conquest and administration. In this context, the theme of eliminating slavery offers a powerful and emotionally charged tool to promote Russia's 'civilizing mission'. Karazin contrasts the danger of being captured and enslaved in pre-Russian Turkestan to the Russian abolitionist efforts making Turkestan a safe place for both the local people and Russian newcomers. At the same time, Karazin's images of slavery in Turkestan clearly highlight one of the main features of his art – humanism, his interest in and attention to the human being, including the native peoples of Turkestan and Iran. As pointed out by a modern Russian scholar, 'Nikolai Karazin is always concerned with the ethical underpinnings of events, so that goodness, conscience, compassion, glory and motherland constitute for him permanent notions, not subject to re-evaluation either in exotic environments or in the heat of pursuits, battles or hostilities.'[12]

Russia's conquest of Turkestan in the second half of the nineteenth century was directly related to Russian policies in Western Europe. Russia was falling ever further behind Western Europe in technological and military development. Even after the emancipation of slaves and other reforms implemented by Alexander II (r. 1855–81), 'agrarian Russia remained economically backward right up to the First World War'.[13] This internal weakness inevitably altered the international position of the empire. After its humiliating defeat in the Crimean War (1853–6), Russia's international prestige in Europe (which had been significant after the victory over Napoleonic France) plummeted and its role in European politics was dramatically reduced. To compensate for the blow to the prestige of the ruling elite, including the military leaders, Russia tried to catch up with its European rivals by imperialist expansion into Central and East Asia. Justifying Russia's conquests in Central Asia, Russian foreign minister Alexander Gorchakov claimed in the famous and oft-quoted dispatch of 1864

---

[11] See, for example, Layton, *Russian Literature and Empire*; Kalpana Sahni, *Crucifying the Orient: Russian Orientalism and the Colonization of Caucasus and Central Asia* (Bangkok: White Orchid Press, The Institute for Comparative Research in Human Culture, 1997); Monica Greenleaf and Stephen Moeller-Sally, eds., *Russian Subjects: Empire, Nation, and the Culture of the Golden Age* (Evanston, IL: Northwestern University Press, 1998); Mark Bassin, *Imperial Visions: Nationalist Imagination and Geographical Expansion in the Russian Far East, 1840–1865* (Cambridge: Cambridge University Press, 1999); Ewa M. Thompson, *Imperial Knowledge: Russian Literature and Imperialism* (Westport, CT: Greenwood Press, 2000); Harsha Ram, *The Imperial Sublime: A Russian Poetics of Empire* (Madison: University of Wisconsin Press, 2003); Izabela Kalinowska, *Between East and West: Polish and Russian Nineteenth-Century Travel to the Orient* (Rochester, NY: University of Rochester Press, 2004); Michael David-Fox, Peter Holquist and Alexander Martin, eds, *Orientalism and Empire in Russia, Kritika* Historical Studies 3 (Bloomington: Slavica, 2006); Katya Hokanson, *Writing at Russia's Border* (Toronto: University of Toronto Press, 2008); David Schimmelpenninck van der Oye, *Russian Orientalism: Asia in the Russian Mind from Peter the Great to the Emigration* (New Haven: Yale University Press, 2010);Vera Tolz, *Russia's Own Orient: The Politics of Identity and Oriental Studies in the Late Imperial and Early Soviet Periods* (Oxford: Oxford University Press, 2011).

[12] Georgii Tsvetov, Introduction to Nikolai Karazin, *Pogonia za nazhivoi* (St. Petersburg: Lenizdat, 1993), 5–7.

[13] Dietrich Geyer, *Russian Imperialism: The Interaction of Domestic and Foreign Policy 1860–1914*, translated by Bruce Little (New Haven: Yale University Press, 1987), 4.

that Russia's expansion was involuntary. According to that document, Russia had to secure its borders from a 'semi-savage' nomadic population as 'all civilized states' were destined to do, and there was no definite limit in sight to the expansion.[14] As a matter of fact, this was close to the truth, as the military expansion was an attempt to find a stable frontier and to protect trade routes from the Kazakhs.[15]

Slavery had played a significant role in Turkestan prior to the arrival of the Russians: Jeff Eden opens his book on slavery in Central Asia by pointing out that 'the region's social landscape had been shaped by a millennium of slavery'.[16] Nomads played a paramount role in the slave trade – as raiders, merchants and slave owners.[17] *Alamans* or raids into the neighbouring lands and attacking caravans provided the main means of obtaining slaves. Many slaves were ransomed by their relatives, with the rest routinely sold in Khiva and Bukhara. Turkmen men often married captured women. Slaves kept by the Turkmen were mostly used in animal herding and domestic slavery.[18] Domestic slaves had to 'watch the flocks, prepare the food, make felts, and weave carpets'.[19]

Central Asians were only allowed to enslave people who belonged to different religions, such as Shi'i Iranians or Orthodox Christian Russians. By the eighteenth century, Central Asian markets mostly drew slaves from Persia and Russia due to the increased presence of Russian and Persian subjects there.[20] Sunni *amirs* and their supporting ulama defined Sh'ism as heresy and sanctioned the enslavement of the Shi'i of Iran. That encouraged Sunni slave raids into Khorasan and eastern Mazanderan,[21] with Persian pilgrims and peasants constituting the majority of those captured.[22] In her book about slavery in Iran, Behnaz Mirzai points out that usually a group of forty to fifty nomads would plunder villages, killing the men and enslaving the women and children. Those slave-raiding expeditions into Iran were only possible due to the weak government control from Tehran in the north-eastern and eastern parts of the country.[23] It comes as no surprise, then, that Russian and Persian slaves received

---

[14] Andreas Kappeler, *The Russian Empire: A Multiethnic History*, translated by Alfred Clayton (Harlow: Longman, 2001), 194.

[15] A. S. Morrison, *Russian Rule in Samarkand 1868-1910: A Comparison with British India* (Oxford: Oxford University Press, 2008), 30. See also Scott C. Levi, *The Rise and Fall of Khoqand, 1709-1876* (Pittsburgh: University of Pittsburgh Press, 2017), 216.

[16] Jeff Eden, *Slavery and Empire in Central Asia* (Cambridge: Cambridge University Press, 2018), 1. Interestingly, a fragment of Karazin's painting entitled 'Vziatie Samarkanda 2 maia 1868 goda' (Conquest of Samarkand on 2 May 1868) appears on the cover of this book.

[17] Ibid., 6.

[18] Yu. E. Bregel, *Khorezmskie turkmeny v XIX veke* (Moscow: Izdatel'stvo vostochnoi literatury, 1961), 67, 156-7, 159-60.

[19] *The Country of the Turkomans: An Anthology of Exploration for the Royal Geographical Society*, ed. Duncan Cumming (London: Oguz Press, 1977), 68. Quoted in William Gervase Clarence-Smith, *Islam and the Abolition of Slavery* (New York: Oxford University Press, 2006), 3.

[20] Megan Dean Farah, 'Autocratic Abolitionists: Tsarist Russian Anti-slavery Campaigns', in *A Global History of Anti-slavery Politics in the Nineteenth Century*, ed. William Mulligan and Maurice Bric (New York: Palgrave Macmillan, 2013), 109.

[21] Abbas Amanat and Arash Khazeni, 'The Steppe Roads of Central Asia and the Persian Captivity Narrative of Mirza Mahmud Taqi Ashtiyani', in *Writing Travel in Central Asian History*, ed. Nile Green (Bloomington: Indiana University Press, 2014), 116.

[22] Farah, 'Autocratic Abolitionists', 109.

[23] Behnaz A. Mirzai, *A History of Slavery and Emancipation in Iran, 1800-1929* (Austin: University of Texan Press, 2017), 75.

most attention from Karazin in his Turkestan works. Though estimates of the slave numbers vary from tens of thousands to hundreds of thousands, all sources agree that the absolute majority of slaves were Iranian. By the time Khiva fell to the Russians in 1873, there were most likely around thirty thousand Iranian slaves and anywhere from dozens to hundreds of Russian slaves.[24] For example, Lieutenant Colonel Alexander Khoroshkhin, ethnographer and writer, and a participant in the Russian conquest, claims that the number of *dogmah* (Persian slaves) was 29,291 by the time of the Russian conquest.[25]

There seems to be a consensus among scholars that while slavery was used in imperial discourse in Russia as a sign of the low civilizational status of Central Asia, abolition of slavery was presented as one of the justifications for the conquest and as a part of Russia's 'civilizing mission' there. For example, according to B. D. Hopkins, Orthodox Christian Russian slaves in Central Asia were 'the most visible enslaved religious group' only because the Russian government used their captivity 'for political and propaganda purposes'.[26] As pointed out by Moritz Deutschmann, a concern about freeing slaves and captives had a long tradition in the history of imperial Russia, for example, in Russian contacts with the Crimean Tatars and the Ottoman Empire. Frequent mentioning of the Turkmen slave trade and its alleged shutdown by the Russians after the conquest of Khiva allowed Russian observers to formulate a sense of cultural superiority.[27] The abolition of slavery in Turkestan was, however, inconsistent and produced only 'mixed results'.[28] On the one hand, Russian administrators in Turkestan employed anti-slavery rhetoric even if they lacked the ability and zeal to implement it.[29] On the other hand, as pointed out by Eden, Russian abolitionism in Central Asia primarily focused on liberation of Russian slaves, not the extermination of slavery in general. Meanwhile, the total number of Russian slaves in Central Asia was 'miniscule compared to the total number of Iranian slaves'. The Khivans had released all the Russian slaves before the city fell to the Russians in 1873 – twenty-one, according to Eden – but anywhere between thirty thousand to sixty thousand mainly Iranian nationals were still enslaved there. It took a major slave uprising to force Kaufman to abolish slavery. His decree, however, was either not followed through vigorously enough by the Russians or simply ignored – enforcing it was especially difficult because the slave trade was decentralized and widely dispersed.[30]

One story by Karazin in which a Persian slave boy plays a key role is entitled 'Atlar'. It reads as a hymn to the Russian conquest presented in an exaggerated, almost grotesque,

---

[24] See Bregel, *Khorezmskie turkmeny*, 159–60; Eden, *Slavery and Empire*, 26–9, 189; Clarence-Smith, *Islam and the Abolition of Slavery*, 14; Farah, 'Autocratic Abolitionists', 109.

[25] Alexander Pavlovich Khoroshkhin, *Sbornik statei, kasaiushchikhsia do Turkestanskogo kraia* (St. Petersburg: Tip. i khromolit. A. Transhelia, 1876), 486.

[26] B. D. Hopkins, 'Race, Sex and Slavery: "Forced Labour" in Central Asia and Afghanistan in the Early 19th Century', *Modern Asian Studies* 42, no. 4 (2008): 636–43, quoted in Farah, 'Autocratic Abolitionists', 109.

[27] Moritz Deutschmann, *Iran and Russian Imperialism: The Ideal Anarchists, 1800-1914* (London: Routledge, 2016), 67–8.

[28] Eden, *Slavery and Empire*, 2.

[29] Farah, 'Autocratic Abolitionists', 110.

[30] Eden, *Slavery and Empire*, 5–7, 204–7.

way. The story is told through the eyes of Mat-Niaz, a Persian slave, who became the first adviser to the emir of Khiva through his outstanding intellectual abilities and high moral qualities. The background of the story is the Russian conquest of Khiva in 1873. Through magic visions presented by the long dead Atlar-mullah, a 'great hero and keeper of the steppes' freedom', the ten-year-old boy can foresee the futility of fighting against the Russians and the great benefits of their future conquests. Inevitable as fate itself, amid a glow of silver light, a great hero arrives from the north riding a white horse: 'In one hand he holds thunder, in another – a green branch covered in early dew. Before him, armed men fall; behind him unarmed men rise up ... blood flows before him; blood turns to flowers and golden bread behind him.' As an old man, Mat-Niaz recognized this vision in the approaching Russian troops and immediately suggested to his master that they surrender and send a peaceful delegation headed by Mat-Niaz himself to the intruders, since the 'sword is useless here ... [t]he will of Allah is done'.[31] He is strongly opposed by the military commander Mat-Murad, his old and treacherous rival, who tries in vain to organize resistance and even to kill his fleeing compatriots with his own hands. When the prediction of Atlar becomes real and the defenders of Khiva are running 'like a flock of sheep', Mat-Niaz brings the legend to its conclusion: 'God grant, he told him, that the dead sands irrigated in blood will come to life as flowering gardens.'[32] Bringing in religious language is another trope to reinforce the inevitability of the Russian conquest. According to Januarius McGahan, a famous American journalist and war correspondent, both Mat-Niaz and Mat-Murad (an Afghan slave, according to McGahan) were ministers of state to the khan of Khiva. While Mat-Niaz belonged to the 'peace party' and was friendly towards the Russians, Mat-Murad 'had a strong hatred of the Russians'.[33] The same two competing characters, the benevolent 'divan-beg' Mat-Niaz and the malicious Mat-Murad, appear in Karazin's novel *S severa na iug* (From the North to the South) in a similar setting: Khiva on the eve of Russian conquest. In the novel, Mat-Niaz again cooperates with the advancing Russians.[34]

In the story 'Atlar', the character of the boy is rendered with undisguised affection, and the descriptions of his artistic abilities and wisdom are brimming with admiration. As pointed out by Eden, in the confrontation between Qajar Iran and the Turkmen over the issue of kidnappings and ransoms, 'Russian sympathies tended overwhelmingly to fall on the side of the Iranians'.[35] At the beginning of the story, Mat-Niaz is described as a good looking boy of ten, 'slender, black-eyed, with a straight and thin nose and a beautifully shaped mouth, not of the Mongol type at all'.[36] Mat-Niaz was sold to the owner of an acting school, a 'kind and gentle old man', who taught the boys to dance,

---

[31] N. N. Karazin, 'Atlar', in *Nedavnee byloe: Povesti i rasskazy. Polnoe sobranie sochinenii*, vol. 15 (St. Petersburg: Izdatel'stvo P. P. Soikina, 1905), 109, 117, 141.

[32] Ibid., 142, 143.

[33] Januarius Aloysius MacGahan, *Campaigning on the Oxus, and the Fall of Khiva*, 2nd edn (London: Sampson Low, Marston, Low, and Searle, 1874), 289. See also Khoroshkhin, *Sbornik statei*, 488.

[34] N. N. Karazin, *S severa na iug. Polnoe sobranie sochinenii*, vol. 7 (St. Petersburg: Izdaniie P. P. Soikina, 1905), 446–58, 479.

[35] Eden, *Slavery and Empire*, 14.

[36] Karazin, 'Atlar', 111–12.

sing and play musical instruments. Mat-Niaz turned out to be a talented actor and spontaneous performer who won the heart of the emir of Khiva with his creative and emotional performance. When the emir visited the school to observe a performance by the students, Mat-Niaz appeared onstage with golden chains on his hands and feet:

> His poses and facial expression showed deep suffering. Everybody, including his old teacher, was surprised. Then the boy began to sing:
> When the wind roams freely across the steppe, it brings coolness and freshness to the tired traveller. If you block its way, the sun will burn everything with its heat …
> Set free the life-saving wind of the steppe.
> When a rose blossoms, filling the air with its fragrance, if the sun is blocked and the rose shuttered in the darkness of night … it will fade … its petals will drop … its fragrance will disappear …
> Give light to the beautiful rose.
> When a fast horse cheerfully carries you on a faraway road, if you drive it [the horse] day and night, drive it without rest, the horse will weaken, its iron legs will bend, its tired heart will stop, and it will drop like a corpse – to the rider's misfortune.
> Let the fast horse rest …
> When joy and happiness play in a person's heart, when even in his labours he finds comfort, if you bind him·in chains, his festive cheer goes silent, his soul tires from forced toil, the human in him is extinguished and only a dumb beast of burden will remain.
> Take off his chains in the name of merciful Allah.[37]

As the old teacher did not know what to think and expected trouble from his guest, the emir ordered the boy's chains be removed. The boy was immediately transformed:

> His eyes were shining with joy and cheerfulness, his lithe, strong body trembled, a bright smile appeared on his face. He took a deep breath, stretched and happily touched the strings [of his saz (a musical instrument)]: 'Eternal glory to him who has granted peace and freedom. God will give him joy and happiness, victory over his enemies, consolation in his family. Glory to him who granted peace …'
> Mat-Niaz threw down his instrument and started to dance … His was a dance unlike anything the guests had ever seen. Their eyes could not keep up with his quick and graceful movements. His face was burning with sincere joy, and when he finished his dance and sat on the carpet, tired and breathless, applause broke out.[38]

This imaginative performance, the hymn to freedom sung by the slave boy, changed the course of his life. The emir brought the boy to his palace, where he became a close

---

[37] Ibid., 133–4.
[38] Ibid., 134–5.

friend to the emir's son. A talented improvisational poet, a wise and kind-hearted adviser, he gained their respect and, gradually, great influence at court.[39]

Persia, 'his mother's motherland', appears in a nostalgic vision presented to the boy by Atlar-mullah one night. Mat-Niaz is also shown a picture of a brutal raid against a Persian village and how one of the Turkmen raiders carries a young and beautiful woman attached to his saddle: 'So young, so beautiful, if she were older, she would have looked exactly like his [deceased] mother.'[40] It is not clear from the story who Mat-Niaz's father could have been: since his mother was a Persian slave, his father must have also been a slave since the boy himself is referred to as a 'Persian slave boy'. If his mother had been a concubine or wife of a local free man, the boy would have been one of the fortunate who were granted 'equal rights as freeborn citizens'.[41] It is also possible, of course, that Karazin was unaware of such details, and making his hero a Persian slave was simply well suited to the framework of the story. In the story, as the boy is whispering 'mother', he is shown another vision of yet another brutal attack on a peaceful village, followed by a horrible scene of beheadings of captives in a city, presumably Khiva or Bukhara, with the severed heads displayed on poles. The above-mentioned glamourous appearance of the Russian warrior immediately follows, presented as a just avenger of the brutal deeds of the Turkmen in Iran.[42]

A hauntingly attractive image of Iran also appears in a song performed for Mat-Niaz by a wandering improvisational poet. This song, one and a half pages long, is about a rose from Khorasan (the province in Iran) – coincidentally the province suffering most from Turkmen raids. Though the sources of most folk songs in Karazin's works are referenced, no source is mentioned for this song. It is possible the author composed it himself – considering how seamlessly its style and language fit into the narrative. Once more, in this song, the desolate Turkmen steppe is juxtaposed to the beauty and fertility of Iran, making the enslavement of Iranians all the more repugnant. The song opens as follows:

A warm and scented wind of Khorasan brought a seedlet into the barren desert wild.

A cold and distant wind of the north brought a drop of water [to the desert] and sprinkled the dry seed.

Life awoke within it, and a young, green little eye peeped out from the sand at the light.

The sprout became a slender branchy rosebush, magnificent roses blossomed on it ...

Glory to you, Wind of Khorasan!

But how long will you be able to blossom here, rosebush, here in this harsh land, where the sun will burn you ...

[39] Ibid., 125–38.
[40] Ibid., 115–16.
[41] Mirzai, *History of Slavery*, 77. See Introduction, Chapter 1 and Chapter 3 of this book for more information on this Islamic manumission practice.
[42] Karazin, 'Atlar', 116–17.

How long will your bright flowers be pouring fragrance into the air …
A burning yellow sand dune will move and cover you.

You are not strong enough to fight against the sun and the sandstorm.

Your weak roots will find no water – you will not be able to drink; your roses will fade, your seeds have no time to ripen … A stranger, a traveller, you will perish here without a trace. And nobody will remember you …

So the rough local children of the desert were telling the rosebush: the grey *dzhizgan* [a local desert plant], saxaul, and thorns …

The rosebush then sings beautiful songs about a nightingale and the hymns it sings to the creator, about two doves and their love duet, about a falcon and his song of war. The beauty of this song enchanted even his enemies:

A burning ray of sun swung like a sword over the daring stranger but upon hearing his song, froze in its course; a heavy sand dune moved – and stopped, charmed by the song … A ferocious storm came, but the magic song resounded louder than its howling … so the merciless destroyer submitted …

Glory to you, child of Khorasan, favoured by God![43]

This poem includes several staples of Persian poetry: a rose, a nightingale and a dove. Its message about beauty prevailing over all threats has a universal appeal. At the same time, it can be seen as a way to place the Russian conquest into the Romantic context of liberating beauty from brutality, possibly Persians from the Turkmen.

The fate of many Iranian slaves freed in Khiva by the Russian conquest turned out to be tragic. Several parties of those Iranians were summarily slaughtered by Turkmen on their way back to Iran. Eden mentions two parties of seven hundred to eight hundred people killed by Turkmen fleeing Khiva after the Russian victory, another group of five hundred people travelling along the Atrek River pillaged and massacred by Teke Turkmen, and finally, five thousand former slaves murdered by some seventeen thousand armed Yomut horsemen. Since Central Asian tribes were not known to slaughter Iranians *en masse*, several factors must have contributed to such an atrocity: the Turkmen were desperate and outraged 'as they realized that the markets and infrastructure for their trade in slaves were collapsing with the Russian advance. What is more, they could see the very cargo they had gone to such lengths to secure literally walking back to freedom before their eyes.' Eden concludes, 'Having dehumanized their Iranian victims for decades already, it is no great surprise that the Turkmens' anger should have found its outlet in astonishing acts of inhumanity.'[44] One of those tragic episodes is documented by Karazin in the drawing entitled *Osvobozhdennye raby-persiiane, vyrezannye turkmenami* ('Liberated Persian Slaves Slain by Turkmen') (Figure 5.1).[45] Karazin's drawing shows dead bodies sprawled over

[43] Ibid., 120–2.
[44] Eden, *Slavery and Empire*, 189–95.
[45] https://rus-turk.livejournal.com/405215.html (accessed 21 November 2018).

THE KHIVA EXPEDITION : LIBERATED PERSIAN SLAVES SLAIN BY TURKOMANS.

Figure 5.1 *Osvobozhdennye raby-persiiane, vyrezannye turkmenami* ('Liberated Persian Slaves Slain by Turkmen').

Source: The *Illustrated London News*, 15 November 1873, 456.

the steppe, some contorted in poses of agony, with wolves and birds gathering around them. Those in the foreground all belong to men, several of them naked, probably robbed of their clothes. The work seems to emanate pain, with the still bodies marking the tragic route that led home. No living human is visible in the steppe. The wheel of a broken carriage in the foreground and a domed silhouette of what must be a tomb in the background intensify the macabre atmosphere of the scene.

In addition to this drawing, Karazin incorporates this or a similar tragic event into his novel *S severa na iug*. One of the main characters, Stepan, after having endured every imaginable and unimaginable hardship in pursuit of his beloved Marina, failed to bring her back and joined a caravan of emancipated Persian slaves. He was 'the only non-Persian' in that huge caravan, and from Iran, he planned to walk on to Jerusalem in a holy pilgrimage. In the novel, no freed Persians who chose to walk back home directly through the territories controlled by the Turkmen were destined to reach their homeland safely. Tekin and other Turkmen gathered together, 'frustrated and angry with the new [Russian] order: "Since we cannot own them [any longer], then let them belong to no one; look at them, dogs, free people [now]; they are even laughing at us, their masters, and threaten us with this alien, Russian force. Just wait and see!" ' They slaughtered the whole caravan, sparing nobody, with Stepan also becoming their victim.[46]

---

[46] Karazin, *S severa na iug*, 514–16.

Karazin presents slavery in Central Asia as a sign of backwardness, where the perils of travel, lack of communication and general lawlessness made any journey there a risky enterprise which often ended tragically. The constant threat of these dangers permeates his literary and visual works. For example, he opens his novel *Na dalekikh okrainakh* with a striking description of the perilous journey from Orenburg to Tashkent, which included crossing the dreaded Karakum desert. The first scenes of the novel, accompanied by a drawing, are terrifying: dreadful sands, wild animals, the remnants of a horse-drawn carriage and the headless corpse of an earlier traveller who fell victim to the *barantachis*, the local bandits.[47] As we learn later, that merchant's wife was captured and sold into slavery. Two travellers are seized with a fear that a similar destiny awaits them: 'Alone, in the deadest part of the sand desert. Help is coming from nowhere.'[48] Those two men, Batogov and Perlovich, appropriate the money they find in the abandoned carriage.

Batogov is later captured and endures a long period of enslavement.[49] While taking his suffering in captivity rather stoically, and with dignity, he encounters another slave – Rakhil, the wife of the man from whose abandoned carriage he and his travelling companion had stolen money. The rough, cynical man is so moved by her suffering, and probably reproached by his own conscience, that he kisses her dirty foot, covered in puss and scabs, and promises that she will be saved 'in two moons'.[50] But just when Batogov finally breaks free, he makes a fatal mistake: he goes directly to Perlovich and tells him the story of Rakhil. He is even grateful for his suffering in captivity, he claims, since only there he met the woman: 'Pale, very thin, just skin and bones, exhausted to the last degree, she looked like a moving corpse. ... If only you could see her.' Batogov has already devised a plan for Rakhil's rescue: a local man will go and arrange for her ransom, so at first they will need 5,000 roubles, and then 'we of course have to support her'. He adds, however, 'You must agree that all that [the stolen money] *belongs to her*. Well, let's say she doesn't need it all, she doesn't need to know about that money.' Batogov is so excited about the rescue that he naively fails to properly evaluate Perlovich's reaction to the news. Perlovich is presented as one of the shockingly 'uncivilized' Russian newcomers who will stop at nothing in order to enrich themselves. Unwilling to part with any of his money, he kills Batogov by offering him a cigar laced with a fatal dose of opium.[51] The end of the novel is profoundly sad: Rakhil keeps looking north with an unconditional faith in the man who promised to rescue her. Even when she dies in misery and despair, she is still facing north.[52]

A drawing entitled 'Plennitsy. Epizod iz nedavnego proshlogo Turkestanskoi zhizni' ('Captive Women. An Episode from the Recent Past of Turkestan') demonstrates the merciless fate of those overcome by local bandits.[53] Two women are lying on bare

[47] N. N. Karazin, *Na dalekikh okrainakh. Polnoe sobranie sochinenii*, vol. 1 (St. Petersburg: Izdanie P. P. Soikina, 1905), 3–7.
[48] Ibid., 5.
[49] Ibid., 86–8.
[50] Ibid., 213–14.
[51] Ibid., 263–6.
[52] Ibid., 270.
[53] *Niva* 37 (1895): 876.

ground in the centre. One is dressed in dark clothes and seems older and quietly sad, as if she has given up all hope. She is resting in a half-reclined position, leaning on her arm. Another figure likely belongs to a younger woman wearing a light outfit, with her head of light hair uncovered, who has thrown herself on the ground. Her face is turned towards the ground as her hands squeeze her head in a gesture of unspeakable despair. Their four Turkmen captors are resting close to them: unlike the women, they are relaxing on a carpet, smoking and smiling, while looking at the chests which they have probably just looted. The suffering of the women can be illustrated by the words of another Russian woman, Katerina, a character from a short story by Karazin. Having been captured on her way from Kazala to Petro-Alexandrovsk, she escaped miraculously and later recalls her sufferings:

> They dragged me out of the wagon by force … pushed and pulled me … then loaded me on a horse, tied up like a sack, and drove into the steppe, away from the road. Only God knows how I suffered during that drive, how I survived … I lost my memory, my body was all crippled … I could not tell the difference between day and night any longer.[54]

The vivid scene with the captured women published in *Niva* in 1895 is accompanied by a short explanation, according to which travel through

> our vast Central Asian territories is currently completely safe and comfortable. It is even hard to imagine that no more than twenty years ago, such a trip was very dangerous: whole caravans used to perish from heat, lack of water and robbers' attacks. This drawing depicts such a tragic episode from the past: bandits attacked a carriage, killed the men and captured two women.[55]

On the one hand, this scene is created by a talented and compassionate artist; on the other hand, the note points out the important improvement brought about by the Russian conquest.

When Karazin travels from Orenburg to Tashkent two decades later, the picture is dramatically different and the journey by then is not only comfortable but also safe and pleasant. In the past, the travel from Orenburg to Tashkent took at least one month; it was the traveller's responsibility to carry everything necessary with him and to be ready to defend himself. But this time, he claims, it 'only' takes two weeks, and he suggests that travellers make sure to have a reliable carriage and pack only tea, sugar, wine and some snacks. The road in the Karakum has become excellent and well-travelled, with sand dunes barely presenting an obstacle any longer. New wells have been dug between the old stations, and new stations have been built. Now there is an 'abundance' of wells, with water a bit salty sometimes, but often the water is excellent, 'cold as ice and clear as crystal'. All the new stations have been built on such wells.[56]

---

[54] N. N. Karazin, 'Staryi Dzhul'dash i ego syn Mamet', in *U kostra: Ocherki i rasskazy. Polnoe sobranie sochinenii*, vol. 12 (St. Petersburg: Izdanie P. P. Soikina, 1905), 168.
[55] *Niva* 37 (1895): 889.
[56] N. N. Karazin, *Ot Orenburga do Tashkenta. Putevoi ocherk* (St. Petersburg: German Goppe, 1886), 4.

Добыча съ берега: Разбойники на берегу Каспійскаго моря. Рис. Н. Каразинъ, грав. І. Кохъ.

Figure 5.2 *Dobycha s berega. Razboiniki na beregy Kaspiiskogo moria* ('Loot from the Shore. Bandits on the Caspian Shore').

Source: *Niva* 16 (1876): 275.

The Caspian Sea and its eastern shore had also been unsafe before the Russian conquest and the construction of the Transcaspian railroad. Parties of Turkmen both traded with the Russians arriving from Astrakhan on boats and captured them when possible. An account and a drawing entitled *Dobycha s berega* ('Loot from the Shore') narrate such a catastrophic episode (Figure 5.2).[57] The text incorporates a recollection by a Russian man, whose father had been the owner of a successful fishing company. The storyteller was a young man then, under thirty. He came to the eastern shore of the Caspian as a member of a boat crew of thirteen men, including his father, and accompanied by his wife Maria for fishing and trading with the Turkmen. But they were betrayed by a Khivan man, whom they had taken into the boat out of pity, and captured by Turkmen.[58] The drawing shows a woman in a torn shirt with her hair loose – she is screaming and struggling with her kidnapper who is holding her behind him on horseback. The looted goods are carried away by the bandits and loaded onto

---

[57] *Niva* 16 (1876): 273–7.
[58] Ibid., 276–7.

animals as the Russian boat is burning in the background.[59] According to the man telling his story, he and his comrades suffered terribly on their march through the sands; out of thirteen men, seven died on the way; the rest were sold separately in Chimbai. They were never to meet again; his father died in slavery; Maria 'got herself employed as the wife of a mullah near Khiva and produced a number of dark kids'. The man himself grew old in slavery, endured beatings and other hardships and was finally freed when the Russians conquered Khiva. The concluding paragraph of the essay proclaims:

> Only now, when Russian troops have occupied this region, when in Mangyshlak and Krasnovodsk permanent fortifications have been built, in order to guard the peace in dead Ust'-Iurt, can we hope that such episodes will happen less and less often, and possibly stop altogether; that the steppe wind and the green sea wave will cover with sand and wash away the last traces of the bloody deeds of the desert knights.[60]

A new era of safety and communication between the metropolis and the new colony of Turkestan undoubtedly opened with the construction of the railroads, as proudly emphasized by Karazin. To Russians and Western Europeans in the nineteenth century, railways were a powerful symbol of technological progress, colonial power and the superiority of the West.[61] Yet military and strategic priorities determined construction: instead of building a direct connection across an easy steppe from Orenburg to Tashkent, the first line started from Krasnovodsk on the Caspian across extremely hostile desert. One of the goals of this construction was to subdue the Turkmen.[62] Karazin was invited as a guest to the opening of the railroad in 1888 – he travelled along it and reflected its history in drawings and the beautiful watercolour album *Zakaspiiskaia zheleznaia doroga* ('The Transcaspian Railroad').[63] In his letters about the trip, the artist pictured the railroad as transforming the life of the area: the plain, 'gloomy, swarming with robberies' in the past, now looks 'comfortable and cultured', with 'the smoke of well-being and peace' rising from Turkmen felt tents. 'Turkmen transition from their free predatory life to peaceful agriculture', the wheel 'replacing the primitive mode of transport on pack animals'; all lead to cheerful prosperity.[64]

Interestingly, the hierarchy within the system of slavery was used to emphasize the worthiness of the Russians who had liberated the slaves and made Turkestan a safe region. This hierarchy ranks Russian slaves as the most prized: an important

---

[59] Ibid., 275.

[60] Ibid., 277.

[61] Brower, *Turkestan and the Fate of the Russian Empire*, 79–81; Jeff Sahadeo, *Russian Colonial Society in Tashkent, 1865-1923* (Bloomington: Indiana University Press, 2010), 120.

[62] Morrison, *Russian Rule in Samarkand*, 34–5.

[63] This album is kept at the State Museum of Oriental Art in Moscow, but its cover and most of its paintings have been published in *Russia's Unknown Orient: Orientalist Paintings 1850-1920*, ed. P. Wageman and Inessa Kouteinikova (Groningen: Groninger Museum, 2010), 56–9.

[64] N. N. Karazin, 'Na puti v Indiiu', *Niva* 38 (1888): 943.

official in Khiva, 'considered Russians to be the best workers; he relied on them and trusted them more than anybody'[65] There is a hierarchy among the slave masters as well, with a generous and rich official in Khiva being a relatively benevolent and generous master, poor Karakalpak fisherman scoring somewhere in the middle and nomad Turkmen being the worst possible masters.[66] According to a comprehensive illustrated volume on 'Russian Central Asia' for which Karazin contributed a number of drawings and some articles, Turkmen were exceptionally merciless towards their captives and slaves:

> Captives and slaves were subjected to cruel treatment, their life was in the hands of their owners; for the smallest fault, or just at a whim, a slave was subjected to harsh torments, or even killed. Slaves were maintained no better than dogs. At night they were shackled in heavy chains or their feet were chained to a heavy log, so that they would not escape. … The position of female slaves was no better than that of male slaves; they were at the total disposal of their mistress, who could exhaust them as much as she wished with unbearable labour and beatings. A female slave's position was not improved if she became the mother of her owner's child. Both her child and she herself retained the status of slaves.[67]

Turkmen women are sometimes shown as routinely cruel. A brief episode in *Na dalekikh okrainakh* reminds readers about Russian characters in Karazin's works who believe the only language the native people understand is force. When the exhausted Rakhil pauses from her hard work of pounding grains for a second in order to wipe sweat from her face, her mistress, one of her master's wives, yells at her immediately: her 'shrill and malicious voice screamed from the tent: – Hey, you, wretched nag, don't you want to quit completely? All you want to do is to sleep, lazy scum. And another voice added – They only work as long as you beat them. I've almost broken my hands on *mine*.'[68] This dialogue takes place most likely between several wives, who were given women captured by their husbands as their slave servants. 'Women here are all raging, like fierce tigers,' confirms Stepan about Turkmen women after his fellow Russian slave examined his back with the marks of severe beatings.[69]

One more aspect of slavery presented by Karazin in his works is related to the institution of *bachas*. It also highlights his talent for showing deep human emotions in regard to the local people and their sufferings. While the word *bacha* means 'a child' or

---

[65] Karazin, *S severa na iug*, 450.
[66] Ibid., 419–20, 434–5, 459–63, 479–81.
[67] *Zhivopisnaia Rossiia. Otechestvo nashe v ego zemel'nom, istoricheskom, plemennom, ekonomicheskom i bytovom znachenii*, vol. 10, *Sredniia Aziia*, ed. P. P. Semenov (St. Petersburg: Tipografiia M. O. Vol'f, 1885), 15–16. According to the Shari'a, such a child was considered freeborn, and the mother's position would usually significantly improve. She was to be freed immediately after her master's death. Most likely, as Karazin suggests, this custom was often not followed by the Turkmen. See Introduction, Chapter 1 and Chapter 3 of this book for more detailed discussions of Islamic manumission practices.
[68] Karazin, *Na dalekikh okrainakh*, 187.
[69] Karazin, *S severa na iug*, 487.

'a young person', the institution of *bachas* in Central Asia included male dancers dressed as females performing in tea houses or private houses. The word also applies to young boys used for sexual slavery or child prostitution. Both meanings were closely related and often overlapping. Many rulers in Central Asia had *bachas* as companion-servants, usually slaves. In his drawings entitled 'Starshii bek kerkinskii i ego bacha' ('The Senior Beg [senior chieftain] of Kerki and his *Bacha*'), an old bearded man is reclining on a carpet leaning against a pillow, with his gaze cast down, looking at the water pipe held by his *bacha*.[70] His facial expression is sad, perhaps contemplative. As the young boy brings the pipe stem to the old man's mouth, he is rather too casually resting his hand on his master's shoulder. This gesture, along with the boy's long hair showing from under his cap, an earring in his ear and his expression of sombre confidentiality as he looks directly into his master's face all imply intimacy between them. It is hard even to estimate the age of the boy, since his face, possibly in make-up, seems too old for his body, which looks small next to the overwhelmingly large figure of the old man on the foreground. The artist, compassionate by nature and sensitive to the mistreatment of the most unprotected, was able to create in this drawing an air of penetrating sadness. Though not as openly revealing as the famed painting by Vereshchagin entitled 'Selling a Slave Boy', it nevertheless seems to convey the same tragic reality of widespread and accepted paedophilia among men of means in Central Asia (and much of the Middle East).[71]

Surprisingly, Karazin describes the beg of Kerki in strongly approving terms as a dignified man and a just ruler to his people. Those observations are based on several personal encounters as well as what the artist learned about the beg. There is a discrepancy between the visual image and the narrative, between the old paedophile in the drawing and the old noble ruler in the narrative. In the narrative, the brother of the Kerki beg who comes to greet the members of the Russian expedition is also accompanied by his *bacha*, 'something similar to the page and sword-bearer, a handsome boy in an unusually large pink turban'.[72]

Karazin describes or at least mentions *bacha* performances in many of his Central Asian works: those descriptions leave little doubt as to the nature of the erotic excitement aroused by the provocative dances of the unfortunate boys. For example, in *Na dalekikh okrainakh*, such a performance by a star dancer in a camp is described vividly and in detail. In the evening, a crowd gathered around carpets spread on the ground:

> A child is standing there ... is this really a child? Large, black eyes are looking with too much expression, in them something un-childlike is seen: impudent and ingratiating, an almost royal pride and dog's abasement glide past each other and alternate in this intent gaze. Those are the eyes of a tiger cub, but at the same

---

[70] *Vsemirnaia Illiustratsiia* 596 (1880): 480.

[71] This heartbreaking painting has become the cover of Brower's book, *Turkestan and the Fate of the Russian Empire*, and has been included in the book *Russia's Unknown Orient: Orientalist Painting 1850–1920*, 89.

[72] N. N. Karazin, 'Samarskaia uchenaia ekspeditsiia', *Vsemirnaia Illiustratsiia* 596 (1880): 471.

time – of a 'public woman'. His beautifully outlined mouth is smiling, revealing bright white teeth. This child is wearing only a long red shirt reaching the ground; his feet and arms to the elbows are exposed. He is standing motionless, with his arms along his sides; from under a red cap embroidered with gold hung almost to his knees long black braids, decorated with gold rattles and cut glass.

... This child is a *bacha*. His name is *Suffi*. This name is known for several hundred *versts*[73] around.

In the front corner [of the carpets] four musicians were seated.

... The musicians at once started to play their instruments. Suffi roused and slowly, as if gliding, started to move around the circle.

... At first the dance consisted of smooth movements of his arms and head; his bare slender legs stepped lightly on the soft carpets; then his movements were becoming faster and faster, the circle spiraled smaller, and finally Suffi was in the centre again. The music stopped. Suffi, without moving his feet, suddenly made a full turn and bent over backwards, almost touching the ground with his head. His whole body was curved into an arch; his black braids spread on the carpets, and every curve of his chest, belly and thighs were clearly visible through the thin fabric of his shirt.

The whole crowd exploded in deafening screams. ... Suffi slowly rose and, slightly reeling, wiping sweat, slowly walked away out of the circle. When he was walking through the crowd, the most flowery compliments were showered on him; dozens of hands were grabbing him, his hands were being caught and kissed as he passed by; even the flaps of his shirt were being kissed.[74]

A very similar narrative is included in Karazin's account of the Amu-Darya expedition in 1879.[75]

Karazin's multimedia works present a vivid picture of slavery in Turkestan, concentrating mainly on Russian and Iranian slaves. Karazin presents us with not only valuable details about slave life unavailable in other sources but also insights into Russian perceptions of these slaves, their cultures and the region in general. On the one hand, the works of Karazin consistently show a very human empathy for the underdog, in this case for the victims of Turkmen brutality. On the other hand, there is a sense that Iranian slaves are being projected through a romanticized lens, and the lamenting of their sad lot in Turkestan might be interpreted as a kind of colonial reflex – one much studied in critical literature – in which representatives of colonial empires tend to side with the ethnic and religious minorities of the regions being colonized. Whether consciously or not, Karazin is inclined to ally himself with the Iranians against the Turkmen majority, the very party resisting Russian conquest. Yet on an artistic level, Karazin's world works as a persuasive illustration of the benevolent impact of the Russian conquest and administration, emphasizing the shared humanity between peoples.

---

[73] *Verst*, a Russian unit of length, equal to 1.067 kilometres.
[74] Karazin, *Na dalekikh okrainakh*, 143–5.
[75] N. N. Karazin, 'Samarskaia uchenaia ekspeditsiia', *Vsemirnaia Illiustratsiia* 581 (1880): 184.

6

Mercy releases: Manumission practices in Tetouan, Morocco (1860–1960)

Josep Lluís Mateo Dieste

Introduction

Slavery occupies a marginalized and masked space in Morocco's collective memory despite vigorous new research by Moroccan and international scholars and other signs of growing awareness, such as the United Nations Educational Scientific and Cultural Organization's (UNESCO's) recognition in 2019 of Gnawa music, of slave origin, as part of the world's cultural heritage and the success of the Essaouira Gnawa music festival. Campaigns by anti-racism activist groups such as 'Je ne m'appelle pas azzi'[1] argue that the un-remembered slaveholding past is part and parcel of the present, reappearing in many forms, from the persistence of unfair conditions for domestic workers to the weight of stereotypes about darker-skinned people. Morocco's historical blindspot for slavery can be partly explained by the gradual nature of the extinction of the practice, a process drawn out at least into the mid-twentieth century. Enslavement persisted in silence, in the hidden life of the household, with individual acts of manumission performed over time.

The aim of this chapter is to rescue this last phase of manumission from oblivion, offering tools for reflection and recognizing the experience of those who lived through it – an ongoing process in many cases. I will place a magnifying glass on one case study I have been working on for the last decade: the city of Tetouan in north-western Morocco and its environs. The city of Tetouan is located 40 kilometres from the Strait of Gibraltar, at the foot of the mountainous area of Jebala; it became a refuge for Muslims and Jews expelled from the Peninsula between 1492 and 1609. The city has retained its Andalusian character through to the present day, although the Jewish population gradually left Tetouan after the creation of the state of Israel. The establishment of the Spanish Protectorate in Morocco (1912–56) kept in power the Tetouani urban

---

[1] 'Je ne m'appelle pas azzi. Une campagne nationale pour lutter contre le racisme ordinaire au Maroc'('I'm not called azzi. A Nationwide Campaign against Everyday Racism in Morocco'), *Libération* (18 March 2014).

bourgeoisie, the very social class that bought slave labour into their homes. The case of Tetouanis is of special interest for the study of the final stage of slavery in the context of changing power relationships in a society under colonial influence.

Sources analysed in this chapter include legal and notary documents on slavery in Tetouan from the mid-nineteenth to the first half of the twentieth centuries and Tetouanese oral sources, mainly former slave-owning families. For this group, freeing slaves was a moral and religious act, recorded in their wills (*wasiya*). Granting emancipation conferred religious merit on the emancipator before death, an assurance of a place in paradise. The records of these acts also allow us to extract valuable information on the personal characteristics and life-paths of these slaves, mainly women, and their role in the urban society of the Maghreb. For all these reasons, I will dwell on the detail and richness of the notary and *ḥabūs* (charitable endowment) data, complemented by Spanish colonial archives and ethnographic fieldwork carried out among Tetouanese families who owned slaves.

While historiographic studies on slavery in Islam and the Arab world are legion, many lacunae remain, such as the rituals and mechanisms of liberation, the moral and religious motivations of the emancipators and the new reality faced by freed women and men.

Since Mohamed Ennaji's foundational 1994 study, *Soldats, domestiques et concubines*, works on slavery in Morocco have multiplied, especially in recent years.[2] Chouki El Hamel's monograph opened new debates on the origin and condition of slaves in Morocco, especially the Bukhara troops recruited by Sultan Mawlay Ismail.[3] Ethnographic studies have also been published on the post-colonial situation of slave and subaltern populations in the southern oases, known as *ḥarrāṭīn*. The social conditions these agricultural workers lived in were very different from those of domestics in urban bourgeois Tetouanese homes. Despite this growing interest in the study of slavery, local historians of Tetouan have not dealt deeply with the issue of contemporary slavery in the city, with the exception of Jaafar Bel Hach Soulami,[4] although the classic works of the colonial period contain profuse sections and documents of great relevance and significance, as in the case of Muhammad Daoud and Ahmad Rahuni.[5]

The role of the domestic slaves who are the protagonists of this study has much in common with that in other Moroccan cities, such as Fez: the Andalusian origin of its notables, the emergence of commercial elites linked to the *makhzan* (state) and the formation of a discrete social class that differentiated itself through endogamy,

---

[2] Mohamed Ennaji, *Soldats, domestiques et concubines. L'esclavage au Maroc au XIXe siècle* (Casablanca: Editions Eddif, 1994).
[3] Chouki El Hamel, *Black Morocco: A History of Slavery, Race and Islam* (New York: Cambridge University Press, 2013).
[4] Jaafar Bel Hach Soulami, 'al-'abidwa al-taqafa al-zanŷiya fi Titwan, fi al-qarn al-rabi'a 'achara al-hiŷri', *Al-muŷtama'u al-titwani, wa al-taturu al-'umraniwa al-ma'amari* 15–16 (2009): 9–29.
[5] Muhammad Daoud, *Tarij Titwan*, 2nd edn (Tetouan: Fondation Muhammad Daoud pour l'Histoire et la Culture, 2014), vol. 7: 228–39, 248, 258; vol. 11: 55, 57–8, 141; vol. 12: 50; Ahmad Rahuni, '*Umdat al-rawin fi tarijTitwan*, ed. Jaafar Bel Hach Soulami (Tetouan: Tettawin-Asmir, 2000–10), vol. 5: 184; vol. 7: 75, 189; vol. 8: 80.

material consumption, cuisine and music, and – of key importance to this study – for whom slaves were a status symbol.[6]

David Goodman, in particular, has dealt with the conditions of domestic slavery in Fez during the final phase of its existence,[7] as well as the ambivalent process of its extinction, analysing manumissions and the colonial policy towards former slaves based on the records of Fez's Shari'a courts.[8] The process of freeing a slave was not always a smooth one, and disagreements over the status of freedmen and inheritances were often brought before Islamic courts. On the other end of the spectrum, manumissions accompanied by financial support often allowed for upward social mobility for newly emancipated men and women.[9]

Methodology and sources

At the methodological level, we wish to distinguish individual manumission within specific social classes from collective abolition, widely analysed both in the Ottoman Empire and in the Muslim West.[10] In the region studied here, the legal mechanism of manumission was maintained during the twentieth century even after the 1922 ban on the slave trade in the French Protectorate zone. In fact, the slave status as such was never formally eliminated in either the French or Spanish Protectorate, due to a colonial policy of permissibility towards the phenomenon.[11]

For the analysis of the liberations and the condition of the freedmen, I have combined handwritten notary documents, interviews and oral history among Tetouanese families, European travellers and journalists, and documents from the administration of the Spanish Protectorate in Morocco. Interviews were conducted in Tetouan between 2012 and 2019, with a total of fifty people (three quarters of them were men over sixty years old), mainly from families who had owned a domestic who

[6] Mohamed Ennaji, 'Young Slaves and Servants in Nineteenth Century Morocco', *Critical Quarterly* 39, no. 3 (1997): 59–68.

[7] R. David Goodman, 'Expediency, Ambivalence, and Inaction: The French Protectorate and Domestic Slavery in Morocco, 1912–1956', *Journal of Social History* 47, no. 1 (2013): 101–31.

[8] R. David Goodman, 'Demystifying "Islamic Slavery": Using Legal Practices to Reconstruct the End of Slavery in Fes, Morocco', *History in Africa* 39 (2012): 143–74. For the question of releases and paternity claims in the French Protectorate zone and in the first years of independence, see Louis Milliot and Jean Lapanne-Joinville, *Recueil de jurisprudence chérifienne*, 4 vols, 1920-1952. The work by François-Paul Blanc and Albert Lourde, 'Les conditions juridiques de l'accès au statut de concubine-mère en droit musulman malékite', *Revue de l'Occident musulman et de la Méditerranée* 36 (1983): 170, collects the most significant litigations of the work of Louis Milliot (*Recueil de jurisprudence chérifienne*, 3 vols (Paris: Éditions E. Leroux, 1920–4)).

[9] This social mobility is also documented in other countries such as Egypt: see Mary Ann Fay, 'From Concubines to Capitalists: Women, Property, and Power in Eighteenth-Century Cairo', *Journal of Women's History* 10, no. 3 (1998): 118–40.

[10] For example, Ehud R. Toledano, *Slavery and Abolition in the Ottoman Middle East* (Seattle: University of Washington Press, 1998); William G. Clarence-Smith, *Islam and the Abolition of Slavery* (London: Hurst, 2006).

[11] Roger Botte, *Esclavages et abolitions en terres d'Islam* (Brussels: André Versaille, 2010). Josep Lluís Mateo Dieste, 'Imágenes y ambivalencias de la política española hacia la esclavitud en Marruecos (1880–1930)', *Historia y Política* 31 (2014): 255–80.

entered the household originally as a slave. This exercise revealed the social factors that so often influence memory, with former masters offering rather sweetened visions of the slave-owning past.[12]

The Spanish colonial documentation comes from consular agents and the High Commissariat of Spain in Morocco, located in the General Archive of the Administration in Alcalá de Henares. For the study of manumissions specifically, the original documents from the nineteenth century up to the first half of the twentieth century are mainly found in the records of the *ḥabūs* of the *zawiyat* (sufi lodges) and mosques of Tetouan, as well as in the Daoud Archive of Tetouan.[13] The analysis of the *ḥabūs* collections has been carried out in collaboration with the historian Khalid Rami. Documents concerning the liberation, sale, purchase or gifting of slaves come from the Daoud Archive.[14]

The *ḥabūs* or *waqf* has been the subject of in-depth study throughout the Islamic world as a primary source for the analysis of Muslim society in its economic and kinship relations,[15] and leveraging it here has been extremely useful for understanding the mechanisms of manumission, linked to notions of charity and moral ideas about the consequences of actions in life on conditions in the afterlife.

Finally, it should be clarified that the terms used in the city to refer to slaves differed in oral and written culture. The most frequent oral term to designate a female slave was *khādm* (pl. *khdam*) or *tata* at a more familiar level, while in written documents the term *ama* predominated. For men, *'abd*, *wasīf* and *raqab* are the most abundant in written literature.

Sociopolitical context and social structure of Tetouan

In Morocco, there were two driving forces behind the enslavement of people from West Africa and the Moroccan south: the need to procure soldiers for the sultans' armies and the need to supply domestic female servants to large and medium landowners, merchants and various notables in urban areas or notables and *shurafā'* (descendants of the Prophet) in rural areas. These domestic slaves were part of the social fabric of the bourgeois classes of Fez, Rabat and Tetouan. Although their main task was domestic work, many of them were sexually exploited. In the explanation of these abuses, we also find accepted wisdom at work, such as the idea that sexual contact with black women provided healing, prophylactic effects and greater sexual pleasure.[16]

---

[12] Josep Lluís Mateo Dieste, 'Remembering the *tatas*: An Oral History of the Tetouan Elite about Their Female Domestic Slaves', *Middle Eastern Studies* 56, no. 3 (2020): 438–52.

[13] For the handling of legal court documents, see Terence Walz, 'Black Slavery in Egypt during the Nineteenth Century as Reflected in the Mahkama Archives of Cairo', in *Slaves and Slavery in Muslim Africa*, vol. II, *The Servile Estate*, ed. John RalphWillis (London: Frank Cass, 1985), 137–60, about Cairo; and Goodman, 'Expediency', about Fez.

[14] I would like to thank Hasna Daoud for her invaluable collaboration in the search for the documents.

[15] Sophie Ferchiou, ed., *Hasab wa nasab. Parenté, alliance et patrimoine en Tunisie* (Paris: Centre National de Recherche Scientifique, 1992).

[16] Ennaji, *Soldats*, 61.

The trans-Saharan slave routes persisted until the end of the nineteenth century. Despite European abolitionist pressure, the slave trade continued from the interior of the continent to the Maghreb. Jean-Louis Miège estimated that between 1840 and 1870 there was still a trade of about four thousand slaves per year to North Africa.[17] This trade continued in significant numbers until the end of the nineteenth century. For example, two thousand slaves were sold annually in Marrakech between 1876 and 1880, and up to seven or eight thousand per year between 1890 and 1894.[18]

This situation provoked the intervention of Euro-American anti-slavery societies, to which the Arab-Muslim world reacted in very different ways. Beginning in 1846, Tunisia allowed any slave to obtain manumission.[19] On the other hand, Moroccan responses to external pressure varied throughout the nineteenth century, both on the part of the sultans and the *fuqahā'* and *'ulamā'*, although the legitimization of slavery would predominate. In 1863, Muhammad IV (r. 1859–73) introduced some reforms, issuing a decree according to which any slave requesting refuge from the *makhzan* would not be returned to his master and the latter would be compensated.[20] The slave trade continued, however, and remained important until the beginning of the twentieth century, as will be seen below. Under the sultanate of Hassan I (r. 1873–94), the British Anti-Slavery Society founded a branch in Tangier and in 1884 tried to convince the sultan that if he did not end slavery, he should at least put a stop to public sales of slaves, especially in the port cities with a significant foreign presence.

In this period of tension between European anti-slavery pressure and the sultan's defence of slavery, we find an exceptional work that raised serious doubts about the legality of the practice of slavery. The Moroccan historian Ahmad bin Khalid al-Nasiri al-Slawi (1834–1897) took a dim view of any possibility of Muslims enslaving other Muslims, arguing that early Islam recognized slavery only in the form of non-Muslim prisoners captured in the course of war. Al-Nasiri's rhetoric, however, set forth in his 1881 book *Kitab al-Istiqsa*, found little resonance in his time, and slavery practices continued.[21]

In the twentieth century, some *'ulamā'* adopted pragmatic positions to maintain consensus with the authorities, such as Muhammad bin 'Abd al-Qader of Fez: in 1905 he issued a fatwa legitimizing the enslavement of the *harrāṭīn* ('freedmen'), of the *ahmar al-jilda* (reddish-brown-skinned) or the concubinage of *harrāṭīn* women with the sultan himself. But other *'ulamā'* and scholars from other areas also condemned the enslavement of people who considered themselves Muslims. In his *Tafsir Luqach* of 1916, the Tetouanese 'Abd al-Wahab Luqach openly rejected the practice of slavery in his city and decried the fact that free people were being sold.[22] His vision was based on

---

[17] Ibid., 173–4. See also Daniel Schroeter, 'Slave Markets and Slavery in Moroccan Urban Society', *Slavery and Abolition* 13, no. 1 (1992): 185–213; and Rahal Boubrik, 'Nineteenth Century Slave Markets: The Moroccan Slave Trade', *Al Muntaqa* 4, no.2 (2021): 63–79.

[18] Ennaji, *Soldats*, 174.

[19] In the 1850s, the Ottoman Empire issued ordinances against the slave trade, with the exception of the Hijaz in the Arabian Peninsula. Ibid., 184; Toledano, *Slavery*.

[20] Ennaji, *Soldats*, 186. Boubrik, 'Nineteenth Century Slave Markets', 76.

[21] Clarence-Smith, *Islam*, 137.

[22] Data obtained thanks to the kind collaboration of Jaafar bel Hach Soulami, a true expert in his work (Tetouan, March 2017).

the first Salafism that came to Morocco through the Islamic university al-Qarawiyin of Fez. The discordant voice of Luqach was part of a renovating vision of Islam. At the same time, his criticism evidenced the existence of slavery in the Tetouan of the first quarter of the twentieth century, despite the decrease in the public slave trade.

In the meantime, European colonialism was penetrating into Morocco, which legally lost its independence with the 1912 treaty between France and the sultan. The Algeciras Conference in January 1906 was a preliminary to colonial penetration, and among the topics discussed in the conference was also the question of slavery.[23] Despite the requests made to the sultan at that conference to put an end to slavery, both the 1912 Protectorate treaty itself – signed between Morocco and France (Treaty of Fez, 30 March) – and the treaty between France and Spain (Treaty of 27 November) on its zone of influence issue. Rather, the treaties were understood to respect the matters of personal status linked to Muslim jurisprudence, such as slavery.[24]

Formally, the condition of slavery was not explicitly prohibited either in the French or the Spanish zone of the Protectorate. In the French zone, however, the Résidence Générale issued an important circular in 1922[25] or 1923[26] that prohibited the trade of slaves in public markets, the acceptance of notary acts of *'udūl* (notaries) certifying possession of a slave and any lawsuit seeking possession of a slave. The circular also urged the liberation of slaves who requested their freedom, as well as of the children not recognized by the masters.[27] Thus, the buying and selling of slaves was dismantled directly, and their possession hindered indirectly, facilitating their liberation.

I would like to emphasize that in the Spanish Protectorate zone, the colonial authorities clearly adopted a *laissez-faire* policy towards slavery through an excessively compromising alliance with local elites. In 1921, the Spanish government was urged by the League of Nations to report on slavery in its area of Morocco and to put an end to its existence.[28] In practice, the Spanish authorities did their best to maintain a neutral stance, designed to avoid negative reactions among Moroccan notables, in keeping with their policy of formal respect for Islam and local customs. This is also reflected in a 1923 report by military interpreter Clemente Cerdeira on slavery in the Spanish zone of the Protectorate. Cerdeira's opinion was openly against the suppression of slavery.

---

[23] 'Carta al Wazir Abdelkrim ben Sliman', Legación de España en Marruecos, Tangier, 24 June 1906. Carton 81/319, Archivo General de la Administración, AGA.

[24] 'Ce régime sauvegardera la situation religieuse, le respect et le prestige traditionnel du Sultan, l'exercice de la religion musulmane et des institutions religieuses, notamment de celles des habous', *Bulletin officiel de l'Empire chérifien*, n° 1, 1 November 1912.

[25] Circular n° 17, S.G.J.P., 12 September 1922. Carton 81/319, AGA.

[26] In the preceding quote I use Spanish sources that refer to the date of 1922. There is a striking confusion about this date, given its historical importance. Goodman maintains that the original document refers to 1923, despite the fact that several French sources also mention the year 1922. See R. David Goodman, 'Reconfiguring Household Slavery in Twentieth Century Fez, Morocco', in *Towards a Global History of Domestic and Caregiving workers*, ed. Dirk Hoerder, Elisa Van Nederveen Meerkerk and Silke Neunsinger (Leiden: Brill, 2015), 401.

[27] Blanc and Lourde, 'Les conditions', 168. See also Botte, *Esclavages*; and El Hamel, *Black Morocco*, 241–69.

[28] 'Informes que solicita la secretaría de la Sociedad de Naciones respecto a la trata de las mujeres y niños en nuestra zona de Protectorado en Marruecos', 1921. Carton 81/10140, AGA.

To justify his position, the author asserted, among other arguments, that the domestic slave enjoyed advantages 'superior in many cases to those enjoyed by women workers among certain civilized peoples.'[29]

In this climate of a pragmatic acceptance, slavery during the colonial era expired gradually, without any active policy to dismantle it. And it was in this general political context that the Tetouanese owner families managed the existence of their domestic women of slave origin, whose numbers must have been in the hundreds at the beginning of the twentieth century. Although we do not have any records or reliable accounting, we can infer that most of the large and medium-sized houses in Tetouan had some *khdam*, and we know that at that time there were in Tetouan about six thousand Jews and about sixteen thousand Muslims, the latter occupying some three thousand dwellings.[30]

The main families mentioned in the *ḥabūs* and manumission documents of the nineteenth and early twentieth centuries belonged to the upper and middle classes of urban society, most of them of Andalusian origin. These families based their status on their economic power and influential ties, both with the *makhzan* and administration authorities and with religious actors such as the *shurafā'* lineages and some Sufi *zawiyat* such as the Raysuniya.[31] As the main buyers of slaves, this social class maintained them as domestic servants in their large Tetouanese homes and, to a lesser extent, as agricultural labour in rural areas such as Jebala. These slaves were acquired through various channels: purchase in the Tetouan market itself (until the 1910s) or in Fez or Marrakech, and even in distant markets, such as the Circassian slaves acquired by La'arbi Bricha in the Ottoman Empire. There was also purchasing in villages in the Jebala area controlled by *shurafā'* families. In other cases, the acquisitions derived from transfers between family members, relatives and close friends, from family inheritances or wedding gifts.[32]

Some of the most powerful families in the city were those with strong ties to the *makhzan* and who worked as customs administrators or merchants, as in the case of Erzini in Gibraltar,[33] or La'arbi Bricha, who provided two Circassian slaves to Sultan Mawlay Hasan I, mothers of the future sultans Mawlay 'Abd al-'Aziz and Mawlay Yusuf.[34] As a reward for their services, Hajj La'arbi and his brothers were granted various offices. Hajj La'arbi was *amin* (administrator) of ports and governor of Casablanca and the Chaouia, as well as a merchant (Figure 6.1).

---

[29] 'La esclavitud en la zona española', Tetouan, 7 June 1923. Carton 81/10140, AGA.

[30] Teodoro Ruiz Cuevas, *Apuntes para la historia de Tetuán* (Tetouan: Editora Marroquí, 1951), 66.

[31] Driss Benyahia, *Médina et ville nouvelle: Tétouan et sa région, le devenir d'une ville du nord-ouest marocain au temps du Protectorat (1912–1956)* (Paris: Université Paris 7, Atelier national de reproduction de thèses, 2014).

[32] For example, there is a marriage certificate dated dhu al-hijja 15, 1265 (1 November 1849). In it, 'Abd al-Rahman, son of the kaid of Tetouan Si Muhammad al-Chaa'ach, marries Fatima Labbadi with a *sadaq* consisting of bridal goods, with a variety of dresses and a slave girl. Document n° 1778, Daoud Archive, Tetouan.

[33] Nadia Erzini, 'Hal yaslah li-taqansut (Is He Suitable for Consulship?): The Moroccan Consuls in Gibraltar during the Nineteenth Century', *Journal of North African Studies* 12, no. 4 (2007): 517–29.

[34] Henri de la Martinière, *Souvenirs du Maroc. Voyages et Missions. 1882–1918* (Paris: Librairie Plon, 1919), 151.

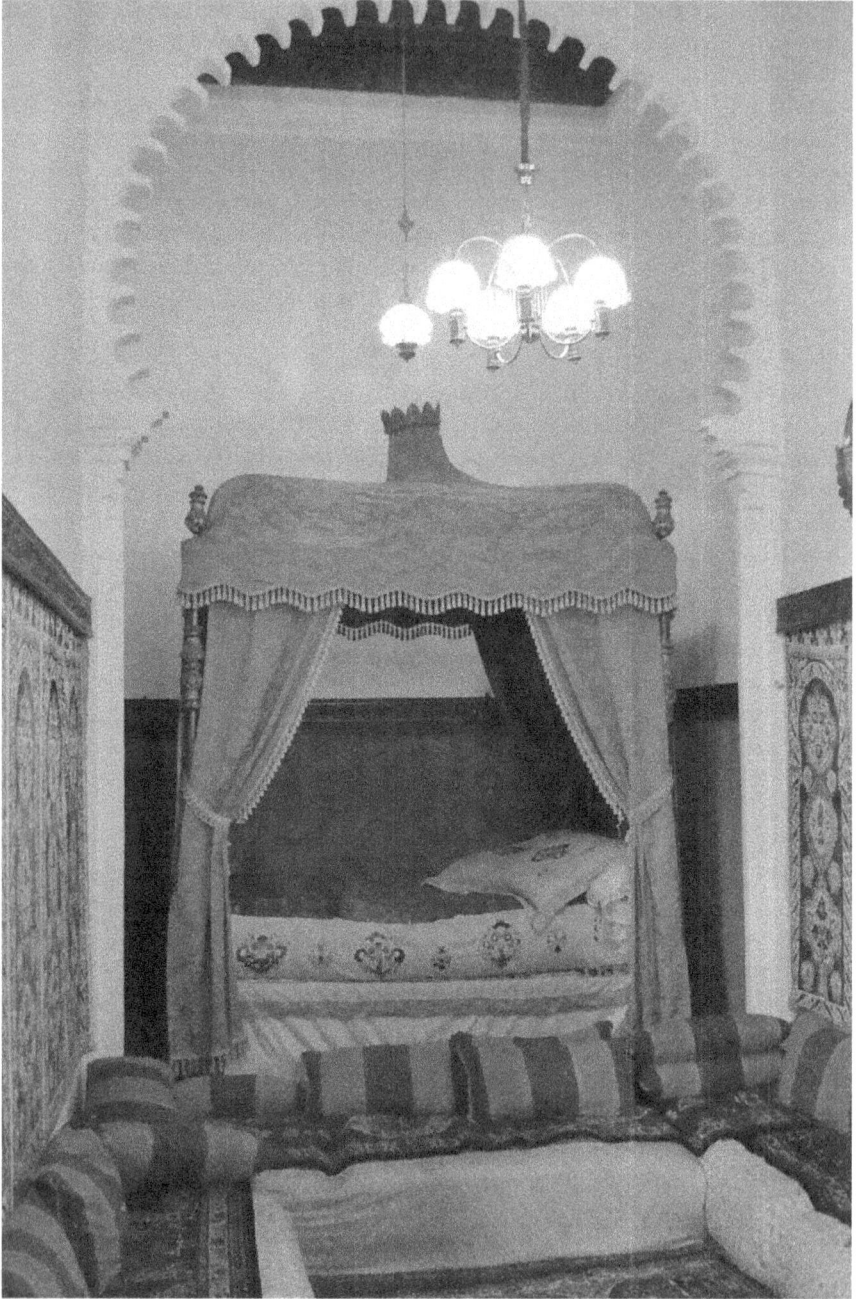

Figure 6.1 Fatima's room (Circassian concubine of La'arbi Bricha), Dar Bricha.

Source: J. L. Mateo.

Many of these powerful men were accompanied by female slaves on journeys, given the reluctance of Tetouanese women to travel outside the city. Thus, while these slaveholding groups were linked to socio-economic and transnational modernity, this milieu actually supported and encouraged slavery: domestic slaves became an element of social distinction and symbolic capital among the wealthy classes. Some of these notables had children with their female slaves, who became known as *umm al-walad* (mother of the children).[35] These women had to be set free upon the death of the owner, although they had no right to inheritance, unlike their children, who if indeed recognized as children of the owner, had the same rights as his other children and were automatically considered free.[36]

Conditions of liberation in the Maliki school

In the Maliki school of law predominant in Morocco, the act of manumission[37] is based on the founding texts of Islam and compilations of jurisprudence such as those of al-Wancharisi in the fifteenth century.[38] Manumission in Maliki law consisted of several formulas.[39] The first was the *mukātaba*, a contract between master and slave, according to which the slave paid a sum of money for his release – money generated by the slave's labour.[40] After manumission, the master–servant bond might remain in force to some extent in the form of patron–client relations. Another type of manumission was based on the *tadbīr*, the master's declaration that upon his death the slave would be freed.[41] The manumitted slave or *mudabbar*, as part of his property, was subject to the rule of the available third: the freed slave's inheritance could not exceed a third of the inheritance that the deceased was entitled to stipulate as free distribution. In addition, the manumitter was obliged to set aside a portion of the resources to support the freed slave. Women released for having given birth to a child of the master belong to the same category. After acquiring the status of *umm al-walad*, the woman could not be sold, and she had to be freed at or before the death of the master. These are the

35 Josep Lluís Mateo Dieste, 'Slave Women and Their Descendants among the Upper Classes in Tetouan, Morocco (1859–1956): Between Recognition and Conflict', *Journal of Family History* 46, no. 2 (2021): 168–90.

36 Cristina de la Puente, 'Entre la esclavitud y la libertad: consecuencias legales de la manumisión según el derecho mâlikí', *al-Qantara. Revista de e studios árabes* 21, no. 2 (2000): 339–60; 'Free Fathers, Slave Mothers and Their Children: A Contribution to the Study of Family Structures in Al-Andalus', *Imago Temporis. Medium Aevum* 7 (2013): 27–44.

37 Malek Chebel, *L'esclavage en terre d'Islam* (Paris: Fayard, 2007), 97–103; Ennaji, *Soldats*, 91–110.

38 Ahmad al-Wancharisi, 'La pierre de touche des fetwas. Choix de consultations juridiques des faquîh du Maghreb (traduites par Emile Amar). Livre deuxième', *Archives Marocaines* 13 (1909): 432–6. It is also necessary to take into account previous legal practices in al-Andalus regarding manumission. Francisco Javier Aguirre Sábada, 'De esclavos a libertos: fórmulas de manumission en al-Andalus en el s. XI, según el Muqni' de Ibn Mugīṯ', *Miscelánea de Estudios Árabes y Hebraicos. Sección Árabe-Islam* 50 (2001): 21–51.

39 Robert Brunschvig, "Abd', *The Encyclopaedia of Islam*, vol. 1 (Leiden: Brill, 1986), 24–40; Ennaji, *Soldats*, 92; De la Puente, 'Entre la esclavitud'.

40 Ahmad Alawad Sikainga, 'Slavery and Muslim Jurisprudence in Morocco', *Slavery & Abolition: A Journal of Slave and Post-Slave Studies* 19, no. 2 (1998): 61.

41 Brunschvig, "Abd', 30.

main forms of liberation for which we have evidence in the Tetouanese documents and which will be analysed here. Other paths to freedom included a verbal declaration by the master and release of a slave for having committed a crime or offence.[42]

Yet manumission was not necessarily a pious practice and did not always adhere to the law when it came to the rights of the freed slave. Ennaji has contested the idea that the slaves were always treated as well as some authors claim. In this regard, there is evidence of complaints sent to the palace of Sultan Hasan I.[43] Many slaves were helpless in the face of abuses of power by those who did not recognize manumission. In practice, manumission did not necessarily alter the working conditions or treatment of the freedmen, who continued to live as de facto slaves, since they had no other alternatives. We have been able to verify this in many cases of domestic servants of slave origin in Tetouan. For slaves without family or any other avenue of support, liberation often amounted to little more than a declaration. In fact, in some of the oral histories I have collected, the boundary between enslaved and free is not at all clear, while the condition of servitude is. Faced with a lack of prospects, freedmen themselves would ask to be put at the service of others or to be drafted into the army, or take on low-status jobs, such as porters or water carriers. In the case of emancipated women without resources, one way to survive was prostitution, as already observed by the khalifa of the bacha (main authority of the city) of Meknes in 1898.[44] The main path to survival for many women in Tetouan was making crafts, such as *naggafa* (female ritual specialist) at weddings, or cooking for big feasts.[45] Confronted with this precarious existence, freedmen unsurprisingly preferred to remain with their former masters, becoming 'slaves of their freedom', as Ennaji so pointedly puts it.[46] Moreover, manumission did not always imply a complete undoing of the ties between master and slave, due to the Quranic principle known as *wala'*. This term refers to the patron–client relationship between owner and slave and also the slave's descendants, even beyond manumission. It goes far in explaining the relations of dependence and inequality between landowners and freed workers in different parts of Morocco, including the region of Jebala, which supplied the city of Tetouan with servants.

The practice of manumission in Tetouan

The liberation of slaves was a common practice, known as *'itq*. 'To free' is *'ataqa*, and one 'freed' is a *mu'atiq/-a*. Documents from the early nineteenth century indicate

---

[42]   In some cases, it was also a strategy to change the master. Julio Caro Baroja gives references to the following practice in the western Sahara until the 1950s: the slave would cut off the ear of a child or an animal belonging to the person to whom he intended to bind. If the former owner could not pay the fine for the damage caused by the slave, then he lost the rights over the slave and the slave became the property of the victim. See Julio Caro Baroja, *Estudios saharianos* (Madrid: Júcar, 1990), 97.

[43]   Ennaji, *Soldats*, 92.

[44]   Ibid., 99.

[45]   Rahuni mentions the existence of some thirty freedwomen engaged in this occupation during the first third of the twentieth century. Ahmad Rahuni, *Historia de Tetuán. Escrita en árabe por el sabio al faquih Sidi Ahmad R'Honi; traducida por Mohamed Ibn Azzuz Haquim* (Tetouan: Editorial Marroquí, 1953), 68.

[46]   Ennaji, *Soldats*, 99.

RABHAH.
A former slave-wife of a native British agent at the Moorish Court,
now free.

Freyonne, Photo., Gibraltar.

Figure 6.2 Rabhah, a former slave-wife, liberated by Budgett Meakin in Tangier.

Source: Budgett Meakin, *The Moors* (London, 1902), 360.

that it was already common for slave owners to order release on the day of their death, as designated in the *wasiya*, or to order the purchase of slaves in order to free them.

This formula is repeated in later years and in the wills of *zawiyat* such as the Raysuniya. This *zawiya* is of great interest because its members belonged mostly to the wealthiest or most politically and religiously influential classes of the city, and nineteenth-century documents paint a vivid portrait of the niche they occupied. In 1868, Sidi M'hammad bin Sidi al-Hajj 'Abdallah al-Khatib willed a third of his inheritance to be allocated for pious acts (known in Islamic jurisprudence as 'the third') and granted freedom to 'a female slave who was his property, on the day of his death, and who will be part of the free Muslims'.[47] In 1879, Rqya bint al-Hajj Muhammad Ragun bequeathed 'the third' towards the purchase of 'a female slave who will be freed on the day of burial'.[48] The practice is repeated among other powerful families such as the Bricha, as shown by the 1884 will of *amin* 'Abd al-Krim bin al-Hajj M'hammad Bricha al-Humaydi, which earmarks 'the third' to free a 'whole [of sound mind and body] female slave on the day of his death, and she will join the free women, and will be given clothes and mattresses and ten *rials*'.[49] The practice continued until the end of the century. In November 1897, 'Abd al-Rahman bin Sidi Muhammad Labbadi bequeathed in his will, in addition to the distribution of three thousand loaves of bread on the day of his burial and other expenses for the ceremony, the release of 'two male slaves and two female slaves who are able to work, and 50 *mizqals* (coin) shall be paid to each of them as an allowance'.[50]

It is worth noting that this pattern was repeated until the arrival of the Protectorate. In 1911, Fatma bint al-Hajj 'Abd al-Krim Bricha ordered in her will that 400 *rials* be earmarked for the purchase of three slaves, who would be freed to enter the path of God.[51] Or in August 1912, a few months before the signing of the Protectorate treaty, Khadduja bint Sidi al-Hajj La'arbi Bennuna bequeathed in her will the release of two female slaves 'as free Muslims, who can work'.[52]

Moral and religious motivations of manumission

Some *hadiths* of al-Bukhari recognize the religious merit of freeing slaves as a way of emulating the Prophet and avoiding eternal damnation. Among other religious motivations was the expiation of the master's trespasses and sins. Freedom might also be granted as a reward for the religious fervour of the slave himself. In short, liberation

---

[47]   The following references correspond to *habūs* documents extracted from the *Hawāla* (register) of different *zawiyat* and mosques of Tetouan. Each reference includes the date of the document in the Islamic Calendar, the name of the mosque or *zawiya* and the reference to the document in the records. Chawwal 24, 1284 (18 February 1868). *Hawāla* of Si 'Ali bin Raysun. Vol. 1, 93.

[48]   Safar 28, 1296 (21 February 1879). *Hawāla* of Si 'Ali bin Raysun. Vol. 1, 114.

[49]   Rajab, 1301 (*c.* May 1884). *Hawāla* of Si 'Ali bin Raysun. Vol. 1, 154.

[50]   Rajab 4, 1315 (28 November 1897). *Hawāla* of Si 'Ali bin Raysun. Vol. 1, 117.

[51]   Cha'aban 21, 1329 (17 August 1911). *Hawāla* of Si 'Ali bin Raysun. Vol. 1, 156.

[52]   Ramadan 8, 1330 (21 August 1912). *Hawāla* of Si 'Ali bin Raysun. Vol. 1, 157.

was considered by Islamic morality and law as a meritorious act that granted religious gain (*ajr*).

The notary acts of Tetouan repeat standardized expressions linked to these concepts of salvation and religious merit. One commonly used formula evokes the moral objective of the will from the point of view of the legatee: for example,'the author of said will intends thereby to do it for Almighty God and for a vast reward in the other world'. Another refers to the liberation of the slave and his or her religious status: for example, 'he [or she] shall be freed and become one of the free Muslims'. We find similar explanations well into the twentieth century, as in a 1922 case of manumission of a female slave in Tetouan, who was purchased from her owner and then 'incorporated into the [community of] free Muslims, with [the attendant] rights and obligations, and no guardianship or taint of slavery remained over her, only the guardianship provided by the Sunna of the Prophet, God's prayer and peace be upon Him'.[53]

The religious merit of leaving *ḥabūs* is also shored up by *hadith*s of the Prophet, which convey moral notions about life and death; according to these notions, one's earthly deeds define one's fate in the hereafter. This explains the acts of piety repeatedly referenced in the wills of the wealthy classes of Tetouan, understood as atonement for sins committed during life. The recipients and beneficiaries of the *ḥabūs* and of these pious deeds were diverse: money was assigned to cover the burial expenses of the legator or payment for prayer in *zawiyat* and mosques; clothes and bread were distributed among the poor (on fixed days of the week such as Thursdays); and, of course, slaves were purchased in order to be liberated, with money, jewels, clothes or furniture donated to assist them in adapting to freedom.

The merits conferred by acts of liberation also explain why many merchants, landowners and *makhzan* men bought slaves in order to free them. Thus, the arrival of slaves responded not only to material questions linked to service but also to religious and moral motivations.

The public ritual of liberation

The manumissions did not take place only on paper but involved a performative element, being made public through a ritual act. Ennaji maintains that this public act made the fact of manumission known to society, so that the freedmen would not lose their rights or fall back into their previous status, since there were known cases of manumitted slaves who were re-enslaved by the relatives of the deceased.[54]

Few of the people I interviewed in Tetouan had heard of the public ritual that took place during burials; among those who had was 'Abd al-Salam Saffar. He was aware of a practice that consisted of publicly displaying the *taḥrīr* (release documents) in the form of a piece of paper folded and attached to a *qasaba* (long cane) carried by a servant behind the coffin.[55]

---

[53] Document nº 15. Purchase and manumission, in Daoud, *Tarij*, vol. 12: 55–6.
[54] Ennaji, *Soldats*, 93–4.
[55] Conversation with 'Abd al-Salam Saffar, 17 May 2012.

We will take a closer look at two Spanish eyewitness accounts of this ritual, from the Protectorate period, that describe the burials of the Grand Vizier Ahmad Erkaina and of the bacha 'Abd al-Krim Labbadi. The former is described as follows:

> The mourning was presided over by the interim Khalifa of the area, with the caid Mesuar and a slave of the deceased, who was the bearer of five passports to give freedom to as many [women] slaves, the last will of the deceased [...] After the burial, a distribution of bread was made among the poor Moors, according to traditional custom.[56]

A second case is the burial of the bacha 'Abd al-Krim Labbadi, who died in 1933 at the age of eighty. Labbadi belonged to one of the main families of Tetouan and kept several domestic servants of slave origin in his palace, as we know from the previous accounts by other Spanish journalists who visited his house.[57] The journalist Ángel Gonzalez Palencia describes Labbadi's burial. One of the male slaves accompanying the coffin held a cane with nine acts of manumission. This number indicates the Labbadi palace housed many slaves. The journalist adds an important detail, commenting that after legal emancipation, the slaves 'will continue to live in the house, serving the children of their former master, in the same way'.[58] That is to say, the freedmen remained dependent on their former owner's patronage, the *wala'*, and continued to serve the family in exchange for room and board.

Gifts linked to manumission by will

One of the most remarkable features of manumission was the donation of a sum of money to the freed person, considered by Islamic law as a pious act. The amounts donated are explicit in the documentation. These quantities could vary, as in the case of Fatima Tobb, who bequeathed to her freed slave Setra and her daughter 20 *mizqal* each. Setra was married to and had children with Salem, a freed slave of Fatma Tobb's husband. When Setra had two more children with Salem, the will of Fatima Tobb's husband, Hajj Muhammad al-Fatah, dedicated 10 *mizqal* to each of them.[59]

When there were several female slaves in a house, they established a hierarchy among themselves, according to their position in the household and proximity to the master – naturally, those who had children with him were closer. In the case of Khatib in 1868, we observe that of the six female slaves in the house, Yaqut and Mbarka each received 100 *mizqals* in the will. Mbarka is defined in the document as his 'eldest *mustawlada* (*umm al-walad*), the mother of his daughter 'Aicha, [who was to receive]

[56] 'Entierro del Gran Visir', *El Imparcial*, 18 November 1924. Author unknown.
[57] Isaac Muñoz, *La corte de Tetuán* (Madrid: Imprenta Helénica, 1913), 68.
[58] Ángel González Palencia, 'El entierro de Lebbadi', in Tomás García Figueras, *Miscelánea*, vol. 47, *España ante África*, 115 (Madrid: Biblioteca Nacional, n.d.).
[59] 1 (fatih) al-qa'ada, 1271 (16 July 1855). *Hawāla* of Jama'a al-Qasba. 26, 3.

100 *mizqals*.[60] The remaining four female slaves received smaller amounts: Brika and Mbrika, 50 *mizqals* each, and Khadija and Raham, 30 *mizqals*, respectively.

In other available documents, the amounts donated remained very similar. In 1873, a granddaughter of the saint Si ʿAli bin Raysun stipulated in her will that a slave girl be bought, freed and given 10 *mizqals*. In 1874, Labbadi stipulated that two girl slaves be freed, 'and each will be given 20 *mizqals* to help them start their lives'.[61] Well into the twentieth century, the same amounts continued to be given. For example, in 1907, Bin Driss freed his female slaves Masʿuda and Juhra, and in addition to other properties discussed below, '10 *mizqals* will be given to each of the two'.[62]

In some cases, in addition to these monetary donations, goods and property were left to slaves who had some special bond with the owner. For example, in 1850, the aforementioned Fatima Tobb bequeathed to Setra, in addition to money, 'a *mtarba* (mattress) and *frach* (furniture)'. Fatima and her husband testify in the will that 'the jewelry worn by Farha [daughter of the slave Setra], a pair of [name unidentified] gold pieces, a pair of *khal-khal* (ankle bracelets) of silver, and silver bracelets worn on her hands, are the property of Farha, and that all those items have been given as property, as a *hiba* (gift)'.[63] This gesture seems to indicate that Farha was wearing the donated jewellery before her release. To prevent them from being taken away, since slaves could not have property, this gift is made explicit in the will document of Fatima and her husband: 'Then the notaries came and saw the girl with the jewels'.[64]

In 1907, Hajj Muhammad bin Driss willed that 'from the third shall come out all the clothes for his two female slaves Masʿuda and Juhra, and furniture and covering, carpets and bedding and the jewelry, which shall be their property'.[65] This example is similar to the will of Khadduja bint Laʿarbi Bennuna, who bequeathed to Setra '20 *rials*, a woolen couch, a pillow and covering, and her *sanduq* (clothing trunk) of dresses, and another [trunk], and silver jewelry'.[66]

Islamic law also provided for a special form of temporary transfer of real estate accompanying acts of emancipation. This formula, known as *ʿamra* (from 'to occupy', 'to fill'), was applicable to both free and enslaved and consisted of ceding the usufruct of a building to a beneficiary for the rest of his/her life. Upon his/her death, the property returned to the *ḥabūs* or to other beneficiaries. This practice was frequent in the city, with the transfer of houses of many different categories to freed slaves, mostly women, who lived in these dwellings until their death. For example, in 1907, Bin Driss bequeaths that

the said house is given to them [freedwomen Masʿuda and Juhra] as *ʿamri*, for the benefit of the house during their whole life, in their lifetime only, and if one of them dies, the other is left alone in the house, and when they both die, the house

[60] Chawwāl 24, 1284 (18 February 1868). *Hawāla* of Si ʿAli bin Raysun. Vol. 1, 93.
[61] End of Safar al-kkair, 1291 (17 April 1874). *Hawāla* of Si ʿAli bin Raysun. Vol. 1, 108.
[62] Qaʿada 1, 1325 (6 December 1907). *Hawāla* of Jamaʿa Jadida Rbat Sfal. 46, 5, 35.
[63] Qaʿada 1, 1271 (16 July 1855). *Hawāla* of Jamaʿa al-Qasba. 26, 3.
[64] Ibid.
[65] Qaʿada 1, 1325 (6 December 1907). *Hawāla* of Jamaʿa Jadida Rbat Sfal. 46, 5, 35.
[66] Ramadan 8, 1330 (21 August 1912). *Hawāla* of Si ʿAli bin Raysun. Vol. 1, 157.

goes back to their [Bin Driss's] grandchildren, and if the grandchildren die, it goes back to the Jadida Rbat Sfal mosque.[67]

From what is recorded in a document 1952 to 1954, we also know that these cessions of occupancy were dynamic and subject to transfer. In this particular case, the freedwoman named Rhimu received a small house as *ʿamri* from a freedman, to which she was entitled until the day of her death. But Rhimu ceded this *ʿamri* to another freedman named Fatah.[68]

In addition to residential buildings, the temporary usufruct of a *farran* (oven), a *hammam* (public bath) or the rent of a house was also bequeathed, as in the case of ʿAicha, freedwoman of Muhammad bin ʿAli al-Maʿarach, to whom he left a house. During her lifetime, she would be entitled to collect rent from this house, and when ʿAicha died, the usufruct would pass to the Ghaylan mosque.[69] To complement these written sources, I will present an oral history that came to me through ʿOmar from his sister, who in turn knew the descendants of the protagonists of this story. The Garsia family died out without descendants, and their two former slaves named Habibti and Fnuni remained in their house. In their will, the Garsias left them the usufruct of the house and a public oven. The freedwomen earned their living by making sweets and eventually adopted a girl. This girl married and had two girls, and their adoptive grandmothers, the freedwomen, financed their university studies in the 1960s.[70] In this case, we observe the agency of the freedwomen in generating their own income and investing the profits in the future of their adopted granddaughters.

An uncertain end and abolition in the twentieth century

Uncertainty loomed over many domestic slaves after notable families began to manumit them during the second quarter of the twentieth century. If, on the one hand, we know that domestic women who were closest and dearest to the families died in the houses, on the other hand, there were also complicated situations, with people left in the streets and forced to look for a living or shelter in charitable institutions. To survive, the freed and their descendants dedicated themselves to various occupations. The most common of these was as a cook for women, on the occasion of great feasts.

Many testimonies of the Tetouanese notable families insist that most of the women were very appreciated and that almost all of them died in the warmth of the families; but there were exceptions, and several of them went through hardship, being sheltered in some charitable institutions in the old medina. It also would cause a certain scandal if a family did not treat an elderly domestic attached to the house properly and expelled

---

[67] Qaʿada 1, 1325 (6 December 1907). *Hawāla* of Jamaʿa Jadida Rbat Sfal. 46, 5, 35.

[68] 1/2 muharram, 1372 (4 October 1952). *Hawāla* of Sidi Muhammad bin al-Faqih. 44.

[69] Rabiʿa al-awal 21, 1310 (13 October 1892). *Hawāla* of the Ghaylan mosque. 114, 116.

[70] Interview with ʿOmar, son of a former minister of the Spanish Protectorate, 20 May 2017.

her from the house. In one case, when the owner died, his son threw the *tata* out of the house, but soon after another family took her into their home until her death as an act of charity.[71]

Narratives from slave-owning families show that the situation of domestics from the middle of the twentieth century often varied between those who stayed with the families and those who had to make a living after their liberation. Let us look at the case of a former slave from one branch of the Torres family, taken into another house for charity. The story narrated to me by those who took her in implies that the old slave, Zohra, was sick, blind and had nowhere to turn. In exchange for her stay, she cooked festive dishes, drawing on her gastronomic skills. The case takes place approximately at the end of the 1950s.[72] Similar examples are repeated among the people in my oral survey. One of the daughters of an old gnawa musician, married to a domestic from Bricha, explained to us how her mother, after leaving her work as a servant, dedicated herself to preparing sweets and cooking food for feasts and rituals.[73] Some of these women also played the role of 'arata (ritual inviters), donning elegant attire and visiting houses to announce, for example, the celebration of a wedding.

In contrast to these trajectories, some authors such as Christelle Taraud[74] maintain that the end of slavery was one of the causes of the increase in prostitution in Morocco. Her study refers to the French zone and the beginning of the twentieth century. I have not been able to find any data on this subject for the northern region, including in Etxenagusia Atutxa's study on prostitution in Tetouan.[75]

It is likely that some women did enter the proliferating sex trade in Tetouan following the arrival of the colonial army. In my oral research, the subject only appeared on a few occasions, in a tangential way, or to highlight the role of the domestics as intermediaries in love affairs or prostitution. It should not be forgotten that domestic servants of slave origin had been an object of sexual exploitation in many of the houses, at the hands of the men of the family, who used them as an initiation into sexuality.[76] The case of emancipated men was somewhat different. During this time period, there were far fewer of them than women. And because of gender stereotypes, they were assigned jobs linked exclusively to physical labour, which did not have the symbolic value that some free women could acquire through their culinary skills. Bachir Haskouri pointed out to me that the occupations of former male slaves or their descendants included smuggling and trading in hashish. Unlike freedwomen, former male slaves had to seek other livelihoods and survived as artisans, soldiers, watchmen, labourers, and musicians or became engaged in smuggling at Ceuta, a Spanish city about 40 kilometres from Tetouan that has historically been a hub for smugglers.[77]

[71] Interview, 21 May 2017. Anonymous reference at the request of the interviewee.
[72] Interview, 10 May 2012. Anonymous reference at the request of the interviewee.
[73] Fieldwork notes, 4 April 2013.
[74] Christelle Taraud, *La prostitution coloniale. Algérie, Tunisie, Maroc (1830–1962)* (Paris: Payot, 2003), 23, 30.
[75] Mª Begoña Etxenagusia Atutxa, *La prostitución en el protectorado español en Marruecos (1912–1956)* (Barcelona: Edicions Bellaterra, 2020).
[76] Interview, 17 March 2017. Anonymous reference at the request of the interviewee.
[77] Email information from Bachir Haskouri, 29 May 2018.

Other freedmen worked as manual labourers: blacksmiths or porters in the harbour.[78] In contrast to these manual jobs, knowledge of the houses and great families of the medina translated into symbolic capital that some managed to turn into the work as a *samsar* (intermediary). Such was the case of 'Abd al-Krim (b. 1943), an old man with a sparse white beard and dark skin, easy to gain access to in the centre of town, a meeting point for his real-estate mediations. He explained that he was the son of servants of the 'Abd al-Wahab family, with peasant origins in Akhmas (Jebala), although he grew up in the house of the Hajjaj family.[79] I should note that it was not easy to gain more specific information about former slaves' origins because of a reticence on their part to discuss it; or perhaps in some cases this generational knowledge has been lost.

As I remarked at the beginning of this chapter, it is far from clear whether or not there was a formal abolition of slavery either during or after the Protectorate. The proof of this ambiguity is that in the 1940s, the British Anti-slavery Society was still active in Morocco. At that time, Morocco had already formally eliminated the buying and selling of slaves, but the legacy of that human trade was evident in most of the houses of notables, officials and merchants. Thus, the *mandub* of Tangier, the highest authority as representative of the sultan, made a will in 1945 in which he manumitted seven female slaves, but only after his death– that is, their state of enslavement did not change when the will was drawn up, although he ceded them the legal third so that they could use part of the garden and house in the condition of *'amra*.[80] Also, as late as in 1950, the *Official Bulletin of the Spanish Protectorate Zone* listed a notary fee of 10 pesetas for 'Manumission. Legacy of freedman. Agreed release' under 'Bequests'.[81]

Some of the people interviewed in Tetouan have suggested that it could be understood that the new Constitution of 1962 essentially ended slavery by declaring equality between persons. This idea was also suggested by François-Paul Blanc and Albert Lourde, according to article 7 of the Fundamental Law of 2 June 1961 and later according to article 5 of the December 1962 Constitution, 'all Moroccans are equal before the law'.[82]

Other informal accounts indicate that in the 1960s, 'something happened' that prompted *taḥrīr*, release documents, to be made for people who had not yet been formally freed. In some cases, the death of the master caused the domestics themselves to propose leaving the house, although this was not always the case, as I have been able to verify, since lack of means often forced them to remain.[83] Some oral narratives of the old owner families recall the negotiations and tensions between masters and servants, following the guidelines of bargaining and discussion.[84] In short, this uncertain final process was mostly informal and the difficulties encountered in documenting it are

---

[78] A 1931 report mentions Abdellah bin Fatah, a 'free slave of Resini', as unloader of the dock in Martil. Intervención local de Río Martín. Servicios locales, 10 December 1931. Carton 81/1007, AGA.

[79] Conversation with 'Abd al-Krim, 21 March 2017.

[80] 'Dahir poniendo en vigor las tarifas de los honorarios a percibir por los aadul y otros en las ciudades y en el campo', *Boletín Oficial de la Zona de Protectorado*, n° 10, 10 March 1950, 232.

[81] Ibid.

[82] Blanc and Lourde, 'Les conditions', 170.

[83] Interview, 10 May 2012. Anonymous reference at the request of the interviewee.

[84] On bargaining in Morocco, see Lawrence Rosen, *Bargaining for Reality: The Construction of Social Relations in a Muslim Community* (Chicago: University of Chicago Press, 1984).

yet more proof of its elusive nature for historians. In this sense, it is necessary to point out not only the lack of narratives available from the liberated women themselves but also the methodological challenges linked to the study of these scarce testimonies. One example is the case of Fatma Barka in Goulmine, in southern Morocco. The story offered by Fatma Barka to the anthropologist was not the life story expected by the researcher but a series of stories strung together according to the interlocutor and the narrator's objectives, highlighting, for example, the life of her master and his prestige, and Fatma's belonging to her owner's family. Her stories were a selection of fragments of the past that allowed her to highlight the time when she joined the family, or the moment of her master's death; this moment was more relevant in her story than her own liberation, and it is not by chance that when in 1994 she received the first identity card of her life, her surname was Barka, that of her buyer.[85]

Conclusions

I propose that the reason for manumissions by slave owners lay in the combination of two inseparable factors, material and symbolic: those groups that accumulated more goods and slaves wanted to appear pious, distributing goods and freeing slaves, for fear of not earning a place in paradise. But it is evident that not only the richest but also the less affluent freed slaves. That is to say, slaves were acquired for their bodily exploitation but also with the purpose of freeing them, thus obtaining religious merit.

In this work, we have been able to confirm the practice of the liberation of slaves in the city of Tetouan during the nineteenth century and well into the colonial period. We have also detailed the legal and ritual mechanisms that accompanied this liberation process. The phenomenon of manumission remained constant throughout this long period and indicates the persistence of a practice associated above all with the wealthy classes of the city. The enrichment of some groups of the elite, linked to the *makhzan* or to their entry into emerging commercial capitalism, increased the level of economic prosperity of that group, so that the acquisition of slaves, far from being a pre-modern or past phenomenon, became instead a symbol of social distinction within the process of modernization. It is for this reason that it was also this group that owned the greatest number of slaves and, subsequently, would free the greatest number of them.

A careful reading of the documentation has revealed the existence of a great variety of situations among the ranks of male and female slaves and their trajectories as freedmen. The consequences of an institution such as the *wala'*, that is, the bond that remains between master and slave even after manumission and is inherited by the following generations, remain to be studied. This institution could indicate the illusion of liberations that in many cases were not such, since they did not break the master–servant bonds between former owners and slaves. The formula that appears in the documents in reference to the purchase of slaves to be freed was that they had to meet the condition of being 'able to work'. This stipulation indicates a possible continuation

---

85 E. Ann McDougall, 'A Sense of Self: The Life of Fatma Barka', *Canadian Journal of African Studies* 32, no. 2 (1998): 285–315.

of the relationship between master and servant even after liberation. Yet documents also demonstrate that for their sustenance, freedmen and freedwomen received money or other forms of support, such as the usufruct of ovens and especially temporary usufruct of houses under the formula of the *'amra*. The trajectories of the manumitted also diverged according to gender. Women who acquired the status of *umm al-walad* had a certain recognition in the family or received higher sums than other slaves. In fact, the best rewarded female slaves were those who had attained a higher degree of proximity to and affection from their owners.

The freed slaves were also given clothes and jewellery by their owners in a double power game, which enhanced the former slaves' status and at the same time reinforced the masters' sense of paternalism towards their subordinates. Yet we cannot ignore that between these slave women and the members of the family, especially the children they took care of, bonds of affection were formed that could also have played a role in explaining the continuity of the relationship between masters and servants even after the liberations. The paths of these freedwomen were certainly varied: according to the oral history collected, in the last quarter of the twentieth century, most women, especially those closest to their owners, died in the houses of their former masters; others went out to make a living with resources provided by their masters or without any means whatsoever.

This past deserves to be remembered in an attempt not only to bear witness to the disinherited of history but also to note the blurred nature of a terminating process without a formal and explicit abolition. This uncertainty left the people and the memory of that period in a liminal state. In other words, those who had abandoned their former category found themselves in an uncertain and even dangerous state, often without being recognized in their new status. Moroccan society and the former colonizers should consider completing this rite of passage from slavery to freedom in their own collective memory.

Part Three

Preserving Identity and Tradition

Afro-Baloch communities in modern Iran and their healing traditions

Maryam Nourzaei

Introduction

The present chapter offers a brief sociocultural description of the Afro-Baloch communities along the coast in the Sistan and Balochistan Province of Iran with special attention to their healing traditions. This large province extending south to the Gulf of Oman is home to a variety of languages and ethnic groups – Iranian, Indo-Aryan and Dravidian but also people of African origin, the descendants of slaves. Following the study performed by Agnes Korn and myself, this chapter uses the term 'Afro-Balochi' to refer to the speech of the Baloch with African roots.[1] Although they do not see themselves as different from other Baloch and do not claim African heritage, the Afro-Baloch are perceived as being different (and as 'black') by other Baloch. These inconsistent perceptions are also the object of this study, which addresses the following questions: what can be said about the African heritage of the Afro-Baloch today? What unique Afro-Balochi traditions and tasks distinguish them from others in the wider society?

How have several generations of interaction with the native Baloch and *Jadgāl* ethnic groups influenced the traditions of the Afro-Baloch?

I got to know the Afro-Baloch communities when I was a teacher at a primary school in a village called Samach on the coast (see Figure 7.1). I noticed that in this village, the Afro-Baloch lived separately, in an area called *golamānī bāzār* (the area of slaves). A typical feature distinguishing them from the rest of the people in the village was their drumming and singing. Every evening, they drummed and sang until midnight. An Afro-Baloch girl worked for the chief of the village from early morning to late evening. She cleaned, washed and cooked. Once I asked the chief's wife about her. The wife said, 'She's the daughter of slaves we bought, but now we've freed them. This girl is the only one who still comes and works for us.' Their physical appearance (dark skin and curly hair) distinguishes them from the ethnic Baloch people in this village, although they dress like the Baloch.

---

[1] Agnes Korn and Maryam Nourzaei, 'Notes on the Speech of the Afro-Baloch of the Southern Coast of Iran', *Journal of the Royal Asiatic Society* 29 (2019): 623–57.

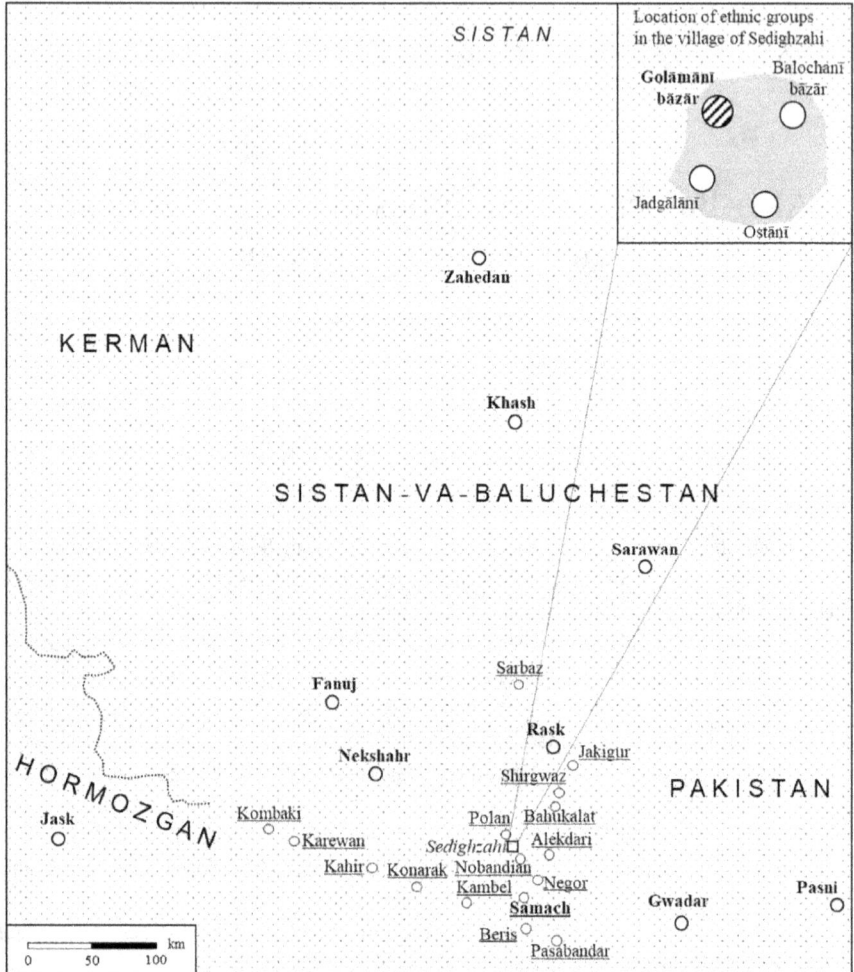

Figure 7.1 The Afro-Baloch settlement in South-eastern Iran.

Source: Taken from Korn and Nourzaei (2019) with some modifications.[2]

I had just one Afro-Baloch student in my class, and she excelled at singing and dancing. During class breaks, she was the only one who did this. Once I asked the daughter of the village chief to dance with her, and she responded curtly, 'I am a Baloch girl, not one to dance like a *ṭēng* (female slave). It's not my job to dance and sing; it's shameful for me.' Her answer made me wonder why a six-year-old girl would give such a sharp rebuke. Over the six months I taught in this village, this schoolgirl's unexpected response kept returning to my thoughts. In 2010, after receiving my master's degree,

²   I am grateful to Christian Rammer for providing a new version of the map.

Figure 7.2 An Afro-Baloch family.

Source: Courtesy of the author.

I finally had an opportunity to explore the reasons behind my student's reaction. I was able to return to the area to carry out extensive fieldwork and visit the Afro-Baloch communities, village by village, to observe their societal structures.

Data and context for this study were collected in direct interviews with both Afro-Baloch and Baloch community members from different cities and villages in four counties along the coast, namely, Sarbaz, Rask, Dashtiyari and Konarak, during several trips between 2010 and 2017. Information about the healing traditions was gathered through direct observation and interviews in Bahukalat village (Figure 7.2).[3]

Scholarly interest in the Afro-Baloch communities of Iran is a relatively recent phenomenon. Together with Korn, I conducted a detailed study of the morphosyntax of the Afro-Balochi language along the coast, and to my knowledge, no one has performed a detailed sociocultural investigation of the Afro-Baloch communities along the coast.[4] Previous studies have focused on the Baloch in general and often relied

[3] I am grateful to the Swedish Riksbankens Jubileumsfond (RJ) for their generous funding of this research (grant number: P20–0076). I wish to thank Abdulaziz Y. Lodhi, Carina Jahani and Agnes Korn for reading and commenting on this chapter, and to the editors, Elena Andreeva and Kevin McNeer, who provided careful comments at different stages of the review process. I would like to express my gratitude to Mohammad Salim Pasand, Abdol Naser Pasand, Mohammad Samadi and other anonymous Balochi speakers for both helping me with my field studies and providing information on these regions. I also would like to thank my Afro-Baloch singers Sabzo, Sarok, Masum, Ragam and other anonymous singers for sharing their beautiful songs and spending time with me. In addition, I wish to convey my thanks to Khayrnesa, the wife of Ragam, for providing me with invaluable information regarding healing traditions and also accompanying me to different villages in the region. My special gratitude goes to the healers *Khalipa* Sarok and *Khalipa* Karim for sharing their knowledge and experiences with me. Finally, I wish to extend my gratitude to Rashid and others for playing their music.
[4] Korn and Nourzaei, 'Notes on the Speech of the Afro-Baloch'.

on published accounts in lieu of first-hand field research. For example, Mahmmud-e Zand-e Muqaddam's study examines Balochistan as a whole in the twentieth century,[5] while Behnaz Mirzai's study is based on accounts written by Muqaddam and Philip Car Salzman.[6]

This chapter begins with an overview of the coastal Baloch communities and their geography, followed by an exploration of Afro-Baloch origins and identity issues, language use, culture, way of life, marriage traditions and education. Current Afro-Baloch roles in larger Baloch society are discussed, specifically Afro-Baloch labour and domestic service as well as public singing and dancing. The chapter concludes with a detailed description of healing traditions in the village of Bahukalat and then provides some thoughts on the origin of this tradition, followed by suggestions for future studies.

An overview of the coastal Baloch communities

The coastal Baloch population consists of the following major sub-ethnic groups (based on my research[7]):

1. The first subgroup consists of those considered to be the main Baloch tribes (such as *hākom, barr, hot, bahrāmzahi, āskāni, rend, nohāni, mullahzahi, hammali*). These are called *asīl* (or 'pure' Baloch).[8] They occupy the top of the region's socio-economic hierarchy. People in this region consider the *Jadgāl* people also to be *asīl* and believe that they are not Baloch but originally came from Pakistan and India.

2. The second subgroup of coastal Baloch society consists of certain professions: *mēd* (fisherman), *dōrzādag* (labourer), *jat* (camel rider), *ostā* (metal worker) and *lūḍī* (singer, performer). The Baloch people themselves believe that these groups are not Baloch and that they originally came from India. Some gave me very vague answers regarding their origin. They mainly work as fishermen, goldsmiths, blacksmiths and in similar skilled and semi-skilled occupations. This group ranks low in the coastal socio-economic hierarchy.

---

[5] Mahmmud-e Zand-e Muqaddam, *Hikāyat-e Baloch* (Tehran: Anjoman-e Āsār va Mafāxer-e Farhangi, 1370).

[6] Philip Car Salzman, *Black Tents of Baluchistan* (Washington: Smithsonian Institution Press, 2000), 241.

[7] Maryam Nourzaei, 'The State of Oral Traditions in Balochi in Iran', in *Oral Narration in Iranian Cultures*, ed. Maryam Nourzaei, Carina Jahani and Agnes Korn (Wiesbaden: Reichert Verlag, 2022), 165.

[8] I have asked people in these regions how they recognize whether a person is *asīl* (original), *borz zāt* (high nature) or *kam zāt* (low nature). According to them, some groups, such as *nawkar* or *golām*, are easy to recognize from their physical appearance and skin colour. Others, such as *ostā* or *dōrzzādag*, are difficult to recognize by their physical appearance and skin colour because they have mixed with others. Since people introduce themselves to each other by using clan names, for instance, *tāīpa/kawm* clans, it is easy to recognize them from their clans.

3. The third major subgroup consists of *nawkar* (servant) and *golām/ṭēng* (female slave) and *ṭī* (male slave). People use the term *sheedī* for persons of African origin who have very dark skin and woolly hair. However, this term is not as common as *nawkar* and *golām/ṭēng*. This third group occupies the lowest rank in the coastal socio-economic hierarchy.

The focus of this chapter is on the third subgroup, the Afro-Baloch community. People outside of this region view all of these groups as ethnic Baloch.[9]

The Baloch people of the coastal region are well known for preserving oral traditions and having a caste-based hierarchy.[10] This is in contrast to speakers of other Balochi dialects in Iran, such as the Sistani Balochi. In fact, the caste system profoundly affects almost all aspects of life of the coastal Baloch, including job opportunities and marriage. Each occupation belongs to one specific caste in society.

The preservation of oral tradition also stands out in this region. In fact, the oral tradition accompanies the local people in all stages of life, from the cradle to the grave. As with the differentiation of labour, the oral tradition is divided between the different social classes. For instance, the upper-caste men recite epic poems. Storytelling, on the other hand, is generally limited to the *lūḍī* class, which is a lower caste.

Types of musical instruments are also associated with different castes. For instance, members of the upper caste play the *ḍambūrag* (long-necked lute) which is considered a respectable instrument for the upper caste. Afro-Balochi men play the *ḍohl* (drum) among other instruments.[11]

The Afro-Baloch communities in Iran

It may at first be surprising to find that people of African origin are living in Balochistan, in the Sistan and Balochistan Province in south-eastern Iran (see Figure 7.1), but contacts between the coastal regions of the Indian Ocean, the Arabian Peninsula and East Africa go back a long time. The presence of Baloch people in the United Arab Emirates (UAE) is well known, but the Baloch also came to East Africa as traders and mercenaries.[12] Conversely, African people were brought to Iran and were settled in particular along the coast in Balochistan, Hormozgan, Buhshehr, Khuzistan,

---

[9] A detailed study of the caste system in this region is beyond the scope of the present chapter.

[10] Maryam Nourzaei, *Participant Reference in Three Balochi Dialects Male and Female Narrations of Folktales and Biographical Tales* (Uppsala: Acta Universitatis Upsaliensis, 2017), 79–82.

[11] Nourzaei, 'The State of Oral Traditions', 166; Nourzaei, *Participant Reference*, 80.

[12] Beatrice Nicolini, 'The 19th Century Slave Trade in the Western Indian Ocean: The Role of the Baloch Mercenaries', in *The Baloch and Others*, ed. Carina Jahani and Agnes Korn (Wiesbaden: Reichert Verlag, 2008), 326–44; Abdulaziz Y. Lodhi, 'A Note on the Baloch in East Africa', in Language in Society', in *Language in Society – Eight Sociolinguistic Essays on Balochi*, ed. Carina Jahani (Uppsala: Acta Universitatis Upsaliensis, 2000), 91–5; Abdulaziz Y. Lodhi, 'Iranian Presence in East Africa', in *Haft kongere wa haft murraka (Elegant Message and Eternal Beautitude), Essays in Memory of Professor Habibullah Amouzegar*, ed. Muhammad Ali Khajeh-Najafi and Muhammad Assemi (Uppsala: Acta Universitatis Upsaliensis, 2007), 267–74: Abdulaziz Y. Lodhi, 'The Baluch of East Africa: Dynamics of Assimilation and Integration', *Journal of the Middle East and Africa* 4, no. 1 (2013): 27–134: Korn and Nourzaei, 'Notes on the Speech of the Afro-Baloch', 2.

Qishm, Kharg and Kish.[13] Mirzai states that 'the presence of Africans in Iran through enslavement was mainly a result of commercial activities, and also this massive involuntary migration and displacement of Africans occurred before the abolitionist movement in the 19th century'.[14]

Farhat Sultana reports that today's inhabitants of African origin are the descendants of slaves who

> were brought to Balochistan from Eastern Africa by Arab conquerors and local traders. Parts of Makran were held by the Sultan of Oman from 1783 to 1958, and during much of the eighteenth and nineteenth centuries Oman also ruled Zanzibar (now in Tanzania), a major slave market. Slaves were brought to Coastal Makran via Oman and Iran and from there many were taken inland to work on the date farms or as domestic servants.[15]

Abdulaziz Y. Lodhi claims that they mainly originated from southern Tanzania and northern Mozambique.[16]

According to Mirzai, after the abolishment of slavery in 1928 in Iran, 'the social position of Africans was not changed; rather they became servants dependent upon their master'.[17]

Geographical distribution

The Afro-Baloch communities are found only in Balochistan, not in the regions of Khash and Zahedan or Sistan. In other words, they have been living with the Baloch people mainly along the coast and as far north as Iranshar and Sarawan. Some groups are also living in Jask in the Hormozgan province of Iran (see Figure 7.1).

The structure of remote villages in Balochistan is highly interesting. Generally, they are divided on the basis of clans such as *golāmānī bāzār* (the area of slaves), *ostānī bāzār* (the area of ironsmiths) and *Balochanī bāzār* (the area of Baloch). In Bahukalat and Samach, for instance, the village has been divided into two main parts: local Baloch and Afro-Baloch. According to the upper-class Baloch account, in this region, the Afro-Baloch people were formerly their slaves. They still live together in the same village. In contrast to the past, they have their own independent life, namely, financially self-sufficient and autonomous (they can make decisions regarding their own and their children's lives).

Some villages, such as Kambel, close to Chabahar, are populated exclusively by Afro-Baloch. I have also seen such villages close to Karewan city, but they are very rare.

---

[13] Mirzai, 'African Presence in Iran', 235.
[14] Ibid.
[15] Farhat Sultana, 'Gwat and Gwat-i leb: Spirit Healing and Social Change in Makran', in *Marginality and Modernity: Ethnicity and Change in Post-Colonial Balochistan*, ed. Paul Titus (Karachi: Oxford University Press, 1996), 30.
[16] Abdulaziz Y. Lodhi, 'Linguistic Evidence of Bantu Origins of The Sidis of India', in *TADIA: The African Diaspora in Asia: Explorations on a Less Known Fact* (Bangalore: Jana Jagrati Prakashana on behalf the Tadia Society, 2008), 301–13.
[17] Mirzai, 'African Presence in Iran', 236.

Origins and identity

In contrast to the African American, Afro-European and Afro-Indian communities, who know that they originated from Africa, the Afro-Baloch communities are not aware of their origin, or perhaps they do not want to tell about their origin (see Chapter 8 in this volume for similar observations regarding Afro-Soqotrans' origin).[18] They refer to themselves either as Baloch or *golām*. Mirzai observed the same with other Afro-Iranian communities who 'do not know their precise origin'.[19] On several occasions, I asked members of the Afro-Baloch communities in different regions along the coast about their origin. All of them gave me virtually the same answer: that they originated in Balochistan and that they are *golām*. Either they have no idea of Africa in their minds or they do not wish to acknowledge this. During my last trip, I asked an Afro-Baloch woman the same question. Interestingly, she told me, 'We are Baloch and we have been here from the beginning.' When asked where their relatives were living, they informed me they were either in the nearby villages or in counties such as Nekshahr or Sarbaz, or even in Karachi or the UAE.

In the remote villages, Afro-Baloch people often continue to see themselves as *golām*. In her stories, another informant refers to herself and her children thus: 'We as slaves were happy when we heard that our chief's wife was pregnant.' The reason for their happiness was that there would be a celebration and they (Afro-Baloch) would benefit from it.

In the large cities, the new generation of Afro-Baloch have replaced their old family names, *golāmi*, with new ones such as *dānāi* (wisdom). However, the Baloch people usually refer to them as *daryāi* (sea-people), indicating they came via the sea to Balochistan. This suggests that the Baloch have mixed ideas about the ways in which Afro-Baloch came to where they are today. When I asked a Baloch man (from one of the khan's families formerly living in Karewan) how they brought Africans to different parts of Balochistan, he said that in former times, the local khans were all related to each other, and they shared the African people among themselves. For instance, the khan of Konarak sent ten Africans (five men and five women) to the khan of Chabahar as a gift. Over time, their population grew and they spread across Balochistan.

There are many interesting legends about how the Afro-Baloch came to Balochistan. Here I will just mention one, which I recorded from a Baloch man from Karewan in 2011. He told me that in the past, the Baloch of their region used to travel to Africa to trade. In the African jungle, they encountered a group of people who were naked and lived like animals. This made the Baloch think about how to capture them and take them to Balochistan. After returning to Balochistan, they discussed this matter with their khans. They agreed to bring *ārag* (dried dates) with them to Africa. They filled a big sack with *ārag*, threw it on the ground and hid themselves. When the Africans came to take the *ārag*, the Baloch captured them. They clothed them and brought them to Balochistan, where they taught them how to behave as the Baloch did. They brought four or five people on each trip. When they noticed that the Afro-Baloch were very

---

[18] Lodhi, 'Linguistic Evidence of Bantu Origins', 304.
[19] Mirzai, 'African Presence in Iran', 231.

strong and able to perform hard labour, such as working on their date farms, as well as domestic jobs, they were encouraged to bring more people from Africa.

The attitudes of the Afro-Baloch towards the ethnic Baloch are interesting. In remote regions, one can still see expressions of Afro-Baloch loyalty to their former masters. In other words, both men and women among the Afro-Baloch exhibit respect for, and loyalty to, the ethnic Baloch. I witnessed how two or three Afro-Baloch women always accompanied their chief's wife when she attended a party, visited a friend or saw the doctor. One of the Afro-Baloch women from the Bahukalat village said to me, 'When our boss's wife got sick and he wanted to take her to Yazd, he talked to my husband; my husband immediately sent me with them. I took care of them for about a month.' During my last trip to this village, the same woman told me, 'I want to accompany you wherever you are going in this region; because you are our boss's guest, you should not be alone. It is shameful for us if you are alone.'

Language use

The Afro-Baloch have forgotten their own languages and have switched over to Balochi. The main reason for this could be that different groups arrived with different language backgrounds and could not communicate with each other. The Afro-Baloch speak the Balochi dialect dominant in the region where they live. For instance, in Konarak, they speak the Konaraki dialect which is different from the Sarbāzi dialect. Their variety is different from the speech of other Baloch in the area, but it seems possible to Korn and myself that limited mobility and access to education play a role in limiting the influence of other dialects and of Persian.

To date, no African language features have been found in their use of Balochi.[20] Nonetheless, ethnic Baloch consider the speech, and in particular the pronunciation, of the Afro-Baloch to be different. This leads us to conclude that Balochi speakers of non-African descent view the Afro-Baloch as a distinct social group. The same is true of Afro-Soqotrans, who are said to have a distinct accent and other linguistic differences when speaking Soqotri, although they no longer use African languages.[21]

Like the Baloch people in this region, the Afro-Baloch are monolingual, which means they speak only Balochi. The only exceptions to this are Afro-Baloch who have been educated in school or who are working on boats, and hence also know Persian, Urdu or Arabic. At home with their children, with each other and with the local Baloch people, they use only the Balochi language.

Culture and way of life

Oral Afro-Baloch accounts, like those of other descendants of slaves around the world, describe miserable lives in the past.[22] The older generation's oral accounts were very

---

[20] See Korn and Nourzaei, 'Notes on the Speech of the Afro-Baloch', 4.
[21] See Chapter 8 in this volume.
[22] In many villages, for example, Bahukalat, I have observed that the Afro-Baloch graveyard is separate from that of the Baloch. In some villages, even their mosques are separate.

painful and saddening to listen to and transcribe.[23] They were forced to toil for the heads of their clans just to get something to eat. One of the saddest oral accounts, recorded from a seventy-year-old Afro-Baloch from Konarak in 2010, states,

> a chief sold his young female slave who had a little baby to the tradesmen. Her little baby was crying alone at home. The baby was crying and crying. Someone from the village came and asked 'Where is its mother?' One of her chief's family said, 'A pain seized her mother and she died, and we took her and buried her.'[24]

After the Iranian revolution in 1979, the political and economic situation of the Afro-Baloch changed considerably. Those who have Iranian identity cards have since received a great deal of assistance and access to services from the government, for example, the Imam Khomeini Relief Committee (although statistics are hard to come by because separate records are not kept for the Afro-Baloch population).[25] In addition, their oral accounts reveal that government authorities supported them against their former masters. One of the oral accounts (recorded from an old man who told me about his father's life story) states,

> His father took his mother, who was a female servant of a Baloch man, to another village. The next day, when it was reported to the Baloch man (or master) that his female servant had been taken by her husband, he followed them in an attempt to kill him and bring home the female servant. His mother complained to the governmental authorities in Polan and said, 'Look, I love my husband, but my chief forced me to come to them, now you tell me, how they made me run [...]' The authorities said to her chief 'You know, it's ok, she's worked before; now she doesn't work, she has a husband and she goes with her husband ...' Finally they rejected this man's claim and his mother stayed with his father in the village.

Today, in more heavily populated areas, the Afro-Baloch own buildings, land, businesses and properties. One Afro-Baloch woman in Rask told me that now they do not need to work for others. In the remote areas, they work on Baloch-owned land as agricultural labourers, but they are paid. I asked an Afro-Baloch in Bahukalat if the farmland belonged to her. She said, 'No, I am just working here; the owner of the land is a Baloch, but I am working on it.'

---

[23] See also the data in Abdolhossein Yadegari, 'Pluralism and Change in Iranian Balochistan', in *The Baloch and Others*, ed. Jahani and Korn, 253–8; Richard Burton, *Sindh, and the Races that Inhabit the Valley of the Indus; with Notices of the Topography and History of the Province* (London: British Library, 1851), 18–114; Hoshang Noraiee, 'Change and Continuity: Power and Religion in Balochistan', in *The Baloch and Others*, ed. Jahani and Korn, 345–64; Nicolini, 'The 19th Century Slave Trade', 339.

[24] This life story is taken from my unpublished Afro-Baloch corpora with Agnes Korn.

[25] Not all Afro-Baloch individuals have identity papers, however. I observed a similar state of affairs among the Brahui, a non-Iranian ethnic group whose language belongs to Dravidian language family.

During my trip in 2017, I noticed that a lot of Afro-Baloch people previously living in a *kapar* (house built of palm branches) had received bank loans and built nice houses, using their *kapar* as a kitchen.

Based on my field observations, the Afro-Baloch share the same religion as the Baloch people, that is, they are Muslims belonging to the Sunni Hanafi school. A distinctive Sunni sect called Zikri also exists in these regions, typically in Zarabad, in the village of Kahir. In the course of my fieldwork, however, I did not observe any Afro-Baloch following the Zikri religion.[26]

Marriage traditions

The Afro-Baloch are regarded as an isolated community in the sense that they practice only endogamous marriage. In the past, their masters arranged their marriages. One oral account states that an Afro-Baloch man went to his uncle with a request to marry his daughter. His uncle said, 'I'm happy to marry off my daughter to you, but you know, she's the servant of such and such a Baloch. You should go and talk to him. If he gives her to you, I'll be happy about this marriage, and who else could be a better husband for her than you.'[27]

There used to be a tradition among the rich Baloch family khans that when their sons or daughters married, the parents gave them around seven *ṭēng* and *ṭī* Afro-Baloch slaves as part of their dowry.[28] This shows that the Afro-Baloch did not have full rights over their own children.

Intermarriage between the Afro-Baloch and *lūḍī* or *med* (who are considered low caste) is very common in these regions,[29] although I have also noted marriages between Afro-Baloch women and non-African men outside of Balochistan, mainly men working as teachers, soldiers or healthcare providers. During my trip in 2017, I met an Afro-Baloch girl married to a Sistani Persian man who lived with the girl's family. A noteworthy peculiarity of this region is that when a girl marries, she and her husband live with her parents until the young family can afford their own home. One oral account from an Afro-Baloch female describes how a military man from outside of Balochistan fell in love with her sister and eventually married her. When

---

[26] For more information on Zikri ritual practices, see Sabir Badalkhan, 'Zikri Dilemmas: Origins, Religious Practices, and Political Constraints', In *The Baloch and Others*, ed. Jahani and Korn, 293–326. The study of religion and belief in these regions is outside the scope of the present study.

[27] Hawrokān's life story, in Maryam Nourzaei, *Documenting Orality: Experiences of Collecting Folk Narratives in Iran*, forthcoming.

[28] I noticed such a case during my childhood. A man from my region took a wife from Balochistan. The girl's family gave her a *moled*, 'female slave', as servant. The servant's name was Shahnaz, but people called her *Shanāz-syā*, 'the black Shahnaz'. She worked there until the end of her life. I also noticed in Chabahar that a Khanzahi family gave seven male and female Afro-Baloch as dowry when their daughter got married to be her servants. I observed a similar case in the city of Iranshar.

[29] Among the Baloch, I have heard that upper class men have (or had) sexual relations with Afro-Baloch women (concubines) but did not marry them officially. The children of such unions are called *golame Khān zātī* (a slave with *Khan*'s blood); see also Muqaddam, *Hikāyat-e Baloch*, 440.

the man decided to take his bride with him to his homeland, she refused and they divorced.

Afro-Baloch marriage ceremonies are much the same as those among the Baloch, lasting three to seven days, though costing considerably less than the ethnic Baloch ceremonies. The guests mainly come from within their own community. As in the Baloch communities, polygamy is common among the Afro-Baloch, meaning that in practice a man can take up to four wives.

School and education

In the past, there were virtually no educational opportunities for either Baloch or Afro-Baloch people in remote regions. Even when there were, women did not have any opportunity to attend school. With increasing access to education and schools in these regions, both boys and girls now attend school. For instance, in Bahukalat, both Baloch and Afro-Baloch girls are educated through high school but do not attend university. When I asked why it was so, the locals explained that people still believed it was enough for a girl to learn how to read and write her name, and they do not take seriously the idea of allowing their girls to get higher education.

In large cities such as Chabahar and Negor, Afro-Baloch children (mainly boys) have received university-level education and even work in the medical sector and at the university. As far as I know from my time living in the area and interacting with the communities, no Afro-Baloch women have yet been enrolled in university-level education.

The social position of the Afro-Baloch communities

The Afro-Baloch people are located at the bottom of the traditional coastal caste hierarchy system; their low social status might be based on their past as slaves, though the caste system is not as strong as it once was, and the traditional social structure has begun to break down. Because changes spread slowly in the remote regions, the tasks discussed below are still mainly reserved for the Afro-Baloch people.

Labour and domestic service

Based on the oral accounts and my own observation in the region, the Afro-Baloch people perform the jobs considered to be the lowest in society. Men and young boys do outdoor work for the head of their clan. Women and girls are involved in cleaning, washing, cooking and other domestic chores. Unlike in the past, however, they are paid for their work. In Chabahar, I witnessed Afro-Baloch women and girls knocking on the doors of prosperous ethnic Baloch and asking whether there was any work for them to do, such as cleaning and washing. In addition, in Nobandiyan, I noticed that some of Afro-Baloch women lived with their chief and others went back to their own family after finishing their daily responsibilities.

At ceremonies for weddings, giving birth, funerals and mourning, all the cooking, washing and cleaning tasks are reserved for Afro-Baloch men and women. The women serve food and drinks at the women's meetings, and the men do the same at the men's meetings. At wedding ceremonies, if the bride and bridegroom's family live far from each other, they usually bring along their own slaves to take care of various jobs.[30]

Until very recently, before the appearance of the telephone and cell phones, inviting people to important events such as weddings or engagement ceremonies was also reserved for the Afro-Baloch. I noticed in a village that the wife of the village chief told her female Afro-Baloch servants to go to the nearby villages and invite people to her daughter's *jol bandag* (engagement ceremony).

Public singing and dancing

Dancing and singing at various events are reserved for Afro-Baloch men and women. Baloch women are not allowed to sing or dance in public due to cultural restrictions in their society. And yet Afro-Baloch women are famous for dancing, singing, musical healing and public performances.

The important occasions when Afro-Baloch sing and dance are celebrations of weddings, engagements, births and circumcisions. They are famous for performing songs such as *līlo* (lullabies), *nāzēnk* (panegyrics), *zahīrok* (poems of homesickness) and *mamabies* (songs for a new mother-to-be), among others.[31]

The tradition of singing songs for a new mother and her baby is generally limited to the Afro-Baloch women in this society. Singing these songs is one of the few kinds of work done by Afro-Baloch women that are highly appreciated by the coastal Balochi society. It is a way for women to gain respect and to emphasize their importance for the community as a whole. People of the higher castes consider the singing of songs for a new mother and her baby to be respectable work. Still, performing these songs is a source of income for the Afro-Baloch people, who receive recompense in the form of food, clothing or money from the father or grandfather of the newborn child. During my last trip in Bahukalat, one of the singers promised to let me record her in the evening. She kept me waiting and did not show up. In the morning she came to me, and when I asked her why she had not come the evening before as she promised, she answered,

> A man came to me from the nearby village while I was working on the land and invited me to come and sing for his new baby. He took me to the party. I sang all night. I thought about you but, you know, he offered me more than you. So, I decided to go there first. I need money for my children.

---

[30]   I took part in a wedding ceremony where the bridegroom's family were from Karachi in Pakistan, and they had brought their own Afro-Baloch servants to help with various jobs.

[31]   *Mamabies* is a term coined by the author. The local people call this type of song *sepet* (praising): see Sabir Badalkhan, 'The Changing Content of Baloch Women's Songs in Eastern Makran', in *Proceedings of the Third European Conference of Iranian Studies*, Part 2, ed. Charles Melville (Germany: Reichert Verlag Wiesbaden, 1999), 107–25.

A sample of a *mamabies* song[32]

Table 7.1 A *Mamabies* Song

rapton be rāhī	'I went to a path'
rāh bī do rāh	'the path became two paths'
man dīton alī šēr ǰāho nemāzā	'I saw (lit. have seen) Ali šēr [brave like a lion] on [his] prayer place'
dračke dēmāo	'there was a bush (lit. a tree) in front of [him] and'
dračk zaperāne	'the bush (lit. the tree) was a saffron bush'
dračk zaperāne	'the bush (lit. the tree) was a saffron bush'
tāke korānan	'its leaves are [as yellow as] pages of the Koran'
allā nabī ǰalloǰalāl	'God, prophet, may His majesty be glorified'
nabīe mohammad sale alā	'prophet Mohammad, Peace upon [him]'
rapton be rāhī	'I went to a path'
rāh bī do rāh	'the path became two pathways'
man dīton alī šēr ǰāho nemāzā	'I saw (lit. have seen) Ali šēr [brave like a lion] on [his] prayer place'
dračke dēmāo	'there was a bush (lit. a tree) in front of [him] and'
dračk zaperāne	'the bush (lit. the tree) was a saffron bush'
dračk zaperāne	'the bush (lit. the tree) was a saffron bush'
tāke korānan	'its leaves are [as yellow as] pages of the Koran'
allā nabī ǰalloǰalāl	'God, prophet, may His majesty be glorified'
nabīe mohammad sale alā	'prophet Mohammad, Peace upon [him]'

Table 7.2 A Sample Lullaby

līlō bāt o līlō manī nonokā ōrdēnā	'*līlō bī* for my little baby'
nonō man tarā rōdēnta	'Little baby, I have raised you.'
līlō bāt o gōgī nēmago sabzḗ mōrt	'*līlo bī* and butter of cows and powder from the green leaves of myrtle.'
gōgī nēmag ča māl dārå	'butter of cows from the livestock owner'

---

[32] See Maryam Nourzaei and Mohammad Salim Pasand, 'Analysing an Afro-Baloch Mamaby Song', to be published in *Essays on Balochi Language and Literature: In Memory of Abdullah Jan Jamaldini*, ed. Sabir Badalkhan and Adriano V. Rossi (UniOr Naples and ISMEO Rome, forthcoming).

līlō bāt o sabzě mōrt o ča mā čabārā	'*līlo bī* and powder from the green leaves of myrtle and [the 'powder from the green leaves of myrtle'] from Chabahar.'
baččī bītag o man dīta	'The baby was born and I have seen [him]'
līlo bāt o čammānī do rōg mǎ bīta	'*līlo bī* Oh his two eyes were bright (lit. there was light in his two eyes)'
ē čammānī do rōg mān bīta	'his two eyes were bright (lit. there was light in his two eyes)'
līlō bāt o līlō manī baččīkā ōrdēnā	'*līlo bī* Oh for my little son'
ē kole ālemān gal zorta	'all these people became happy'
līlō bāt kol gō gwānzagā šahm gepta	'*līlo bī*, the house with the cradle became bright.
baččī manā xodā dāta	'God has given me the little baby.'
līlō bāt o šāhēn kāder o raxmānā	'*līlo bī* and [my Lord] powerful like a king and merciful.'
līlō līlalō, līlō bāt	'*līlo līol olīlo bī*'
līlō bāt o līlōī kanǎ dǎ bewāspī	'*līlo bī* Oh I keep līlo bī until he sleeps'
bwāsp ke wāp tarā rōdēnī	'sleep! because sleep makes you grow'
līlo bāt o bīwābī tarā ranǰēnīt	'*līlo bī* Oh sleeplessness makes you unhappy'
šāgēn gwānzagā o mēdēn band	'the teak cradle and the band (made of goat hair)'
līlō bāt o šāgēn gwānzag taī wāb ǰāhen....	'*līlo bī* Oh the cradle is your sleeping place'
šāgēn gwānzag taī wāb ǰāhen	'the cradle is your sleeping place'
līlō bāt o mīdēn band taī pāsbānant	'*līlo bī* and the band (made of goat hair) is your protection'

Healing traditions

The traditional art of healing is commonly practised in the Sistan and Balochistan Province. There are several types of healing practices. The healer is called a mullah (a Muslim learned in Islamic theology), *pīr* (saint), *shaykh/shay* (leader), *khalipa* (leader) and *jādūger* (magician). Today, both mullahs and *jādūgers* do very good business. In fact, their business is growing and gaining more prestige in society. People go to them and ask for help with various problems such as depression, infertility, mental disorders, jaundice, seizures, paralysis, love problems and even finding a job. In contrast to the mullah and *jādūger*, healers such as *pīr*, *shaykh* and *khalipa*, whom people believe to be *xodāye dōst* (God's friend), are disappearing from this region. Once when I was sick, my grandmother took me to *Shaykh* Almkhan, a famous *pīr* who lived in the mountain in Koren Region close to Zahedan and died in 2009. I still remember that the room was packed with patients. He only prayed orally and gave the patients some salt and a string made of camel hair, because he did not have enough education to write a prayer to place in a *tāwīz/tāīt* (amulet), as is often done.[33]

The healing tradition with music and dance is the most distinctive cultural expression of the Afro-Baloch communities, particularly in this region. This tradition among the Afro-Baloch is disappearing as well. It is called *por kanag* (going into a trance). Even though the Baloch people live in the same villages as the Afro-Baloch, they are unaware of this tradition; some of the Baloch people do not even want to acknowledge this tradition because they do not believe in it. In contrast to the other traditions, such as *mamabies*, the healing tradition has spread to neither the Baloch nor the *Jadgāl* communities. I asked the female *khalipa* called Sarok, 'Who are your patients?' She said, 'The patients only come from our own clans. They are my cousins and close relatives; no one is a stranger.' When I asked if she had ever cured a Baloch patient, she answered, 'Baloch people do not bring their patients to us.' This tradition is not very common among Muslims, but it is found among East African Muslims and Afro-Indian Sidi.[34] The Baloch generally believe that only the Afro-Baloch people are victims of *gwāt* (lit. 'wind') /jinn because they are spiritually weak. I was often told by Baloch that the Afro-Baloch engaged in drumming rituals late into the night simply because 'they love drumming, they are crazy'. The native community seemed little interested in attempting to understand the nature of or motivations behind the drumming.

Previous studies on healing traditions have focused on Afro-Iranian and the Afro-Baloch communities in Pakistan.[35] The first study, described in a book entitled *Zār va Bād va Baloch* ('Zār (a form of spiritual possession) and Wind and the Baloch'), was carried out in Chabahar by Ali Riyahi in the 1970s.[36] He gives a brief description of the Balochi traditions and beliefs including *zār*.[37] Yet today, neither Baloch nor Afro-Baloch are aware of *zār* generally, much less of the types of *zār* Riyahi describes. Riyahi's study also makes mention of the tradition of female circumcision in the Afro-Baloch communities,[38] but this too is no longer practised.

---

[33] A detailed account of healing traditions in this region is the subject of a future article.
[34] Lodhi, 'Linguistic Evidence of Bantu Origins', 304.
[35] Iraj Bashiri, 'Muslims or Shamans: Blacks of the Persian Gulf', https://www.angelfire.com/rnb/bash iri/Gulf/gulf.pdf (accessed 9 August 2023); Sultana, 'Gwat and Gwat-i leb', 7.
[36] Ali Riyahi, *Zār va Bād va Baloch* (Tehran: Kitābḫāna-e Ṭahūrī, 1977).
[37] I would like to thank Guiti Shokri and Ali Hassouri (Stockholm) for introducing this book to me. My special thanks go to Riyahi's wife, Tehran, for scanning the book and sending it to me.
[38] Riyahi, *Zār va Bād*, 3.

Moreover, the Iranian scholars who have addressed healing traditions have not performed thorough investigations.[39] The most recent work on healing traditions among the Afro-Baloch is a documentary film by Mirzai.[40]

Later in this chapter, I will give a brief description of the healing practices among the Afro-Baloch in Bahukalat based on my field observations in 2017 and direct interviews with the healers.[41] Prior to that, it is necessary to introduce some terms and concepts.

Jinn / *gwāt*

For the Baloch people, *gwāt* and jinn are two different classes of entity: a *gwāt* is an evil spirit in the air who does not have a solid body as a jinni does. A *gwāt* can exist as male or female and can be either Muslim or *kafir* (unbeliever). The Afro-Baloch people, however, do not distinguish between them.[42]

Based the Afro-Baloch oral accounts, the jinn/*gwāt* typically live in graveyards, under date palms, by the sea, by a *kawreāp* (a puddle) in old and dark places, in the forest, in dirty places, such as *pasīl* (toilets), and ruins.

Khalipa/gwātī māt

In contrast to the Afro-Iranian terms for healers *bābā zār* (father of *zār)* and *māmā zār* (mother of *zār*), the Afro-Baloch healers, regardless of gender, are called *khalipa/gwātī māt* (mother of the wind).

I met in person a male *khalipa* called Karimok in the Bahukalat village (Golāmanī bāzār). He was a charming man, around forty years old, who was proud of being called *khalipa*. I asked him how he happened to become a *khalipa* and whence he acquired this knowledge. He explained to me that a *khalipa* gained supernatural knowledge from either a mullah or a *shaykh/shay* belonging to the Baloch community. He further said,

> Before I became a *khalipa,* I used to work as a well digger. One day, while I was working inside the well, several jinn attacked me. I felt weak and fainted. The people took me out [and laid me] on the ground. I did not feel well for three or four days. They took me to a doctor in Chabahar. I stayed in the hospital for three weeks, but I did not feel better. Then, my family took me to a *shay* in our nearby village. When the *shay* recited Koranic verses, I fell unconscious, and my jinni appeared in front of the *shay*. The *shay* saw with his supernatural knowledge that I would be useful

[39] Muhammad Reza Darvishi, *Ā ynah va Ā vaz* (Tehran: Hawzeye Honari, 1376), 34; Muqaddam, *Hikāyat-e Baloch*, 212.
[40] *The African-Baluchi Trance Dance* (2012) [Documentary Film] Dir: Behnaz A. Mirzai, http://www.afroiranianlives.com/index.htm (accessed 26 July 2019).
[41] Maryam Nourzaei (2022), *Mamabies among the Afro-Baloch Community Social Status and Cultural Heritage of a Low Caste Community in Iran*, Endangered Languages Archive, archiving code 0697 (documentary project). I am recording and filming this tradition, along with other traditions, village by village, in these regions. I have a good relationship with the community, and its members are actively involved in the project.
[42] When I asked, the healers informed me that jinn and *gwāt* are the same.

for the people and had the power to fight jinn and evil things. The *shay* then put his hand on my back and called me *khalipa*; you know a *shay* doesn't put his hand on anyone's back. I was very lucky that the *shay* chose me as one of his followers. Since then I have been a *khalipa* and have cured many patients. It is a hard job to fight with the jinn. Once a year, I go to the *shay* to enhance my supernatural power. I do not need to be trained, visiting the *shay* is enough.

Khalipa is a new term used instead of *gwātī māt*. This could be due to the influence of Balochi culture. People prefer to use *khalipa* rather than *gwātī māt*. Riyahi introduces terms such as *bābā zār* and *māmā zār* in his work.[43] I have not heard these terms in the Bahukalat and Chabahar regions. It might be that people do not use them today or simply that they have forgotten them. In addition, the words *bābā* and *māmā* are not Balochi words and not used by Baloch speakers in this region; the most common words are *pet/abok* (father) *māt/mamok* (mother).

A *khalipa/gwātī māt* can be male or female. The *khalipa* is a person who has been affected by the jinn and has supernatural powers to fight them. In contrast to a mullah or a *shaykh*, who cures their patients by giving them *tāwīz/dāīt/dam* (amulets), the *khalipa* cures patients by means of *leb dayag* (dancing) and *por kanag* (going into trance). In addition, both the *khalipa* and the patient go into a trance *por* (complete). A mullah and *shaykh* must have an Islamic education, but for a *khalipa* this is not necessary. For instance, *Khalipa* Sarok cannot even read or write her name.

The afflicted

According to the information provided by *Khalipa* Sarok, 'A person can be affected by a single jinni or several at the same time.' Both men and women can be affected by the jinn: for instance, if someone passes one of the above-mentioned places alone at night, she/he will be affected by them. Women are the main victims, because women's thoughts are considered dirty and their hearts full of jealousy. Women can be affected by male jinn and men by female ones. An unborn child inside the mother's belly can also be affected by the jinn. I asked the *khalipa* how she cures a baby inside the mother's belly. She said, 'We take the woman to the *shaykh/shay* and the *shay* gives the woman a *kolband* (a black string) to tie around her waist until the baby is born.' This practice is an exception, since in all other cases, it is suggested that the Afro-Balochi healers cure a patient just by dance and music.

Symptoms

The symptoms of a person affected by a jinni are described by *Khalipa* Sarok as follows: the person looks pale, feels dizzy and experiences pain in the head and heart; her/his heart is full of fear, she/he is weak and always afraid and in a state of panic.

---

[43] Riyahi, *Zār va Bād*, 5.

Musical instruments used

The following musical instruments are used during healing practices: *ḍambūrag* (long-necked lute), *nal* (flute), *change-soroz* (bowed lute), *soroz* (lute), *do nalī* (double flute), *ḍohl* and *rēl* ('recorded music'). In addition, rhythmic chanting of *sorod* (singing) and clapping are used. The choice of instruments depends on the *gwāt*/jinn: for instance, some *gwāt* go into a trance with the *nal*, some with the *change-soroz*, others with *ḍohl* or with clapping and *sorod*; still others go into a trance with a combination of all of these. The *khalipa* invites musicians from other villages to come and play the music for the ritual. When I asked whether they belong to Sarok's clan, she replied, 'No, they do not belong to my clan.'

A band with instruments costs a lot, and the patient must bear all the costs. During the ceremony, a person in the audience told me that a group of musicians today was so expensive that many patients could not afford it and, therefore, used recorded music instead.

The singers praise the famous saints such as Kalandar and Abdolghader-e Gilāni/Jīrānī/Ghos, and ask for help from them while singing *sorod*.

A study of these songs demonstrates that many of them include Arabic phrases. Judging by inaccuracies in pronunciation, these songs could be new for the healers (see song 2). One reason for using these Arabic phrases might be that since 1979, Islamic clerics consider it to be *haram* (forbidden) to praise saints and ask them for help. Instead, they encourage people to praise God and the prophets and their followers and ask only them for help.

Two healing songs are presented below. These songs consist of two parts: the first part is recited by the *gwātī mat* and the second part by the participants. As shown in the following songs, the participants recite only a single word. The first column shows lines recited by the healer, while the second shows the participants' responses.

Food sacrifice

In addition to music and dance, food plays an important role in the ritual ceremony. The following items are used as sacrifice: meat (1 goat), rice (11 kilos), *halwā* (wheat pudding, half a kilo), eggs (2), sweets (1 kilo), apples (half a kilo), oranges (half a kilo), juice (2 bottles) and fresh goat milk (2 litres). I was not told the reason behind these specific quantities.

In addition to the food sacrifice, the patient should prepare the following: *zaprān* (saffron), *ṭēl* (coconut oil), *sōrēn ṭēl* (scented oil), *golāp* (rose water), perfume, scents, *mesrī šakar* (crystal sugar), *spedēn mask* (white musk), *agarbaṭṭī* (joss stick), *rehān* (basil) and *sōčkī* (incense).

Healing traditions in Bahukalat

All the items listed above are necessary for the ceremony, which means that the healing tradition costs a lot for the patient's family. In fact, it is more expensive than visiting a doctor. During my fieldwork expedition in 2017, I asked how much it costs. The *khalipa*

Table 7.3 Song 1: *Kalandar*

Gwātī māt ('healer')	Participants
saxī šābāzē kalandar ('Kalandar is Sakhi Shabaz')	*kalandar* ('Kalandar')
saxī jerānī ('Sakhi Jerani')	*kalandar* ('Kalandar')
kalandar jān ē ('he is dear Kalandar')	*kalandar* ('Kalandar')
kalandar jān ē ('he is dear Kalandar')	*kalandar* ('Kalandar')
saxī lālrānī ('[he is] very generous')	*kalandar* ('Kalandar')
saxī jošānī ('[he is] very generous')	*kalandar* ('Kalandar')
saxī jošānī ('[he is] very generous')	*kalandar* ('Kalandar')
kalandar jānē ('he is dear Kalandar')	*kalandar* ('Kalandar')
nabī tī nāmē ('[Kalandar] Nabi is your name')	*kalandar* ('Kalandar')
Nabī tī nāmē ('[Kalandar] Nabi is your name')	*kalandar* ('Kalandar')
allāh allāhē ('God is God')	*kalandar* ('Kalandar')
allāh allāhē ('God is God')	*kalandar* ('Kalandar')
saxī šāhbāzē ('[Kalandar] is Sakhi shabaz')	*kalandar* ('Kalandar')
saxī lārānī ('[he is] very generous')	*kalandar* ('Kalandar')
saxī jošānī ('[he is] very generous')	*kalandar* ('Kalandar')

Table 7.4 Song 2: *Šhadon Lāhellāh*

Gwātī māt ('healer')	Participants
šhadon lāhellāh ('there is no deity except God')	*elellāh* ('only God')
šhadon lāhellāh ('there is no deity except God')	*elellāh* ('only God')
Morīdā̊ hamā pīr ('I am follower of that saint')	*elellāh* ('only God')
morīdānī pīr ('the saint of the followers')	*elellāh* ('only God')
sakī šābāz o ('Sakhi Shabāz and')	*elellāh* ('only God')
Šadon lāhelāh ('there is no deity except God')	*elellāh* ('only God')
Šadon lāhelāh ('there is no deity except God')	*elellāh* ('only God')
Morīdā̊ hamā pīr ('I am the follower of that saint')	*elellāh* ('only God')
Morīdānī pīrā̊ ('I am the followers of saint')	*elellāh* ('only God')
ašhadan lāhelāh ('there is no deity except God')	*elellāh* ('only God')
Ašhadan lāhelāh ('there is no deity except God')	*elellāh* ('only God')
Ahadan lāhelāh ('there is no deity except God')	*elellāh* ('only God')
Morīdā̊ tī pīr ('I am your follower, the saint')	*elellāh* ('only God')
Ašhadon lāhelāh ('there is no deity except God')	*elellāh* ('only God')
ašhadon lāhelāh ('there is no deity except God')[44]	*elellāh* ('only God')
Morīdānī pīr ('the saint of the followers')	*elellāh* ('only God')

---

[44] Transcriptions are based on oral recordings, I kept the singers' original pronunciations of what seems to be the same word, for example, *šadon* and *ašhadon*.

told me that the musical group alone costs 2,000,000 Iranian tomans (about $154) excluding other costs such as food and sacrifice. A *khalipa*'s services cost 1,000,000 Iranian tomans (about $77).

Despite the high costs, the Afro-Baloch hold that for some situations, healing is necessary. I have heard two different accounts of how the Afro-Baloch seek healing.

The first account: When a person gets sick, they first take the patient to a doctor. If the doctor confirms that the patient does not have any physical problem, they take the patient to a mullah. When the mullah confirms that the patient has not been affected by *jādū* (magic), then they take the patient to a *shaykh/shay*. If the *shay* says that the patient has been affected by *nīmonene* (a jinni), then the patient's family take her/him to a *khalipa*. This seems to be a modern tradition, because the first person they consult is a doctor.

The second account, which might be more traditional, is first to consult with a *khalipa*. The *khalipa* is the one who decides where the patient should go for treatment. The patient's family either invites the *khalipa* to their home or they go to visit the *khalipa*. The main idea is that both the *khalipa* and the patient must be in the same place during the treatment. The *leb* (dancing) lasts three nights. Only the *khalipa* and the patient are dancing while other participants are singing.

In other cities, such as Konarak, the *leb* lasts from three to seven nights. *Khalipa* Sarok also informed me that in the past it lasted from three to seven nights.

I will explain the first-, second- and third-night ceremonies in detail in connection with the second account.

The first night, ǰost gerag *(asking questions)*

The main goal of the first night, which is called *ǰost gerag*, is to determine the cause of the patient's problem. No food is served during the first and second nights, but the patient's family must prepare a dinner for the musicians.

The *khalipa* arranges the ceremony and invites the music group. The ceremony starts around 8 pm, after evening prayers, and continues until around 10 pm. It takes only one or two hours. The patient must be washed and dressed in white. During the treatment, both female and male patients should cover their faces with a light cloth called *shall*.

The *khalipa* and other people who previously have been affected by the jinn spread a clean and unused white blanket. Everyone in the community comes and joins in this ceremony.[45] The people sit in a circle. The middle of the room is reserved for the *khalipa* and the patient. The *khalipa* invites the patient to sit on the blanket. The *khalipa* burns *sōčkī*, first for himself, then for the patient and finally in the four corners of the room. The music plays, the singers sing and the audience claps along. While the *khalipa* listens to the music, he begins slowly moving his body from head to foot, dances and goes into a trance. The audience claps for him. They call this *por byag* (ready to go into a trance).

While the *khalipa* is *por* and dancing, he slowly approaches the patient. He touches the patient's left shoulder. Then, the *khalipa* becomes unconscious and speaks in a

---

[45] One of my Baloch informants in this village said that when he was a little boy, he used to go and watch their ceremony; however, his father told him not to go there.

different language.[46] They believe that the *khalipa* himself has jinni and he can contact the jinn afflicting the patient by touching the patient's shoulder. The *khalipa*'s jinni tells him what the cause of the illness is and how the patient can be cured. For instance, if the *khalipa*'s jinni recognizes that the patient's problem can be cured by a doctor, the *khalipa* suggests that the patient go and visit a doctor. If the *khalipa*'s jinni finds that *jādū* has influenced the patient, then the *khalipa* sends the patient to a mullah. If the *khalipa*'s jinni discovers that the patient has been attacked by *pari* (fairy),[47] then he sends the patient to a *shaykh/shay*. If the *khalipa*'s jinni recognizes that the patient has been affected by a jinni, then he suggests that the patient should be prepared for *leb* and *por kanag*. At the end of this ceremony, the *khalipa* asks for *pānī* (water).[48] People give him a glass of water.

The second night, **por kanag**
The main activity of the second night's ceremony is that the *khalipa* makes the patient dance and comes in contact with the patient's jinn. The ceremony starts at around 8 pm and does not last beyond midnight. As on the first night, the *khalipa* prepares for the ceremony, spreading a clean blanket in the middle of the room. Both men and women attend. The *khalipa* burns *sōčkī* for himself, then for the patient and finally in all four corners of the room. The *khalipa* asks the musicians to begin playing. The audience claps along. Once more, the *khalipa* burns *sōčkī* for the patient in order to make him or her dance.

The *khalipa* takes rose water, fresh basil, water and coconut oil and recites *dam jant* (some verses from the Quran); makes a special drink (a mixture of rose water and fresh basil) and gives it to the patient; and then massages the patient with coconut oil from head to toe. Due to cultural restrictions, if the patient is a woman and the *khalipa* is a man, the *khalipa* asks a woman to do the massage.

The *khalipa* puts a hand on the patient's left shoulder in order to connect with the jinn and again burns *sōčkī*. The patient slowly starts to dance. The body movement begins with the head and goes all the way to the feet. The choice of dance depends on the patient's jinn; for instance, some jinn prefer to dance while the patient is sitting, while others prefer to dance while the patient is standing. The patient dances to the point of exhaustion and falls down on the floor unconscious. The *khalipa* approaches and begins to massage and touches the patient's left shoulder with the hand. Then the patient regains consciousness, starts to dance and goes into a trance.

The *khalipa* begins by asking the patient's jinn questions to figure out how many of the jinn are operating, what their wishes are and their reason for attacking the patient. For example: 'Why have you come to this person? What do you want in order to leave this person? Some patients (or, it is believed, the jinn within them) reply that this person will not buy me certain clothes, but if she/he buys me the clothing then I will leave her/him in peace.' Then, the *khalipa* proposes a compromise by promising to give

---

[46] The language is *Jadgāli*, which they believe is the jinn's language.
[47] The *khalipa* told me that *paris* do not have feet to walk; instead, they have wings and fly.
[48] The word pānī is from *Jadgāli* and *Kholosi* – Indo-Aryan languages spoken in this region – not Balochi.

the jinn blood, *halwā* and delicious food the next evening. The patient's family must fulfil these conditions before the last night of the ceremony, otherwise the jinn will not leave the patient.

The third night, wātān *(sacrifice and meal)*

The third night is different from the previous two nights. The goal is to feed the jinn and make an agreement with them to leave the patient.

After the afternoon prayer, the *khalipa* slaughters a goat. In the Afro-Baloch healing tradition, a goat is always slaughtered for this ceremony. The *khalipa* mentions that the jinn do not accept just any kind of goat. It must be a big, fat, healthy male.

The *khalipa* collects the blood in a copper bowl, puts a silver ring in it and leaves the offering of blood on the roof of the house for the jinn. He cuts the goat meat into small slices. The idea is that the entire goat must be cooked and served. The *khalipa* cleans the head, trotters and stomach, and cooks two separate dishes from them: one for the audience and the other one for himself and the patient, which is called *jenni warag* (the jinn's food). At this point, no one should touch the food. Only the *khalipa* and the patient are allowed to taste the food.

After the evening prayer, around 8 pm, when the food is ready, the *khalipa* separates some of the cooked meal for the patient and the rest for the people. In addition, the *khalipa* makes *halwā* and boils eggs. The *khalipa* arranges a large *sopra* (table cloth). He puts food, rice, different types of fruit (see the section 'Food sacrifice'), *halwā*, eggs, water, fresh milk, juice and sweets on the *sopra*.

A close relative of the patient applies henna to the patient's feet and hands in the morning at around 11 am. They regard the red colour of henna as a symbol of health. At noon, the family wash the patient's body and dress him or her up in white. They bring the patient back to the same room where the ceremony took place on the previous nights.

Similar to those nights, they spread a white blanket in the middle of the room and make the patient sit on it. The rest of the people sit in a circle around the patient, clapping. The *khalipa* burns the *sōčkī* for himself, then for the patient and finally in the four corners of the room. He then orders the musicians to begin playing. While the music is playing and the singers are singing, the *khalipa* massages the patient's body with coconut oil until both the *khalipa* and the patient go into a trance. They both start to dance and continue until they get tired.

The *khalipa* calls for the jinn's food, fruits, sweets and so forth to be brought in. People set up a *jol* (chamber) on top of the blanket like a tent. Both the *khalipa* and the patient sit inside this *jol* and eat their meal while the music plays, the singers sing and the people clap along. One of the *khalipa*'s followers goes inside the *jol* and washes the *khalipa*'s and patient's hands after their meal. The *khalipa* saves the remaining food for breakfast the next day for him and the patient.

After serving the food, the *khalipa* and the patient both begin to dance and go into a trance. They dance for an hour or more. The patient becomes tired and *behōš bī* (unconscious). The *khalipa* massages the patient's body again with the coconut oil until the patient is revived.

Finally, the *khalipa* makes the patient's jinn swear by the prophet Suleman's ring to leave the patient in peace. In addition, he makes an agreement with them not to bother the patient for a certain number of years (e.g. four years, five years or even for the patient's entire life). He announces the end of the ceremony and the people return home.

In the morning, the *khalipa* comes to the patient. They eat the rest of the food and give the leftovers to the children. Then the *khalipa* looks for the bowl of blood that was left for the jinn. He makes sure that it is empty and the jinn have drunk it up. He takes the ring and gives to it the patient to wear. If the jinn do not drink the blood, the ceremony must be repeated from the beginning. The healer told me that this only occurred very rarely.

Prohibitions during the treatment

During the healing treatment, a patient should neither attend *nekāh sar* (a wedding celebration), funeral and mourning ceremonies, nor visit a *čelagī* (a woman who has given birth to a baby within the past forty days). In addition, a married patient should not sleep with her or his spouse. If a patient does not follow these prohibitions, the jinn will return and will not leave the patient in peace for the rest of her/his life.

Some thoughts and reflections

This healing tradition with music and dance is only recorded in the Afro-Baloch communities.[49] It has not spread to the wider Balochi and *Jadgāli* communities, and I hypothesize that it is of African origin and possibly represents a remnant of an African culture that once existed in this region.[50] If so, these people probably brought this tradition to Balochistan along with others, for example, the singing of *mamabies*. Having lost their language, they have retained these traditions to preserve their identity, which is in line with Mirzai's ideas.[51] Interestingly enough, as mentioned earlier, in contrast to the healing tradition, the singing of *mamabies* has spread to the Balochi and *Jadgāli* communities, and the Afro-Baloch use it as a source of income. This recalls the cultural niche of Afro-Soqotrans in the following chapter, who no longer speak their native African languages but are in high demand for their African dances and music and are often hired by wealthy Gulf Arabs to play at celebrations.

There is no documented material from earlier stages of these traditions, and therefore it is difficult to discuss much about what they were like before their integration with Balochi cultures in these regions. Some questions, however, might still be raised regarding these traditions. One question that might be asked is where these singers get

---

[49] This tradition is highly endangered and has already disappeared in some Afro-Baloch villages, such as in Iranshar and Sarawan counties.

[50] Professor Abdulaziz Y. Lodhi of Uppsala University informs me that these ceremonies are similar to those found among the Swahili people of East Africa and the Afro-Indian side of Gujarat (personal communication, 10 March 2019).

[51] Mirzai, 'African Presence', 245–6.

their songs from. Based on my own observations, it is mostly local Baloch poets who contribute the lyrics both for the healing and *mamabies* traditions; but the tradition of healing through songs and dancing comes from Africa. Thus, well-known poets in these regions offer their songs (called *sena*) to the main Afro-Baloch singers to be performed on these occasions. This leads to another question: what was the original content of these songs? Since we do not have enough recorded material, it is again difficult to answer. My hypothesis is that the content, themes, motifs and other details of these songs have been changing over time. One wonders whether and to what extent increased Islamization affected the tradition and culture of Afro-Baloch.

Some suggestions for future studies

The Sistan and Balochistan Province remains an extremely poorly explored region when it comes to this kind of research. Based on my personal observations, even within the Afro-Baloch communities there are differences in the practice of healing traditions. It would be interesting to make a comparison between these regions and analyse to what extent these traditions have been influenced by the Islamic movement since 1979.

Transmuted memories: Slavery and its shadow on the island of Soqotra

Kevin McNeer and Sarali Gintsburg

Since it appeared on the historical map, Soqotra has had an association with slavery. A first-century CE Greek navigation guide relates that traders from East and West brought rice, grain, fine Indian fabrics 'and on occasion female bodies [i.e. slaves]'[1] to the island in exchange for tortoise shells. In later centuries, slave-trading routes criss-crossed Soqotra, as recorded in Arabic 'pilot songs' – the poetic recitations of landmarks and dangers that sailors used as guides. One such song from the fifteenth century advises stopping at Soqotra when sailing from Sindh to Zanj,[2] a major axis of the Indian Ocean slave trade.[3] Another, composed in 1802, describes the journey from the slave-purchase markets of Arabia to the slave-supply markets in Zanzibar – 'the land of masters and slaves' – as running past Soqotra.[4] An early-twentieth-century report tells of traders from Arabia and Africa providing African slaves as payment for large quantities of ghee on the island,[5] and other accounts bear witness to slavery

---

[1] Lionel Casson, *The Periplus Maris Erythraei: Text with Introduction, Translation, and Commentary* (Princeton: Princeton University Press, 1989), paragraph 31.

[2] That is, from present-day Pakistan to East Africa. Teodor Shumovskii, *Tri neizvestnye lotsii Akhmada Ibn Madzhida, arabskogo lotsmana Vasko da-Gamy, v unikal'noi rukopisi Instituta vostokovedeniia* (Three Unknown Pilot Songs of Ahmad Ibn Majid, the Arabian Pilot of Vasco da Gama, in a Unique Manuscript at the Institute of Oriental Studies) (Moscow/Leningrad: Academy of Sciences of the USSR, 1957), 18.

[3] The descendants of East African slaves still live in the Pakistani province of Sindh and surrounding areas. For more on slave-descendant communities, see Chapter 7 in this volume, and Helene Basu, 'History on the Line: Music and the Formation of Sidi Identity in Western India', *History Workshop Journal* 65 (Spring 2008): 161–78.

[4] Robert Bertram Serjeant, 'Ḥaḍramawt eo Zanzibar: The Pilot-Poem of The Nākhudhā Saʿīd Bā Ṭāyiʾ of Al Hāmīʾ, *Paideuma: Mitteilungen zur Kulturkunde*, 1982, Vol. 28, *From Zinj to Zanzibar: Studies in History, Trade and Society on the Eastern Coast of Africa* (Frankfurt am Main: Frobenius-Institut, 1982), 109, 121, Arabic on 117: بلاد الموالى و ألخدام. From 1964, when Serjeant transcribed the song, to 1977, when the Yemeni scholar Muhammad Abd al-Qadir Ba-Matraf published a version of it, the issue of slavery in Yemen's past seems to have acquired a certain sensitivity. Instead of Zanzibar as 'the land of masters and slaves' in the penultimate quatrain, the newer version has 'the land of cloves'. Serjeant considers it probable that this is 'a substitution for the original allusion to slaves, unpalatable since slaving and slave-owning have gained such ill-repute' (111).

[5] Henry Ogg Forbes, *The Natural History of Sokotra and Abd-el-Kuri* (Liverpool: The Free Public Museums, 1903), xxxviii.

existing up until 1967, a crucial turning point in Soqotra's modern history, when the Soviet-backed National Liberation Front took power, abolishing the practice.

What makes the case of Soqotra unusual is that despite ties to Africa, Arabia and Asia through an active sea trade, the archipelago remained relatively isolated, a way station between markets more than a destination. The four islands – the largest being Soqotra itself (3,650 square kilometres[6]) and the object of this study, with a current population of around fifty thousand[7] – lie over a hundred miles south of Yemen and East of Somalia in the Arabian Sea. This separation from the mainland produced a unique language, culture and biosphere: over a third of the plant life[8] and part of the human gene pool exist nowhere else.[9]

How did this relative isolation influence the nature of slavery on the island, if at all? Close readings of sources show that while slavery on Soqotra mirrored slavery practices in the Gulf region, Africans on Soqotra at times occupied positions of power or heightened status – even as slaves – especially over the population of the interior, traditionally considered to have the most ancient roots on the island and called *badū* (Bedouins) or *jabalieh* (mountain folk). They subsisted as herdsmen, as opposed to the fishermen and merchants of the coast, mostly mainland Arab or African stock. And despite some reports of slavery ending on Soqotra as early as the late 1800s, the island's peripheral position and prolonged resistance to British jurisdiction allowed for the practice to continue – especially in the sultan's court – despite the regional push for abolition in the nineteenth century.

With these questions in mind, the first part of the chapter provides an overview of slavery on Soqotra, focusing on the modern period and the road to abolition in the twentieth century. Sources leveraged are etic and emic, ranging from Greek and Arab travelogues and poems to European reports to Soqotri oral works, often generations old but only recently published and translated – the latter constituting a rich and neglected storehouse of information about daily life, attitudes and experiences on the island.

The second part of the chapter looks at the nature of Afro-Soqotran traditions and identity today, several generations removed from abolition in 1967. It is based on the authors' recent fieldwork on Soqotra and engages a blacksmith and a musician from the Afro-Soqotran community, almost all of whom are the descendants of slaves. These two individuals agreed to be interviewed and observed at their craft, and an exploration of these encounters illuminates elements of African culture

---

[6] Vitaly Naumkin, *Ostrova arkhipelaga Sokotra (ekspeditsii 1974–2010)* (Islands of the Archipelago of Soqotra (Expeditions 1974–2010)) (Moscow: Yazyki slavianskoi kul'tury, 2014), 8.

[7] Anthony Miller and Miranda Morris, *Ethnoflora of the Soqotra Archipelago* (Edinburgh: The Royal Botanic Garden Edinburgh, 2004), 13. Population figures vary: another source has 43,000 as of 2004, in Catherine Cheung and Lyndon DeVantier, *Socotra: A Natural History of the Islands and their People* (Hong Kong: Odyssey Books and Guides, 2004), 5. Only two of the other three islands are populated, and their inhabitants number in the hundreds.

[8] Miller and Morris, *Ethnoflora*, 8.

[9] Viktor Cerny, Luísa Pereira, Martina Kujanová, Alzbeta Vasikova, Martin Hájek, Miranda Morris and Connie Mulligan, 'Out of Arabia—The Settlement of Island Soqotra as Revealed by Mitochondrial and Y Chromosome Genetic Diversity', *American Journal of Physical Anthropology* 138 (2008): 439–47.

preserved through generations. While on the one hand, the performers showcase this Africanness – it is a large part of what makes them popular on the island and in the larger region – on the other, they de-emphasize, mask or even decline to recognize African roots in conversation with the authors. Potential motivations for this are examined in the context of recent political events and cultural shifts.

An overview of slavery on Soqotra

While European travellers, beginning in the early modern era, have left numerous accounts of enslaved Africans on the island, earlier sources and recently recorded Soqotri folklore depict a more varied hegemony, with groups at times exchanging hierarchical roles: Africans have been masters as well as slaves, and some slaves have had a share of power on the island.

A ninth-century poem – one enjoying a renaissance among islanders today – by a woman known as Fatima al-Soqotriyya, or al-Zahra, describes Christians, likely from Abyssinia,[10] overrunning the island, seizing and violating its Muslim women. In her poem, Al-Zahra appeals to Imam as-Salt[11] of Oman to save and avenge the Muslim population of Soqotra:

> The Christians have outrageously wronged your viceroy and seized
> Women – and they did not fail to possess what they wished.
> …
> Tell the Imam of whom virtue is expected
> That girls of great faith and beauty have been ruined.
> …
> For they [the Christians] have completely taken away the women of Islam.
> The [women] cry out in terror and sorrow.[12]

The poetic plea seems to have achieved its desired effect: Imam al-Salt reportedly gathered his forces, ordering them to liberate Soqotra and even take the fight to the Zanj on the Horn of Africa.[13]

Periods of African lordship over Soqotra are also recorded in the eleventh-century Egyptian *Book of Curiositie*s, which reports that the island's Nestorian Christians had been forced into a kind of fealty to the East-African Zanj, 'who cut off the route of their

---

[10] Naumkin, *Ostrova arkhipelaga Sokotra*, 42. For a discussion of Soqotran historian Ahmad Said Khamis Al-Anbali's position that the Christian attackers were among the island's inhabitants, see Nathalie Peutz, *Islands of Heritage: Conservation and Transformation in Yemen* (Stanford: Stanford University Press, 2018), 213–14.

[11] (237 AH/AD 857-8 – 273 AH/AD 886), Robert Bertram Serjeant, 'The Coastal Population of Socotra', in *Socotra: Island of Tranquility*, ed. Brian Doe (London: IMMEL, 1992), 138.

[12] Nur Al-Din Abdullah bin Humayyid Al-Salimi, *Tuhfat al-a'yān bisirat ahl 'umān* (A Gift to the Seeing of the Story of the People of Oman), vol. 1 (Cairo: Matba'at al-shabab, 1931), 138–9. Translated by Kevin McNeer relying on Naumkin and Serjeant's translations.

[13] Peutz, *Islands of Heritage*, 213; Al-Salimi, *Tuhfat*, vol. 1, 151–2.

boats'.[14] Fifteenth-century navigator and pilot-song composer Ahmad Ibn Majid sang of a man from the Horn of Africa who seized Soqotra during the Abbasid Caliphate, until the islanders 'devised a ruse against him – they made him and his comrades drunk and murdered them'.[15]

In the ensuing decades, however, initiative shifted from Africa to Arabia, and around the turn of the fourteenth and fifteenth centuries, Soqotra was incorporated into the Mahra Sultanate, based on the mainland in Qishn, a coastal town in Yemen. In 1615, Sir Thomas Roe writes that Soqotra is governed by an Arab born on the island but having roots on the South Arabian coast, and that this king 'hath amonge his slaves divers Abbassines'.[16] Roe, a former esquire in the Court of Queen Elizabeth turned courtier-adventurer,[17] was on a mission to the Great Mogul Court in India when he anchored at Soqotra. With Elizabethan curiosity, in his travelogue he examines Soqotra's social structure, finding that slaves rank not last but second from the top among four castes: (1) the Arabs – who conquered the island, (2) the slaves, (3) the mountain-dwelling Bedouins (whom he considers Christian) and (4) the 'true ancient naturals', or aboriginal population.[18] Roe's seventeenth-century outline of the island's social hierarchy, confirmed by subsequent visitors, holds true today in many ways, especially the core distinction between the coastal and hinterland populations: Arabs and Africans on the coast, and the *badū* aborigines throughout the mountainous interior. The aborigines, as seen in Roe's account and repeatedly in later descriptions, were looked down upon as primitive. Yet for their part, the *badū* categorized the coastal groups as *men rinhem* (from over the sea i.e. foreign),[19] and their sense of the superiority of the hinterland way of life is evident in oral works. In one *badū* tale, a desirable woman has a choice between three suitors: a goatherder, a date palm farmer and a fisherman; unsurprisingly, she chooses the mountain herdsman.[20]

Slaves on Soqotra were seen to rank higher on the social ladder largely because they belonged to the sultan's court, another element that persisted well into modern times (and was not uncommon in the Gulf)[21] – although, according to Roe's description, no one but the sultan himself seems to have commanded much respect. The slaves, 'when they Come to him [the king], kisse his foote, and those doe all his worke and make

[14] Yossef Rapoport and Emilie Savage-Smith, eds, *An Eleventh-Century Egyptian Guide to the Universe: The Book of Curiosities* (Leiden: Brill, 2014), 481, Arabic text on 108: و أكثر مبايعتهم للزنج الذين يقطعون الطريق على المركاب

[15] Serjeant, 'Coastal Population of Socotra', 144.

[16] Sir Thomas Roe, *The Embassy of Sir Thomas Roe to the Court of the Great Mogul, 1615–1619, as Narrated in his Journal and Correspondence* (London: The Hakluyt Society, 1899), 34.

[17] Ibid., v.

[18] Ibid., 33–4. Roe sees a stark gap between the slaves and natives: 'natural' at this time often meant 'like an idiot or fool', A. L. Rowse, *The Annotated Shakespeare* (New York: Greenwhich House, 1988), 512; *The New Shorter Oxford English Dictionary*, meaning I.4.

[19] Serge Elie, 'Communal Identity Transformation in Soqotra: From Status Hierarchy to Ethnic Ranking', *Northeast African Studies* 16, no. 2 (2016): 30.

[20] 'Isa Gum'an al-Da'rhi, Ahmed 'Isa al-Da'rhi, Dmitry Cherkashin, Maria Bulakh and Ekaterina Vizirova, *Corpus of Soqotri Oral Literature*, vol. I, ed. Vitaly Naumkin and Leonid Kogan (Leiden: Brill, 2015), 224.

[21] John O. Hunwick, 'Black Slaves in the Mediterranean World: Introduction to a Neglected Aspect of the African Diaspora', *Slavery & Abolition* 13, no. 1 (1992): 10, 17.

his Aloese', while the native Soqotrans 'obey him and dare not speake without lycence (as appeared when one seemed of quality spake, he [the king] asked him how de durst open his Mouth in his presence), but approching kisse his hand'.[22] If nothing else, at least the slaves, being the 'second sort', were clothed:

> The 4 sortt are a Savage People, poore, leane, naked, with long hayer, eating nothing but rootes, hidinge in Bushes, conversing with none, afrayd of all, without howses, and almost as Savage as beasts ;[23] and by conjecture the true ancient naturails of this Island.
>
> … They make a poore Cloth of their woole for the slaves.[24]

Soqotri folklore preserves depictions of African slaves asserting power that may be echoes of real events. In 1905, Austrian Orientalist David Heinrich Müller published a Soqotri folktale under the title of 'Der starke Sklave. (*Mébḥel ʿed.*)' (The Strong Slave) that he recorded from his informant. It begins:

> In times of old, the people gathered together to feast, and amongst them there happened to be a strong slave. A man brought a basket of dates, and he [the slave] consumed them; a man brought a pot of butter, and he drank it up; a man brought a camel, and he ate its bones; a man brought a billy goat, and he ate its bones; a man brought a sheep, and he ate its bones; and none could stand up to him.[25]

But the people stage a rebellion of attrition by leaving the slave to fend for himself while they disperse 'to their own places'. Over the course of his year of solitude, the slave-tyrant is reduced to such a pitiable state that one of his canines drops out and he is unable to eat.

In the twenty-first century, Vitaly Naumkin and Leonid Kogan recorded a similar but more elaborate tale called 'The Story of the Makon':

> In times of old, the Makon was on the crown of Hagher. For the Makon had been built by that time. And there were a few men who ruled the Makon. Among them was one Swahili, and that Swahili was a strong man.[26]

---

[22] Roe, *Embassy*, 33.

[23] The picture of an aboriginal people in the region living a primordial existence is echoed by other sources and prefigured in *Periplus Maris Erythraei*, which noted that the inhabitants on the Omani coast in and around Khor Ruri 'for the most part dwell in caves' (170).

[24] Roe, *Embassy*, 34. Similar observations about the native population are made by the Portuguese officer Duarte Barbosa a century earlier: 'This folk has its own language, they go naked, covering only their private parts with cotton cloths, and some with skins.' He differentiates them from 'the brown men [on the island], who call themselves Christians', apparently Abyssinians. Duarte Barbosa, *The Book of Duarte Barbosa*, trans. Mansel Longworth Dames (London: The Hakluyt Society, 1918),

[25] David Heinrich Müller, *Südarabische Expedition*, vol. II (Vienna: Alfred Hölder K.u.K. Hof- und Universitäts-Buschhandler, 1905), 108.

[26] Naumkin and Kogan, *Soqotri Oral Literature*, vol. I, summary on 1–2, story and commentary on 64–93.

The word 'slave' (*mébḥel*) is not used here: the minor tyrant is now a 'Swahili man' (*ᶜag suwāḥil'i*), that is, an African/slave/former slave, in contemporary Soqotri usage, who is a strong man (*ᶜag ᶜeẓ*).[27] The setting in this tale is bleak and foreboding: the Makon atop the Hagher Mountains (lit. 'on the skull of the Hagher'[28]) seems to be a kind of fortress, inhabited by a junta of tough guys led by the despotic Swahili. Embedded in the story is the mountain-coastal dichotomy outlined earlier – the Swahili being literally a 'shore dweller' asserting power in the mountains (the term 'Swahili' comes from the Arabic *sāḥil*, 'coast, shore').

This version, recorded over a century after 'The Strong Slave', is less realistic and direct in its treatment: the Swahili's tyranny consists of forcing any uncircumcised boy – in other words, pre-teenage[29] – who passes by to make a vow that is all but impossible to fulfil. The price of failure is execution. But then one clever youngster does what no one before him could: he fulfils the 'impossible' task in the time allotted: the Swahili is decapitated, the Makon dismantled and its despotism brought to an end. Could these tales have roots in slave revolts or periods of African rule on the island?

Soqotri folktales also provide glimpses of slave agency and solidarity. One, dating back at least to the late nineteenth century, gives us the purchase price for a slave named Hasran, which means 'loss'. Since slave-dealers often gave slaves Arabic names 'redolent of happiness, good fortune, and favour from God',[30] partly as a marketing tool, the name 'Loss', redolent as it is of bad fortune, would catch any listener's attention. Loss's owner, having bought him in the island capital Hadibo, sells him to a sheep herder for a low price of 100 dirhams just to be free of him, since the slave is too clever for his own good. The seller frankly explains, 'Whoever buys this slave has a "loss"; and whoever sells this slave has a "loss"'. But the obtuse shepherd ignores the warning and buys the slave. Loss wastes no time getting into trouble: he has a grappling hook forged by a blacksmith, fashions a rope and breaks into the sultan's home from the rooftop to steal a large sum of money. Afro-Soqotrans have traditionally been the island's metalworkers,[31] and native listeners are likely to assume the blacksmith was also a slave or of African descent. Later, Loss is happy to share his ill-gotten gains with his master, but things end badly for both when they are killed by the sultan.[32]

Slaves often appear in Soqotri tales involving the sultan's court, where, as will be explored later, some wielded significant power. In one story, a slave acts as matchmaker and helps the sultan find a bride; in another, slaves serve as enforcers of royal justice for thieves: 'the Sultan's slaves and servants would stand up and bind his hands [to be severed]'.[33] In the 1950s, an Afro-Soqotran doctor showed English explorer Douglas

---

[27] For another example of softened language in the modern era, see footnote 4 above regarding 'the land of masters and slaves'.

[28] Naumkin and Kogan, *Soqotri Oral Literature*, vol. I, 76, note 1.

[29] Ibid., 76–7.

[30] Hunwick, 'Slaves in the Mediterranean', 13.

[31] 'The blacksmiths and silversmiths, most of the sailors and pearl-fishers, the house-builders, the carpenters and menders of boats are African.' Douglas Botting, *Island of the Dragon's Blood* (London: Hodder and Stoughton, 1958), 82.

[32] Müller, *Südarabische Expedition*, vol. II, 'Der Unglückssklave', 84–7.

[33] Naumkin and Kogan, *Soqotri Oral Literature*, vol. II, 334, where a slave helps the sultan find a bride, and 314, regarding punishment for thieves.

Botting a severed hand 'in a jar of preserving spirit … like an old wrinkled brown glove' that the sultan's black executioner had cut from a goat thief.[34]

The Soqotri oral tradition almost certainly holds more references to slavery than appear at first glance, considering the island poets' fondness for enigmatic language.[35] The subject of one work chant, for example, is a black 'hornless goat' – *fidedo* in Soqotri, also reportedly slang for an Afro-Soqotran.[36]

Table 8.1 A Work Chant

First group:	Whose is the hornless she-goat?
Second group:	The black one?
First group:	The one with no horns??
Second group:	And no ears?
First group:	Whose is the hornless she-goat?
Second group:	The black one?
First group:	She gave birth to a male kid.
Second group:	And then would not suckle it.[37]

The combination of the 'black', the implication of an owner ('Whose is the hornless she-goat?') and a rejected child are suggestive. Another poem ostensibly about a hornless goat will be examined below.

The long-drawn-out demise of slavery on the island 'left to itself'

At the dawn of the nineteenth century, just as the abolition movement was about to gain momentum, slavery on Soqotra followed much the same pattern as in other areas around the Arabian Gulf. In addition to the ever-present slaves in the sultan's court, many slaves of African origin – as well as other individuals, often essentially economically enslaved *badū* – worked as pearl divers and fishermen.[38] They were dependent on outside financial backing, which kept them permanently in debt, as boats and equipment were owned by others – the fishing nets on Soqotra were the sultan's property.[39]

---

[34] Botting, *Island of the Dragon's Blood*, 66–7. A black-and-white photo of a thief's severed hand dangling from a tree can be seen at the Soqotra Folk Museum.
[35] Miranda Morris, 'The Use of "Veiled Language" in Soqoṭri Poetry', *Proceedings of the Seminar for Arabian Studies, Vol. 43, Papers from the 46th meeting of the Seminar for Arabian Studies held at the British Museum*, London, 13–15 July 2012 (2013), 239.
[36] Peutz, *Islands of Heritage*, 223. Our informants were not aware of this secondary meaning of the word, which may exist only in other dialects.
[37] Miranda Morris, *The Oral Art of Soqotra: A Collection of Island Voices* (Leiden: Brill, 2021), 40–1.
[38] For a detailed description of conditions slaves lived and worked in around the Arabian Gulf, and the economic entrapment of fishermen, see Chapter 4 in this volume.
[39] Serjeant, 'Coastal Population of Socotra', 175. It should be remembered that the *badū* were practically slaves themselves. In Elie's words,

In 1807, the first great blow to slavery in the Middle East and elsewhere was delivered when Great Britain abolished the slave trade in the empire. While the British Empire did not officially include Soqotra, it did control many of the Gulf sheikhdoms that kept the slave-trading networks alive around the archipelago. Thus, slavery's fitful and stubborn demise on Soqotra had begun, although it would not be completed until 1967.

In 1833, slavery itself was abolished in the empire, but enforcement of either this or the previous edict proved problematic, and British administrators left long paper trails complaining of their inability to adequately police the waterways.[40] British lieutenant James Wellsted writes that in 1834, Soqotrans provided his expedition across the island with 'two slaves to attend the camels, fetch firewood, etc.'[41] Wellsted liked them and repeatedly emphasizes his sympathy for the slaves on Soqotra:

> During the heavy showers which fell this night, our slaves were offered the interior of the tent: but they preferred remaining outside, lying on the ground, and wrapping themselves over with the thick mats which were used during the day to cover their camels. These slaves accompanied me during the whole of our tour, and more merry, more willing, or more faithful servants it would be impossible to obtain.[42]

The slaves, he adds, were not opposed to 'a glass of spirits'.

The wheels of the British Empire turned slowly, but anti-slavery sentiment continued to gather momentum. A British husband-and-wife exploration team, the Bents, write on a visit to Muscat near the turn of the century that abolition is 'undoubtedly the burning question in Arabia'.[43] The number of freed slaves was increasing, and the British were trying to manage them. In an odd hypothetical of history, Soqotra might have become a slave-refuge: 'Lieutenant Fellowes in 1872, in command of the *Briton*, was sent from Aden to Socotra to see if that island, and nearby Abd-al-Kuri, were suitable for liberated slaves; but Fellowes decided against both.'[44] The difficult living conditions and scarcity of food on the island were not considered favourable.[45]

The *badū*'s exclusive dependence on the environment for their livelihood was punctuated by seasonal hunger, which compelled them to offer their services to the Sultan and his kin as well as to the wealthier members of the other groups who came 'from over the sea' in exchange for food and clothing. This situation engendered a subcategory of pastoralists called *akhdām*, or voluntary 'Bedouin' servants (Elie, 'Community Identity', 40–1).

[40] Dr Mark Hobbs, 'Britain's Ineffectual Efforts to Suppress the Slave Trade', *Qatar Digital Library*, 16 December 2014, https://www.qdl.qa/en/britain's-ineffectual-efforts-suppress-slave-trade (accessed 11 August 2022).

[41] James Raymond Wellsted, 'Memoir on the Island of Socotra', *Journal of the Royal Geographic Society* 5 (1835): 138. Wellsted was also travelling with a former slave from Sudan, a young man freed by the British in Egypt whom Wellsted now employed as a personal helper, and of whom he was very fond.

[42] James Raymond Wellsted, *Travels to the City of the Caliphs*, vol. 2 (London: Henry Colburn, 1840), 199.

[43] Theodore and Mrs. Theodore Bent, *Southern Arabia* (London: Smith, Elder, 1900), 60.

[44] K. Ingham, ed., *Foreign Relations of African States: Proceedings of the Twenty fifth Symposium of the Colston Research Society Held in the University of Bristol, April 4th to 7th, 1973* (London: Butterworth, 1974), 104.

[45] Mafia, Lamu and Dar es Salaam were also considered.

In 1873, the British were finally able to have the Zanzibar slave markets closed, under threat of a blockade. In 1880, the slave markets on the Yemeni coast, Mukalla and Shihr, were shut down.[46] German botanist Georg August Schweinfurth, who travelled around the south coast of Arabia in 1881, reported that 'slavery does not exist there on a large scale', with the trade wholly suppressed at some ports – such as Zanzibar, Mukalla and Muscat – thanks to steep penalties and rigorous surveillance, but not at others, such as Aden. Schweinfurth spent a month on Soqotra and was convinced the island had no part in the slave trade, having witnessed boats from Zanzibar trading only in goods:

> You perceive that Socotra might be a very convenient place for slave-trading, but that it is not so. Slaves are almost unknown on the island. There are some, however, in the small villages on the coast, which are inhabited by Arabs. ... There are in these villages a great number of negroes free or manumitted by their masters in Zanzibar or in Muscat. These families have already reached the second or third generations. Others have recently come from Muscat, &c., but all of them enjoy perfect liberty. Socotra is a sort of refuge for these people. The Red Sea is the very reverse.[47]

And yet Schweinfurth seems overconfident in the effectiveness of British measures. Later travellers continue reporting slaves on the island. In 1897, the Bents repeatedly note the presence of slaves, describing Qalansiya as having 'a considerable Negroid population in the shape of soldiers and slaves'.[48] Elsewhere, they remark about a wedding that 'on the morning of the festive day the Sokotrans, negro slaves being apparently excluded, assembled in a room'[49] and that 'slaves ... are employed in fertilizing the palm trees'.[50]

Julian Hansen van Rensburg considers the Bents were likely mistaken because their account is 'at odds to the report submitted by Schweinfurth',[51] but Schweinfurth himself notes the presence of some slaves in the coastal villages of Soqotra and

---

[46]   Robert W. Stookey, *South Yemen: A Marxist Republic in Arabia* (Boulder: Westview Press, 1982), 45.

[47]   Georg August Schweinfurth, 'Socotra's Isle Visited: Dr. Schweinfurth, the Traveler, Tells his Experience', *New York Times*, 8 August 1881. Schweinfurth's confidence about the absence of slavery on Soqotra is odd when he himself repeatedly alludes to the difficulties of monitoring the slave trade: 'To put down the slave trade in the Red Sea effectively, it would require a small fleet of steam cutters constantly searching every vessel without exception', adding that the movements of the cruisers patrolling the area were communicated to the slave vessels in advance, the cruisers were often not allowed to land men to pursue fugitives and that treaty with the Ottoman Empire needed to be reframed.

[48]   Bent, *Southern Arabia*, 346.

[49]   Ibid., 350.

[50]   Ibid., 368. The Bents spent one night in the area called Suq (in Arabic) or Shiq (in Soqotri), on the outskirts of the island capital, where the Afro-Soqotran population is concentrated to this day. While they did not use the word 'slaves' regarding the population there, they did describe it as 'a wretched hamlet of Somali' (ibid., 394).

[51]   Julian Jansen van Rensburg, *The Maritime Traditions of the Fisherman of Socotra, Yemen*, doctoral thesis (University of Exeter, 2012), 107–8. He is referring to Schweinfurth, 'Recollections of a Voyage to Socotra', in *Records of Yemen: 1798- 1960*, vol. 4, ed. D. Ingrams and L. Ingrams (London: Archive Editions, 1993), 190.

acknowledges that 'the stoppage which the vessels trading between these two ports make at Socotra escapes observation, for this island is so completely left to itself'.[52] Throughout the region during this period, slavery was in an ongoing state of abolishment and reappearance, and the Bents observed it other places where it was officially prohibited: in 'Yemen, the Hadhramout, the Mahra country, and Dhofar – slavery is universal'.[53]

Several years later, Scottish naturalist Henry Forbes writes of his expedition of 1898–9 that the guide assigned to him, Ali, was the sultan's slave, so 'all Ali's pay would go into His Highness's pocket', and that traders from Zanzibar and Mukalla (Yemen) sometimes paid mountain dwellers for large quantities of ghee with African slaves.[54] Similar observations, as will be seen, are made by travellers well into the twentieth century.

Writing about the continuation of the Red Sea slave trade after the British-Egyptian convention of 1877 that officially suppressed it, Diane Robinson-Dunn enumerates some of the slave traders' ruses:

> [Slaves] were transported by night in light 'drought' boats in groups of 20 or fewer, and rarely more than 100. These boats were quick, easily manoeuvred and capable of outrunning a British cruiser, especially along the coast; the vessels themselves were inconspicuous and could blend easily with the life of the ports, engaging in fishing and pearl-diving and only transporting slaves when a profitable opportunity arose. Moreover[,] slave traders could monitor the movements of British cruisers and plan their activities around them, an unintended consequence of the publicity surrounding British efforts in the Red Sea.[55]

While the British enshrined different degrees of abolition in treaties with many governments in the region, there is no record of any such demand made of the Mahra Sultanate on Soqotra, perhaps because the island was not considered important – it had a small population, lacked a good harbour and no longer produced profitable exports – and simply because the Mahra sultans had proven themselves difficult to deal with: in 1835, when the British were seeking to buy Soqotra outright, the sultan 'had refused to sell the island, or even cede a portion of it as a coaling depot'.[56] Once an agreement was finally signed in 1876, followed by two protectorate treaties in 1886 and 1888, slavery was not addressed,[57] in contrast to agreements the British had struck with

---

[52]   Schweinfurth, 'Recollections of a Voyage', 190.

[53]   Bent, *Southern Arabia*, 60. They added that 'there is no doubt about it the slaves are treated very well and lead happy lives', as opposed to in Oman.

[54]   Forbes, *Natural History*, xxxiii, xxxviii. Other items bartered for ghee were rice, calicoes, amber, Maria Theresa dollars and Indian coins.

[55]   Diane Robinson-Dunn, *The Harem, Slavery and British Imperial Culture: Anglo-Muslim Relations in the Late Nineteenth Century* (Manchester: Manchester University Press, 2006), 36.

[56]   *A Collection of Treaties, Engagements and Sanads Relating to India and Neighbouring Countries*, compiled by G. U. Aitchison, vol. XI (Delhi: The Government of India Manager of Publications, 1930), 35.

[57]   Ibid., 36.

Soqotra's Arabian and African neighbours in the nineteenth century for the abolition or 'suppression of the slave trade'.[58]

Thus, the archipelago seems to have languished in something of a time warp, 'left to itself and escaping observation', to paraphrase Schweinfurth. Was the Mahra Sultanate's move from Qishn, on mainland Yemen, to Soqotra in the late nineteenth century partly due to the growing abolitionist movement and restricted access to new slaves in mainland Yemen? Although slavery in Yemen was officially abolished only in 1962, changing attitudes towards the practice may have been felt earlier and more strongly on the mainland, where the port slave markets had been closed and were more easily monitored. Removal of the sultanate to an island of only mild strategic interest, more or less 'under the radar' – especially given the habit of colonial rulers to leave local governing structures largely intact – would have allowed for the court to hold onto its slaves without much fuss.

References to slaves and Afro-Soqotrans by twentieth-century visitors are primarily associated with the sultan's court – not unusual in the Islamic world, where from the Maghreb to Egypt to the Ottoman Empire slaves historically served as court advisors, soldiers, executioners and enforcers.[59] Botting notes during a visit to Soqotra in the 1950s that the police force comprises 'a dozen or so Africans armed with old rifles' and the court executioner is 'Abdulla, a very large, very black negro [with] a bald, shiny head and a tuft of wiry beard on his chin. He suffered from elephantiasis and had a scrotum the size of a football.'[60] The royal executioner's appearance also made a strong impression on traveller Tim Mackintosh-Smith: 'Photographs taken during a British administrator's visit in the early 1960s show him [the sultan] peering warily from beneath an enormous Saudi *iqal*, surrounded by a handful of courtiers and flunkeys. These included the executioner, a huge slave with severe elephantiasis.'[61] It was this same Abdulla who sawed off the goat thief's hand preserved by a doctor in Hadibo. Rensburg spoke with the executioner's grandson in 2009: 'A full-time fisherman in his 60s, Saad Dabowed Mousa … said that his grandfather had been brought from Sudan as a slave and was the Sultan's chief executioner.'[62]

But not all Afro-Soqotrans in the court were merely physical enforcers or servants. Sean Stilwell observes of court slaves in Kano (now Nigeria), 'They used their proximity to the throne to acquire power, while developing wide ranging expertise in matters both civil and military.'[63] The last sultan's wazir, Sheikh Ibrahim bin Khaled, was a

---

[58]   These included Muscat (ibid., 202), Mukalla (160), Shihr (161), Bahrain (252), Abu Dhabi (252, 254), Dubai (252, 254), the Persian Gulf and even Somali tribes (106).

[59]   The reasons for this have been fruitfully explored in Miura Toru and John Edward Philips, eds, *Slave Elites in the Middle East and Africa* (London: Kegan Paul International, 2000). In that volume, Sean Stilwell writes that 'royal slaves were neutral, subjugated beings, who were brought into the circles of power because, as slaves, they could make no legitimate claims to independently possess power or status' and were thus perceived to be more loyal. Sean Stilwell, 'The Power of Knowledge and the Knowledge of Power: Kinship, Community and Royal Slavery in Pre-Colonial Kano, 1807–1903', in *Slave Elites in the Middle East and Africa*, ed. Toru and Philips, 121. See also Bent, *Southern Arabia*, 60.

[60]   Botting, *Island of the Dragon's Blood*, 69, 47.

[61]   Tim Mackintosh-Smith, *Yemen: Travels in Dictionary Land* (London: John Murray, 2007), 231.

[62]   Rensburg, *Fisherman of Socotra*, 108.

[63]   Stilwell, 'Power of Knowledge', 121.

consummate politician of African descent. Botting writes of him: 'Although of slave origin (his mother was a negress) Ibrahim had, by training and personality, attained the rank of Prime Minister on Socotra' and is 'highly intelligent, speaks perfect Arabic (comparatively rare on Socotra, even among the coastal inhabitants), has picked up a little Swahili, and is anxious to learn English'.[64] A report by a British expedition to the island in March of 1967, on the eve of the sultanate's extinction, also singles out the wazir: 'On Socotra the Sultan has a State Council of five members and his wazir, Ibrahim b. Khalid, is his close friend – he calls himself al-Thuqali but his real name is, they say, al-Nubi, the Nubian, which implies slave descent'.[65]

According to Serge Elie, the vizier's name also denotes that he hailed from a privileged class of Sudanese called the *Nūbān*:

> The *Nūbān*'s presence on the island is presumptively dated from the seventeenth century when they first came in contact with Soqotra as shipmates on the dhows plying the trade routes between East Africa and the Arabian gulf. Subsequently, they settled almost exclusively in the two northern coastal towns of Hadiboh and Qalansiyah, where they practiced fishing, became the Sultan's soldiers, and were known as the most successful cultivators of date palm trees.[66]

Unlike other Afro-Soqotrans, according to Elie, they intermarried with other groups and were known for their literacy thanks to study of the Quran.

In the 1950s, a retired servant from the sultan's household still spoke Swahili and recounted to Botting how he had been taken from Pemba Island near Zanzibar, yet another testimonial to the persistence of slave acquisitions: 'I was born there. I lived there till I was six. Then the Sultan came and brought me here to work for him. I came without my baba or mama and I have never been back. I was a very little boy but I still remember it'.[67] He recalled the beauty and fertility – the bananas, paw-paws and coconuts – of his native island and wished to see it once again: 'He spoke for a long time, digging up shadowy, transmuted memories'.[68]

While some of the slaves serving the sultan might boast of numbering among the island's elite, nominally free Afro-Soqotrans not associated with the court occupied a low social niche, comparable to, although perhaps better than, on mainland Yemen in the twentieth century.[69] Botting remarks that a brothel in the island capital is 'full of negresses',[70] and the British report from 1967 observes that most Afro-Soqotrans are not fully enfranchised:

---

[64] Botting, *Island of the Dragon's Blood*, 64.
[65] Serjeant, 'Coastal Population of Socotra', 163.
[66] Elie, 'Communal Identity', 37.
[67] Botting, *Island of the Dragon's Blood*, 81–2.
[68] Ibid., 82.
[69] 'The lower groups (*akhdam* and *subayan*) are commonly descended from former slaves, and have remained outside the mainstream of traditional Yemeni life.' In Tareq Y. Ismael and Jacqueline S. Ismael, *The People's Democratic Republic of Yemen: Politics, Economics and Society: The Politics of Socialist Transformation* (London: Frances Pinter and Boulder, 1986), 8.
[70] Botting, *Island of the Dragon's Blood*, 68.

The people of the coastal area and of the town are mixed Arab, Indian and African from the Swahili coast. … The African element have their own *muqaddam* or headman, but cannot own property. They are considered to be the descendants of slaves and they are employed by the Arabs but nevertheless form a separate community.[71]

Regarding assimilation, Robert Bertram Serjeant writes,

There seems to be no feeling on the island against intermarriage with different races or even colours – except that slaves (khaddam) in places like Hadibuh (still actually slaves in the sense of being a possession and unable, for instance, to leave the island without the consent of their masters), do not marry outside their own class. They are looked after by their master, who they call 'amm, uncle, who arranges for them to be married with their own kind.[72]

Indeed, a recent study of the island's gene pool indicates little intermarriage between the African and Arab/native populations.[73] The Afro-Soqotrans had their own burial ground, but so did the *badū*, the hinterland Soqotrans, as did the 'Whites [presumably Europeans], the Arabs, Sayyids, Sultans'.[74]

And yet there are signs that the segregation was in some respects voluntary. Serjeant notes that the black community has its own headman (*muqaddam*) and that 'the Whites do not want to be separate from the Blacks, but the Blacks do not want the Whites in their organization'.[75] The Afro-Soqotran doctor who showed Botting the hand in the jar remarked to him that 'only the Bedouin steal. They are like birds in the corn. It's their nature,'[76] reflecting the social stratification noted by Roe that, for some coastal islanders, places indigenous Soqotrans at the bottom of the social ladder.

Slavery consigned to the dustbin of history

It was the end of the sultanate – the erasure of rule by birthright and the old economic order – that brought slavery on the island to an end. While the British had provided the first great impulse to end slavery in the region, it took their exodus and the arrival of Soviet-backed revolutionaries to abolish it fully. On 1 August 1967, the British left South Yemen, and the People's Democratic Republic of Yemen came into being. From August through October, as region after region fell, over a dozen local sultans

[71] Brian Doe, 'The Socotrans', in *Socotra: Island of Tranquility*, 31.
[72] Serjeant, 'Coastal Population of Socotra', 165–6.
[73] Cerny et al., 'Out of Arabia', 439–47.
[74] Serjeant, 'Coastal Population of Socotra', 168.
[75] Ibid.
[76] Botting, *Island of the Dragon's Blood*, 67.

and sheikhs fled or were arrested; in some cases, they were executed, often with their families.[77]

Soqotra held out the longest, fending off an initial attack in March 1967,[78] but on 30 November, a detachment of the National Front disembarked on the island and put an end to the last pocket of monarchic rule in South Yemen.[79] The Mahra Sultanate was finished. The day it fell, 30 November 1967, was declared Independence Day for the new socialist republic.[80] The old ways were to be swept into the dustbin of history: 'The revolutionary leaders announced that all sectarian distinctions were now erased, along with those of birth and race.'[81]

The last sultan, 'Isa b. 'Ali b. Salim b. Sa'd al-Taw'ari al 'Ifrayr, was imprisoned in Aden but eventually released. In 1974, however, the National Front convened a 'people's court' on Soqotra that one young foreign officer reluctantly agreed to witness, after insistent invitations, as guest of honour.[82] The sultan's two brothers, a nephew and others were executed, including the capable vizier of Sudanese ancestry – al-Nubi. His brother, Peutz was told, 'escaped death by rowing out to sea in a wooden dugout, where he sat out five long days, staring back at the land'[83] – the land over which his brother had ruled.

The sultan's palace, just outside the island capital of Hadibo, is now dilapidated and deserted, something to show curious tourists. The executions inflicted a social trauma on the entire island, which otherwise has not seen the levels of political or sectarian violence visited upon mainland Yemen and much of the Middle East – or the modern world, for that matter. For decades, open discussion of the subject was taboo, but the year 2003 saw 'ancient grudge break to new mutiny' when audio cassettes reached Soqotra bearing a poem about the killings. The poem, called *hajar al-asas* or 'The Foundation Stone', a reference to the sultanate, addressed the executions with a directness not heard before. It was composed by a Soqotran expatriate living in Oman and had the effect of an explosive charge. The poet declared that *fidadi* ('hornless goats' – Afro-Soqotrans) had been the perpetrators of the executions. In Peutz's words, the poet 'drives his point home by representing them as former slaves who have forgotten their true "work" and station: clearing the airstrip, transporting earth and stones, with a whip at their heels. ... He then undermines the relative financial and political successes attained by some in recent years.'[84] Was this partly resentment at the privileged status of court slaves who benefited from a proximity to power that, in the eyes of some islanders, they later betrayed? The son of one of the executed played the poem loudly outside the shop of one of the alleged executioners. A fight broke out in the street.

[77] Vitaly Naumkin, *'Krasnye volki' Iemena. Natsional'nyi front v revoliutsii* (The 'Red Wolves' of Yemen: The National Front in the Revolution) (Moscow: IV RAN (Institute of Oriental Studies), 2017), 222; Stookey, *South Yemen*, 232.

[78] Naumkin, *Krasnye volki*, 197.

[79] Ibid., 222.

[80] Naumkin, *Ostrova arkhipelaga Sokotra*, 60.

[81] Stookey, *South Yemen*, 233.

[82] Personal interview, November 2019.

[83] Peutz, *Islands of Heritage*, 220.

[84] Ibid., 223. Our discussion of the poem and the social shockwaves it caused is taken from Chapter 5 of *Islands of Heritage*, which provides a penetrating discussion of the events and their context.

The Afro-Soqotran population today

Today, Afro-Soqotrans share in a Soqotran identity: they speak Soqotri as their mother tongue (African languages such as Swahili having been forgotten), they own property and some have risen to higher level government posts. They are, of course, officially recognized as Yemeni citizens.

Yet even after four hundred years, the contours of Roe's social divisions have not been wholly worn down by the sands of time: the distinction remains between mountain-dwelling natives and mainland Arabs and 'Abbassines', or those of African origin, living along the coasts. Afro-Soqotrans are often referred to by other island groups as *muwalladīn*,[85] used for people born into a culture or land without ancestral roots there, that is, non-Arabic ethnic groups living in traditionally Arab societies. The term can also convey a ruder connotation, something like 'half-breed'.

Afro-Soqotrans live on the coast and tend to labour in well-defined niches: fishing, date plantations and construction.[86] A few also work as professional musicians and performers. This niche, however profitable, is regarded by some as one of the least respected occupations on the island.[87] The Afro-Soqotran community resides, rather compactly, in distinct neighbourhoods, or *ḥafas*, which may be casually referred to as *makān al-'abīd* (the slaves' place).[88] While Afro-Soqotrans are native speakers of Soqotri, indigenous Soqotrans[89] told us that the variety of Soqotri spoken by the Afro-Soqotrans is characterized by a specific accent and can be difficult to understand.[90] Intermarriages between members of the African community and the local population do not seem common.[91]

In 2019, the authors visited Soqotra as members of a Russian-Yemeni research expedition and rather unexpectedly had the chance to interview two members of the Afro-Soqotran community in the island capital Hadibo, one in the traditionally Afro-Soqotran neighbourhood of Shiq. The interviews below demonstrate subtle structuring mechanisms of African identity at work among members of this community. The two individuals interviewed were a blacksmith and a musician, both eager to emphasize directly and in less obvious ways that they were of purely Soqotran origin. This led us to contemplate what the nature of today's Afro-Soqotran identity might be – should we even be using the term 'Afro-Soqotran'? – and why the Africanness of this identity

---

[85] On the euphemistic character of this term in Yemen, see Elie, 'Communal Identity', 50–3.
[86] The low status of Afro-Soqotrans, and to some extent the coastal population, from the perspective of the autochthonous *badū*, is marked in vernacular poetry and conversational labels.
[87] Peutz, *Islands of Heritage*, 251–2.
[88] Elie, 'Communal Identity', 42.
[89] I.e. non-Arab and non-Africans of the island's hinterland: ibid., 39.
[90] Sarali Gintsburg and Eleonora Esposito define this as Heritage African language ('The Asymmetric Linguistic Identities of African Soqotris: A Triadic Interaction', in *Language and Identity in the Arab World*, ed. Fathiya Al Rashdi and Sandhya Rao Mehta (London: Routledge, 2022), 241).
[91] The social status of Afro-Soqotrans might be likened to that of the Sidis, descendants of African slaves in India who were recently granted a special status. Sidis, however, continue to live on the margins of Indian society. Beheroze Schroff, '"Goma Is Going On": Sidis of Gujarat', *African Arts* 46, no. 1 (Spring 2013): 18–25.

is being de-emphasized or, indeed, suppressed. Is this an instance of *mankurtizatsiya*, the stripping away of an individual's cultural and familial past as part of a political program,[92] or are other motivations at work?

In our ethnographic analysis, we have focused on typical markers of identity building: music and dance, and speech and clothing.

The Afro in Afro-Soqotran

Music and dance

Music is often considered a foundational element of any culture. The use of drums is not seen as part of the musical heritage of Soqotra: traditional Bedouin poetry and dances are performed either solo or with the accompaniment of a wind instrument and tambourine. The primacy of rhythm, what Africa scholar Ruth Finnegan calls 'the famous "beat"', has historically been the domain of Africa, where drums are the instrument *par excellence*.[93]

Afro-Soqotrans are well known among the Soqotran population for their talents as dancers and drummers, and they are regularly invited as paid performers to weddings and other important celebrations. And yet Afro-Soqotri drumming became an object of controversy in the years surrounding Yemeni unification in 1990, when a surge in Islamic zeal led to the framing of drum music as 'the devil's work', a religiously forbidden (*ḥarām*) practice encouraging mixed-sex dancing and distracting from prayer. Peutz spoke with one Afro-Soqotran drummer who was even promised a new home by proselytizers if he would only abandon his passion for percussion. In the end, he refused, 'I am sorry; I can't stop drumming. Drumming was passed down from my parents to me and from their parents to them.'[94] Soqotrans of African descent have also been associated with witchcraft,[95] and we ourselves heard stories from locals about mysterious, even tragic, events involving African sorcerers. Africa has historically had a reputation for witchcraft, one that could tarnish even emigrants, as in the case of Omanis who fled Zanzibar for Oman but were treated poorly in their native land as arrivals from Africa – the land of sorcery.[96]

---

[92] A term derived from Kyrgyz author Chingiz Aitmatov's 1980 novel *I dol'she veka dlitsa den'* (And Longer Than a Century Lasts the Day) in which war prisoners have their heads wrapped in camel hide and are left in the desert for days, during which time the head-wrapping shrinks in the heat and the prisoners lose their former identity – including any memory of their roots.

[93] Ruth Finnegan, *Time for the World to Learn from Africa* (Staines-upon-Thames: Balestier Press, 2018), 91.

[94] Peutz, *Islands of Heritage*, 251–2.

[95] Serjeant, 'Coastal Population of Socotra', 142. Although all of the islanders have been associated with sorcery at some point in history, including in Marco Polo's account. See Peutz, *Islands of Heritage*, 13.

[96] See Marc Valeri, 'Nation-Building and Communities in Oman since 1970: The Swahili-Speaking Omani in Search of Identity', *African Affairs* 106, no. 424 (July 2007): 479–96.

The smithy and the dance with no name

I can take any empty space and call it a bare stage.[97]

Peter Brook

In 2019, the authors visited a blacksmith in his one-room workshop near the market in the island capital of Hadibo. He and his family live in a house next door. One of our Soqotran hosts had shown us a smartphone video of the blacksmith dancing to a drumbeat as he worked his forge, and told us that wealthy Gulf Arabs paid top dollar to watch him at work. We wanted to see the show.

Affan, the blacksmith, is of African descent, and the spirit and form of his performance gave every indication of having roots in Africa, echoing performances previous travellers had seen by Africans on the island. Several elements stand out from 'native' Soqotran and Arabic performance culture: elements of costumes and role playing – 'a combination of mimetic ritual dance and elements of drama'[98] – the centrality of drumming and the setting itself at a smithy, metalwork being the traditional domain of Afro-Soqotrans.[99] By contrast, observes Soqotran historian Ahmad Said Khmais Al-Anbali, native forms of group performance on the island involve 'neither instruments nor dance movements': the Bedouin Soqotri ṣāmihir, for example, a group singing event, or more traditionally 'an exchange of colloquial poetry, spoken verses set to different tunes… without demanding anyone stand up [and perform] certain movements'.[100]

When we arrived at the blacksmith's workshop, it was deserted but for Affan, and in some way it resembled a small theatre: we sat opposite the forge as opposite a stage. A price was agreed upon, and the blacksmith asked what we wanted him to make, proposing a knife or an auto part; we chose a knife. He cranked the bellows to heat the forge, and as he began to work, other Afro-Soqotrans from the neighbourhood arrived, many of whom picked up plastic petrol containers, metal bins or whatever else was at hand and began drumming. Others clapped in unison. The lead drummer was a professional musician and set the pace, altering the rhythm at intervals.

The knife began to take shape, and the blacksmith waved it tantalizingly at the lead drummer, as if to hypnotize him. Then the blacksmith placed a plastic petrol container on his head and approached the drummer like a stalking animal. Several times he closed in on the drummer and backed away to continue working: heating and hammering the knife. Work and performance were interwoven. All the while, more spectators were gathering in the workshop and on the street outside. Soon the role-playing began again: the blacksmith donned a pair of cow horns on a headband. He again engaged the drummer, charging and retreating, closer and closer each time until they touched noses – the customary Soqotran greeting – which seemed to defuse the

---

[97] Peter Brook, *The Empty Space* (New York: Atheneum, 1969), 9.
[98] A. Graham-White, 'Ritual and Drama in Africa', *Educational Theatre Journal* 22, no. 4 (December 1970): 339–49.
[99] See Naumkin and Kogan, *Soqotri Oral Literature*, vol. I, 76–7; and Wellsted, 'Memoir on the Island of Socotra', 193, on the crudeness of knife-making in the Soqotran highlands.
[100] Ahmad Said Khamis Al-Anbali, *Tārikh jazirat suqutrā* (A History of the Island of Soqotra) (Al-Ain: Matba'at al-sahābat, 2006), 210.

Figure 8.1 As he works his forge, a blacksmith impersonates a wild animal in a performance resembling the African *ngoma* dance. Neighbours have gathered in his workshop, drumming on bins and clapping to provide a beat.

Source: Photo by Kevin McNeer.

theatrical tension building between them. But at that instant, the blacksmith turned and lunged at other members of the audience, in particular the clapping children, who screamed in fear and delight. Later, the drummer 'tamed' the bull-blacksmith, who rolled on his back (Figure 8.1).

After this crescendo, the drumming and clapping died down and soon stopped. The blacksmith put the finishing touches on his work – filing the blade and carving the bone handle – in hushed silence. The entire performance lasted about an hour, after which we were presented with the knife.

Elements of this performance – role playing, a mock attack on the audience and aggression transformed into submission – have parallels in an Afro-Soqotran dance that Botting saw in the 1950s:

> One old African gave a special performance all by himself, an improvised dance which was patently a throw-back to the dances of his native Africa. It was a war dance and he was a warrior. He advanced with slow undulating motion towards me, holding his stick like a rifle. When he came within shooting distance, about two feet away, he screamed, aimed his rifle and fired. 'Gow! Gow!' he yelled.[101]

Then one of Botting's Soqotran companions poked the man in the navel, and the dancer collapsed in mock death throes, as if he'd been shot himself – an aggression-turned-submission like that of the horned blacksmith. When Botting asked the

[101] Botting, *Island of the Dragon's Blood*, 87.

dancer the next day whether the dance was from Africa, he replied, 'No, it was in my head. It came out like a river in spate and I couldn't stop it. Now it's all run away.'[102] This is similar to the answer the blacksmith gave the authors almost seventy years later: 'Everybody has his ideas.' We asked repeatedly what the name of the dance was, but the blacksmith insisted it had no name, that it was only *ḥarakāt mā fī ism* – 'movements, no name'.[103]

In the 1950s on Soqotra, however, this kind of dance had a name, a very African name. The 'war dance' Botting witnessed was a part of a larger African dancing event that a native told him was *ngoma*, an African term for a trancelike healing dance. What's more, it was on the street, and the cream of island society turned out to see it – 'the most elegantly dressed Arabs, including the entire foreign community, the Affraria Government and many others'.[104] But in 2019, the blacksmith described songs and celebrations on the island using only terms in Arabic (*mawlid* – the festival of the Prophet's or a Saint's birthday) and Soqotri (*ṣāmihir* – discussed above). Has it become less fashionable to advertise the Africanness of Africa-rooted culture on Soqotra in the ensuing half-century?

The term *ngoma* describes a wide variety of dances in eastern, central and some parts of southern Africa. It seems to have originated as a healing dance, although the form is highly flexible and adaptable: it may be short or last all night and may have Christian or Islamic elements and involve dialogues in a variety of languages, but *ngoma* in all of its manifestations has common features: the primacy of drumming and rhythm that create a trance-like atmosphere, interaction between dancer and audience and a narrative of affliction – or spirit-possession – and subsequent healing.[105]

While the incarnations of *ngoma* seen on Soqotra are light and humorous compared to descriptions of similar dancing on mainland Africa, they display key elements of African-mainland *ngoma*. The blacksmith explains the inspiration for the dance as coming from his interaction with *aš-šabāb* – 'the guys' – around him, affirming the social nature of his dance. The donning of the horns and mock charge imply a state of possession: one that seizes and releases the blacksmith during his work, drawing him into conflict with the spectators, and is defused when the nose of the 'possessed' blacksmith touches the nose of the drummer.

It is worth noting that the tradition of *ngoma* is also maintained in at least one other African diaspora community: among the Sidis in the province of Gujarat, India, where it is known as *goma*. There, too, the dance is a social phenomenon, a community-structuring mechanism.[106]

---

[102] Ibid., 88.

[103] For a detailed analysis of the interview, see Gintsburg and Esposito, 'Asymmetric Linguistic Identities'.

[104] Botting, *Island of the Dragon's Blood*, 87.

[105] John M. Janzen, '"Doing Ngoma"; A Dominant Trope in African Religion and Healing', *Journal of Religion in Africa* 24 (November 1991): 290–1.

[106] Shroff's '"Goma Is Going On"', 18–25; and Basu's "Music and the Formation of Sidi Identity', 161–78, also support the idea that music and dance are among the key identity markers in this community.

The choice of 'costume' is also telling. When asked about the cow horns, the blacksmith insisted they had no special meaning: *ana mā ta'allamtha hākada sāwēt el-qurūn hagg el-bagra u sāwēthum ya'ni kull wāḥed 'ala fikratu* ('I didn't learn it [from anyone], I just took the cow horns, and I put them like that; I mean everyone has his ideas'). Cow horns, however, are a popular element of dance in many parts of Africa, where cultural values are intertwined with cattle breeding, and cattle serve as a reference point in the perception of the world.[107] Dances involve the use of horns, whether authentic or stylized, in Western Africa: in Ghana and Mali,[108] Burkina Faso,[109] Senegal and Guinea-Bissau.[110] In Central Africa, animal horns are an essential part of a shaman's toolkit – among the people of Azande, they are used as containers for keeping medicine – as well as an important element of various ritual dances.[111] In Eastern Africa, performances and ritual dances involving animal horns worn on the head as a symbol of bravery seem to be common in various Nilotic tribes involved in cattle breeding, one example being the *kambala* dance practiced in Southern Sudan, Ethiopia, Kenya and northern Uganda.[112]

Out of the rich variety of dance existing in eastern, central and southern Africa, it is *ngoma* that members of African diaspora across the Indian Ocean preserve. Rebecca Gearhart sees East African society, especially on the coast, as structured through the tradition of performing *ngoma*. This African genre of dance, Gearhart explains, played an important role in the process of Swahilization, so that non-Bantu speakers who were either brought to the east coast as slaves, or relocated there for economic reasons, were eager to participate in *ngoma* performances to generate a powerful sense of belonging to the Swahili super-culture. Until the 1960s, every household on the coast had a member involved with one of the numerous local music and dancing associations.[113] Remnants of the Swahili *ngoma* likely play the same role in the Afro-Soqotran community, offering its members a way to remain connected to their African heritage and identity.

---

[107]   See, for instance, Calvin Schwabe and Isaac Kuojok's study on Dinka's healers' perception of human anatomy and diseases through those of the cattle ('Practices and Beliefs of the Traditional Dinka Healer in Relation to Provision of Modern Medical and Veterinary Services for the Southern Sudan', *Human Organisation* 40, no. 3 (Fall 1981): 231–8); Zeremariam Fre's study on the animal-centric pastoral practices of the Beni-Amer (*Knowledge Sovereignty among African Cattle Herders* (London: UCL Press, 2018)); and Akanmu G. Adebayo's paper featuring the Fulanis' tradition of tracing their origin to their cattle through oral narratives ('Of Man and Cattle: A Reconsideration of the Traditions of Origin of Pastoral Fulani of Nigeria', *History in Africa* 18 (1991): 1–21).

[108]   Francis Thackeray, Wazi Apoh and Kodzo Gavua, 'Adevu and Chiwara Rituals in West Africa Compared to Hunting Rituals and Rock Art in South Africa', *South African Archaeological Bulletin* 69, no. 199 (2014): 113–15.

[109]   Constantine Petridis, 'Buffalo Helmets of Tussian and Siemu Peoples of Burkina Faso', *African Arts* 41, no. 3 (Autumn 2008): 26–43.

[110]   Peter Mark, 'The Senegambian Horned Initiation Mask: History and Provenance', *The Art Bulletin* 69, no. 4 (December 1987): 626–40.

[111]   Edward Evan Evans-Pritchard, *Witchcraft, Oracles and Magic among the Azande* (Oxford: Clarendon Press 1976), 72–3, 95, 106.

[112]   N. L. Corkill, 'The Kambala and Other Seasonal Festivals of the Kadugli and Miri', *Nuba, Sudan Notes and Records* 22 (1939): 205–19.

[113]   Rebecca Gearhart, 'Ngoma Memories: How Ritual Music and Dance Shaped the Northern Kenya Coast', *African Studies Review* 48, no. 3 (December 2005): 21–47.

A second visit to the Afro-Soqotran community: The drummer

Our second interview took place several days later, with Saud, a drummer well known on the island and mainland, such as in Abu Dhabi, where he is invited to play at weddings and other celebrations. For a fee, Saud agreed to talk to us about his life and career as a drummer and do some drumming.

We met him in the Afro-Soqotran neighbourhood of Shiq, on the outskirts of Hadibo. As we walked towards Saud's house, differences between Shiq and Arab-Soqotran Hadibo drew our attention. Some of the houses were built from coral rag cemented with clay, a technique seen in other coastal areas of Soqotra, such as the western port of Qalansiyya, and that Serjeant posited was African in origin.[114] Other dwellings, especially inland, are usually made of stone. The practice of building houses with blocks of coral rag cemented with clay is common along the East African coast from Somalia to Mozambique.[115]

On our way to the drummer's house, we saw mainly Afro-Soqotrans. Unlike in Hadibo, where Soqotran women are expected to wear black abayas and, in many cases, a black niqab when outside, the Afro-Soqotrans prefer colourful, long dresses and brightly coloured, long scarves as head coverings. Only a few hide the lower part of their face, for which they use the same bright head scarf. Both men and women prefer relaxed dress and bright colours, and in the case of men, loosely arranged belts and headwear. In other words, while indigenous Soqotrans and Afro-Soqotrans formally follow similar clothing norms, Afro-Soqotrans have their own style (Figure 8.2).

The appearance of contemporary Afro-Soqotrans brings to mind an observation by Frederick Olmsted about Afro-Americans in Washington, DC, in 1852: 'In their dress, language, manner, [and] motions all were distinguishable almost as much by their color from the white people.'[116] He also noted a predilection for colourful dress.

> They take a real pleasure, for instance, such as it is a rare thing for a white man to be able to feel, in bright and strongly contrasting colours, and in music.[117]

---

[114] Serjeant, 'Coastal Population of Socotra', 169.

[115] Stephanie Wynne-Jones and Jeffrey Fleisher, 'Swahili Urban Spaces of the Eastern African Coast', in *Making Ancient Cities*, ed. Andrew T. Creekmore III and Kevin D. Fisher (Cambridge: Cambridge University Press, 2014), 111–44.

[116] Frederick Law Olmsted, *The Cotton Kingdom: A Traveller's Observations on Cotton and Slavery in the American Slave States, 1853–1861*, vol. 1 (New York: Mason Brothers, 1961), 34.

[117] Ibid., vol. 2, 221. This is consistent with other observations made about the dress of African slaves in the eighteenth and nineteenth centuries in the United States, where even at the turn of the twentieth century, former African slave women wore headgear typical of West Africa, which 'served as a symbolic link to later generations of Georgia black women and to their cultural heritage on both sides of the Atlantic'. For a deeper investigation of African-American dress, see Patricia K. Hunt, 'Clothing as an Expression of History: The Dress of African-American Women in Georgia, 1880–1915', *The Georgia Historical Quarterly* 76, no. 2 (Summer 1992): 459–71.

Figure 8.2 The straw hat and colourful dress of this girl in the Afro-Soqotran neighbourhood of Shiq are characteristic of female islanders of African descent.

Source: Photo by Kevin McNeer.

Transposed roots: *ḥaggana* – our very own

When we arrived, Saud introduced us to his wife and his granddaughter, who were busy in the entryway making straw hats to sell. This is one of the crafts and identity markers that contribute to maintaining Afro-Soqotran identity. Neither the *badū* of the interior nor the non-African coastal population wear straw hats, despite the fact that the former actively produce basketry and mats of straw. Such hats are worn exclusively by Afro-Soqotrans, particularly women; similar hats are woven in coastal Tanzania.[118]

We passed through a small courtyard and into another room, where we sat on the floor opposite Saud. In the course of our conversation, we asked about his background, drumming and band – whose members are mostly from his family. Saud insisted he did not know his exact age, providing a rather broad range of between seventy and a hundred. We might guess he was around seventy. Saud explained to us that he learned how to play the drums when he was still a child: *min zamān, min zamān* ('[I've known drumming] for ages, for ages') – as if his possession of the skill had no starting point,

---

[118] Moreover, sources indicate that already in the sixteenth century, people of Malindi (modern Kenya), Mafia (Zanzibar Archipelago), Ngoji (modern mainland Tanzania) and the Comoros were known for their well-crafted, wide-brimmed straw hats (see Jeremy G. Prestholdt, 'As Artistry Permits and Custom May Ordain: The Social Fabric of Material Consumption in the Swahili World, circa 1450 to 1600', in *PAS Working Papers Number 3*, ed. Jonathon Glassman Jane I. Guyer and Roseann Mark (Evanston: Northwestern University 1998), 29). Similar to how African slaves from Upper Guinea brought to America the technology of cultivation and processing indigo (see Gwendolyn Midlo Hall, *Slavery and African Ethnicities in the Americas: Restoring the Links* (Chapel Hill: The University of North Carolina Press, 2005), 66, 90), we find that Africans in Soqotra are involved in producing straw crafts (hats, baskets, etc.).

not unlike his family lineage on the island. His knowledge of drumming, he insisted, came from his own mind – like Affan's dance; yet Saud added that he also learned, in his words: *min an-nās illi mātu* ('from people now dead'). Saud repeatedly emphasized his Soqotran identity: *el-laḥn ḥaggna el-laḥn ḥaggna huwa soqoṭri baʕad ḥilw lli ḥaggna hna ḥilw men al-Imārāt* ('our melody, our melody which is Soqotri, it's sweet. Ours here is sweeter than the Emirati'). His preference for all things Soqotri applies to dress as well: *al-malābis ḥaggna ḥagg Soqoṭra tamām muš mitil lli ḥagg el-Xalīg* ('the way we dress, the dress of Soqotra is nice, not like that of the Gulf').[119]

Saud has mastered several types of drums and drumming styles, including Arabic ones. He spoke about the difference between various beats used on Soqotra and emphasized a specific 'native' beat called *ndīmo*, for which the drum is always placed vertically, never horizontally. After a demonstration of a variety of drumbeats, we were invited to see Saud's collection of drums in a small shed outside where a kitten was sleeping. The majority of the percussion instruments hanging on the walls were from Soqotra and various parts of Yemen, such as Mukalla and Aden (Saud would point at the non-Soqotri drums and say *hāda baḥr*, 'from across the sea'). There was a small drum that attracted our attention, and we asked its name and origin. Saud said it was called *nyawawa* but immediately changed the subject.

The drum is not seen as an integral part of the native musical heritage of Soqotra,[120] as indicated above by Al-Anbali; therefore, the profession of drummer does not fall within the realm of traditional jobs forming the Soqotran identity. To describe the varieties of drums he owns, Saud used two clearly African terms: *ndīmo* and *nyawāwa*. The first, *ndīmo*, is a Bantu word that in its Swahili form – *(n)dīmo* – means 'a lime fruit', describing the conical shape of the drum. The second, *nyawāwa*, comes from Dholuo language (Nilotic family), where it is used to describe the passage of evil spirits through a village and the process of expelling them with voices and drums.[121] Although neither Saud nor Affan alluded to any manner of communication with spirits, the dance of Affan and the drumming of Saud bear clear similarities with such practices.

Lingering questions for outlanders looking in

Why did our subjects deflect enquiries into their ancestry and the origin of their crafts? Maryam Nourzaei notes a similar 'ghosting' of African roots while working with Afro-Baloch in southern Iran,[122] which makes one wonder whether other African diaspora communities in the Gulf and Indian Ocean also demonstrate an apparent ambivalence towards their heritage. In the case of Soqotra, one factor coming readily to mind is the Islamization, coupled with Arabization, of the island since the unification of North and South Yemen in 1990. Elie describes the new

---

[119] For a detailed transcript and analysis of our conversation with Saud, see Gintsburg and Esposito, 'Asymmetric Linguistic Identities', 236–54.

[120] Peutz, *Islands of Heritage*, 251.

[121] For further detail, see Gintsburg and Esposito, 'Asymmetric Linguistic Identities', 242.

[122] See Chapter 7 in this volume.

Yemeni government's push to create a unifying national identity as 'the promotion of an Islamic sensibility partly to delegitimize allegiance to the secular ideals of the previous Socialist regime; and the prioritization of Arab ethnicity'.[123] Also, new money coming into Soqotra from the wealthy countries of the Gulf and the significant Soqotran diaspora there may also be contributing to the attractiveness of the Arab-Islamic model, a model that has difficulty accommodating rituals involving elements of possession, a part of African tradition. In the larger context of social change on the island, it should also be noted that many Soqotri traditions are frowned upon as un-Islamic.

And yet our informants prioritized their Soqotran identity over a Yemeni or pan-Arab one. Could the societal stress of the Haybak executions, the tensions from the purported participation of Afro-Soqotrans, be rearing its head here? And during the sultanate, it was Afro-Soqotrans, if only a handful, who enforced the ruler's law on the island. Perhaps the insistence on an exclusively Soqotran identity is partly a strategy for avoiding sectarian strife?

Or is our informants' simultaneous showcasing and masking of their African heritage a choice to merge with mainstream Soqotri and broader Arabo-Islamic culture through 'cultural bricolage',[124] a strategy also practiced in varying degrees by slaves and former slaves in North America? This bricolage ensures members of the Afro-Soqotran community inclusion in the island-wide social hierarchy while allowing them to maintain links with their African heritage. Another way to understand their role is through Homi Bhabha's concept of hybridity. Dominant and excluded cultures, Bhabha argues, form a hybrid relationship, where the dominant culture becomes 'contaminated' by linguistic, racial and cultural traits of the excluded one.[125] Indeed, while descendants of African slaves imitate Soqotrans in order to become accepted, the 'autochthonous' population similarly imbibes elements of African culture: African musicians and dancers are routinely invited to perform at Soqotran weddings, and some African crafts have become part of the daily life of all the islanders.

And yet we caught glimpses of behind-the-scenes tensions. One informant, who takes tourists on trips across the island, told us of a near fight between members of his Soqotran crew when one jokingly called an Afro-Soqotran 'a slave'. The latter had to be restrained from dousing him with a pot of boiling water. We asked the same informant to give us a polite formula for asking Afro-Soqotrans about the island's history of slavery and were told not to use the word 'slave' at all, in either Soqotri or Arabic. At the same time, the Afro-Soqotran/Soqotran division was repeatedly rejected by islanders in our presence. Afro-Soqotrans told us they see themselves as simply Soqotran, and non-African Soqotrans told us they see Afro-Soqotrans as Soqotran, despite differences in language use and cultural practices evident in daily life. 'Afro-Soqotran' is, after all, a term foreign researchers have adopted, not an emic one.

---

123 Elie, 'Communal Identity', 26.
124 Shane White and Graham White, 'Slave Clothing and African-American Culture in the Eighteenth and Nineteenth Centuries', *The Past and Present* 148 (August 1995): 149–86.
125 See Homi Bhabha, *Location of Culture* (London: Routledge, 1995).

Miranda Morris describes Soqotrans 'as the careful guardians of their islands' biodiversity'.[126] Reading about Soqotra, one often encounters words such as 'custodians' and 'stewards' to describe the islanders' interaction with their natural environment. Might these descriptors also apply to Soqotran society, to the efforts and strategies of the islanders to curate and preserve their human community despite tensions and grievances from the past – their insistence, in our presence at least, on a shared Soqotran identity?

[126] Miller and Morris, *Ethnoflora*, v.

Part Four

Slavery in a Post-Slavery World

Enslaved by the street: Contemporary forms of slavery among the street children of Cairo

Dina Al Raffie

Introduction

In *Politics*, Aristotle argued that some men were free, while others were 'slaves by nature'.[1] These slaves were 'property with a soul'.[2] This form of slavery, whereby human beings could be owned, transferred and sold by other human beings, was not only legally recognized and regulated by states but also socially and culturally accepted as a fact of life. This began to change rapidly and in a rather unprecedented manner in the nineteenth and early twentieth centuries, which renders the abolition of slavery a recent development in the history of man, with the last state to formally abolish legal or de jure slavery being Mauritania in 1981.

Yet the abolition of slavery and its consequent criminalization in both international and domestic legal frameworks has not automatically eliminated slavery or, more to the point, practices *resembling* slavery. Whether or not practices resembling slavery constitute slavery per se is a point of contention among scholars, and an in-depth review of that debate is available elsewhere.[3] This chapter adopts a consensus viewpoint on the continued existence of slavery: that under certain conditions, the same constituent elements or 'incidents' of slavery understood as ownership (in the traditional sense of chattel slavery) present themselves in contemporary situations and lived experiences as forms of modern slavery.

At its core, one of the most important differences between modern slavery and traditional chattel slavery is the legality of the practices associated with the former. Save for a category of certain cultural activities/practices that fall within a grey area of contemporary definitions of slavery, modern slavery is illegal and mostly employed by

---

[1] Peter Garnsey, *Ideas of Slavery from Aristotle to Augustus* (Cambridge: Cambridge University Press, 1996), 13 (citing Aristotle, *Politics* 1252a24–b15 and 1259a38–1260b26).
[2] Moses I. Finley, *Ancient Slavery and Modern Ideology* (Princeton, NJ: Wiener, 1998), 141.
[3] See, for example, Janne Mende, 'The Concept of Modern Slavery: Definition, Critique, and the Human Rights Frame', *Human Rights Review* 20, no. 2 (July 2018): 229–48.

illicit networks that thrive in areas characterized by weak, corrupt or absent governance, often compounded by conflict and poverty. Thus, while enslavement based on the 'racialised legal ownership of persons'[4] has officially ceased to exist, certain vulnerable social groups continue to be party to master–slave structural relationships despite the existence (theoretically, at least) of established legal frameworks available for their rescue and protection from such situations.

This chapter investigates an example of such relationships that presents itself across several countries and cultures, namely, that of street children. Accurate figures on this global phenomenon are difficult to obtain for a variety of reasons. First, discrepancies exist on how to categorize street children, and who precisely fits the definition of a street child – a definition of which will be provided below. Government bodies responsible for generating data on street children might exclude those who only temporarily 'work the streets' but otherwise have a home or family to return to at the end of the day, artificially reducing the official number of street children.[5] Similarly, children officially registered in, but largely absent from, rehabilitation centres or shelters are often not included in official figures.[6]

Paradoxically, children who *are* entirely homeless and live on the streets or at unregistered locations often fly under the radar, beyond the reach of data collectors. This is exacerbated by the fact that many street children seek to avoid interaction with government authorities, which is why much of the information available on such children is obtained through the efforts of civil society and nongovernmental organizations (NGOs) that are perceived by street children as less of a threat than the authorities. There are also obvious political reasons for manipulating figures: first and foremost, to present a rosier picture of the situation; many of those reasons have to do with countries saving face.

Notwithstanding these challenges, the United Nations Children's Fund (UNICEF) estimates that millions of children around the world either work primarily on the streets or are homeless and spend all their time on the streets.[7] Further, as they are 'absent from official statistics, these children remain politically and socially invisible, amplifying their marginalization and exposure to rights violations'.[8] It is precisely this marginalization – often accompanied by a lack of legal identity – that allows for forms of exploitation that strongly resemble slavery.

The factors driving children to adopt the streets as their home vary, as do the reasons behind the inefficacies and limitations of the law in addressing the issue. This chapter deals with the phenomenon in Egypt, bringing together a wide variety of sources, from social research to Egyptian film and television.

---

[4] Katarina Schwarz and Andrea Nicholson, 'Collapsing the Boundaries between De Jure and De Facto Slavery: The Foundations of Slavery beyond the Transatlantic Frame', *Human Rights Review* 21, no. 4 (March 2020): 392.

[5] Claudia Cappa and Mark Hereward, 'Fulfilling the Right of Street Children to Be Counted', *UNICEF* (blog), 11 December 2019, https://blogs.unicef.org/evidence-for-action/fulfilling-right-street-child ren-counted/ (accessed 25 August 2022).

[6] Ibid.

[7] 'The State of the World's Children 2006: Excluded and Invisible', UNICEF, November 2005, https:// www.unicef.org/media/84806/file/SOWC-2006.pdf, 40–1 (accessed 25 August 2022).

[8] Cappa and Hereward, 'Fulfilling the Right of Street Children to Be Counted'.

Long before the existence of large, structured government initiatives and NGOs to deal with the phenomenon, the entertainment industry was engaging it. Films broaching the issue of street children go at least as far back as the 1950s and reveal continuities in root causes up to the present day. The entertainment industry is a valuable window for both the general public and researchers, given how it can address controversial issues in an artistic space, often nominally fictional and less likely to provoke local sensibilities and government ire. Films and documentaries not only raise awareness of the complexity of social problems but also reflect how the root causes and nature of these problems develop over time. Critically, in those countries where confronting and demanding accountability from governments on social problems is not an available channel of redress, portraying taboo issues in film has always been an alternative through which these issues can be raised, signalling the need for governmental action without coming into direct confrontation with the political elite.

This chapter begins by briefly reviewing scholarship on modern slavery to demonstrate the many ways in which street children are subject to conditions that effectively render them 'slaves'. The aim is not to argue that street children, by definition, fit the category of enslaved individuals but rather to parse out the ways in which many of them are routinely subjected to conditions and circumstances that effectively amount to modern forms of slavery, as well as to highlight the challenges hindering effective solutions. It also puts forward a revised and strengthened definition of enslavement that demonstrates how street subcultures manifest conditions that further entrench children in exploitative and stigmatized roles, not only making them easy prey for illicit forces that exploit and enslave them, but also effectively rendering them slaves to the street itself. Unlike the conventional forms of organized slavery of the not-so-distant past, the solution to which was abolition – that is, criminalizing the practice and institution of slavery – many factors enabling slavery today are socioeconomic, cultural and psychological, and thus require more holistic approaches above and beyond the legal.

With this new conceptual framework of modern slavery in mind, the chapter will focus on its root causes through an exploration of both scholarship and popular entertainment in Egypt, concluding with an examination of the ways modern slavery and its offshoots are maintained, both internally, within the street children's milieus, and externally, by criminal and quasi-criminal networks.

The conditions of modern slavery

The aggressive push to abolish slavery started almost two centuries ago, and traditional or chattel slavery, understood as the legal ownership and trade in humans, has by now been outlawed across the world – with the last country officially to outlaw the practice being Mauritania.[9] This said, the lead up to abolition perhaps finds its best expression in the attempts of the fledgling League of Nations to enshrine the prohibition in

---

[9] Bernard Lewis, *Race and Slavery in the Middle East: An Historical Enquiry* (New York: Oxford University Press, 1992), 79.

international legal conventions that would progressively become binding on all nations as they successively subscribed to international legal norms laid out by intergovernmental organizations (IGOs) – most importantly, the UN.[10]

One of the earliest and perhaps most relevant conventions is the 1926 Slavery Convention, which was the outcome of efforts by the *Temporary Slavery Commission* – established in 1924 – to identify 'slavery in all its forms' and initially motivated by the fact that slave trade continued in large parts of Africa, Asia and the Arabian Peninsula, and, as some scholars have argued, provided a pretext for intervention in these 'uncivilized' parts of the world by European colonial powers.[11] Notwithstanding the colonialist and imperialist motivations that may have underpinned these efforts, the resulting text of the convention remains the primary backdrop against which subsequent legal theories and legislation on slavery have been developed and argued.

The most important passage of the convention, the wording of which has allowed for the expansion of the scope of activities considered modern day slavery, defines slavery as

> the status or condition of a person over whom any or all of the powers attaching to the right of ownership are exercised … [and all parties to the convention should do all that is possible] … to prevent and suppress the slave trade [and] … bring about, progressively and as soon as possible, the complete abolition of slavery in all its forms.[12]

Since the abolition of the slave trade, legal theorists and scholars have increasingly focused on the question of whether this definition is relevant, given the effective end and criminalization of chattel slavery.[13] At the same time, commissions established to revise the definition in the twentieth century have regularly deemed the original definition sufficient, arguing that it readily lends itself to interpretations that have facilitated the development of an international legal foundation for prosecuting a wide range of activities and relationships that constitute a form of slavery or 'slavery-like practices'.[14]

Legal scholars and initiatives as well as governmental bodies involved in establishing the parameters for judging whether a practice may be tantamount to slavery have focused primarily on two phrases in the first clause of the convention's text: the '*status or condition*' of the person over which '*any or all of the powers* attaching to *the right of ownership*' are being exercised.[15] The former (status or condition) differentiates

[10] For review of the history of modern conventions on slavery, see Jean Allain, 'The Definition of Slavery in International Law', *Howard Law Journal* 52, no.2 (Winter 2008): 239–76.

[11] Jean Allain, 'The Legal Definition of Slavery into the Twenty-First Century', in *The Legal Understanding of Slavery: From the Historical to the Contemporary*, ed. Jean Allain (Oxford: Oxford University Press, 2014), 199–219, 200–2.

[12] Joel Quirk, 'Defining Slavery in All Its Forms: Historical Inquiry as Contemporary Instruction', in *The Legal Understanding of Slavery*, 258.

[13] Ibid., 253–77.

[14] Allain, 'The Legal Definition of Slavery', 212.

[15] Article 1(1), 1926 Slavery Convention: https://www.ohchr.org/en/instruments-mechanisms/instruments/slavery-convention#:~:text=(1)%20Slavery%20is%20the%20status,right%20of%20ownership%20are%20exercised (emphasis added).

between what legal scholars refer to as de jure versus de facto realities. Thus, whereas 'status' here defines a reality in which slavery is legally recognized, 'condition' focuses on circumstances surrounding a situation that entails/constitutes forms of de facto slavery absent any legal recognition.

The question that followed – and remains subject to debate – is which conditions amount to slavery and how are they to be defined? Which practices are tantamount to slavery, and should they be recognized and criminalized as such?

The existing debate remains underdeveloped despite newly conceived productive parameters for speaking about modern slavery. Many practices falling within these parameters are not typically criminalized as such. For example, human trafficking is considered an example and manifestation of modern slavery even though it is criminalized as human trafficking and not as slavery per se. Among the differing approaches to elaborating definitions, this chapter finds the focus on powers attaching to ownership – and how to define ownership – to be especially instructive.[16]

Since slavery is no longer institutionalized, it is necessary to describe the nature of powers attaching to ownership that when exercised over an individual might amount to slavery. Robin Hickey concludes that ownership fundamentally relates to the power to 'use, manage, profit from, and discard' belongings or possessions, and that when applied to slavery, these 'incidents' of ownership are useful for elaborating the powers implied in Article 1 of the 1926 Convention.[17] Thus, while 'no legal system permits that one person (the slaveholder, call him SH) may hold a legally enforceable claim-right in respect of another person (call that other S), and correspondingly no court will entertain litigation by SH in respect of interferences with S',[18] some contemporary 'slaveholders' behave as though they have the right to 'control and use S' and produce the same outcomes and effects.[19] Enslavement is necessarily about not only the restriction and curtailment of individual freedoms and liberties but also the suppression of individual agency and the subjugation of individuals such that others exercise overwhelming control – directly or indirectly – over them. Historically, this has often been for economic purposes, that is, economically benefitting from labour to the disproportionate and/or exclusive benefit of the master or slaveowner. The motivating factors for de facto enslavement, however, are not limited to economics but include sociocultural and religious purposes.[20]

There still exist various sociocultural and religious norms that enable practices and relationships resembling slavery, and these are problematic because they are the product of normative environments in which the practices in question are morally and often legally sanctioned. Scholars highlight several examples of relationships in which – at least theoretically – a master–slave relationship is wholly or partially observed yet culturally or religiously sanctioned and still widely practiced. Commenting on the historical connection between marriage, reproduction and slavery, Joel Quirk

---

[16] Robik Hickey, 'Seeking to Understand the Definition of Slavery', in *The Legal Understanding of Slavery*, 220–41.
[17] Ibid., 235.
[18] Ibid., 233.
[19] Ibid., 234.
[20] Quirk, 'Defining Slavery in All Its Forms', 268–76.

points out that some marriage relationships today can be likened to these historical matrimonial forms of bondage:

> When someone is forced into marriage and their subsequent experience of married life is principally defined by their partner exercising powers attaching to rights of ownership over their productive and reproductive capacity... and they are unable to exit the marriage owing to threat of violence and other sanctions, then their individual circumstances may very well amount to slavery according to the 1926 definition.[21]

Conditions and relationships present both among street children within the milieu as well as those enforced by individuals or organizations external to the milieu recreate forms of bondage similar to those described above. This leads to a second defining feature of modern slavery: the de facto slave may not believe in the possibility of release – be it due to social sanctions restricting access to emancipatory alternatives or psychological intimidation.

It is important to emphasize perceived barriers to emancipation as well as real-world ones. The former are often the product of violence or the threat of violence used to enforce obedience. Enforcement agents may be organized gangs and illicit networks external to the milieu, as well as members of the street children's milieu itself.

Enslavement also persists due to a lack of real-life alternatives, a situation exacerbated by the illegal or illicit nature of the activities in which the enslaved and exploited are often forced to participate and by legal and societal repercussions that render escape unrealistic. As discussed in the following section, it is equal parts society's resistance to reintegrating street children into the mainstream as it is the reality of the children's frequent involvement in criminal activities and other deviant behaviour that create a fertile environment for their exploitation and effective 'enslavement'. Thus, a key ingredient in manifest examples of modern slavery is the 'master's' or 'slaveholder's' ability to exploit the individual by capitalizing on conditions that render said individual more vulnerable to relationships in which s/he falls under significant or complete control of another, with few to no real or perceived chances to escape these conditions.

The above review, as is characteristic of the overall debate on terminology and definitions of modern slavery, while leaving much to be desired in the way of specificity, highlights several features central to contemporary understandings of slavery showing how the practice has changed since its abolition as a legally recognized institution. The importance of keeping the debate alive – as witnessed through successive international workshops and initiatives – lies in the recognition that enslavement, as opposed to slavery, persists to varying degrees in the world today and that there is a need to acknowledge and challenge it where it does.

The challenge, however, lies not only in reaching a global consensus on the inherent rights and liberties of individuals in their relationships to others, but also in appreciating the complex intangible factors that allow certain categories and groups of people

---

[21] Ibid., 271.

to be subjected to enslavement. As the remainder of the chapter seeks to illustrate, jurisprudence and the existence of legal mechanisms to protect against enslavement are only one side of the coin. The other side consists of the sociocultural, religious, psychological and economic factors that create a breeding ground for exploitation in the first place, and whose resolution is arguably far more important if we are to put an end to the phenomenon of street children and their exploitation and enslavement.

Street children: Definitions and motives

'Street children' are a heterogenous group whose vulnerabilities are the product of various factors that challenge consensus on a standard definition of what constitutes a street child. Most NGOs view street children through a 'victimhood' lens, focusing on their vulnerability, while governmental entities – particularly law enforcement – tend to view them as criminal and a danger to society. The lens through which street children are viewed impacts on approaches employed to address the phenomenon. As Rebecca Göthe observes, the nature of public sentiment exerts a degree of influence over the nature of policies developed to address the challenge:

> When street children are conceptualized as deviants and threats to public order, policy approaches tend to be correctional, reactive or repression-oriented. When they are instead seen as victims, through an emphasis on the harsh living conditions of the street, rehabilitative or protection-oriented models are often favored.[22]

The common denominator across definitions of street children is that they are children for whom the street serves as the primary source of livelihood and community. Following a consensus definition forwarded in a study on street children and the Egyptian justice system, street children can be broadly defined as 'those children (male or female) younger than 18 who spend a large proportion of their time on the street, who have minimal or no contact with their families, and who because of minimal adult supervision are more vulnerable to a variety of hazardous conditions'.[23] The lack of adult supervision or contact with family distinguishes street children from other children spending time on the street, who have a home to which they consistently return. Additionally, when considering the motivations that underlie the decisions made by many children to leave their families and take to the streets, it becomes apparent that a desire to escape abuse and abysmal conditions in the home is a significant push factor and commonality among profiles of youth across country studies.[24]

---

[22] Rebecca Göthe, 'Public Perceptions of Street Children in Cairo: The Criminalization of Street Children and the Role of the Public' (dissertation, Lund University, 2016), 17.
[23] Nawal H. Ammar, 'The Relationship between Street Children and the Justice System in Egypt', *International Journal of Offender Therapy and Comparative Criminology* 53, no. 5 (2008): 558.
[24] Sarah Thomas de Benítez, ed., *State of the World's Street Children: Violence*, Consortium for Street Children, https://www.streetchildren.org/resources/state-of-the-worlds-street-children-violence/, 16–23 (accessed 25 August 2022).

Unlike the street children depicted in earlier Egyptian films, today's street children are rarely stolen from their families or abandoned as newborns near mosques or orphanages as a result of non-sanctioned relationships – although challenges to children born out of wedlock in Egyptian society persist and recent reports suggest that the theft and sale of babies and children into human trafficking rings is not an uncommon practice.[25] Besides organized crime and exploitation, a slew of push factors propels children to run away, the outcome being their socialization into street milieus that – for reasons discussed below – prevent them from wanting or being able to successfully reintegrate into family or foster care.

Many of today's street children are on the street because they *choose to be*, although there are some examples of children forced out of their homes by parents or guardians. The majority, however, do have homes and families yet opt for the street because it presents a better alternative. Reports and studies surveying children's reasons and motivations for living on the street list child abuse and neglect among the most important, while other factors such as peer pressure and forced labour also rank high.[26] As in other countries where the phenomenon is manifest, abysmal living conditions and abusive or negligent child-rearing drive children to run away. Most street children hail from impoverished or lower-income neighbourhoods where few amenities are available for them to play in safe and clean conditions outdoors, and this is often coupled with little to no education and a high primary school dropout rate.[27]

At home, living conditions are often cramped and children have little privacy or a space to which they can withdraw from parents and siblings. The close quarters in which children coexist with their adult guardians expose them to adult practices and behaviours that they try to emulate. The children may 'see their parents having sex and want to copy them, initially with siblings, hence rape and harassment' becoming commonly experienced forms of violence within the home.[28] Incest is also not uncommon in such settings, as many children come from broken homes characterized by divorce and the presence of step-parents who may sexually harass, rape or otherwise violently treat children whom they feel no responsibility towards because they are not their biological offspring.

Children are often also socialized in a home environment characterized by domestic violence. A lack of contraceptives coupled with high reproduction rates, sometimes with the aim of producing young labourers to contribute to family earnings, places a strain on parents who are uneducated and under- or unemployed. Children – especially stepchildren – are seen as a financial burden and often bear the brunt of parental aggression and abuse, particularly by step-parents with little wish to expend limited financial resources on them.[29]

---

[25] Suzi Mohamed Rashad, 'Child Trafficking Crime and Means of Fighting It: Egypt as a Case Study', *Review of Economics and Political Science* (June 19, 2019): 12–13.

[26] For example, Ammar, 'Relationship between Street Children and the Justice System in Egypt', 559.

[27] Iman Bibars, 'Street Children in Egypt: From the Home to the Street to Inappropriate Corrective Institutions', *Environment and Urbanization* 10, no. 1 (1998): 203; Ammar, 'Relationship between Street Children and the Justice System in Egypt', 559.

[28] Ammar, 'Relationship between Street Children and the Justice System in Egypt', 559.

[29] Mirna Abdulaal, 'Dreams of a Safe Home: How Banati Foundation Fights against Child Abuse in Egypt', *Egyptian Streets*, 13 October 2019, https://egyptianstreets.com/2019/10/10/dre

Violence against children at home is normalized in mainstream notions of child-rearing in Egypt, particularly in lower-income or impoverished rural areas that prioritize harsh discipline over nurturing approaches to bringing up children. A co-commissioned survey by UNICEF and the Egyptian Council for National Childhood and Motherhood found that '92% of [those surveyed] said that beating their children was completely normal'.[30] Consequently, children may fail to develop meaningful bonds with their parents and guardians and grow to fear rather than trust them. Where other push factors exist, the street quickly becomes an initially attractive alternative – and one of the few available – because of the relative freedom it grants runaways.

As street children soon learn, however, this freedom is conditional and, for many, short-lived, since the transition to the street often means little more than replacing one set of abusers with another. Although conventional wisdom and media representations depict exploitation by criminal gangs as the primary danger faced by street children, a deeper examination of available studies suggests a continuum running from internal exploitation (within street society) to external exploitation (by entities outside the street milieu), where some conditions and practices arguably amount to modern slavery, while others involve a form of self-inflicted 'enslavement'.

In this chapter, the latter is understood to be a result of requirements of street life that make it almost impossible for the children to successfully reintegrate into society. Instead, continued dependence on the street milieu pulls its inhabitants into repeated cycles of exploitation, violence and abuse. These cycles do not always necessitate organized exploitation by networks and gangs seeking to benefit economically – or otherwise – from children, but rather are the outcome of systematic forms of violence and abuse that render children perpetual slaves to the street as a result of the social stigmata attached to their wilful or unwilful participation in a plethora of taboo or illegal practices.

Exploitation from within

Many forms of exploitation derive from the basic need to survive on the street. Street children in different settings face a variety of options for survival, but all must share the street with others and thus become integrated into an existing subculture that is paradoxically both a means of survival and a source of immediate danger. While very little on-the-ground, immersive research has been carried out on these milieus, an exception is a recent study of street children in Egypt, conducted over several years, that finds underappreciated layers of exploitation existing *within* the street milieus themselves.[31]

---

ams-of-a-safe-home-how-banati-foundation-is-fighting-against-child-abuse-in-egypt/ (accessed 25 August 2022).

[30] Ibid.

[31] Kamal Fahmi, 'Working with Street Kids: Unsettling Accounts from the Field', in *Marginality and Exclusion in Egypt*, ed. Ray Bush and Habib Ayeb (London: Zed Books, 2012), 169–90.

The street is its own ecosystem. Its denizens are at times subservient to prevalent social and cultural norms, while at others challenge these very same norms through their stigmatized status. The above-mentioned study describes this ecosystem based on fieldwork in which researchers and social care workers were able to immerse themselves in the street children milieu over time in order to better understand it. The ethical dilemmas and challenges facing the researcher in this environment are many, but what emerges is a story of power hierarchies and various forms of exploitation in the form of initiation rites and pecking orders in what are essentially street gangs of children. These street hierarchies are not necessarily based on age but on time spent on the street and a reputation for being a seasoned street figure that commands the respect of others. This respect and veneration is often, unfortunately, a result of the children's ability to force compliance through forms of violence or abuse or through coping mechanisms and tactics that often entail sacrificing the well-being of others within the milieu. Various examples, including that of street girl Mervat's agreement with the police, are cited below. Initiation rites not only ensure passage into the street children milieus but also guarantee a degree of protection, acceptance and recognition by others within it. As noted in the study, street milieus are a place in which children 'develop a network of niches in the heart of the metropolis in order to resist exclusion and chronic repression'.[32]

However, being in these milieus has several shortcomings: exploitative power hierarchies exist within them as well as the often-violent practices through which these power hierarchies are consolidated. This is because many of these practices violate mainstream social conventions, particularly with regard to sexual relations. Researchers note the prevalence of 'deviant [sexual] behavior' within these milieus, as well as frequent sexual assault inflicted upon children by others within and without the milieu.

While some of the behaviours in question – such as same-sex relations and premarital sex[33] – are consensual and at times intimate and loving, more prevalent forms of sexual assault include the practice of being 'forcefully taken', that is, raped, by stronger or more dominant boys.

Worryingly, sexual abuse seems to be normalized, as best expressed in one street child's observation that 'it's only natural; when you are young you get taken, and when you grow up you take'.[34] It is not surprising, then, that, absent intervention, the exploited become the exploiters, and there is perhaps no better Egyptian example than the infamous 'El-Tourbini' or 'Express Train' (aka Ramadan Abdel Rehim Mansour).

Tourbini's case shocked Egyptians when it came to light. A runaway and street child himself, El-Tourbini was arrested and prosecuted alongside six other gang members for the brutal rape and murder of over thirty street children.[35] His modus operandi – on which his name was based – was luring street children onto train carriage roofs,

[32] Ibid., 171.
[33] Identified as such due to being social taboos and/or criminalized in Egypt.
[34] Fahmi, 'Working with Street Kids', 187.
[35] John R. Bradley, *Inside Egypt: The Land of the Pharaohs on the Brink of a Revolution* (New York: Palgrave Macmillan, 2009), 199–200.

where they were raped, tortured and often killed and thrown onto the train tracks. El-Tourbini was put to death with one other accomplice, also a runaway and street child.[36] While El-Tourbini arguably represents the extreme of violent exploitation within the milieu, focused studies profiling perpetrators of sexual violence and assault against street children find much of it within the milieu, disproportionately targeting girls and young women.

In a study by Nada Khaled and Suliman El Daw surveying violence, abuse and substance use among street children in Greater Cairo and Alexandria, the authors note that 'sexual abuse was many fold more common among girls'[37] and that forced sex was 'reported to be perpetrated mainly by street boys (61%)'.[38] Additionally, the main clients soliciting prostitutes among street children were themselves street children (46 per cent).[39] The cycles of sexual abuse and violence do not remain within the milieu, however, and the dual factors of high demand for child prostitutes and the danger of becoming one quickly drive some street children to adopt the tactic of sexually exploiting others to save their own skin.

Mervat – a street girl aged twelve – essentially peddles her peers for sex to a police informant and tea maker in exchange for protection, both from corrupt policemen as well as other street children who might have her in their sights as a target for sexual abuse. Mervat, 'witty, as well as good looking',[40] and dedicated to resisting the pressure to behave and dress more like a male in order to avoid sexual assault by her male peers, takes on the role of a pimp, luring new street girls into meetings with the informant and tea maker in return for protection from both. 'Group solidarity and intense individualism appear to go hand in hand. Selfless sharing and selfishness are equally widespread,'[41] and those who survive and resist exploitation are those who know how to balance the two.

Stigma and cycles of abuse inside and out of the milieu

The street children milieu is only one source of potential exploitation of children, and many more exist outside of it. The sad fact is that in order to survive, street children are often forced into activities that are either illegal or seen as deviant by society at large. This makes them easier to blackmail and control. For example, same-sex relations are criminalized in Egypt, as is premarital sex, especially for women. Consequently, children born out of wedlock are not recognized by the state and thus have no legal status, stripping them of any protections and rights that the state would otherwise

---

[36] Ibid.; Manal el-Jesr, 'Killing Kids', *World Street Children News*, 10 January 2007, https://streetchild rennews.wordpress.com/2007/01/09/killing-kids/ (accessed 25 August 2022).
[37] Khaled H. Nada and El Daw Suliman, 'Violence, Abuse, Alcohol and Drug Use, and Sexual Behaviors in Street Children of Greater Cairo and Alexandria, Egypt', *AIDS* 24, Suppl 2 (2010): 542.
[38] Ibid., 543.
[39] Ibid.
[40] Fahmi, 'Working with Street Kids', 185.
[41] Ibid., 186.

afford to those with a birth certificate.[42] This lack of a legal identity also renders these individuals far more vulnerable to exploitation and various forms of trafficking because, as far as the state is concerned, they do not exist.

Same-sex relationships and pregnancies among non-married street children or their 'clients' in prostitution and child trafficking rings are common. The inability to resort to official entities for care and protection forces street children to rely on the aid of not only shelters – when they exist – but also health practitioners and government officials (mostly police officers) that often extort them in return for protection and illicit access to resources. Because the children do not have the means to pay for these services, they are made to remunerate in other ways. Forms of payment commonly include anything from providing sexual services to moving illicit goods, such as drugs, for the 'creditor'.

The punitive approach adopted by many governments towards street children arguably perpetuates conditions for their exploitation. The situation is complicated by the fact that criminal activity is often the primary source of income for many street children; thus, a criminal-punitive approach is usually adopted because it seems logical and is justified from a legal perspective. The result is a quick fix: the problem is literally locked up rather than addressed as a factor of larger sociocultural, economic and political issues. A more immediate problem with the punitive approach, however, is that it destroys the children's trust in state institutions and predisposes them to exploitation by both corrupt law enforcement officials and criminal networks and gangs that further cement the street child's criminal legal status through forcing him or her into participating in illicit activities. The underdeveloped nature of the juvenile detention system in Egypt only contributes to the problem.

Thus, notwithstanding amendments to Egypt's Child Law No. 12 (1996) that recognizes a category of children as being *vulnerable to danger*, the law still includes provisions that allow police to arrest 'children under 18 for a variety of activities [that include] … being habitually absent from school and suffering from mental illness or diminished mental capacity'.[43] These and other activities, like begging, sleeping on the street or 'mixing with suspected persons' are standard fare for street children, yet their status and situation are rarely taken into consideration when they are arrested and tried.

Furthermore, because of the low age at which Egyptian law establishes criminal liability – recently amended to twelve years of age[44] – Egyptian legislation fails to discriminate adequately between children twelve years and above and adults, based on the belief that the former are similarly able to distinguish right from wrong. This leads to higher rates of arrest and incarceration of children who, despite the existence of special detention and correctional centres for juveniles and minors, often end up

---

[42] For review of laws and legal rights of these children, see Laura M. Thomason, 'On the Steps of the Mosque: The Legal Rights of Non-Marital Children in Egypt', *Hasting's Women's Law Journal* 19, no. 1 (2008): 121–47. See also Rashad, 'Child Trafficking Crime', 8.

[43] Ammar, 'Relationship between Street Children and the Justice System in Egypt', 561.

[44] 'ICMEC Egypt National Child Protection Legislation', *International Center for Missing & Exploited Children*, October 2018, https://www.icmec.org/wp-content/uploads/2018/10/ICMEC-Egypt-National-Legislation.pdf (accessed 25 August 2022).

sharing prison space with adults. Sweeping provisions for arrest not only leave many children at the mercy of policemen (many of whom are corrupt and often abuse their authority by extorting the children for money, drugs or sex) but also expose them to further potential abuse at the hands of adult criminals. Not to mention the detrimental impact that imprisonment alongside adults may have on the children's development.

As Nawal Ammar notes, a major shortcoming of an underdeveloped juvenile (detention and correctional) system is that it leaves little room for the development of 'skills and behavioral modification [that would enable children] ... to mature out of being "troublemakers" '.[45] The importance and relative success of rehabilitation for street children are echoed in other studies[46] and suggest a need for more of these initiatives to reintegrate children. Although correctional facilities do exist in which children are held separately from adults, they tend to be under-resourced and understaffed, and because of implementation issues associated with laws theoretically meant to protect juveniles, the result is more frequently the temporary or permanent holding of children in prisons alongside adults. The juvenile justice system 'remains either piecemeal or left to nonprofit organizations'[47] and is thoroughly underdeveloped. The involvement of several ministries (Ministry of Justice, Ministry of Interior and Ministry of Social Solidarity) in the process of elaborating procedures associated with juvenile care and delinquency further stalls the process of fine-tuning and implementing a cohesive and coherent body of laws specific to minors. And this is due to not only the 'heavy bureaucratic burdens'[48] of each but also 'frequent disagreement in ministerial priorities'[49] that results in a fragmented and inconsistent approach to reforming the juvenile justice system. Absent clear guidelines on what should be done, street children (among other minors arrested on criminal offenses) often find themselves in prison with adults.

Street children's brush with law enforcement and the existence of police records on them is yet another impediment to their reintegration into society. One of the earliest Egyptian movies showcasing the challenges facing the reintegration of rehabilitated street children as adults is the 1955 *Ja'alouni Mojriman* ('They Made Me a Criminal') (Figure 9.1).[50] The movie starred some of Egypt's most prominent movie stars at the time – including Rushdy Abaza, Farid Shawqi and Huda Sultan – and sought to capture the socio-legal dynamics contributing to the street children phenomenon. The plot follows the life of Sultan (Farid Shawqi), a boy whose mother was illegitimately betrothed in a *'urfi* marriage to a rich man who, upon dying, left the two impoverished – Egyptian law does not grant inheritance rights to children born in such civil marriages. Sultan's mother soon follows his father in death. After he is rejected by his uncle, who refuses to acknowledge any kinship to him while simultaneously squandering his

[45] Ammar, 'Relationship between Street Children and the Justice System in Egypt', 566.
[46] G. Hosny, T. M. Moloukhia, G. Abdel Salam and F. Abdel Latif, 'Environmental Behavioural Modification Programme for Street Children in Alexandria, Egypt', *Eastern Mediterranean Health Journal* 13, no. 6 (January 2007): 1438–48.
[47] Ammar, 'Relationship between Street Children and the Justice System in Egypt', 566.
[48] Ibid.
[49] Ibid.
[50] *Ja'alouni Mojriman* (1955), [Film], Cairo: Dollar Film.

Figure 9.1 In the Egyptian movie *They Made Me a Criminal*, Sultan convinces the ringleader of a criminal gang to take in abused street children.

inheritance, Sultan ends up being recruited into a criminal street gang. The boy is eventually arrested and forced to serve time in a correctional facility. Upon release, he attempts to find a job with the help of an *imam* who has taken him in.

The film briefly traces Sultan's difficulties as various locals refuse to give him a job when they learn he spent time in a correctional facility. He is forced to lie about his background and is hired as a milkman but loses his job after again unsuccessfully trying to contact his uncle. The movie follows Sultan as he finds the ringleader of his old criminal street gang, with whom he briefly works as a means to rescue children and bring down the gang. Sultan's affections for a cabaret performer Yasmina (Huda Sultan) who rejects Sultan's playboy uncle in favour of Sultan leads to a violent cabaret brawl orchestrated by the uncle that lands Sultan in prison again. Only thanks to a clever ploy devised by the cabaret performer is the uncle tricked into confessing. Sultan is eventually freed and reunited with Yasmina.

The movie highlights not only how a run-in with 'the law' can hobble an individual's future but also how the legal system in Egypt fails to safeguard the rights of women. In many of the earlier films on street children, a recurring plot is that of a female houseworker or low-income woman being coerced into a relationship with a richer man, who takes her on as a mistress. When the mistress inevitably gets pregnant – contraception and family planning remain fringe concepts among much of Egyptian society even today – the man either discretely provides for the mother and child (as in the case of Sultan's mother) or else forces the woman to get rid of the child.

In the movie *Dahab* ('Dahab'),[51] a wealthy, gambling, alcoholic playboy and his wife task their niece with killing the man's illegitimate newborn by the housemaid in order to avoid scandal. The niece abandons the little girl (later named Dahab or 'Gold') on the doorstep of a mosque – a common place for abandoned babies in the Muslim world. The child is soon found by a poor musician and street entertainer who decides to take her in. A few years later, the man and girl happen across the house of Dahab's wealthy father and the niece recognizes the man, whom she had spotted rescuing Dahab from the mosque's doorstep on the night she abandoned her. Although still a beggar at this point, Dahab's talents as a performer are soon discovered by a cabaret owner, and she quickly amasses wealth for herself and her adopted father. Only when her biological father, having gambled away his fortunes, discovers from the niece that his illegitimate daughter is alive and wealthy, does he attempt to claim her as his own. The movie ends well (with custody eventually given to Dahab's foster father), as do many of the older Egyptian black-and-white films on street children; it rarely ends well, however, in the real world for street children or those who conceive them out of wedlock or within the context of unrecognized marriage contracts.

Despite advances in personal status laws in Egypt, women still face many challenges because society and the law continue to place the responsibility of 'proper' sexual conduct at the feet of women. Then and now, avenues for obtaining abortions, even when the woman has been raped or otherwise coerced into sex, are few and expose women to major health risks as well as potential further exploitation. Abortions are illegal unless the pregnancy poses a risk to the mother's life. As one women's rights advocate in Egypt explains, Egyptian society is 'male-centered. A woman's body belongs to a father, a brother, then to a husband or a brother-in-law in case of the death of the husband … a premarital sexual relationship is sacrilege … women's moral independence and their ability to make choices for themselves are not integrated'.[52]

In a society that still very much emphasizes chastity and virginity as marriage prerequisites for women, both forced and consensual sexual experiences of street girls effectively bar options for them to reintegrate into a society where a family life would be possible – they are tainted goods regardless of whether or not they were forced into having sex. Even with the existence of clandestine clinics that will accept money for illegally performing abortions, the cost is prohibitive for street girls who will either opt to keep the baby, try and obtain illicit drugs to carry out a 'homemade abortion', or else abandon the baby – and not always at the doorstep of an orphanage or mosque, as is the tradition. 'You have no idea,' states an aid worker, 'how many newborns are found dead in dustbins.'[53]

[51] *Dahab*, 1953, https://www.youtube.com/watch?v=_2eLxCutxSg (accessed 25 August 2022).
[52] 'Abortion: Why Egypt's Children Are Being Dumped on the Streets', *Middle East Eye*, 5 October 2015, https://www.middleeasteye.net/news/abortion-why-egypts-children-are-being-dumped-streets (accessed 25 August 2022).
[53] Ibid.

Reintegration is doubly challenging for women and girls. As with many other honour/shame societies, premarital sex – whether consensual or not – is a source of dishonour that taints the individual and significantly reduces their chances of getting married and starting a family. It is female chastity that determines family honour. Virginity is still prized by prospective suitors in Egyptian societies, and street girls are the least likely to be able to afford hymen restoration procedures, which remain in demand due to the false yet widespread belief that if women do not bleed on their wedding night, it signifies a broken hymen, that is, premarital sexual relations. Because sex and pregnancy out of wedlock on the street are almost a given, the prospects of marriage and starting a family – especially if the girls have children on the street – are almost impossible. As with abortions, there are no figures on hymen restoration procedures in Egypt, but it is difficult to find clandestine clinics that will perform them, and they come with a high price.

Insights from inside all-female shelters not only demonstrate the value of chastity and being 'untouched' but also exhibit a disturbing mentality that exists among street girls housed together in these shelters. Nelly Ali, a British-Egyptian blogger and humanitarian worker with extensive experience covering the street children phenomenon in Egypt, writes on one shelter's policy of separating virgins from mothers. The policy is developed to help the virgins safeguard their chastity from the mothers and other non-virgin street girls among them, who, Ali realizes, are conspiring to try and forcibly break another girl's – Laila's – hymen. The girls in question are mostly young, single street mothers who understand that they are unlikely to escape the stigma of single motherhood on the street and are condemned to a life in the shelters. 'I hate Laila, she is better than me, I know she is better than me and I hate her … I will break her so she is like us, so she is not better than me,' says one of the single street mothers.[54]

Attempts to help alleviate the stigma through providing reproductive healthcare, including contraception, have led to societal and governmental accusations that aid organizations are helping fuel immorality by facilitating freer (because safer) sexual relations between girls and boys. The thoroughly flawed operative assumption here is that a lack of contraception will encourage less sexual contact on the street – an idea debunked by studies on the prevalence of both consensual and non-consensual relations among street children.[55] Further, in the absence of a more comprehensive government-supported initiative to reintegrate street children and address the issues

---

[54] 'Street Children: The Hymen and the Stamp of Shame', *Nelly Ali* (blog), 8 November 2012, https://nellyali.wordpress.com/2012/09/11/street-children-the-hymen-and-the-stamp-of-shame/ (accessed 25 August 2022).

[55] Several studies already cited here document both types of sexual relations among the children. For example, in Fahmi, 'Working with Street Kids', the author notes that the researchers 'observed that both boys and girls were often involved in sexual relationships that were not necessarily exploitative but had more to do with exploration, intimacy and even love'. On the other side of the divide are the studies that demonstrate a plethora of both consensual-exploitative (i.e. prostitution) and non-consensual (i.e. rape) relationships among children within these milieus that are unrelated to the provision of contraceptives or lack thereof, for example, Nada & Suliman, 'Violence, Abuse, Alcohol and Drug Use'.

leading to their presence on the street, two important and undesirable outcomes remain overlooked.

The first is that the lack of contraceptive devices provided to street children leads to more children being born into the street milieu, which leads to more children growing up on the street. More dangerously, this leads to a rise in sexually transmitted diseases (STDs) among street children, leading to higher rates of HIV infection (among other STDs) in the population overall. This makes reintegration and rehabilitation both more costly for the government – as it now also has to contend with healthcare costs associated with sick children – as well as more challenging for the children in question.

While less attention is given to premarital sexual relations among men in many patriarchal societies, the fact of boys being forcibly taken or sodomized by other men is a source of deep humiliation and shame that, even when not immediately traumatizing to its victims in the street milieu, render the men in question less masculine and tainted in the eyes of women and society as a whole. As depicted in various films and studies mentioned throughout this chapter, street children are often marked with razor cuts or else branded as a means of punishment which only adds to their 'undesirable' appearance, further isolating them from society and leaving the scars as constant reminders of the abuse. More ominously for the women and girls, it permanently identifies them as no longer chaste. As Nelly Ali observes,

> [The gangs that] ... rape them will knife their face – usually a curved scar under the eyes to mark them as no longer being virgins, 'spoilt goods', and this scar would result in a thick piece of flesh hanging from their face serving as a reminder of the horror they faced but also as a deterrent to society at every attempt the girls tried to reintegrate back into it.[56]

Several of the films reviewed here showcase this practice of branding or cutting street children as a form of punishment. Ringleaders of criminal street gangs enslaving children and profiting from their street activities, criminal or otherwise, will burn or disfigure children attempting to escape or caught skimming from the proceeds of their street activities, be it money or drugs.

One of the first and most famous films to come out in colour in Egypt showcasing this practice among other elements of criminal gangs is *Al-Afareet* ('The Devils'), starring Egyptian pop singer Amr Diab.[57] In the film, a drug trafficking gang avenges the killing of some of its members by murdering the policeman who leads the operation to interdict their drug activities. In the process, they steal his newborn baby girl to give to the female ringleader of a criminal street gang (Figure 9.2). The girl is raised to beg and steal until, after a concert in which she introduces herself to the singer (and discretely steals his wallet), she shows up at his doorstep to return the wallet and makes the case for being given a chance to perform with him on television.

[56] 'The Stamp of the Street', *Nelly Ali* (blog), 21 February 2016, https://nellyali.wordpress.com/?s=curved+knife (accessed 25 August 2022).
[57] *Al-Afareet*, 1990, https://www.youtube.com/watch?v=hesFbe-G1f4 (accessed 25 August 2022).

Figure 9.2 Belya is assaulted by the gang's boss, who demands to know what information she has divulged to the police.

Not long after, the girl (Belya) explains her situation and admits to Diab that she and the other street children are being made to sell and transfer a 'white powder' (heroin) for the ringleader, at which point Diab takes a petrified Belya to report the gang's activities to the police (Figure 9.3). Although terrified at the thought of encountering the authorities, Belya goes along with Diab, only to be found in the back of his jeep outside the police station by three other street children dispatched by the ringleader to find her and bring her back. Upon her return, Belya is threatened with branding by hot iron for divulging information to Diab and the police about the criminal gang's activities and held in a cage-like sleeping area where she is tied up and prevented from leaving the gang's safe house.

Earlier in the film, Diab caves in to the girl's request for a chance to develop her singing and acting abilities. He introduces her to the producer and hostess of a children's television show who is the birth mother – Karima – she was stolen from as a baby.

Ironically, and in an accurate cinematic reflection of society's response to street children, upon discovering that Belya is a street girl in need of shelter and protection from the criminal street gang, Karima dismisses her and angrily tells Diab never to bring her back to the studio. Her initial urge is to dissociate herself for fear that mixing with a criminal and beggar could damage the show's (and Karima's) reputation as well as invite legal consequences. Belya and another young street girl are finally reunited with Diab and Karima when the criminal network is dismantled, and Belya is promised that they will not be given to a shelter or orphanage and will instead receive foster care from 'mama Karima'.

Figure 9.3 The ringleader gathers the street children around her, issuing instructions and tasks, before dispatching them back onto the street.

Karima's attitude towards Belya, as well as that of Sultan's employers, reflects another major challenge to street children: reintegration and rehabilitation. Having grown up on the street affects children's chances of reintegration into mainstream society, even when options exist for that very purpose. The fact of sexual abuse and violence to which many of these children are exposed, as well as their forced or wilful participation in criminal activity, contributes to their enduring stigmatization, even when they are taken off the streets.

Society at large is highly suspicious of street children, notwithstanding their age or knowledge of the circumstances and conditions that drive their involvement in illicit activities or deviant behaviours. Although beyond the scope of this chapter, some scholars argue that the tendency to demonize street children traces its history back to societal developments in the industrial age, with Arnon Bar-On suggesting that in many respects, street children and beggars represented a sort of competition to the bourgeoisie in their desire to monopolize capital and the labour supply.[58]

On a far more basic level, however, the existence of street children challenges the image of 'functioning' mainstream society by reminding people of their society's failures. Street children are the product of societal deficits and ailments that should

---

[58] Arnon Bar-On, 'Criminalising Survival: Images and Reality of Street Children', *Journal of Social Policy* 26, no. 1 (1997): 65.

be corrected, avoided or eliminated. Street children hold a mirror up to society that exposes the deep-seated failings that produce the subculture. Children in general 'are held in one of two regards or combinations thereof. On the good scapegoat we project our ideals, and so protect adoringly; conversely, on the bad scapegoat we project our guilt, and consequently fear.'[59] Street children are the ultimate 'bad scapegoat', in that they mirror a collective guilt and overall sense of helplessness among a mainstream whose primary strategy in dealing with the children is, at best, apathy, and, at worst, demonization or dehumanization. The children are tolerated yet disappear into the depersonalized backdrop of the cityscape, in plain sight but invisible, doomed to be perpetual slaves to the street.

Conclusion

Several international legal conventions developed over the better part of the past century have sought to spell out the conditions and characteristics of modern slavery, and these have since served as a primary source for crafting legislation in many countries. Modern slavery lacks the permanency of the institutions of chattel slavery, as both the practice and institution of holding, trading in and profiting from the labour of individuals have been outlawed. This said, conditions recreating master–slave relationships in the context of modern criminal and illicit networks that exercise several or all of the 'powers of ownership' over others persist, perpetuating the phenomenon of slavery despite global abolition and criminalization.

The most common form of organized slavery today is arguably human trafficking, where human beings are coerced into forms of labour from which human trafficking networks economically benefit. Besides organized crime and exploitation, however, far more insidious forces coalesce to create for vulnerable groups self-fulfilling cycles of violence and exploitation that generate practices and conditions resembling slavery.

Street children are one subcategory of endangered children worldwide particularly vulnerable to these cycles. When not explicitly targeted by criminal networks, many are compelled to leave their homes, escaping domestic conditions that are a result of complex sociocultural, psychological and economic factors reflective of larger societal ills beyond their control. Once 'settled' in street subcultures, children must adopt personalities and strategies that entrench them in cycles of exploitation and criminality that perpetuate conditions of actual or approximate enslavement.

For those few taken off the streets and reintegrated into society, education and employment options are stymied by insufficient funding as well as the stigma attached to their pasts. While few reliable statistics or large-scale studies exist on the fate and future of those street children who do make it into adulthood, literature and media suggest that common trajectories involve continued association with the street: being

[59] Ibid., 64.

exploited by gangs and sometimes evolving into exploiters themselves within the very same gangs.

It is against the backdrop of society's rejection and the justice system's crime-focused approach to the children that professional criminal networks operate. And these represent the main sources of external exploitation. Besides criminal gangs, street children are easy prey to networks forcing them into prostitution and pornography and, more recently, trafficking of body organs. While trafficking is a crime under Egyptian law,[60] implementation measures are complicated by an underdeveloped juvenile support system as well as laws that prosecute a wide gamut of behaviours associated with habitation on the street *as minors*. The overwhelmingly punitive approach not only creates distrust in institutions but also leaves ample room for their abuse and exploitation both by criminal networks and corrupt police officials benefitting from the children's dependence on them to stay out of prison.

These cycles of enslavement and exploitation persist because the underlying issues luring children to the streets are not adequately addressed. Although funds are allotted to shelters, orphanages and other facilities to aid children, absent efforts to tackle the root causes, it is likely that the phenomenon will persist and continue to grow.

---

[60] Important elements of the relevant law – Article 2 of Law 64 of 2010 in this case – include those which criminalize the exploitation of vulnerability, with a special reference to children. Among other things, trafficking is understood as 'abusing vulnerability or need ... It is also any form of exploitation; prostitution, sexual exploitation – children included – coercion, servitude, slavery, begging, organ removal, human tissue or part of it.' Because human trafficking is acknowledged as one form of modern slavery, many of the situations in which street children find themselves as a result of their precarious existence on the street represent modern forms of slavery.

Yazidi women and girls held as slaves under the Islamic State: Healing wounds and reassessing doctrines

Lana Ravandi-Fadai

Sexual slavery was a key component of the Islamic State's (IS) radical programme, and many Yazidi and other girls and young women suffered this physical, emotional and spiritual indignity during the IS reign of terror from roughly 2014 to 2017. While the female slaves did serve a 'function' – pleasure objects for male fighters and in some cases for producing a new generation of fighters – the women filled no economic niche, as did the slave pearl divers of the Gulf or domestic servants of the Maghreb. The centuries-long practices of slavery across the Middle East described in other chapters were underpinned by economics and governed – and restrained – by religious ideology, but the engine for IS slavery was religious ideology, and in the case of Yazidis, this was exacerbated by 'an ancient calumny, the accusation that they [Yazidis] worship the devil'.[1] This chapter examines the practice of sexual enslavement of Yazidis by IS and the subsequent process of reintegration for these women into their native communities. While some Yazidi women now living in Europe, such as Nobel Peace Prize laureate Nadia Murad,[2] have spoken out about their ordeals, the condition of many victims remaining in Iraqi Kurdistan is more difficult to assess.

Because the central role of doctrine in the IS phenomenon poured oil on the fire of a pre-existing debate within the Islamic community about the textual canon and slavery, intensifying the struggle for control of interpretations of the Islamic tradition, this chapter places sexual bondage under IS within the larger debate among Islamic scholars over reforms to Islamic doctrines.

A short introduction to the Yazidi ethno-confessional group is in order. Scholars consider Yazidis a branch of the Kurdish peoples, although many Yazidis consider themselves a separate group.[3] They live primarily in the northern part of

---

[1] Gerard Russell, *Heirs to Forgotten Kingdoms: Journey into the Disappearing Religions of the Middle East* (New York: Basic Books, 2014), 40.
[2] This chapter references her account of her captivity: *The Last Girl: My Story of Captivity, and My Fight against the Islamic State* (New York: Tim Duggan Books, 2017).
[3] P. G. Kreyenbroek, *Encyclopedia of Islam*, new edn, s.v. 'Yazidi' (Leiden: E.J. Brill, 1986), 313.

Iraqi Kurdistan in the provinces of Nineveh and Duhok (but also in other parts of the Middle East, with large diasporas in Germany – perhaps almost two hundred thousand people[4] – Russia, the Caucasus, Belgium and elsewhere), where they speak the Kurmanji dialect of Kurdish, and sometimes Arabic, and practice Yazidism, a syncretic religion that appeared in the eleventh century and echoes aspects of Zoroastrianism, Islam, Judaism, Nestorian Christianity and Sufism.[5] Yazidis undergo baptism, as in Christianity, and circumcision, as in Islam and Judaism; they believe in the divine nature of fire, as do Zoroastrians; and they pray five times a day, as do Muslims and Zoroastrians.[6]

In March 2019, I travelled to Iraqi Kurdistan with colleagues from the Institute of Oriental Studies in Moscow, visiting Erbil, Duhok, Lalish, Sulaymaniyah and other cities. I had also been in Erbil in 2014, when IS detachments were entrenched not far from the city, held at bay by a defensive ring of Peshmerga fighters.[7] Even within this ring, it was impossible to travel without bodyguards, and the roads were choked with security checkpoints. But in 2019, the danger had largely passed. Our group met with the Head of the Department for Yazidi Affairs in Kurdistan,[8] Kheyri Bozani, and the Kurdish social activist Asso Urmi to discuss the situation with Yazidis in Iraqi Kurdistan and the fate of Yazidi refugees from the area of Sinjar (also called Shingal) (Figure 10.1).

On the night of 2–3 August 2014, Peshmerga military formations of Iraqi Kurds numbering around eight thousand fighters were ordered out of Sinjar for reasons that remain unclear, after which IS entered the city and committed atrocities against the peaceful population.[9] Images of the tragedy flew around the world and shocked humanity. By the end of the IS terror, over 10,000 Yazidis had been killed;[10] up to 5,000 women and children forced into slavery – official statistics put the number of female captives at 3,548; and around 360,000 Yazidis became refugees – 65 per cent of the total Yazidi population in Iraq.[11] For the first time in their history, Yazidis were forced to abandon their land and its holy sites en masse. On our 2019 trip, we visited refugee camps in the Dohuk, Sulaymaniyah and Erbil provinces, where Yazidis live alongside Kurdish refugees from Darashakran and other places in Syria. In 2019, it was estimated

---

[4] Von Lena Gilhaus, 'Jesiden in DeutschlandAbschied von Afrin', *Deutschlandfunk*, 26 March 2008, https://www.deutschlandfunk.de/jesiden-in-deutschland-abschied-von-afrin-100.html (accessed 4 September 2022).

[5] Kreyenbroek, 'Yazidi', 313.

[6] A. Naumov, 'Prinuditel'nyi brak, iznasilovanie, smert': Kakuiu sud'bu "Islamskoe gosudarstvo" gotovit zhenshchinam Yazidov?' ('Forced Marriage, Rape, and Death: What Fate Is the Islamic State Preparing for Yazidi Women?') *Лента.ру* (internet journal), https://lenta.ru/articles/2015/10/14/yazidi_plight/ (accessed 14 June 2022).

[7] 'Peshmerga' in the Surani Kurdish dialect means something akin to 'ready for death', from *pesh* (before, in front of) and *merg* (death).

[8] Under the Ministry of Religious Affairs of the Regional Government of Kurdistan.

[9] Interview with General Kasim Shasho of the Kurdish Army, Rudaw news agency: http://rudaw.net/arabic/onair/tv/episodes/episode/hevpeivin19092014 (accessed 1 June 2022).

[10] https://en.qantara.de/content/pursuing-prosecution-in-germany-justice-for-yazidi-survivors-of-islamic-state-genocide (accessed 29 August 2002).

[11] *KRG Clarifications of the Findings of the 2021 Country Report on Human Rights Practices: Iraq* (Kurdistan Regional Government Presidency of the Council of Ministers, June 2022), 31.

Figure 10.1 The Baadre refugee camp in Iraqi Kurdistan in 2019.

Source: Courtesy of the author.

that 64,554 people lived in 39 camps in these areas.[12] What struck me first was the scale of the camp – a sea of tents stretching to the horizon; and what struck me most were the local children. An entire generation has grown up in tents, often together with livestock. These young people have no experience of any other life.

We also visited the holiest Yazidi site, the temple in Lalish, at the invitation of its prior, Sheikh Abubakr. In addition to speaking with Yazidi pilgrims from around the world, religious figures and the head of the local Shingal clan, I met most of the twenty-four girls and young women living in the area who had been liberated from slavery under IS. These beautiful girls were from eight to ten years of age when taken into slavery. It was impossible for me to process what they must have gone through for days, months and, in some cases, years. One girl was held as a concubine for three years. Yet despite sufferings beyond their years, beyond the comprehension of most, these young women seemed unexpectedly, almost shockingly, carefree. When one religious leader proposed that I ask them directly about what had happened to them, I was taken aback and reluctant to risk reopening their wounds (Figure 10.2).

Their enslavers were as shameless in ideology as in deed: they openly resurrected and promulgated principles justifying slavery, despite the fact that many had grown up in Western countries, where public discourse is saturated with discussions of

---

[12] 'Winterization Needs for the Displaced Populations in the Kurdistan Region – Iraq', report published by the Joint Crisis Coordination Centre under the Ministry of the Interior of the Kurdistan Regional Government (7 November 2019), 2.

Figure 10.2 The author and a colleague walk with Yazidi girls born and raised in the Baadre refugee camp in Iraqi Kurdistan, 2019.

Source: Courtesy of the author.

human rights. To fathom the unfathomable, the resurgence of slavery in our time, it is necessary to examine the aims of the self-styled IS in its war against unbelievers, seen as 'God's work'. The IS strategy is made all too clear by steps taken to erase historical monuments of other faiths in IS-controlled territories in Iraq and Syria from 2014 to 2019. In addition to the killing – often through beheading – and persecution of living representatives of other faiths, hundreds of religious buildings, including Christian churches and pre-Christian ruins, were damaged and destroyed.[13] Part and parcel of the negation of other belief systems was the objectification of their practitioners: old justifications for enslavement and slave-trading were re-instituted, with non-Sunni Muslims and other 'unbelievers' targeted: Shiites, Christians[14] and Kurdish Yazidis.[15] According to the principles that IS developed, Muslims were required to obey a strict

---

[13] A joint declaration by sixty-five countries 'in support of human rights of Christians and other communities, especially in the Middle East', made on the initiative of the Vatican, Russia and Lebanon at the 28th session of the UN Council on Human Rights in Geneva on 13 March 2015: http://www.mid.ru/foreign_policy/humanitarian_cooperation/-/asset_publisher/bB3NYd16mBFC/content/id/1092273/pop_up?_101_INSTANCE_bB3NYd16mBFC_viewMode=print&_101_INSTANCE_bB3NYd16mBFC_qrIndex=0.

[14] In Iraq, the number of Christians has dropped by a factor of 10 since 2003, from 1.5 million to 150,000. In Syria, since the beginning of the civil war in 2011, the Christian population has decreased from 2.2 million to 1.2 million, by almost half. For more detail, see A. V. Fedorchenko and A. V. Krylov, Fenomen 'Islamskogo gosudarstva' (The Phenomenon of 'The Islamic State'), *MGIMO University Messenger* 41, no. 2 (2015): 174–83.

[15] Ibid.

interpretation of Shariʻa Law, while *kuffar* (sing. *kafir*) were either to be killed or enslaved. All Shia were considered *kuffar*, or unbelievers.[16]

Islamic State-controlled territories became the scenes of rape, torture, murder and enslavement of large numbers of Yazidi women and others belonging to non-Sunni confessional groups. This wave of cruelty hit the Yazidi community with devastating effect, especially for pre-teen Yazidi girls forced into concubinage (young boys were also taken captive to be raised as *ashbal al-khilafah*, 'cubs of the Caliphate'[17]). Most who survived[18] – through ransom or escape – remain in refugee camps in Iraqi Kurdistan and face severe challenges in overcoming these traumas.

For over a millennium, Yazidis have maintained a unique, syncretic form of faith with practices strange to outsiders, some of which may strike them as paganistic – a prohibition on eating lettuce or wearing blue clothing, carrying balls of soil (called *barat*) from the shrine of Lalish as talismans, kissing the spot first touched by rays of the morning sun and praying towards the sun.[19] The seventy-two persecutions Yazidis count throughout their history[20] were often connected with the attributes of the Yazidi deity, which even today arouse suspicion among neighbours. Yazidis worship Malak Taʻaus, the 'Angel-Peacock', whom they consider the highest of the archangels and who refused to bow down to God's creation – man – out of reverence for God, that is, because such an act of prostration would be disrespectful to God.[21] In mainstream Islamic tradition, it was Iblis – or Satan – who refused to bow down to man, thus the association of Malak Taʻaus with Satan. In Yazidi tradition, Malak Taʻaus spent seven thousand years in Hell for his refusal to prostrate himself, filling Hell with tears. Then God forgave him and elevated him to the status of highest of the archangels.[22] This age-old association of the Yazidi deity with Satan is so deeply rooted in parts of the Middle East that in the 1990s, a Yazidi member of the Iraqi parliament felt compelled to protest against the use of the word 'Satan' (often used in Arabic imprecations) during proceedings because other parliamentarians gave him accusing looks each time it was pronounced.[23] Former British diplomat Gerard Russell describes how, in 2011, his Kurdish taxi driver declared he would not eat any Yazidi food: 'That Melek Taoos they worship – that's the Devil.'[24]

The seeds of xenophobia lay in the soil; IS had only to nurture them. The severest IS attacks were carried out in August 2014 in the city of Sinjar and environs. Yazidi men and boys over ten years of age were killed (at times given a choice between death and

[16] A. B. Shirokorad, *Bitva za Siriiu. Ot Vavilona do IGIL* (The Battle for Syria: From Babylon to IS) (Moscow: Veche, 2016).

[17] 'Daesh Training Camp for Children Uncovered in Syria', *Sputnik*, 5 June 2018, https://sputniknews.com/20180605/daesh-training-camp-children-1065124765.html (accessed 3 September 2020).

[18] Figures published on 4 April 2021 by the Office of Rescued Yazidi Abductees, a Kurdish Regional Government initiative headquartered in Erbil.

[19] Kreyenbroek, 'Yazidi', 314–15; Murad, *Last Girl*, 18.

[20] Russell, *Heirs to Forgotten Kingdoms*, 41.

[21] This view dovetails intriguingly with some Persian Sufi readings of Iblis' transgression, see Hamid Algar, 'EBLIS', *Encyclopædia Iranica*, online edn (2004), https://www.iranicaonline.org/articles/eblis (accessed 3 September 2020).

[22] Naumov, 'Prinuditel'nyi brak, iznasilovanie, smert''.

[23] Russell, *Heirs to Forgotten Kingdoms*, 60.

[24] Ibid.

conversion to Islam), while women and younger children were taken to other cities and then sold in open-air or private slave markets. They were beaten, subjected to torture and poorly fed. Their new 'husbands' raped them.[25] One Yazidi girl named Nur recounted how she had been bought by an old man who invited ten of his friends to sleep with her, which they did, one by one, including her 'husband'.[26] Badeeah Hassan Ahmed, who was eighteen at the time, describes a private slave market:

> I picked up fragments of their Arabic, spoken in accents I didn't recognize, as well as languages I'd never heard before. Some of the men were old. Others were young. … Women … hoping to be unseen, shimmied their bodies away when the men approached them.
>
> When an older man with a bald head and a gray beard pointed at two Yazidi girls about my age who looked related, a Daesh [IS] soldier yelled at them to stand, He ordered them to open their mouths, and the older man studied their teeth. The Deash soldier next demanded the girls hold out their hands. The older man, dressed in a black dishdasha [traditional robe], examined their fingernails. Then he pulled up their dresses and looked at their legs. The girls were asked to turn around as the potential buyer gazed at their hair. I watched as urine dripped down one of the girl's legs, pooling on the floor.[27]

Another case was that of Roza Barakat, seized by IS fighters in Sinjar when she was eleven years old. She was taken to Syria, sold, resold and raped repeatedly. In order to escape future sales, she was forced to convert to Islam and marry a Lebanese man living in Raqqa, the capital of the purported IS caliphate. He brought food and clothing to IS fighters and treated her better than her previous 'spouses'. She gave birth to a son at the age of thirteen. In 2019, IS was defeated, but Roza was afraid to return to her family lest they reject her – as her IS captors had declared they would. Her 'husband' was killed on the road, and her son died in an airstrike. Later, she learnt that her entire family had either been killed by IS or disappeared. Now she is living in a Yazidi community in the Syrian village of Barzan, where she was warmly welcomed back and is recuperating from the horrors she experienced.[28]

Statistics on the scale of the tragedy have been gathered by the Ministry of the Interior of Iraqi Kurdistan. In the Sinjar Region, 96 per cent of the 308,300 Yazidi residents were able to relocate to safer areas of Iraqi Kurdistan in time to escape the horrors of IS. By the end of 2016, only around 3,200 Sinjar Yazidis had returned, while the majority still languish in refugee camps, in exile from their homes. Up to 5,500 Yazidis were killed by IS,[29] and over 9,000 taken prisoner, both men and women.

---

[25] Naumov, 'Prinuditel'nyi brak, iznasilovanie, smert''.

[26] Ibid.

[27] Badeeah Hassan Ahmed with Susan Elizabeth McClelland, *A Cave in the Clouds* (Toronto: Annick Press, 2019), 93–4.

[28] S. Kullab, 'Adrift after Enslavement, Yazidi Teen Says She Can't Go Home', *Associated Press News*, 10 February 2022, https://apnews.com/article/islamic-state-group-middle-east-europe-iraq-syria-64e612ac557d2d8de6bc3b597b8403e0 (accessed 4 October 2023).

[29] P. Nicolaus and S. Yuce, 'Sex Slavery: One Aspect of the Yazidi Genocide', *Iran and the Caucasus* 21 (2017): 196–229.

As of May 2022, 6,400 Yazidis had been liberated from captivity, while almost 3,000 reportedly remain IS captives despite the fact that Sinjar was cleared of IS fighters in November 2015. Amazingly, these captives were said to remain in IS captivity within the massive Al-Hol camp in northern Syria, a 'mini-state' that became a refuge for IS as well as its victims after the organization was driven from the last territories it had occupied.[30]

Almost all of the Yazidi women subjected to sexual slavery (by IS fighters or local Sunnis) were pressured to convert to Islam. Their captors, to the astonishment of the women, often prayed just before or after raping them, sometimes telling their victims they were turning them towards the true faith by raping them, thereby saving their souls. While some texts in the Islamic tradition do condone enslavement in time of war, justification of such 'methods of conversion' based on traditional texts is far-fetched, to say the least. For example, Surah 16 Ayah 125 of the Quran explicitly states: 'Call [others] to the way of God through wisdom and good news and debate well with them. For truly, your Lord knows best who has strayed from His path and who follows the straight path.'[31]

Systematic rape, abduction, threats and other forms of violence and indignity that Yazidi women and girls were subjected to wrought lasting emotional and physical damage. This is confirmed by a survey of twenty-three Yazidi women from fifteen to forty-five years of age (with a mean age of twenty-five years) conducted in a refugee camp in Iraq in May 2017. All were driven from their homes in August 2014. Although none were old, 62 per cent rated their health as poor, 17.2 per cent as relatively good/good and only 3.4 per cent as excellent (the remainder did not answer). Of these women, 79.3 per cent lived through intense trauma: capture, terror and threats (about half of the women), loss of a home, hunger and thirst (65 per cent of all the women), and rape (8.7 per cent). Chronic stress and depression combined with the oppressive conditions in tent camps have taken their toll. Although 40 per cent of the women reported a need for medicines, they do not have them due to the prohibitive cost.[32]

The net of IS sexual bondage was cast wider than Yazidi women. High numbers of male fighters meant a high demand for females to satisfy them and a push to recruit from other countries, including Europe, which supplied a number of volunteers for 'sex-jihad'. Several hundred sex slaves were born in Great Britain, Sweden, France, Spain and other European countries. Volunteers also flew in from the United States, Australia, Africa, Brazil and some Asian countries. Later, and in increasing numbers, women from the former Soviet republics, especially Kazakhstan and Russia, began to join IS 'sex brigades'.[33] Most of these 'under-loved' women naively supposed they

[30] A. Beliaeva, 'Obnarodovano kolichestvo iraktsev-yezidov, nakhodiashchikhsia v plenu u IGIL (The Number of Iraqi-Yazidis in IS Captivity Has Been Published)', *SalamNews*, 31 May 2022, https://www.salamnews.org/ru/news/read/461286 (accessed 14 June 2022).

[31] Nicolaus and Yuce, 'Sex Slavery', 196–229.

[32] P. Jäger, 'Stress and Health of Internally Displaced Female Yazidis in Northern Iraq', *Journal of Immigrant and Minority Health* 2 (2019): 257–63.

[33] J. Cook and G. Vale, *From Daesh to 'Diaspora': Tracing the Women and Minors of Islamic State* (London: ICSR, 2018), https://icsr.info/wp-content/uploads/2018/07/ICSR-Report-From-Daesh-to-%E2%80%98Diaspora%E2%80%99-Tracing-the-Women-and-Minors-of-Islamic-State.pdf (accessed 14 June 2022).

would become the wives of brave jihadists and live romantic and adventurous lives. In secular European societies, where the pursuit of gender equality is prioritized, the traditional role of the male as breadwinner and protector of wife and family has long been undergoing a radical change and, from the perspective of many traditional cultures, diminishment. Some argue that traditionally minded women are searching for that once prized icon, the knight on a white stallion, and that Western volunteer 'pleasure girls' found it in today's radical Islamic fighters: a man with a rifle sprinting through wildlands and facing off against 'evildoers' in the name of justice and religion. Could this be what compelled some of these women to abandon the secular enlightenment and material comfort of Western Europe to find fighter-husbands in Iraq and Syria?[34] At least one young woman, in Australia, began trying to recruit other women online after she decided to join IS at the age of nineteen.[35]

The category of women most vulnerable to IS recruitment was the religious and single – including single mothers, young women of student age and those who had problems with their parents. Islamic State recruiters prowled social media sites looking for women in these categories and targeting certain internet forums – especially ones associated with Islam. Once a target had been located, experienced recruiters would begin to work over their potential prey, usually behind fake online identities. Eloquent language and photographs of handsome men supposedly fighting in Syria out of pure principle provided appealing bait; the target was then engaged in 'meaningful' discussions about life. The reeling-in process might require months, but in time, the woman or girl would become attached to her online interlocutor. The result was that the target would leave for the Middle East to join the man – sometimes taking her children and also putting them at risk.[36]

Only after travelling to her IS hosts would the woman or girl realize she had been misled. She would often be told that her pen-pal-husband had been killed in combat and be placed in a special 'distribution center' whence she would be given or sold to some fighter. More often than not, this was not the last transfer, with women frequently passed from man to man. 'Husbands' not infrequently beat and raped their 'wives', then gifted or sold them to others.[37] Thus, there were two categories of IS sex slaves: those forced into slavery and those who entered into it willingly – albeit without full knowledge of what they had chosen.

Some of the liberated women and girls recounted how their captors forced them to take contraceptive pills based on the idea that the rape of 'infidel' captives is sanctioned in Islam if measures are taken to prevent pregnancy.[38] But experiences varied. Many of the captive women did get pregnant but were able to have abortions performed, not

---

[34] 'Kak zhivut seks-rabyni "Islamskogo gosudarstva"' ('How the Sex Slaves of the "Islamic State" Live'), *Kaktus Media*, 4 August 2016, https://kaktus.media/doc/342560_kak_jivyt_seks_rabyni_isl amskogo_gosydarstva.html (accessed 14 June 2022).

[35] Naima Brow, 'Mother of Australian "IS Bride" Begs Government "Please Bring My Daughter Home"', *SBS News*, https://www.sbs.com.au/news/dateline/article/exclusive-mother-of-aus tralian-is-bride-begs-government-please-bring-my-daughter-home/g7x8g1wjx (accessed 4 September 2022).

[36] Ibid.

[37] Ibid.

[38] Interview by the author with victims, March 2019.

wanting a child by their rapist (although abortion is forbidden among Yazidis), while others were forced to have abortions because their captors believed it was not permitted to have children from 'infidel' slaves; still others gave birth in captivity. A number of these children – according to accounts that cannot be independently verified – are said to have been left behind by their mothers, while other mothers could not bear to leave their newborns and took them upon liberation. I was told in Kurdistan that some of these children were baptized in the sacred Zamzam spring at Lalish, according to the Yazidi practice, and accepted by Yazidi society, although officially children of 'mixed parents' are not accepted.[39]

Radical Islamists put together a set of instructions concerning conduct towards slaves: 'Questions and Answers on Captives and Female Slaves', published in 2014 and translated into English by Human Rights Watch:

Question 1: What is al-sabi?[40]

Al-Sabi is a woman from among ahl al-harb [the people of war] who has been captured by Muslims.

Question 2: What makes al-sabi permissible?

What makes al-sabi permissible [i.e., what makes it permissible to take such a woman captive] is [her] unbelief. Unbelieving [women] who were captured and brought into the abode of Islam are permissible to us, after the imam distributes them [among us].

Question 3: Can all unbelieving women be taken captive?

There is no dispute among the scholars that it is permissible to capture unbelieving women [who are characterized by] original unbelief [kufr asli], such as the kitabiyat [women from among the People of the Book, i.e., Jews and Christians] and polytheists. However, [the scholars] are disputed over [the issue of] capturing apostate women. The consensus leans toward forbidding it, though some people of knowledge think it permissible. We [IS] lean toward accepting the consensus....

Question 4: Is it permissible to have intercourse with a female captive?

It is permissible to have sexual intercourse with the female captive. Allah the almighty said: '[Successful are the believers] who guard their chastity, except from their wives or (the captives and slaves) that their right hands possess, for then they are free from blame [Koran 23:5–6].'...

Question 5: Is it permissible to have intercourse with a female captive immediately after taking possession [of her]?

If she is a virgin, he [her master] can have intercourse with her immediately after taking possession of her. However, if she isn't, her uterus must be purified [first]....[41]

Question 6: Is it permissible to sell a female captive?

---

[39] Ibid.
[40] 'Prisoner of war' in Arabic.
[41] That is, wait for her period.

It is permissible to buy, sell, or give as a gift female captives and slaves, for they are merely property, which can be disposed of as long as that doesn't cause [the Muslim ummah] any harm or damage.[42]

Forceful arguments have been fielded from the Islamic world, based on the Quran, Hadith and Islamic legal tradition, to demonstrate the vacuity of 'IS Islam', that the acts permitted in the IS catechism above – sex with pre-pubescent girls, rape – demonstrate a grossly selective interpretation of traditional Islam, which in fact encouraged the freeing of slaves and set forth conditions for doing so in many ways more humane than analogous rules in the Roman Empire or the antebellum United States, among other historical examples.[43]

In September 2014, 126 Sunni theologians, scholars and community leaders from around the world issued *al-risalat al-maftuhah*, an 'open letter' in the form of a pamphlet in Arabic and English to Abu Bakr al-Baghdadi, the titular head of IS at that time. Signatories relied on the opinions of Sunni religious and legal authorities from all periods of Islamic history and decried the distortion of Islamic tradition and its authoritative texts, specifically the Koran, to justify the crimes IS boasted of in its media outlets as acts of the faithful. The pamphlet criticized the harsh and radicalized interpretation of Shari'a Law, and acontextual citations of Ayat (Quranic verses) to fashion false justifications for murder, pillage and rape. The self-proclaimed IS 'caliphate' could not be considered legitimate, since a caliphate can be established only through the consensus of the Muslim population at large, whereas in the case of IS 'a group of no more than several thousand has appointed itself the ruler over a billion and a half Muslims'.[44] The signatories also argued that any appeal to wartime ethics was inapplicable in the case of the Yazidis, since 'they neither fought you nor Muslims'.[45] Moreover, not only are the Yazidis not 'Satanists', but they also are protected by the Quranic formulation *ahl al-kitab*, 'People of the Book' (sometimes translated as 'People of the Scripture') – Christians, Jews and Sabians (usually interpreted as Zoroastrians and adherents of closely related faiths) – with other religions added by later Islamic scholars commenting on the text. The Quran 'emphasizes the community of faith between the possessors of the earlier scriptures and the adherents of the new revelation',[46] and the adherents of these earlier scriptures (parts of 'the Book') are

---

[42] Human Rights Watch, 'Slavery: The IS Rules', 5 September 2015, https://www.refworld.org/docid/55ed6f124.html (accessed 25 August 2022).

[43] One example being that children born of a slave but sired by a master were automatically free according to the Islamic principle of *umm al-walad*. See Chapter 1 in this volume for more detail. Others are 'the presumption of freedom' and 'the ban on the enslavement of free persons except in strictly defined circumstances'. See Bernard Lewis, *Race and Slavery in the Middle East: An Historical Enquiry* (Oxford: Oxford University Press, 1990), 5.

[44] 'Open Letter to Dr. Ibrahim Awwad al-Badri, Alias "Abu Bakr Al-Baghdadi", and to the Fighters and Followers of the Self-Declared "Islamic State"', *Issuu*, 19 September 2014, https://issuu.com/openlettertobaghdadi/docs/arabic_english_open_letter_to_baghd?embed_cta=embed_ba dge&embed_context=embed&embed_domain=www.lettertobaghdadi.com&utm_medium=refer ral&utm_source=www.lettertobaghdadi.com&embed_id=14632537%2F10405725, 23 (accessed 24 August 2022).

[45] Ibid., 18.

[46] G. Vajda, *Encyclopedia of Islam*, s.v. 'AHL al-KITAB'.

accorded particular respect – although in other parts of the Quran and Hadith, they are also censured as having strayed from the true path. The letter argues that Yazidis are Magians, and indeed, Yazidi territories were referred to as 'Magian' in the twelfth century,[47] probably meaning Mazdean, another term for Zoroastrianism.[48] It is true that similarities between Yazidism and Zoroastrianism and its offshoots abound: a concern with issues of pollution and purity and respect for the elements of earth and fire, but the most significant qualifier is that Yazidism, like Islam, Christianity and Judaism, is a monotheistic religion.[49] It is unacceptable, the letter argues, to kill any representative of the 'People of the Book' regardless of whether the individual chooses to convert to Islam; and there can be no question of any sanction for rape, torture or enslavement. Thus, the murder and exile of Yazidis and the rape of Yazidi women are blatant crimes. Moreover, signatories argue, slavery in the Islamic world 'has been considered forbidden for over a century. Indeed all the Muslim countries in the world are signatories of anti-slavery conventions.'[50] The abolishment of slavery, the authors argue, was, in fact, 'one of Islam's aims'.[51] It is likewise forbidden in Islam to force children to participate in combat or killings, as IS did with Yazidi children: 'Some are taking up arms and others are playing with the severed heads of your victims.'[52] Signatories categorically condemned the use of enslaved women as concubines, adding that such a practice only spread 'corruption and lewdness'.[53]

But have the signatories of the al-Baghdadi letter glossed over unsavoury aspects of traditional Islamic scripture – or, at the least, its complexities and contradictions – to further their humanistic arguments? While urging kindness to slaves and encouraging manumission, 'The Qur'ān, like the Old and New Testaments, assumes the existence of slavery. It regulates the practice of the institution and thus implicitly accepts it.'[54] Concubinage is also recognized. And what about individuals who in no way qualify as 'People of the Book'?

Unlike the signatories of the open letter, Hocine Drouiche, vice-president of the Conference of Imams of France and imam at a mosque in Nimes, does not see the texts in the Islamic tradition as blameless and merely the subject of perverse interpretation by radicals. Drouiche published a three-part analysis of contemporary violence in Muslim lands and the state of Islamic law in which he bemoans the fact that

---

[47] Kreyenbroek, 'Yazidi', 313.
[48] A more historically accurate formulation might have been that Yazidis are the inheritors of a form of Magian/Zoroastrian belief or share a more ancient source with Zoroastrianism. Christine Allison, 'YAZIDIS i. GENERAL', *Encyclopædia Iranica*, online edition (2004), http://www.iranic aonline.org/articles/yazidis-i-general-1 (accessed 3 September 2020).
[49] While the monotheism of Yazidism fits the spirit of the Quranic formulation, in a literal sense Yazidis are not 'of the Book' or 'of the Scripture', as they do not seem to have fixed scriptural texts. Whether this had any influence on IS prejudice is difficult to say. Kreyenbroek, 'Yazidi', 314; Russell, *Heirs to Forgotten Kingdoms*, 43.
[50] 'Open Letter', 19.
[51] Ibid., 18.
[52] Ibid., 20.
[53] Ibid., 19.
[54] Lewis, *Race and Slavery in the Middle East*, 5. Lewis provides a summary of Quranic positions on slavery and the relevant passages on pp. 5–6.

many Muslim clerics and some professors at Al-Azhar University in Cairo, the most authoritative university in the Muslim world, continue to justify the enslavement of non-Muslims – even girls – based on certain texts in the Islamic tradition. A female dean and professor of *fiqh* (Islamic law) at the university, Suad Salih, a proponent of women's rights in other areas,[55] has spoken in support of the right to enslave non-Muslims during war.[56] Salih is one of several religious scholars with such views, who consider Shari'a Law above international legal and humanitarian norms. Although Muslim countries have signed onto the Geneva Convention and thereby agreed to protect the rights of POWs and civilians, Al-Azhar and other Islamic educational institutions continue to publish, distribute and teach texts that sanction the enslavement and rape of non-Muslims, texts that should be 'burnt', according to Drouiche.[57] He argues that some conservative Muslim theologians and Salafists[58] are justifying the actions of IS and discrediting Islam even when many of Islam's leading thinkers call for renouncing such principles as atavisms impeding the evolution of a progressive Islamic theology. Drouiche argues Suad Salih should apologize before all the non-Muslim victims of sexual aggression, because pronouncements like hers embolden radicals to commit such crimes, arming them with an 'Islamic' justification.[59] Drouiche calls for nothing short of 'a profound internal reform of Islam' to bring its principles into accordance with those of international law and convention and to enshrine the sanctity of any life regardless of religion. He argues this should begin with a thorough overhauling of teaching materials and approaches in leading Islamic universities.[60]

Dina Al Raffie sees the reluctance on the part of some religious authorities to offer 'a more robust theological counterargument' as part of a struggle for ideological authority that has led to unintended consequences:

> Religious institutions seek to maintain their control over these outdated blueprints for state and society, since their institutional power and authority derive largely from a continued monopoly over the interpretation of religious law. This dynamic translates to an ineffective response to Islamists, whose worldview is guided by some of the same pre-modern notions of governance found in the sharia. But it also helps explain the general trend of unwitting intellectual collaboration between the Muslim clergy and political Islamists against a Muslim intelligentsia with whom

---

[55] Wendy Kristianasen, 'Egypt: Islamic Sisters Advance', *Le Monde Diplomatique*, September 2005, https://mondediplo.com/2005/09/12woman (accessed 26 August 2022).

[56] https://www.youtube.com/watch?v=sOy11srPcp0 (accessed 26 August 2022).

[57] H. Drouiche, 'Imam Drouiche: Raping Christians and Yazidis Cannot be Considered an Islamic Right (I)', *AsiaNews*, 2 January 2018, https://www.asianews.it/news-en/Imam-Drouiche:-rap ing-Christians-and-Yazidis-cannot-be-considered-an-Islamic-right-(I)-42986.html (accessed 14 June 2022).

[58] Neo-orthodox Muslim reformers advocating a return to the pious and simple faith of early Islam.

[59] H. Drouiche, 'Daesh Is Not Alone in Justifying Sexual Slavery, There Is Al Azhar Too (II)', *AsiaNews*, 2 February 2018, https://www.asianews.it/news-en/Daesh-is-not-alone-in-justifying-sexual-slav ery,-there-is-al-Azhar-too-(II)-43002.html (accessed 14 June 2022).

[60] H. Drouiche, 'Imam Drouiche Slams Rape Jihad, a Crime Against Humanity (III)', *AsiaNews*, 2 May 2018, https://www.asianews.it/news-en/Imam-Drouiche-slams-rape-jihad,-a-crime-against-humanity-(III)-43016.html (accessed 26 August 2022).

they disagree, yet whose ideas present significant potential for developing effective counternarratives to violent extremism.[61]

Yazidi doctrines have also been tested and subjected to re-evaluation following the IS trauma. As a small ethno-confessional group surrounded by other – often expanding, at times aggressive – groups, the Yazidi community has been vigilant in protecting its identity over the ages. Strict concepts of purity and pollution have honed Yazidi society's sense of honour (*namus* in Kurdish).[62] Traditionally, if a Yazidi female enters into a relationship with a man from another religion, she must be exiled from the community or the entire clan is considered polluted, and no distinction is made between relations marital or non-marital, voluntary or forced, any and all of which constitute dishonour for the female and her family.

But in a world in which cultures are mixing with ever more frequency, and especially in the face of the IS tragedy, Yazidi customs evolved to preserve group identity have at times turned in upon themselves to work against the group like an autoimmune disease, one that IS exploited and one that threatened to exile a large segment of the female population from their community through no fault of their own. Honour killings are sometimes carried out: when male relatives kill Yazidi girls for their romantic liaisons in order to purify the clan.[63] One of the most notorious instances was the stoning to death of a seventeen-year-old Yazidi woman in 2007 by her family and locals.[64] The killers reportedly suffered no punishment, and the police were informed that the victim committed suicide. Such honour killings have occurred even among diaspora communities such as in Germany, where a girl's father murdered her in the forest because she had fallen in love with a Pakistani. He was seized, dragged to his home and doused with boiling water. A 'polluted' girl is compared to a worm-ridden apple that needs to be thrown out so as not to spoil the bushel.[65] It should be no surprise, then, that Yazidis raped by IS fighters or local Sunni men often feared returning home, lest their relatives reject them or worse – and IS captors played upon this fear. Nadia Murad writes that she was told, 'You are ruined … No one will marry you, no one will love you. Your family doesn't want you anymore.'[66]

For this reason, in the wake of IS, the two leading Yazidi spiritual leaders, Baba Sheikh and Baba Chawish, relaxed their customary strictness and declared all female victims fully restored after bathing in the Zamzam spring and visiting the Sheikh Adi shrine – in other words, after undergoing a ritual cleansing. Any punitive action against them was forbidden. The leaders spoke personally with and comforted each victim.[67] There have been no cases of honour killings.

---

[61] Dina Al Raffie, 'After the Islamic State, Renewed Urgency for Religious Reform', *The Washington Institute for Near East Policy*, 3 October 2023, https://www.washingtoninstitute.org/pdf/view/1801/en (accessed 9 June 2023).

[62] The word *namus* is used across the Middle East by many peoples in the senses of 'honor, good name, modesty' and is rooted in the Greek *nomos*: law, custom.

[63] Nicolaus and Yuce, 'Sex Slavery', 196–229.

[64] Ibid., 209.

[65] Ibid., 209–10.

[66] Murad, *Last Girl*, 261.

[67] Nicolaus and Yuce, 'Sex Slavery', 210–12.

Badeeah Hassan Ahmed recounts her experience of the ceremony:

> Majida [her sister] passed me a Chira [a burning wick called the 'sacred fire']. I lit
> it and followed her into the main temple, where the tomb of the twelfth-century
> mystic Sheikh Adi was located. I'd visited this place in my mind many times when
> I was in captivity. Now, I felt I had come home.
>
> After we'd rested in the sun, Majida joined me for a private meeting with Baba
> Sheikh and Baba Chawish. I was nervous.
>
> ....
>
> Both leaders wore calm expressions. Baba Chawish asked about my family and
> about who was here with me.
>
> ....
>
> I started to cry then, sobbing like a baby.
>
> Baba Chawish leaned forward. 'Dear girl, you did nothing wrong. You don't
> need forgiveness. Stay connected to the good power of the universe. In time, you
> will heal and feel the power of good running through you again.'
>
> After that, we prayed together.
>
> When our meeting was over, Baba Chawish accompanied me to the White
> Cave, where some of the Faqras, the girls and women who dedicate their lives
> to spirituality, Lalish, and advancing their own souls, had already gathered. Baba
> Chawish had me kneel down. I dipped my hands into the water of the sacred spring
> and then drew them across my face, dampening my skin. The Faqras splashed
> water on me as Baba Chawish said another prayer.
>
> The final part of the ceremony involved me changing into a white dress made
> from fabric from the same tree used for Baba Sheikh and the Faqras' robes and that
> we used to wrap the Berat [balls of soil from Lalish carried as talismans]. The belt
> he gave me was red, signifying love.[68]

Ahmed, however, is now living in Germany; and not all of the Yazidi were taken back
in by their families, with the suicide rate among former slaves high. Another serious
barrier to rehabilitation is the traditional ban on children by men of another faith. Not
all the Yazidi women aborted children from Muslim partners, and some even decided
to remain with IS so as not to be separated from their children rather than return to a
family circle that seemed certain to reject them. But here religious leaders felt unable
to bend tradition, and this problem remains unresolved.[69]

A wider shockwave from this tragedy is increased mistrust among Yazidis of their
Muslim neighbours ('Arabic was a language that had once reminded me of a love
poem. I hated the sound of it now,' writes Ahmed).[70] Yazidis consider that neither their
Sunni neighbours (Arabs and even Kurds) nor the Peshmerga made sufficient efforts
to defend them from the IS onslaught, despite forehand knowledge of the coming
slaughter. The Peshmerga left the area not long before IS arrived, for reasons still not

---

[68] Ahmed, *Cave in the Clouds*, 224–5.
[69] Nicolaus and Yuce, 'Sex Slavery', 212–13.
[70] Ahmed, *Cave in the Clouds*, 134.

clear. Some neighbouring Sunnis are said to have risked their lives to shelter Yazidis or relocate them to safe areas – but the opposite is also reported, with claims that some Sunnis helped IS in return for substantial payments. And according to some Yazidis, many Sunnis simply stood by while the tragedy unfolded despite their long-standing ties with the Yazidi community. Still others joined IS, and among them were those who took Yazidi women they knew as sex slaves.[71]

An acute source of disappointment for the Yazidi community was the behaviour of *kerifs*, who have traditionally played a role analogous to that of a godfather in the European tradition and are usually from a neighbouring community rather than from inside the Yazidi community: Muslims in Iraq, and Armenians or Georgians in the Caucasus.[72] After a young Yazidi male undergoes the ritual of circumcision, he and his *kerif* become 'blood brothers', and the latter is bound to protect his Yazidi 'brother' in the future. A practical function of this tradition is to maintain friendly ties with neighbouring peoples. But one can often hear Yazidis charge that in their time of need, the majority of *kerifs* abandoned their Yazidi brothers to the whims of fate, fearing IS reprisals. There are still harsher claims, that some Sunnis even led IS fighters to Yazidi hiding places and participated in the crimes against them – against those whom they had pledged to shelter.

While the trauma of IS has introduced some flexibility into Yazidi customs, it has also turned the Yazidi community in upon itself and away from the peoples around it. Interaction between Yazidi and Muslim communities, and even with Kurdish communities, is fraught with increased mistrust. If before, many Yazidis considered themselves Kurds, now greater numbers of them are insisting on an ethnic identity wholly separate from the Kurds. Likewise, despite attempts by the Kurdistani government to promote integration and a spirit of unity between Kurds and Yazidis, Muslim Kurds are more likely to see Yazidis as 'infidels'.[73] A bitter truth that must be admitted is that, despite defeat on the battlefield, IS in some ways achieved its goal – at least temporarily – of weakening other faith communities by fracturing relations between them. The full scale of the damage is impossible to measure. Nadia Murad describes how her younger brother had become 'obsessed with the violence sweeping through Iraq and Syria. The other day I had caught him watching videos of Islamic State beheadings on his cell phone, the images shaking in his hand, and was surprised that he held up the phone so I could watch too.'[74]

Nonetheless, I have sensed a recent positive change in local attitudes towards Yazidis. If during my first visit to Kurdistan in 2014, prior to the IS tragedy, I caught a feeling from among Muslims – even if unspoken – that Yazidis were very much 'other', then during my visit in 2019, Kurdish officials and others seemed paternalistic, intent on efforts to integrate and heal wounds. And while Yazidi attitudes towards their Muslim neighbours in Iraq remained scarred, the Yazidis have become more

---

[71] Ibid., 214–15.
[72] Lana Ravandi-Fadai, 'Faithful Custodians of Ancestral Tradition', *in The Kurds: Legend of the East*, ed. V. V. Naumkin and I. F. Popova (Moscow: Arbor Publishing Group, 2019), 103.
[73] Nicolaus and Yuce, 'Sex Slavery', 196–229.
[74] Murad, *Last Girl*, 10.

open to the outside world, according to Murad Ismail, a Yazidi activist and head of the Sinjar Academy, which offers local Yazidis educational opportunities. Before the catastrophe of 2014, Yazidi women could not leave their village without permission from a family guardian. Now they travel throughout Iraq and even to Europe without such permission. Previously, the majority of Yazidi women received only a grammar-school-level education, while today many enrol in university. Two driving schools have cropped up in Sinjar.[75]

The Caucasus and other neighbouring regions provided a haven for Yazidis in centuries past, but the West has become an important refuge today, with Germany playing an outsized role. Around 85,000 Yazidi females have emigrated there from Iraq and Syria since 2014. At the beginning of 2015, 1,000 Yazidi women and children were brought to Germany as part of a special humanitarian programme initiated by the German state of Baden-Württemberg. Their testimonies were collected for investigations of IS crimes.[76] Likely the most well-known Yazidi woman in the world now is 29-year-old Nadia Murad, a laureate of the Nobel Peace Prize, partly in recognition of her 2017 memoir, *The Last Girl: My Story of Captivity, and My Fight against the Islamic State*.[77] Her family was almost completely annihilated, and Nadia has dedicated herself to documenting and punishing IS crimes and to informing the world about the sufferings of Yazidis in the face of silence on such crimes. She provided exhaustive testimony to German investigators and has encouraged other Yazidi women to do the same. Over one hundred victims have thus far been able to present their cases in Germany. The case of genocide against the Yazidis is being investigated by a special department of the Federal Prosecutor in Karlsruhe, which strives to afford Yazidi women who have agreed to speak out with the most secure and comfortable conditions for doing so.[78]

The problem of post-trauma assimilation is a persistent one, however. A former worker at a refugee camp in northern Iraq says Yazidis are still reluctant to accept survivors of sexual bondage as full-fledged members of Yazidi society. 'Some family members accept them; others do not. This is a catastrophe regardless of whether the Yazidi community wants to speak about it.' He adds, 'All of these new rules that Yazidi women are enjoying are still contingent on permission from a male guardian. For real change to take place in women's status, much time is needed.'[79]

What can be said by way of a conclusion? The Yazidis were subjected to horrors in 2014: thousands of men were killed, and thousands of women were forced into slavery – many raped and made sex slaves. Their number was augmented by naïve young women travelling from Europe to join IS in the hopes of winning the love of men they saw as

[75] C. Schaer, 'After Tragedy, New Freedoms and Opportunities', *Qantara.de*, 10 January 2022, https://en.qantara.de/content/iraqs-yazidi-women-after-tragedy-new-freedoms-and-opportunities (accessed 14 June 2022).

[76] M. Hein, 'Justice for Yazidi Survivors of Islamic State Genocide', *Qantara.de*, 12 August 2019, https://en.qantara.de/content/pursuing-prosecution-in-germany-justice-for-yazidi-survivors-of-islamic-state-genocide (accessed 14 June 2022).

[77] See bibliographic information in footnote 2.

[78] Hein, 'Justice for Yazidi Survivors'.

[79] (Dengê laliş). № 603. 3.07.2022.

brave, strong and pious. The tragedy for the Yazidis has been intensified through their perceived betrayal by the Peshmerga and Kurdish and Sunni Arab neighbours, some of whom were godparents to their children. Many Yazidis are convinced that the failure to protect their small and vulnerable population was no accident, and that some of those groups even joined IS and participated in the crimes. Although the majority of leading Muslim theologians loudly criticized IS, there were some who supported actions against 'unbelievers'. And yet these events have led to a certain opening up to the world – to Europe and especially Germany – where many Yazidi women have settled and begun to lead active lives again, although with uncertain ramifications for the preservation of traditional Yazidi culture.

Within the Yazidi community, religious leaders have indeed relaxed traditional norms regarding women who have had carnal relations with outsiders, paving the way for reintegration into the community for those remaining in Iraq, but the issue of children born of IS fathers has proven more difficult to resolve. Yazidis acknowledge neither converts to Yazidism nor apostates and have maintained their traditional ban on incorporation of children of 'mixed marriages' into the community. In March 2021, the Iraqi Parliament passed a 'Survivors Law' granting special support to Yazidi women held captive by IS: pensions, plots of land and educational, employment and other privileges. The law originally included a clause regarding children sired by non-Yazidi fathers, but this was removed at the request of Yazidi religious authorities, who argue that the children are Muslim by Iraqi law and thus cannot be considered Yazidis either legally or spiritually. To further complicate matters, their inclusion in the Yazidi community could be a source of future strife with Muslims who consider the children Muslim. A female Yazidi parliamentarian, Khaleda Khalil, commented, 'We are trying to find a solution to the dilemma, but the problem is multifaceted: it is religious, social, humanitarian and legal.'[80]

---

[80] Qhasan Khazar, 'Qanun najiyat alaizidiyat ... masir majhul al atfal aba'uhum min "daeish"' ('A Law for Yazidi Women Survivors... the Fate of Children Whose Fathers Are from ISIS is Unknown'), *Al-Araby*, 24 March 2021, https://www.alar aby.co.uk/society/ قانون-الناجيات-الأيزيديات-مصير-مجهول-لأطفال-آباؤهم-من-%22داعش%22 (accessed 4 September 2022).

Selected Bibliography

Ahmed, Badeeah Hassan, with Susan Elizabeth McClelland. *A Cave in the Clouds*. Toronto: Annick Press, 2019.

Al-Anbali, Ahmad Said Khamis. *Tārikh jazirat suqutrā* [A History of the Island of Soqotra]. Al-Ain: Matba'at al-sahābat, 2006.

Al-Tajir, Mahdi A. *Bahrain 1920–1945. Britain, the Shaikh and the Administration*. London: Groom Helm, 1987.

Al-Tirmanini, 'Abd al-Salam. *al-Riqq Madihu wa Hadiruhu*. Kuwait: al-Majlis al-Watani al-Thaqafa wa al-Funun wa al-Adab, 1979.

Allain, Jean. *The Legal Understanding of Slavery: From the Historical to the Contemporary*. Oxford: Oxford University Press, 2014.

Allen, Richard. *European Slave Trading in the Indian Ocean, 1500–1850*. Athens: Ohio University Press, 2014.

Allison, Robert J. *The Crescent Obscured: The United States and the Muslim World, 1776–1815*. New York: Oxford University Press, 1995.

Alpers, Edward A., and Matthew S. Hopper. 'Speaking for Themselves? Understanding African Freed Slave Testimonies from the Western Indian Ocean, 1850s–1930s'. *Journal of Indian Ocean World Studies* 1 (2017): 60–88.

Alpers, Edward A. *East Africa and the Indian Ocean*. Princeton: Markus Wiener, 2009.

Ammar, Nawal H. 'The Relationship between Street Children and the Justice System in Egypt'. *International Journal of Offender Therapy and Comparative Criminology* 53, no. 5 (2008): 556–73.

Anon. *An Affecting History of the Captivity & Sufferings of Mrs. Mary Velnet, an Italian Lady Who Was Seven Years a Slave in Tripoli, Three of which, She Was Confined in a Dungeon, Loaded with Irons, and Four Times Put to the Most Cruel Tortures ever Invented by Man*. Boston: William Crary, c. 1802.

Anon. *An Authentic Narrative of the Shipwreck and Sufferings of Mrs. Eliza Bradley, the Wife of Capt. James Bradley of Liverpool, Commander of the Ship Sally Which Was Wrecked on the Coast of Barbary, in June 1818*. Boston: James Walden, 1820.

Anon. *History of the Captivity and Sufferings of Mrs. Lucinda Martin, Who Was Six Years a Slave in Algiers; Two of Which She Was Confined in a Dark and Dismal Dungeon, Loaded with Irons, for Refusing to Comply with the Brutal Request of a Turkish Officer*. Boston: Lemuel Austin, 1810.

Anon. *Narrative of the Captivity of John Vandike, Who Was Taken by the Algierines in 1791: An Account of His Escape in 1791, Bringing with Him a Beautiful Young English Lady Who Was Taken in 1790; the Ill Usage She Received from Her Master; the Whole in a Letter to His Brother in Amsterdam*. Leominster: Chapman Whitcomb, 1801.

Anon. *Neapolitan Captive: Interesting Narrative of the Captivity and Sufferings of Miss Viletta Laranda, a Native of Naples, Who, with a Brother, Was a Passenger on Board a Neapolitan Vessel Wrecked near Oran, on the Barbary Coast, September 1829, and Who Soon After Was Unfortunately Made a Captive of by a Wandering Clan of Bedowen Arabs, on Their Return from Algiers to the Deserts, and Eleven Months after*

Providentially Rescued from Barbarian Bondage by the Commander of a Detached Regiment of the Victorious French Army. New York: Charles C. Henderson, 1830.

Anon. *Ravissement de l'Hélène d'Amsterdam, contenant des accidens étranges tant d'Amour que de la Fortune, arrivez à une Demoiselle d'Amsterdam en plusieurs endroits du monde, & principalement en Turquie où elle a été Esclave* [The Ravishment of Hélène of Amsterdam, Containing Strange Mishaps of Love as well as Fortune That Befell a Maiden of Amsterdam in Numerous Places across the World, and Principally in Turkey Where She Was a Slave]. Amsterdam: Timothée ten Hoorn, 1683.

Anon. *Turkish Barbarity: An Affecting Narrative of the Unparalleled Sufferings of Mrs. Sophia Mazro, a Greek Lady of Missolonghi, Who with Her Two Daughters (at the Capture of That Fortress by the Turks) Were Made Prisoners by the Barbarians, by Whom Their Once Peaceable Dwelling Was Reduced to Ashes, and Their Unfortunate Husband and Parent, in His Attempts to Protect His Family, Inhumanly Put to Death in Their Presence*. Providence: G.C. Jennings, 1828.

Araz, Yahya. 'Cariyeler, Efendiler ve Pusuda Bekleyenler: Osmanlı İstanbul'unda Hamile ve Çocuk Annesi Cariyeler Üzerine Düşünceler (1790–1880)'. *Kebikeç* 37 (2014): 233–60.

Ardakani, Sadri Navvabzadeh. *Amr-i Baha'i dar Ardakan. The Baha'i Faith in Ardakan*. Edited by Vahid Rafati. Hofheim: Baha'i Verlag, 2009.

Austin, Ralph. 'The 19th Century Islamic Slave Trade from East Africa (Swahili and Red Sea Coast): A Tentative Census'. In *The Economics of the Indian Ocean Slave Trade*, edited by William G. Clarence-Smith, 21–44. London: Frank Cass, 1989.

B***, Mlle Sidonie [pseud.]. *Marche´aux esclaves et harem: Épisode ine´dit de la piraterie barbaresque au XVIIIᵉ siècle* [Slave Market and Harem: An Unpublished Episode of Barbary Coast Piracy during the Eighteenth Century]. Paris: Ernest Leroux, 1875.

Baepler, Paul, ed. *White Slaves, African Masters: An Anthology of American Barbary Captivity Narratives*. Chicago: University of Chicago Press, 1999.

Basu, Helene. 'History on the Line: Music and the Formation of Sidi Identity in Western India'. *History Workshop Journal* 65 (Spring 2008): 161–78.

Bayda, Aqa Sayyid Abu'l-Qasim. *Tarikh-i Bayda* [Bayda's Narrative]. Edited by Siyamak Zabihi Moghaddam. Hofheim: Baha'i Verlag, 2016.

Bekkaoui, Khalid. *White Women Captives in North Africa: Narratives of Enslavement, 1735–1830*. Basingstoke: Palgrave Macmillan, 2011.

Bent, Theodore, and Mrs Theodore. *Southern Arabia*. London: Smith, Elder, 1900.

Bibars, Iman. 'Street Children in Egypt: From the Home to the Street to Inappropriate Corrective Institutions'. *Environment and Urbanization* 10, no. 1 (April 1998): 201–16.

Botte, Roger. *Esclavages et abolitions en terres d'Islam*. Brussels: André Versaille, 2010.

Botting, Douglas. *Island of the Dragon's Blood*. London: Hodder and Stoughton, 1958.

Boubrik, Rahal. 'Nineteenth Century Slave Markets: The Moroccan Slave Trade'. *AlMuntaqa* 4, no. 2 (2021): 63–79.

Bregel, Yu. E. *Khorezmskie turkmeny v XIX veke*. Moscow: Izdatel'stvo vostochnoi literatury, 1961.

Brower, Daniel. *Turkestan and the Fate of the Russian Empire*. London: Routledge, 2003.

Cacchioli, Niambi. 'Disputed Freedom: Fugitive Slaves, Asylum, and Manumission in Iran (1851–1913)'. *UNESCO*. Available online: http://portal.unesco.org/culture/en/files/38508/12480962345Disputed_Freedom.pdf/Disputed%2BFreedom.pdf (accessed 16 July 2023).

Chebel, Malek. *L'esclavage en terre d'Islam*. Paris: Fayard, 2007.

Chetwood, William Rufus. *The Voyages and Adventures of Captain Robert Boyle, in Several Parts of the World.* London: J. Watts, 1726.

Clarence-Smith, William G. *Islam and the Abolition of Slavery.* London: Hurst, 2006.

Cooper, Frederick. *Plantation Slavery on the East Coast of Africa.* Portsmouth: Heinemann, 1997.

Daoud, Muhammad. *Tarij Titwan*, 12 vols. Tetouan: Fondation Muhammad Daoud pour l'Histoire et la Culture, 2014 (2nd edn).

Drouiche, H. 'Imam Drouiche: Raping Christians and Yazidis Cannot Be Considered an Islamic Right Part I–III'. *AsiaNews.* Available online: https://www.asianews.it/news-en/Imam-Drouiche:-raping-Christians-and-Yazidis-cannot-be-considered-an-Islamic-right-(I)-42986.html (accessed 16 July 2023).

Eden, Jeff. *Slavery and Empire in Central Asia.* Cambridge: Cambridge University Press, 2018.

El Hamel, Chouki. *Black Morocco: A History of Slavery, Race and Islam.* New York: Cambridge University Press, 2013.

Elie, Serge. 'Communal Identity Transformation in Soqotra: From Status Hierarchy to Ethnic Ranking'. *Northeast African Studies* 16, no. 2 (2016): 30.

Ennaji, Mohamed. *Soldats, domestiques et concubines. L'esclavage au Maroc au XIXe siècle.* Casablanca: Editions Eddif, 1994.

Fahmi, Kamal. 'Working with Street Kids: Unsettling Accounts from the Field'. In *Marginality and Exclusion in Egypt*, edited by Ray Bush and Habib Ayeb, 169–90. London: Zed Books, 2012.

Fedorchenko, A. V., and A. V. Krylov. 'The Phenomenon of "The Islamic State"'. *MGIMO University Messenger* 41, no. 2 (2015): 174–83.

Fisher, Allan G. B., and Humphrey J. Fisher. *Slavery and Muslim Society in Africa: The Institution in Saharan and Sudanic Africa and the Trans-Saharan Trade.* London: C. Hurst, 1970.

Fisher, Humphrey J. *Slavery in the History of Muslim Black Africa.* London: Hurst, 2001.

Gintsburg, Sarali, and Eleonora Esposito. 'The Asymmetric Linguistic Identities of African Soqotris: A Triadic Interaction'. In *Language and Identity in the Arab World*, edited by Fathiya Al Rashdi and Sandhya Rao Mehta. London: Routledge, 2022.

Goodman, R. David. 'Demystifying "Islamic Slavery": Using Legal Practices to Reconstruct the End of Slavery in Fes, Morocco'. *History in Africa* 39 (2012): 143–74.

Goodman, R. David. 'Expediency, Ambivalence, and Inaction: The French Protectorate and Domestic Slavery in Morocco, 1912–1956'. *Journal of Social History* 47, no. 1 (2013): 101–31.

Gordon, Murray. *Slavery in the Arab World.* New York: New Amsterdam Books, 1989.

Harms, Robert, Bernard K. Freamon and David W. Blight, eds. *Indian Ocean Slavery in the Age of Abolition.* New Haven: Yale University Press, 2013.

Hopper, Matthew S. *Slaves of One Master: Globalization and Slavery in Arabia in the Age of Empire.* New Haven: Yale University Press, 2015.

Human Rights Watch. 'Slavery: The IS Rules', 5 September 2015. Available online: https://www.refworld.org/docid/55ed6f124.html (accessed 16 July 2023).

Huntress, Keith. *A Checklist of Narratives of Shipwrecks and Disasters at Sea to 1860, with Summaries, Notes, and Comments.* Ames: Iowa State University Press, 1979.

Jayasuriya, Shihan de Silva, and Richard Pankhurst, eds. *The African Diaspora in the Indian Ocean.* Trenton, NJ: Africa World Press, 2003.

Karazin, N. N. 'Atlar'. In *Nedavnee byloe: Povesti i rasskazy. Polnoe sobranie sochinenii*, vol. 15, 109–43. St. Petersburg: Izdatel'stvo P. P. Soikina, 1905.

Karazin, N. N. *Na dalekikh okrainakh. Polnoe sobranie sochinenii*, vol. 1. St. Petersburg: Izdanie P. P. Soikina, 1905.

Karazin, N. N. 'Samarskaia uchenaia ekspeditsiia'. *Vsemirnaia Illiustratsiia* 581 (1880); 183–4.

Karazin, N. N. *S severa na iug. Polnoe sobranie sochinenii*, vol. 7. St. Petersburg: Izdaniie P. P. Soikina, 1905.

Karazin, N. N. 'Staryi Dzhul'dash i ego syn Mamet'. In *U kostra: Ocherki i rasskazy. Polnoe sobranie sochinenii*, vol. 12, 131–92. St. Petersburg: Izdanie P. P. Soikina, 1905.

Karazin, N. N. *Ot Orenburga do Tashkenta. Putevoi ocherk*. St. Petersburg: German Goppe, 1886.

Kemball, Arnold B. 'Suppression of the Slave Trade in the Persian Gulf'. In *Selections from the Records of the Bombay Government*, No. XXIV.

Khoroshkhin, Alexander Pavlovich. *Sbornik statei, kasaiushchikhsia Turkestanskogo kraia*. St. Petersburg: Tip. i khromolit. A. Transhelia, 1876.

Korn, Agnes, and Maryam Nourzaei. 'Notes on the Speech of the Afro-Baloch of the Southern Coast of Iran'. *Journal of the Royal Asiatic Society* 29 (2019): 623–57.

Lee, Anthony A. 'Africans in the Palace: The Testimony of Taj al-Sultana Qajar from the Royal Harem in Iran'. In *Islamic Slavery*, edited by Mary Ann Faye. New York: Palgrave Mcmillan, 2018.

Lee, Anthony A. 'Enslaved African Women in Nineteenth-Century Iran: The Life of Fezzeh Khanom of Shiraz'. *Iranian Studies* (May 2012).

Lee, Anthony A. 'Half the Household Was African: Recovering the Histories of Two Enslaved Africans in Iran, Haji Mubarak and Fezzeh Khanum'. *UCLA Historical Journal* 26, no. 1 (2015): 17–38.

Lee, Anthony A. 'Recovering the Biographies of Enslaved Africans in Nineteenth-Century Iran'. In *Changing Horizons of African History*, edited by Awet T. Weldemichael, Anthony A. Lee and Edward A. Alpers. Trenton, NJ: Africa World Press, 2017.

Levi, Scott C. *The Rise and Fall of Khoqand, 1709–1876*. Pittsburgh: University of Pittsburgh Press, 2017.

Lewis, Bernard. *Race and Slavery in the Middle East: An Historical Enquiry*. Oxford: Oxford University Press, 1990.

Lodhi, Abdulaziz Y. 'A Note on the Baloch in East Africa, in Language in Society'. In *Language in Society: Eight Sociolinguistic Essays on Balochi*, edited by Carina Jahani, 91–5. Uppsala: Acta Universitatis Upsaliensis, 2000.

Lodhi, Abdulaziz Y. 'Iranian Presence in East Africa'. In *Haft kongere wa haft murraka* [Elegant Message and Eternal Beautitude], *Essays in Memory of Professor Habibullah Amouzegar*, edited by Muhammad Ali Khajeh-Najafi and Muhammad Assemi, 267–74. Uppsala: Acta Universitatis Upsaliensis, 2007.

Lorimer, John G. *Gazetteer of the Persian Gulf, Oman, and Central Arabia*, vol. I *Historical*, vol. II *Geographical and Statistical*. Calcutta: Superintendent of Government Printing, 1908.

Malmiri, Muhammad Tahir. *Tarikh-i Amriy-i Yazd* [History of the Cause in Yazd]. Bundoora, Victoria: Century Press, 2013.

Malmiri, Muhammad Tahir. *Tarikh-i Shuhaday-i Yazd* [History of the Martyrs of Yazd]. Le Caire, 1926. Reprinted Karachi: Baha'i Publishing Trust, 1978.

Marsh (Crisp), Elizabeth. *The Female Captive: A Narrative of Facts, which Happened in Barbary in the Year 1756*. London: C. Bathurst, 1769.

Mateo Dieste, Josep Lluís. 'Remembering the *Tatas*: An Oral History of the Tetouan Elite about their Female Domestic Slaves'. *Middle Eastern Studies* 56, no. 3 (2020): 438–52.

Mateo Dieste, Josep Lluís. 'Slave Women and Their Descendants among the Upper Classes in Tetouan, Morocco (1859–1956): Between Recognition and Conflict'. *Journal of Family History* 46, no. 2 (2021): 168–90.

McDougall, E. Ann. 'A Sense of Self: The Life of Fatma Barka'. *Canadian Journal of African Studies* 32, no. 2 (1998): 285–315.

Médard, Henri, Marie-Laure Derat, Thomas Vernet and Marie Pierre Ballarin, eds. *Traites et Esclavages en Afrique Orientale et dans l'océan Indien*. Paris: Karthala, 2013.

Meetelen, Maria ter. *Wonderbaarlyke en Merkwaardige Gevallen van een Twaalf Jarige Slaverny, van een Vrouwspersoon genaemt Maria ter Meetelen, Woonagtig tot Medenblik* [The Wondrous and Remarkable Story of the Twelve-Year-Long Slavery of a Lady Named Maria ter Meetelen, a Resident of Medenblik]. Hoorn: Jacob Duyn, 1748.

Mirzai, Behnaz A. 'African Presence in Iran: Identity and Its Reconstruction'. In *Traites et Esclavages: Vieux Problemes, Nouvelles Perspectives*, edited by O. Petre-Grenouilleau, 229–46. Paris: Société Française d'Histoire d'Outre-mer, 2002.

Mirzai, Behnaz A. *A History of Slavery and Emancipation in Iran, 1800–1929*. Austin: University of Texas Press, 2017.

Mirzai, Behnaz A. 'The Slave Trade and the African Diaspora in Iran'. In *Monsoon and Migration: Unleashing Dhow Synergies*, edited by Abdul Sheriff, 3–34. Zanzibar: ZIFF, 2005.

Morrison, A. S. *Russian Rule in Samarkand 1868–1910: A Comparison with British India*. Oxford: Oxford University Press, 2008.

Mulligan, William, and Maurice Bric, eds. *A Global History of Anti-slavery Politics in the Nineteenth Century*. New York: Palgrave Macmillan, 2013.

Murad, Nadia. *The Last Girl: My Story of Captivity, and My Fight against the Islamic State*. New York: Tim Duggan Books, 2017.

Nada, Khaled H., and El Daw Suliman. 'Violence, Abuse, Alcohol and Drug Use, and Sexual Behaviors in Street Children of Greater Cairo and Alexandria, Egypt'. *AIDS* 24, no. 2 (July 2010): 39–44.

Naumkin, Vitaly, and Leonid Kogan, eds., with 'Isa Gum'an al-Da'rhi, Ahmed 'Isa al-Da'rhi, Dmitry Cherkashin, Maria Bulakh and Ekaterina Vizirova. *Corpus of Soqotri Oral Literature*, vol. I. Leiden: Brill, 2015.

Naumkin, Vitaly. *Ostrova arkhipelaga Sokotra (ekspeditsii 1974–2010)* [Islands of the Archipelago of Soqotra (Expeditions 1974–2010)]. Moscow: Iazyki slavianskoi kul'tury, 2014.

Naumov, A. *Prinuditel'nyi brak, iznasilovanie, smert': Kakuiu sud'bu "Islamskoe gosudarstvo" gotovit zhenschinam Yazidov?* [Forced Marriage, Rape, and Death: What Fate Is the Islamic State Preparing for Yazidi-Women?]. Available online: https://lenta.ru/articles/2015/10/14/yazidi_plight/ (accessed 14 June 2022).

Nicolaus, P., and S. Yuce, 'Sex Slavery: One Aspect of the Yazidi Genocide'. *Iran and the Caucasus* 21 (2017): 196–229.

Nicolini, Beatrice. 'The 19th Century Slave Trade in the Western Indian Ocean: The Role of the Baloch Mercenaries'. In *The Baloch and Others: Linguistic, Historical and Socio-Political Perspectives on Pluralism in Balochistan*, edited by Carina Jahani, Agnes Korn and Paul Titus, 2nd edn, 326–44. Wiesbaden: Reichert Verlag, 2008.

Onley, James. *The Arabian Frontier of the British Raj: Merchants, Rulers and the British in the Nineteenth-Century Gulf.* Oxford: Oxford University Press, 2007.

'Open Letter to Dr. Ibrahim Awwad al-Badri, Alias "Abu Bakr Al-Baghdadi", and to the Fighters and Followers of the Self-Declared "Islamic State"'. *Issuu,* 19 September 2014, 23. Available online: https://issuu.com/openlettertobaghdadi/docs/arabic_english_o pen_letter_to_baghd?embed_cta=embed_badge&embed_context=embed&embed_ domain=www.lettertobaghdadi.com&utm_medium=referral&utm_source=www.lette rtobaghdadi.com&embed_id=14632537%2F10405725 (accessed 24 August 2022).

Peutz, Nathalie. *Islands of Heritage: Conservation and Transformation in Yemen.* Stanford: Stanford University Press, 2018.

Powell, Eve M. Troutt. *Tell This in My Memory: Stories of Enslavement from Egypt, Sudan and the Ottoman Empire.* Stanford: Stanford University Press, 2012.

Powell, Eve M. Troutt. 'Will the Subaltern Ever Speak? Finding African Slaves in the Historiography of the Middle East'. In *Middle East Historiographies: Narrating the Twentieth Century,* edited by Israel Gershoni et al. Seattle: University of Washington Press, 2006.

Rashad, Suzi Mohamed. 'Child Trafficking Crime and Means of Fighting It: Egypt as a Case Study'. *Review of Economics and Political Science* 8, no. 4 (2019): 2631–3561.

Ravandi-Fadai, Lana. 'Faithful Custodians of Ancestral Tradition'. In *The Kurds: Legend of the East,* edited by V. V. Naumkin and I. F. Popova. Moscow: Arbor Publishing Group, 2019.

Ricks, Thomas M. 'Slaves and Slave Traders in the Persian Gulf, 18th and 19th Centuries: An Assessment'. In *The Economics of the Indian Ocean Slave Trade in the Nineteenth Century,* edited by William G. Clarence-Smith, 60–7. London: Frank Cass, 1989.

Ricks, Thomas M. 'Slaves and Slave Trading in Shi'i Iran, AD 1500–1900'. *Journal of Asian and African* Studies 36:4 (2001): 407–18.

Riyahi, Ali. *Zār va Bād va Baloch.* Tehran: Kitābḫāna-e Ṭahūrī, 1977.

Sahadeo, Jeff. *Russian Colonial Society in Tashkent, 1865–1923.* Bloomington: Indiana University Press, 2010.

Schick, İrvin Cemil, ed. *Avrupalı Esireler ve Müslüman Efendileri: 'Türk' İllerinde Esaret Anlatıları* [European Captive Women and Their Muslim Masters: Narratives of Captivity in 'Turkish' Lands]. Istanbul: Kitap Yayınevi, 2005.

Schimmelpenninck van der Oye, David. *Russian Orientalism: Asia in the Russian Mind from Peter the Great to the Emigration.* New Haven: Yale University Press, 2010.

Schroeter, Daniel. 'Slave Markets and Slavery in Moroccan Urban Society'. *Slavery and Abolition* 13, no. 1 (1992): 185–213.

Schwarz, Katarina, and Andrea Nicholson. 'Collapsing the Boundaries between de Jure and de Facto Slavery: The Foundations of Slavery beyond the Transatlantic Frame'. *Human Rights Review* 21, no. 4 (2020): 391–414.

Segal, Ronald. *Islam's Black Slaves: The Other Black Diaspora.* New York: Farrar, Strauss and Giroux, 2001.

Serjeant, Robert Bertram. 'The Coastal Population of Socotra'. In *Socotra: Island of Tranquility,* edited by Brian Doe. London: IMMEL Publishing Limited, 1992.

Sheriff, Abdul. 'The Slave Trade and Its Fallout in the Persian Gulf'. In *Abolition and Its Aftermath in the Indian Ocean, Africa and Asia,* edited by Gwyn Campbell, 103–19. London: Routledge, 2005.

Sherwood, Marika. *After Abolition: Britain and the Slave Trade since 1807.* London: I.B. Tauris, 2007.

Sikainga, Ahmad Alawad. 'Slavery and Muslim Jurisprudence in Morocco'. *Slavery & Abolition: A Journal of Slave and Post-Slave Studies* 19, no. 2 (1998): 57–72.

Spivak, Gayatri Chakravorty. 'Can the Subaltern Speak?' In *Marxism and the Interpretation of Culture*, edited by C. Nelson and L. Grossberg, 272–313. Basingstoke: Macmillan Education, 1988.

Sultana, Farhat. 'Gwat and Gwat-i leb: Spirit Healing and Social Change in Makran'. In *Marginality and Modernity: Ethnicity and Change in Post-Colonial Balochistan*, edited by Paul Titus, 28–50. Karachi: Oxford University Press, 1996.

Taraud, Christelle. *La prostitution coloniale. Algérie, Tunisie, Maroc (1830–1962)*. Paris: Payot, 2003.

Thomason, Laura M. 'On the Steps of the Mosque: The Legal Rights of Non-Marital Children in Egypt'. *Hasting's Women's Law Journal* 19, no. 1 (2008): 121–48.

Toledano, Ehud R. *As If Silent and Absent: Bonds of Enslavement in the Islamic Middle East*. New Haven: Yale University Press, 2007.

Toledano, Ehud R. *Slavery and Abolition in the Ottoman Middle East*. Seattle, London: University of Washington Press, 1998.

Toledano, Ehud R. *The Ottoman Slave Trade and Its Suppression: 1840–1890*. Princeton: Princeton University Press, 1982.

van Rensburg, Julian Jansen. *The Maritime Traditions of the Fisherman of Socotra, Yemen*. Doctoral thesis, University of Exeter, 2012.

Wellsted, James Raymond. *Travels to the City of the Caliphs*, vol. 2. London: Henry Colburn, 1840.

Zilfi, Madeline C. *Women and Slavery in the Late Ottoman Empire: The Design of Difference*. New York: Cambridge University Press, 2010.

Index

www.ingramcontent.com/pod-product-compliance
Lightning Source LLC
Chambersburg PA
CBHW071854270326
41929CB00013B/2224